Foundation and Destruction

Nikopolis and Northwestern Greece

Foundation and Destruction
Nikopolis and Northwestern Greece

The archaeological evidence for the city destructions,
the foundation of Nikopolis and the synoecism

Edited by Jacob Isager

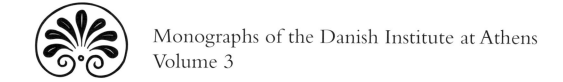

Monographs of the Danish Institute at Athens
Volume 3

Foundation and Destruction.
Nikopolis and Northwestern Greece

The archaeological evidence for the city destructuctions,
the foundation of Nikopolis and the synoecism

General editor: *Jacob Isager*
Graphic design and Production by: *Freddy Pedersen*

Printed in Denmark on permanent paper
conforming to ANSI/NISO Z39.48-1992

The publication was sponsored by:
The Carlsberg Foundation
The Danish Research Counsil
Landsdommer V. Gieses Fond
University of Southern Denmark

Monographs of the Danish Institute at Athens
Volume 3

ISBN 877288734-6
ISSN 1397 1433

Distributed by
AARHUS UNIVERSITY PRESS
University of Aarhus
DK-8000 Århus C
Fax (+45) 8619 8433

73 Lime Walk
Headington, Oxford OX3 7AD
Fax (+44) 1865 750 079

Box 511
Oakville, Conn. 06779
Fax (+1) 860 945 9468

Cover illustration: Lupa Romana from the sima found at the Augustan Tropaeum.
By the courtesy of the 12th Ephorate of Prehistoric and Classical Antiquities, Ioannina.

Contents

Introduction

Jacob Isager

In 1984 the first international congress was held on the theme, Nikopolis, the city founded by Caesar Augustus after his victory in the naval battle of nearby Actium in 31 BC. A large group of scholars met in the city of Preveza close to the site of Nikopolis to present their papers on this important theme, so evidently neglected until then. The proceedings of the congress, edited by E. Chrysos, were published in 1987 and, as the first, major publication which treated in monograph form a wide range of historical, archaeological, art historical, religious, and other aspects, it certainly awakened the interest of the international scholarly world to this city, which came to play such an importing role in the development of Northwestern Greece in the Roman Imperial and early Byzantine periods. The much sought after monograph marked the start of a new era for the investigation of Nikopolis and the impact of the synoecism. Many further topics were taken up later by other scholars. A very fruitful discussion, for example, of the status of the city now seems to have ended with an almost universal agreement upon the fact that Nikopolis was not a Roman *colonia* and did not receive colonists. It had the status of a *civitas foederata*.

Other problems which had already been considered include the following: The foundation of Nikopolis was a result of a synoecism of numerous Greek cities in Epirus, Acharnania and Aetolia, whose inhabitants were forced to leave their former dwellings and establish themselves in the newly built city. An important question raised was to what extent the former cities were left deserted as a result of the synoe-

cism. Another problem was the inhabitants' relation to their former rural properties and the possible redistribution of this land. Many of these Greek cities still awaited archaeological research, which could give us indications of their possible destruction or reduction.

For Nikopolis itself still remained, as it does today, the huge tasks of making systematic investigations in the city area and locating the administrative and religious centre or centres of the city. The unique rostral monument erected on a hill just north of the city by Augustus to celebrate his victory at Actium for all eternity was at the time of this first Nikopolis conference almost unexcavated. Systematic, archaeological surveys in the vast hinterland of the newly established city were then only in preparation.

In his contribution to the proceedings of 1987, James Wiseman proposed a plan for an investigation of the city and its region, which focused on registration, conservation and restoration of the existing monuments inside and outside the city and a regional survey which included geophysical prospecting and other types of remote sensing. This project, eventually, became reality as a joint venture between the 12 Ephoria of Classical and Prehistoric Antiquities in Ioannina, represented by Konstantinos Zachos, and Boston University, represented by James Wiseman.

When the Danish Institute in Athens in 1997 took the initiative to arrange a new symposium on the foundation of Nikopolis and its effects upon the surrounding region, the picture had completely changed. The Archaeological Service of Ioannina had begun a systematic excavation of the

Rostral monument of the Actian victory, and through a series of investigations and excavations inside and outside Nikopolis it had also thrown new light on the relationship between the city and the surrounding region. It also contributed to more precise dating of the material from the Roman period in Northwestern Greece.

The Greek–American survey campaigns had, as well, covered a large area of the region west, north and east of the city of Nikopolis and this together with the geophysical soundings on the northern coast of the Ambracian Gulf had established much new and more precise knowledge of the landscape and its changes.

Finally, as far as the regions south of Nikopolis across the Strait of Actium, that is Akarnania and Aetolia, are concerned, in collaboration with the Archaeological Service of the Ephoria of Patras, the German, Danish, and Dutch survey campaigns, investigations and excavations had contributed to unveil the history of Greek sites, which were affected by the Roman invasion of Greece and the foundation of the new, central city.

Thus, the common interest in bringing together for the first time the Greek and foreign scholars working in the area affected by this change of the urbanistic pattern, was evident. Konstantinos Zachos, Head of the Ephoria of Ioannina, Professor James R. Wiseman, Boston University, and Professor Peter Funke, University of Münster supported the idea of the Symposium from the start and have given advice and help during the preparations. So has the director of the Danish Institute at Athens, Signe Isager, who gave shelter to the Symposium at the Institute and made arrangements with the Italian School for a larger auditorium for three public lectures. Acting as host, she introduced the Symposium and the public sessions and together with her staff she took care in the best possible manner of all the different arrangements and administrative matters. I am most grateful to them all.

The theme for the Symposium, held at the Danish Institute at Athens in March 1999, was "Northwestern Greece before and after the foundation of Nikopolis". A main focus was the consideration of the archaeological evidence for the effect of the synoecism of the Greek city centres in Epirus, Acharnania and Aetolia into this new central city. In which state were the Greek cities at the time of the synoecism and to which extent were the city sites abandoned in connection with the synoecism? What was the impact of the new metropolis on its wide ranging hinterland? How was the land of the former city centres administred?

The new evidence presented at the Symposium brings us a long step forward in our endeavour to answer these question and suggests where to proceed with further investigations:

Strabo is our main source for the changes in the urban and political patterns in the area, brought about by the Romans, and Isager (University of Southern Denmark) takes up this controversial text. According to Strabo, Epirus was not part of Greece and its inhabitants were called *barbaroi*. The concept of *eremia*, desolation, emptiness, is likewise connected by Strabo with Epirus, sacked by Aemilius Paullus after 167 BC, and some scholars have taken the text at face value as evidence of an Epirotic landscape left in total emptiness. New archaeological evidence contradicts this, and doubt has been raised as to the validity of the information given by Strabo. Yet, as Isager argues, an analysis of Strabo's use of the concepts *barbaroi* and *eremia* shows that Strabo in other contexts uses them only to designate the less civilized, the less urbanized. The concepts are employed not only in descriptions of progress away from barbarism, but also in the reverse process where cities are reduced to mere villages. This reverse process took place in Epirus and civilization was only brought back to Epirus with the foundation of Nikopolis by Caesar Augustus. With this reading of Strabo, there seems to be no conflict be-

Nikopolis. View from the theatre. Drawing by Carl Haller von Hallerstein, 1810. Bibliothèque Nationale et Universitaire de Strasbourg.

tween Strabo and the evidence provided by the archaeological investigations.

The excavation of what was the most important construction in Nikopolis, the Victory Monument founded by Octavian at Nikopolis in memory of the battle of Actium in 31 BC, is presented in a preliminary report by Zachos, who is the leader of the excavation. The monument is situated on a hillside north of Nikopolis with a magnificent view to the Ionian Sea and the Ambracian Gulf, its main axis corresponding to the main axis in the city plan. The excavations have not only confirmed the description of the monument, given by Dio, but also given us much new and detailed information about this unique construction.

The monument is built on two terraces, supported by two retaining walls, facing south. Along the perimeter of the upper terrace a pi-shaped stoa opened to the south, forming an atrium. A kind of open-air sanctuary, a temenos was thus created. The southern facade of the podium opening to the lower terrace, carried a Latin inscription on its upper part and much of it has been preserved. Beneath this, the podium facade shows carved anchor-shaped sockets, which held bronze rams from ships captured in the battle, as many as 36 in all. A massive six and a half

kilo bronze fragment from a ram is what is left from them.

Various structures were discovered in the area within the pi-shaped stoa: two statue pedestals, and a monumental altar with fragments of a frieze, which suggests representations of battle and triumphal scenes. A large number of roof tiles with stamps and different types of terracotta revetments was found as well. One type shows a depiction of the *Lupa Romana* and the twins.

The monument thus constitutes at the same time a victorial monument and a sanctuary presumeably dedicated to Apollo. The victorial monument is created in Roman tradition with a series of rams and an impressive triumphal inscription in Latin. The lay-out recalls the upper terrace of the Asclepieion on Kos and the Late Republican sanctuaries in Latium.

The Nikopolis Project, a joint Greek-American archaeological and geological survey of Southern Epirus, directed by James Wiseman from Boston University and Konstantinos Zachos of the 12 Ephoria of Antiquities in Ioannina, aimed broadly at understanding the changing relationship between humans and the landscape they exploited from prehistoric to mediaeval times. In his paper, Wiseman discusses the evidence for changes in the landscape and for changing patterns of settlements from 2nd century BC through Late Antiquity. He also presents results of the investigations in areas which were affected by the synoecism connected with the foundation of Nikopolis. A program of geological and archaeological studies of the Northern coastal plain of the Ambracian Gulf has revealed the startling fact that the period from about 2,500 BC until the 5th century AD was a time of maximum marine intrusion into the Ambracian embayment, so that the northern shore of the gulf lay at the foot of the mountains. The floodplain which now extends some 12 km south to the shore of the gulf was created later. The survey did not include the plain of Arta (ancient Ambracia) and could not confirm the dating of the traces of centuriation found here, which has been connected with the founding of Nikopolis.

At the Nikopolis Peninsula the Mazoma embayment east of Nikopolis seems to have extended 500 meters further inland, thus creating a small harbour just outside the walls of Nikopolis. A more important harbour south-east of Nikopolis is found at the Ormos Vathy, an inlet from the Gulf, which in antiquity extended further inland. Here the harbour town has been identified, covering more than 16 ha. and a Roman bath has been found.

In the Lower Acheron Valley geological coring has given new evidence for the changes of the coastline and the creation of the Acherousian Lake. The site of Castri was chosen for a systematic urban survey. The preliminary conclusions of the survey show that there was no long-term deserted landscape in Roman times. Within a century after the founding of Nikopolis earlier sites were being revived and new sites grew up. Only from the 6th century AD is a reduction of population indicated.

An area close to Nikopolis, the Ayios Thomas Peninsula south east of the city, was investigated as part of the Nikopolis Project survey, and Stein (Boston University) presents in her paper the effects there from the foundation of the new urban center. Substantial changes in land use took place, most radically a centuriation of at least the western part of the peninsula. The survey has identified Roman sites in this area and the location of these has been correlated with the already proposed centuriation system for the area south of Nikopolis. The sites located on the survey seem to fit into such a centuriation scheme. Farmsteads are found aligned with the rural network, among them one, which by its dating can confirm an Augustan date for centuriation scheme.

The Roman and late Antique ceramic material collected by the Nikopolis survey project is presented by Moore (Boston University) with double aim of reconstructing southern Epirote trade with Italy and other parts of the Mediterranean after 31 BC and showing evidence of a change in the production technology of cooking vessels before and after the foundation of Nikopolis. The distribution pattern of imported amphorae and tablewares is significantly different from that of locally produced coarsewares. The imported wares were found at large villa sites and in the harbour area near Nikopolis, while the local wares were more evenly distributed, even in areas where habitation is thought to have ended with the synoecism, thus showing a gradual resettlement. A shift in the selection of clay resources in the 1st century AD may indicate a political reorganisation of the region. During the Roman and Late Antique periods, a local production of coarse cooking-vessels and tablewares in imitations of popular forms imported from Italy, Asia Minor and North Africa is maintained. There is no evidence of amphora production, and the quantities of amphorae, though always rather small, increases from the 1st through the 5th centuries AD, showing increasing contact to the Mediterranean trade network.

Angeli and Katsadima from the Ephoria of Ioannina discuss two architectural structures of the Roman era on the coast of southern Epirus north of Nikopolis. The *frigidarium* of a bathing complex, found near Riza and dated to the 3rd - 4th centuries, indicates the presence of a villa (*rustica*?) of a well-to-do landowner. The same conclusions can be drawn from the existence of a water reservoir recorded 3 km. south of Riza (now destroyed). It was in use from the mid 1st century AD to Byzantine times. Nearby a mausoleum has been partially excavated and fragments of sarcophagi have been found. It can be dated to the 2nd century AD. The bath and the mausoleum testify to the existence of a sizable landed estate and represent a prosperous elite presence in the countryside. The basis of its owners wealth has not yet been revealed, but surely land exploitation formed part of it. An interesting question is: do these complexes indicate Roman presence here or were the owners Greeks, adopting Roman building customs? We have no indication. Possibly, the landlords had their residence in nearby Nikopolis, and to draw conclusions from the epigraphical material found here, it had an almost exclusively Greek population.

A presentation of the results of the Greek-German investigations of Kassope, the city in whose territory Nikopolis was founded, is made by Schwandner (DAI, Berlin). The city was established as a *synoikismos* of the Kassopaeans just before the middle of the 4th century BC seemingly with the city-plan of colonial, coastal cities in southern Italy and Sicily as a model. The city seems to have been affected by the destructions and plunderings of Aemilius Paulus after 167 BC. The municipal Katagogion and the Prytaneion were destroyed by fire, but no destruction level was recognizable in the city's private houses. As shown in the paper by Gravani, the stratigraphical material suggests an abrupt decline in the city's population after 167 BC. Around 140 BC, the situation seems to have stabilized and the city flourished until the foundation of Nikopolis in the territory of the Kassopaeans, who were then forced to leave their homes and resettle in the new city.

They brought with them their statues of heroes and honourable citizens, and even the temple of the city goddess Aphrodite seems to have been transferred to Nikopolis. The total absence of any statue fragments in the Agora and of even the smallest fragment of the temple's superstructure seem to indicate this. Only one house of the 12 excavated shows further use in the first century AD. Kassope remained abandoned until the Late Medieval period.

One group of finds from Cassope, the mould made relief bowls is discussed by Gravani (University of Ioannina) in connection with the establishment of a stratigraphical chronology. Around 1981 fragments and pieces and a few whole mould made bowls were recovered during the excavations. The appearance of relief bowls in Cassope at the end of the 3rd century coincides with their diffusion in other Hellenistic centres. Locally produced mould made bowls represent about 80% of this category of vases. The clay came from local deposits. It has been possible to distinguish six groups according to their characteristic decorative patterns. Three of them point to the existence of three different workshops and the other three are related to workshop groups. Workshop A seems to have formed a common repertoire, enriched or imitated by the workshop B and the workshop group. The production peak for workshop A and B is dated before 167 BC, a period in which Cassope enjoyed independence from the Epirotic League. Thus, the use of decorated relief bowls, presumedly imitating bowls made of precious metal or glass, reflects a desire to display luxury. The activity of workshop C is dated after 167 BC. It has a different repertoire and it reflects probably the settling of new inhabitants in Cassope. The production of locally made bowls ceased in late 2nd century BC and the greatest number of imported ones date to this period. In the 1st century BC relief bowls were replaced by other kinds of drinking vessels.

The island and city of Leukas, south of Nikopolis, is another locality affected by the synoecism. Building both on earlier investigations and recent ones made by the Archaeological Service of Ioannina, Pliakou from this Ephoria discusses the history of Roman Leucas and shows that the suggestion, based on Strabo, that Leucas was left "deserted" after the foundation of Nikopolis cannot be confirmed by the archaeological evidence, which demonstrates that inhabitance of the urban area inside the walls of the city of Leucas continued at least until the 1st century AD. Only from that time is it likely that the population gradually decreased. A Roman grave found inside the walls indicates a change in or collapse of the city structure. This change is further shown by a recent discovery of a large farmhouse between the city walls and the northern cemetery. Roman graves attested almost only in this cemetery indicate human presence until the 3rd century AD. Pliakou concludes that the city's key position at the channel between Leucas and the mainland on the sea route which gives safe passage from Nikopolis to centres like Patras and Corinth, was the conclusive factor for the continuation of inhabitance in Leucas.

The great task of collecting the evidence from all the sites in Epirus where remains can be dated to the Roman period, that is from the 2nd century BC until late antiquity, is taken up by Karatzeni (Ephoria of Ioannina). The material presented by her confirms that the foundation of Nikopolis did not result in total abandonment of the former settlements in the hinterland. Ambracia is pointed out as a city, which seems to have been inhabited until the 4th century AD, yet in reduced conditions. The general picture of southern Epirus that emerges from her investigation is the following. In the period of Roman domination, the mountanous areas were abandoned and the settlements, for the most part small unwalled villages, were gathered at the coast and in the plains, at the river basins and at the main roads. The number of urban centres was small. Of the ealier centres only Ambracia seems to have survived. A final abandonment, caused by barbaric invasions, of most of the cities and settlements in the area, took place in the 6th century AD. Only Nikopolis survived for four more centuries.

Butrint (Bouthroton) situated in the southwestern part of the Epirotic region of Chaonia (now the southernmost part of modern Albania), at the coast opposite the island of Corfu, is the theme for the paper by Ceka (University of Tirana). He describes the development of the city from an Corcyrean emporium in the 7th century BC until it became a Roman colony at the time of Augustus. It avoided destruction by Aemilius Paulus and preserved its institutions. The process of its transformation into a Roman colony, begun by Caesar and completed by Augustus, is documented by literary sources as well as by archaeological data (e.g. an Augustan aqueduct and the rebuilding of the Prytaneion in *opus reticulatum)*, showing a change of political institutions and a new organisation of public space, and a different pattern in the agrarian territory. It has not been possible to indicate any specific effects on Butrint from the foundation of Nikopolis and the synoecism. A new road connecting the two cities may be dated to the times of Hadrian and further studies of the architectural remnants of both cities may reveal a closer connection at that period.

The ancient polis Stratos in Acarnania is another city affected by the Nikopolitaean synoecism. In recent years it has been investigated through a Greek-German excavation and survey project. Stratos is situated in a wide fertile plain, the Stratiké, close to the river Acheloos. With a city-wall (5th century BC) of almost 8 km in lenght, it was one of the largest towns in Northwestern Greece. Its city area seems to have been reduced with a *diateichisma*-wall only with Roman occupation after 168 BC or perhaps in connection with the foundation of Nikopolis and the installation of a Roman colony at Patras.

Funke (Universität Münster) describes the purpose, methods, and results of the excavations in Stratos and of the Stratiké Surface Project, which have been carried out in close collaboration with Lazaros Kolonas of the Ephoria of Patras. The excavations on the Agora have revealed that the major part of the public buildings here date to the late 4th century BC. As to the Roman period, a small altar with an attachment-ring for sacrificial animals, dating to 2nd – 4th century AD, is – apart from a few coins and potsherd – the only evidence from this period found inside the city walls. It is suggested that a new unfortified centre was created 3 km southwest of Stratos, where a Roman bath has been found. A general change in the urbanistic pattern from pre-Roman fortified settlements to non-fortified settlements on lower elevations in the Roman period is discussed in the paper by Lang. The maps of the distribution of sites, given by her, show a change in the land use, but the continuity seems not to have been totally disrupted by the Nikopolitaean synoecism and the new colony at Patras. There is also evidence for a revival of activities in many settlements during the early Imperial era.

The city-excavations have revealed that the theatre has well preserved parts of the orchestra and of the stage-building with access from both sides through ramps. It shows three building-phases during the 4th and 3rd century BC and gives important information on the development of the Greek theatre. The stratigraphical data from the city-excavation have delivered a foundation for the dating of the material from the Stratiké survey, which covered an area of about 100 square km. Among the 133 sites, from the Greek and Roman period, already located, the site Spathari stands out because of the discovery of well preserved, decorated roof elements from an Archaic temple (550/40 BC) and elements from a later Hellenistic phase (2nd - 1st centuries BC) as well.

The paper of Lang (Universität Rostock) is dedicated to methodological considerations related to the Stratiké survey and she discusses various dimensions of topography in relation to the development in the Stratiké. Problems when dealing with continuity and discontinuity at an intersite level and well as at an intrasite level are pointed out. She looks at the distribution of the sites occupied one (the majority) to five times, and reflects on the closing down of places in different areas. On the intrasite level, the continuity and discontinuity can be viewed in temporal and functional changes. A more specific method of site-function-analysis is defined based chiefly on the examination of pottery with the aim to establish different categories of function. Sites with the same function are assumed to produce the same set of ceramics in an analogous-comparative model.

Freitag (Universität Münster) is part of an international team of epigraphists, who have as their objective to collect and study all the epigraphical material from ancient Acarnania. The first step in this program is a registration of the epigraphic material in the museums of Agrinion and Thyrion. In his paper Freitag relates the history of the epigraphic investigations in the area and gives a report on the current work, pointing out the more important inscriptions. Milestones which have been found allow us a view into the Roman infrastructure in the area, providing evidence for a Roman road system in Acarnania from the first century AD, shortly after the foundation of Nikopolis. At the museum of Thyrion are found the well-known inscriptions mentioning Roman-Aetolian treaties of alliance from 212 BC and 94 BC, which, apart from their historical value may lead to a better interpretation of treaties between Rome and other Greek cities. Ancient Thyrreion is named among the cities annexed to Nikopolis and expectedly it is assumed to have been deserted after the synoecism. The existence of a relatively large number of epitaphs from the Roman period forces a reconsideration of this. The reorganizing of the area and the settlement policy after 30 BC seems to have been rather more complex than suggested by the sources.

The last two contributions investigate the distribution of cults and the pattern for placing sanctuaries in Northwestern Greece. The development and the changes found in the cults reflect the transformation of the regions.

The transfer of cult, cult-statues, and even temples has been connected with the Nikopolitean synoecism and Apollo came to enjoy a special position as the god who favoured the side of Octavian in the sea battle at Actium and secured the emperor's victory. Tzouvara-Souli (University of Ioannina) presents the history of the cult-places of Apollo in Northwestern Greece, demonstrating their affinities and the enduring existence of the worship of Apollo from the Archaic to the Roman period. The most famous Apollo sanctuaries were found in the colonies established by Corinth in Northwestern Greece (Ambracia and Apollonia being the most important) and it spread from there to the areas affected by Corinthian influence. After Actium and the Nikopolitean synoecism, the local cults of Apollo were transformed radically. The cult, its symbols, and the festival games at Nikopolis obtained new importance not only in Greece, but in most parts of the Roman Empire. As a protector of Octavian, Apollo Actius was given a place on the Palatine in Rome close to the dwelling of the Emperor.

Houby-Nielsen (University of Lund) from the Danish Kato Vasiliki (ancient Chalkis) Project in Aetolia, has studied the tradition and the pattern for placing sanctuaries in Aetolia and she extends her area of investigation to Achaia, where the city of Patras was made the centre of Augustus' largescale synoecism policy. We are told by Pausanias that the Aetolian people were to be incorporated in Nikopolis, and images from Aetolia and Acarnania was brought to this city. Yet, some important cults and cult statues (Artemis Laphria and Dionysos) were transferred from Aetolian Kalydon to Patras. Houby-Nielsen suggests that Augustus here acted in respect of the significance which former non-urban cults had to the Aetolians and Acharnians. She documents the fact that from the Geometric to the early Hellenistic period the most solid evidence for sacred architecture stems from cults, placed outside nucleated settlements, and even when the monumentalization of urban functions increased including city walls, the most costly temples were found outside city walls or close to these. Cults such as those for Artemis, Dionysus and Demeter, originating in smaller rural communities, seem to have been maintained after a synoecism as unprotected cults outside the city-walls and may have been regarded as vital for new cities.

The excavations at Aetolian Chalkis have given no evidence for habitation in the Roman period, so it must be assumed that the inhabitants of this city were transferred to Nikopolis or, more likely, to Patras, situated on the opposite shore of the Corinthian Gulf.

The last contribution brings us to the southern limits of the area, which was affected by foundation of Nikopolis. This area also formed part of the hinterland of Patras, another city taken into consideration by Augustus in his plans for centralizing the population into few administrative centres. I want to conclude this introduction by stressing the difference in the models of organization, exemplified in the these two cities.

In the case of Patras a Roman colony was installed in an already existing Greek city, which at the same time was made centre for a synoecism of Greek settlements in the surrounding region. A city with a mixed population of Greeks and Romans was thus created.

In the case of Nikopolis another model was used. A new city, built in Roman design, a metropol with all its facilities, was founded in the plain, in an open position between the Ionian See and the Ambracian Gulf. By synoecism it received a Greek population transferred from surrounding Greek city-settlements. Thus,

Nikopolis was created as a Greek city with a population which may have amounted to around 90.000. It was called Nikopolis, a city of Victory and a symbol of peace, and, as its fate has shown us, peace was a prerequisite for its existence.

Finally, I want to thank all the speakers who from their different angles have given their contribution to the common theme. All the evidence, brought together here for the first time, has given us an overall and nuanced picture of the very complex process of transformation, which took place in Northwestern Greece in the Roman period.

My thanks go as well to the other participants in the Symposium, who made their contributions in creating many fruitful discussions. We all want to express our gratitude to the Danish Humanities Research Council and the Carlsberg Foundation for their support of the symposium and for providing together with Landsdommer V. Gieses Fond and the University of Southern Denmark the economic basis for the printing of the acts and, finally, to the Director of the Danish Institute at Athens, Signe Isager, for accepting them as a volume in the Institute's series of monographs. Robin Lorsch Wildfang is thanked for revising the English translations.

Eremia in Epirus and the Foundation of Nikopolis

Models of Civilization in Strabo

Jacob Isager

One possible starting point for the history of the Romanization of Northwestern Greece might be the victory of the Romans at Pydna followed by their cruel destruction of the cities of Epirus and the enslavement of what must have been the greater part of the inhabitants. This event has made a during impact on the way in which ancient authors relate the history of Roman Epirus, for a picture of ruined cities and landscapes emptied of their inhabitants and their former sources of wealth seems to overshadow the later history of Epirus. This picture has in fact hindered us from learning in more detail the history of Epirus from ancient authors. Epirus was left in its emptiness and needed no further interest from authors or readers. The plunderings of Sulla and more generally the fact that many of the decisive battles in the Roman civil wars were fought in Greece have only contributed to this picture.

One result of this meagre information for the history of Northwestern Greece in the last two centuries before our era is the still ongoing discussion of the question of truth in Strabo, when he speaks about the area's desolation and emptiness, *eremia*, seemingly down to Augustan times.

Some scholars have taken the text of Strabo at face value, but now the archaeological evidence seems to contradict this claim. The value of his remarks on the desolate landscape of Acharnania and Aetolia has recently been put in doubt by, for example, the German scholars from the Stratike survey.[1] Funke[2] connects Strabo's sombre picture with the author's more general idea of early Roman Greece as a Greece in decline. The studies of Susan Alcock as well suggest that Strabo's remarks on a decadent Greece must be taken with a pinch of salt:[3]

"The general concurrence of the sources in their negative presentation of Roman Greece does not necessarily prove its truth, but rather the degree to which a rhetoric was shared: depopulation and decline had become natural ingredients for representations of a defeated Greece".

Alcock seems close to reducing Strabo's representation of Roman Greece to rhetoric and topicality. At the same time she advices us to assess the strengths and the limitations of the literary texts and it is that I intend to do in the reading of Strabo, which I will present in this paper, focusing on the vocabulary and the concepts used by Strabo to describe the development of Epirus in the Hellenistic and early Roman period. A prerequisite for this must be a general evaluation of the vocabulary he uses to define a geographical area politically and economically. What are his framework and his models? What are the images he wishes to create in his reader's mind and how do they reflect reality?

Eremia, desolation is not the only concept used by Strabo in his description of Epirus. He also uses barbarism. In a recent article[4] Hatzopoulos first discusses the fact that the Epirotic tribes are called *barbaroi* by Strabo and other ancient authors, and then enumerates all the evidence for the Greekness of the Epirotes. They were Greek-speaking tribes, they traced their origin back to the Achaian heroes, shared their religion with other Greeks and had full access to the Panhellenic festivals, where only Greeks could take part.

What has not been discussed by Hatzopoulos in his article is why Strabo named the tribes of Epirus barbarians. The question is, does Strabo even dispute that the Epirotes were Greeks? It seems evident to me that Strabo when naming these tribes barbarians does not refer to the their language[5] or even to their Greekness and we have to look for other connotations of the word barbarian in the language of Strabo. Here, I will connect Strabo's concept of barbarism with his use of the concept of desolation, *eremia*.

It is important to keep in mind how Strabo places Epirus in his geographical map. It is found in Book 7, where Strabo treats Central Europe and the Balkans including Macedonia and Epirus. Then, in Book 8 he begins his decription of the different areas of Greece. He quotes Ephorus when stating, that when you proceed from Illyria going south along the coast, Acharnania constitutes the beginning of Greece proper[6]. But Strabo does not make Acharnania a starting point for his description of Greece.

He envisages Greece as a continuous range of peninsulas and arranges his description according to this vision and he starts with the southernmost part the Peloponnesos, which he pronounces "the acropolis of Greece as a whole"[7] – the smallest, but most renowned part (8. 2 ff.). It is treated in Book 8. Athens and Attica follow in Book 9. The last part of Book 9 and all of Book 10 contain descriptions of the rest of mainland Greece and the islands. Acharnania is found in Book 10. Strabo thus turns the expected geographical model upside down and creates a hierarchic system governed more by his historical and literary interests than by any geographical logic[8].

Strabo and Epirus

In Strabo's geographical system we should thus not expect Epirus to be placed on any significant level.

Evidently, Strabo follows Ephorus in the opinion that Epirus is not really part of Greece. Epirus (and Macedonia) is treated by Strabo together with the Balkans, before he begins his chapters on Greece (7. 7. 1).

"And even to the present day the Thracians, Illyrians and Epeirotes live on the edges [of Greece] (though this was still more the case formerly than now); indeed most of the country that at the present time is indisputably Greece is held by barbarians – Macedonia and certain parts of Thessaly by the Thracians, and the parts above Acarnania and Aetolia by the Thesproti, the Cassopaei, the Amphilochi, the Molossi, and the Athamanes – Epeirotic tribes.[9]"

In book 7 (5. 1) we find the same opinion expressed, when Strabo enumerates the remaining areas of Europe, which he will treat in the following chapters: "In this part we find Greece and the tribes of the Macedonians and of the Epirotes." They are not part of Greece.

Yet, Strabo seems to have revised his view in Book 8 (1. 1), where Macedonia is included as a part of Greece:

"I have now encompassed in my survey all the barbarian tribes in Europe as far as the Tanais and also a small part of Greece, Macedonia. I shall now give an account of the remainder of the geography of Greece. This subject was first treated by Homer..."[10]

When we read a little further, we can see, however, that Strabo has not changed his view about Epirus:

"My account ended, on the west and the north, with the tribes of the Epeirotes and of the Illyrians, and, on the east, with those of the Macedonians as far as Byzantium. After the Epeirotes and the Illyrians, then, come the following peoples of the Greeks: the Acarnanians, the Aetolians, and the Ozolian Locrians." [11]

As I have already stated: Strabo (8. 1. 3), quoting Ephorus, pronounces Acharnania the beginning (*arche*) of western Greece. Acharnania borders on the Epirotic tribes.

In 7. 7. 6 we get the following information: When one sails into to the mouth of the Ambracian Gulf, the coast on the right is inhabited by Greek Acarnanians, while on the left of the mouth Nikopolis and the Epeirote Cassopaeans are found.

Even in an Augustan context when Nikopolis is mentioned, a marked contrast between Greeks and Epirotes is expressed.

From these quotations of Strabo we can infer two things:
1) If we consider Strabo's geographical distribution of the landscapes of Northwestern Greece he seems to follow the ancient tradition when he does not make Epirus part of Greece. Its inhabitants are called *barbaroi*. What that designation means is not stated. He seems to use the word barbarian in the old and traditional sense: ethnically non-Greek. But it hardly makes sense. Even when Epirus is mentioned in an era, when Nikopolis constitutes a metropolis with Epirus as well as Acharnania and even part of Aetolia as its Hinterland, Strabo does not seem to modify or change his general opinion of Epirus. But he states that Macedonia now has become part of Greece.

2) The Epirotes are consistently called tribes, *ethne*, and that may infer an connotation of barbarism in the meaning of not-civilized.

The most discussed part of Strabo's description of Epirus is the one, in which he tells about the effects of the sack of Epirus which was ordered by the Roman senate as a reward to the soldiers of Aemilius Paulus for defeating king Perseus of Macedonia in 167 BC:

"Now although in earlier times the tribes in question were small, numerous and obscure, still, because of the density of their population and because they lived each under their own king, it was not at all difficult to determine their boundaries; but now that most of the country has become depopulated and the settlements, particularly the cities, have disappeared from

sight, it would do no good, even if one could determine their boundaries with strict accuracy, to do so, because of their obscurity and their disappearance. This process of disappearing began a long time ago, and has not yet entirely ceased in many regions because the people keep revolting; indeed, the Romans, after being set op as masters by the inhabitants, encamp in their very houses. Be this as it may, Polybius says that Paulus, after his subjection of Perseus and the Macedonians, destroyed seventy cities of the Epeirotes (most of which, he adds, belonged to the Molossi), and reduced to slavery one hundred and fifty thousand people. Nevertheless, I shall attempt, in so far as it is appropriate to my description and as my knowledge reaches, to traverse the several different parts, beginning at the seaboard of the Ionians Gulf – that is, where the voyage out of the Adria ends."[12]

Here we get the information that in an earlier period many, small, and unknown tribes lived in settlement (*katoikiai*) among which there were cities (*poleis*). Because of their prospering populations (*euandria*) and the fact that they were ruled by a king, their boundaries were well defined. All in all, a very positive description of a community, which one would not expect to be described as barbarian. But this is the past, Strabo announces, now the area is depopulated (*eremos*), and as the cities have disappeared, there is no need to seek for boundaries. What remains is obscurity. The inhabitants have contributed to the disappeance of their cities by revolting (*apostaseis)*. The process began long ago and has not yet stopped and that is why the Roman encamp in their houses, chosen as masters by the inhabitants, themselves.

One main problem with the text is to sort out the indications of time. "Earlier" clearly indicates the period before the Roman interference in Greece. "Now" must indicate Roman times, but it is difficult to decide if it indicates a period before or during the lifetime of the author or both. Which are the revolts mentioned in the text as still going on now? Can they refer to the Roman civil wars in the first century BC, in which Greece was very often involved and during which Roman soldiers would encamp in the destroyed cities.

Or does "Now" rather designate the period going back to a time before Paulus' intervention in Epirus, the description of which concludes Strabo's discussion of the causes for the disappearance of cities? In that case Strabo wishes to tell us that Paulus' sack of the cities put an end to the revolts and that afterwards the soldiers encamped in the ruined and empty cities. The revolts and Paulus' destruction of the cities together caused the *eremia* in Epirus. In either case Strabo does not make further comments on this nor does he make himself a judge of the question of wright or wrong, as Plutarch does in his biography of Paulus. Here (§29) he says, that the Roman Senate was to blame for the cruel and meaningless decision to sack Epirus, which Paulus had no opportunity to oppose and which he most unwillingly executed.

Strabo thus stresses the fact that in earlier times Epirus was characterized by *euandria* and *poleis*, a statement he repeats a little later in Book 7:

"Now although in those earlier times, as I have said, all Epirus and the Illyrian country were rugged and full of mountains, such as Tomarus and Polyanus and several others, still they were populous; but at the present time desolation prevails in most parts, while the parts that are still inhabited survive only in villages and in ruins. And even the oracle at Dodona, like the rest, is virtually extinct."[13]

Summarizing here, we can state that Strabo gives us the following image of the development in Epirus:

Despite it rugged and mountainous character Epirus was formerly characterized by prospering cities. Now the cities have disappeared and the people live only in villages (*komedon*), and desolation (*eremia*) prevails.

How does this decription fit into Strabo's more general conception of civilization, as it has been pieced together from his various descriptions of people and places? In recent years especially French, Belgian, and Dutch scholars have made important contributions in this field[14].

When one compares Strabo's ethnographic decriptions it becomes clear that the concepts of civilization and barbarism are closely connected[15] and that Strabo does not consider them opposites or mutually exclusive. Very seldom a people is considered as just barbarian. It will be defined less barbarian, more barbarian or most barbarian, that is more or less civilized. In principle, the further away from Roman civilization you are the more barbaric you are, but Strabo does not confine himself to a concentric model with Rome as the centre. He operates with many other factors. Barbarians are to be found inside the Roman Empire as well and one's status as a barbarian can stem from the distance one lives from a given civilized centre. This phaenomenon, called *ektopismós*, can also be caused by geographical or climatic conditions or social and political isolation. As to the climatic conditions, Strabo is in agreement with other ancient authors when he states, that the Mediterrean climate offers the best climate for highly developed civilization.

If we look at the geographical factor we find that people who live a nomadic life or a life in the mountains are normally considered barbarian, whereas people who live as farmers in the plains are placed on a much higher level of civilization. But to this can be added another factor: each people's ability to make the best of the possibilities offered by nature even when provided with less than agreeable conditions.

When describing a landscape Strabo first estimates its physical potential and then the degree of development reached by its inhabitants. A landscape with few possibilities is pronounced rugged (*trachus*) whereas a landscape with optimal qualities is described with expressions like *eudaimo-*

nia, happiness, and *eukarpia*, rich in crops. Good conditions for agricultural basics – grain, wine, and olives, are essential to a life of happiness[16].

The degree of civilization also manifests itself in the ability of a given society to organize itself socially and politically. In his general description of Europe in Book 2 (2. 5. 26) Strabo points to the Greeks as a good example of this principle: though occupying mountains and rocks, they used to live happily because they demonstrated forethought (*pronoia*) in politics, in the arts and in the science of living.

Strabo also presupposes the polis as the optimal basis for the politically well organized society. The highest degree of civilization is found in the highest degree of urbanization. So a polis-life based on agriculture is first on our list of civilized conditions. Tribes living in villages, although basing their life on agriculture, are to be placed on a much lower level on the scale.

Strabo places any given society on a scale ranging from a high degree of barbarism to a high degree of civilization. But he makes a very important addition: He sees Greek and Roman civilization as a catalyst in the ongoing process away from barbarism. He, however, speaks not only of progress. A society may also be reduced to a lower level of civilization, that is to say to a barbarism of sorts.

Strabo offers several examples of this reverse process. In 5. 4. 11 Strabo tells us the results of Sulla's subjugation of the Samnites: "And truly their cities (*poleis*) have now become mere villages (*komai*) ...some have utterly vanished... No one of these deserves to be regarded as a city, but I, for my part, am thus going into detail,... because of the glory and power of Italy". In general Strabo does not think villages worthy of any mention, but he makes an exception here.

I would like to give two other examples of this process which, as well, can illuminate the conditions in Epirus as described by Strabo. In 3. 2. 15 he speaks of the Turditanians in Spain:

"Along with the happy lot (*eudaimonia*) of their country, the qualities of both gentleness and civility have come to the Turditanians; and to the Celtic peoples, too, on account of their being neighbours to the Turdetanians, as Polybius has said, or else on account of their kinship; but less so the Celtic people, because for the most part they live in mere villages (*komedon*). The Turdetanians, however,....have become Latins and they have received Romans as colonists, so that they are not far from being all Romans. And the present jointly-settled cities (*synoikismenai poleis*), Pax Augusta in the Celtic country, Augusta Emerita in the country of the Turdulians, Caesar-Augusta near Celtiberia, and some other settlements (*katoikiai*), manifest the aforesaid civil modes of life."

Strabo 3. 3. 5 mentions the tribes in the area of Tagus in Spain:

"...and although the country was blest (*eudaimon*) in fruits, in cattle, and in the abundance of its gold and silver and similar metals, most of the people had ceased to gain their livelihood from the earth, and were spending their time in brigandage and in continuous warfare both with each other and with the neighbours across the Tagus, until they were stopped by the Romans, who humbled them and reduced their cities (*poleis*) to mere villages (*komai*), though they improved some of their cities by adding colonies thereto (*synoikizontes*). It was the mountaneers who began this lawlessness, as was likely to be the case...[17]

In his book on *Barbarie et civilisation chez Strabon* Thollard[18] has made a list of the concepts used by Strabo to denote barbarism and civilisation.

He lists the geographical conditions for barbarians: mountains, woods, a northern position, isolation. This is the opposite of non-barbarians living near the coast, in the plains, in contact with the Romans.

As to the economic resources the barbarians dwell in poor, rugged, frosty and barren landscapes[19], while civilized regions are blessed with happiness, excellent soil, and fertility[20]

The barbarian way of living is characterized by permanent war conditions, brigandage, and negligence[21], while the opposite is expressed with notions of peace, leasure, and agriculture[22].

If we look at the social life of the barbarians we get a picture of unsociable persons, living in lawlessness in scattered villages, with their own dialect or language, living from day to day, without rules and education in contrast to those living in a civilized – that is Romanized way – in well ordered societies; law abiding citizens dwelling in cities.[23]

To Thollard's list, one might add well-defined borders as another criterion for the well-ordered society.

If we compare the vocabulary used by Strabo to describe the development in Epirus with the afore mentioned definitions of barbarism/civilization which his text allows us to extract we get the following picture:

Despite its mountainous and rugged character and its tribal system Epirus was once able to produce cities (*poleis*) with a prospering population (*euandria*). A well organized society with well defined boundaries. A clear case of people fighting successfully against the poor conditions given by nature. It is tempting to compare this description with Strabo's general description of Greece quoted above, for the status given would hardly be characterized as barbarian. But the status of Epirus then changed, not following the expected line of progress. This change was caused first by the people revolting and finally by the destruction, which the Roman Senate ordered of most of the cities and the following enslavement of a large part of the population. Revolution, that is unlawful war, which could even be comparable to brigandage[24], is one of the signs of barbarism in the Strabonian model. Another indication is the change in settlements from cities to villages with no organization and no fixed boundaries. The country

has been depopulated (the opposite of the former *euandria*) and isolation/desolation prevails. This *ektopismos* is another indication of barbarism. So the reader of Strabo's text can reach only this conclusion:

From a former civilized status Epirus has regressed and now has all the symptoms of a reversed status, that of a barbarian state. And Strabo allows himself to conclude that as long as this country keeps a barbarian and less urbanized status, it is of no interest to his reader. Therefore, it requires no further comments from him[25] – at least not until the situation is changed again with the foundation of Nikopolis.

Eremia, isolation or desolation, is part of the definition of the non-urbanized, barbarian landscape with its inhabitants living in villages and is not, as far as I can see, an indication of the totally devastated landscape. As stated by Luigi Gallo, Strabo's use of the concept of *eremia* seems closely connected with the existence of cities; the fewer cities the more *eremia*; the more cities the more *euandria*. Strabo seems not to take the size of the cities into consideration[26]. I wish to point out, that Nicopolis is an exception. This single city is considered reason enough for the *euandria* in this area.

In this connection I wish to mention Strabo's own definition of the term *ekleipsis*, " being extinct", which is found in his description of the tribes Talares and Aethices, who lived in the Pindus mountains.

"The term *ekleipsis* is to be taken in one of two meanings; either the people vanished and their country has become utterly deserted, or else merely their ethnic name no longer exists and their political organisation no longer remains what it was. When, therefore, any present political organisation that survives from an earlier time is utterly insignificant, I hold that it is not worth mentioning, either itself or the new name it has taken; but when it affords a fair pretext for being mentioned, I must needs give an account for the change.[27]

I feel convinced that *eremia* in relation to Epirus and to the future hinterland of Nikopolis is to be understood as *ekleipsis* in the second sense mentioned by Strabo: the political organisation no longer remains on its former level. The designation *eremia* is part of the vocabulary used by Strabo to describe a less urbanized country characterized by villages and isolated from larger urbanized centres.

At the same time he signals that this country is ready for a new step along the line of progress towards a higher degree of civilization, caused by the foundation of a new city by Caesar Augustus.

A similar model of development is mentioned by Strabo in connection with Spain as mentioned above, where new jointly-settled cities (*synoikismenai poleis*), and other settlements (*katoikiai*), were established as examples of the new civil mode. A jointly-settled city with surrounding, subordinate settlements is exactly the model that Strabo (7. 7. 6) tells us was used in the case of Nikopolis:

"In later times, however, the Macedonians and the Romans, by their continuous wars, so completely reduced both this [Ambracia] and the other Epeirote cities because of their disobedience that finally Augustus seeing that the cities had utterly failed, settled what inhabitants were left, in one city together – the city on this gulf which was named by him Nicopolis, and he so named it after the victory he won in the naval battle before the mouth of the gulf over Antony and Cleopatra the queen of the Egyptians, who was also present at the fight. Nicopolis is populous, and its numbers are increasing daily, since it has not only a considerable territory and the adornments taken from the spoils of the battle, but also, in its suburbs, the thoroughly equipped sacred precinct – one part of it being in a sacred grove that contains a gymnasium and a stadium for the celebration of the quinqennial games, the other part being on the hill that is sacred to Apollo and lies above the grove. These games – the Actia, sacred to Actian Apollo – have been designated as Olympian, and

they are superintended by the Lacedaemonians. The other settlements are dependencies of Nikopolis. In earlier times also the Actian Games were wont to be celebrated in honour of the god by the inhabitants of the surrounding country – games in which the prize was a wreath – but at the present time they have been set in greater honour by Caesar."

A new polis has been founded and it is blessed with *euandria*. It is surrounded by dependent settlements, *peripolioi katoikiai*.[28] Strabo used exactly the same vocabulary to describe the former higher status of urbanization in an Epirus ruled by kings, before the Greeks and the Macedonians, to quote Strabo (6, 4, 2), "revolted and led the Romans to conquer them". Caesar Augustus seeing that the cities had failed (*ekleleimmenas*) restored the landscape of Epirus to its former glory by creating a new and more developed example of urbanization, that is to say Nikopolis surrounded by subordinate settlements. Hereby he showed a foresight which is the prerequisite for the creation of a new city, – the same foresight (*pronoia*) that, according to Strabo (2. 5. 26), quoted above, was once shown by the Greeks. It is now part of the political ingeniousnes of the Romans[29].

Augustus saw that the cities had failed (*poleis ekleleimmenas*). I have already referred to Strabo's use of the concept of *ekleipsis* and I shall repeat my interpretation of *ekleipsis* in this context as indicating a change from a higher to a lower level of civilization. Strabo does not want us to think that Augustus found a deserted and empty landscape with few inhabitants, but rather a landscape characterized by small scattered villages indicating a decayed, more simple, and, according to Strabo's model, barbarian level of urbanization.

I am well aware that Strabo's choice of material for his Geography is often dictated by a literary tradition going back to Homer, and that he did not always feel it necessary to describe the physical and social reality of a given geographical locality,[30] — but I will not go so far as Susan Alcock does, when she says that our written sources especially Strabo are governed by rhetoric and topicality more than reality. Strabo has inherited the concept of barbarism in Epirus from authors such as Ephorus and Thucydides, but he has endeavored to fit the history of Epirus into his model of civilization and has incorporated his notion of barbarism as part of it. But if one focus only on this concept and that of *eremia*, as well, out of their Strabonian context, the message of the text appears distorted and will not show us the reality which Strabo wished us to see. In my reading of Strabo this reality seems to be even more in accordance with the results of the archaeological investigations in the area.

Notes

NOTE 1
Lang 1994, Strauch 1996, 59 and 179, and Funke 1991, see note 2.

NOTE 2
Funke 1991, 184. Strabo writes for the educated reader. His use of commentaries to Homer, especially Apollodorus' Commentary to the Catalogue of Ships, shows his preference for Homer. Homer is a main source, but Strabo supplies with information from other authors, preferring historical informations to geographical ones. Cf. Baladié 1978, 7-14.

NOTE 3
Alcock 1993, 30.

NOTE 4
Hatzopoulos 1997, 140-145.

NOTE 5
Cf. Hammond in Sakellariou 1997, 60.

NOTE 6
Strabo 8. 1. 3.

NOTE 7
The translations of Strabo are by H. L. Jones (Loeb ed.). Strabo 8. 1. 3: "the acropolis of Greece as a whole; for apart from the splendour and power of the tribes that have lived in it, the very topography of Greece, diversified as it is by gulfs, many capes, and, what are the most significant, large peninsulas that follow one another in succession, suggests such hegemony for it".

In Strabo's hegemonic description the Peloponnesus is the first peninsula. A second peninsula embraces the first and extends from Pegae to Nisaia. The third includes the second and the first, extending from the Crisaean Gulf to Thermopylae. A larger fourth peninsula is created by drawing a line from the Ambracian Gulf to the Maliac Gulf and Thermopylae, and this can be extended to an even larger peninsula starting again from the Ambracian Gulf, but reaching as far as the Thermaean Gulf and Thessalonike. It is unclear if he follows

Ephoros here, as maintained by Laserre in Strabon, Tome VII (Livre X), Paris 1971, 5.

NOTE 8
Cf. R. Baladié, Strabon, Géographie, Tome V (Livre VIII), Paris 1978, 3-4.

NOTE 9
Strabo 7. 7. 1. Cf. Baladié i Strabon Tome IV (Livre VII) Paris 1989, 133 note 9: Il se déduit de ce passage que, pour Strabon, la Macédoine, la Thessalie, l'Acarnanie et l'Étolie font partie de la Grèce. Ce ne fut pas toujours le cas pour la Macédoine; cf. livre VIII de la présente édition p.50 n.2. D'autre part, pour lui, les tribus épirotes (Thesprotes, Cassopaiens, Amphilochiens, Molosses, Athamanes) ne sont pas des Grecs.

NOTE 10
Cf. Baladié, in Strabo, Tome V (Livre VIII), Paris 1978, 215.

NOTE 11
Strabo 8. 1. 1. For the concept of barbarism in connection with Aetolia se Antonetti 1990, 134-143.

NOTE 12
Strabo 7. 7. 3.

NOTE 13
Strabo 7. 7. 9: τότε μέν οὖν, ὡς εἶπον, καίπερ οὖσα τραχεῖα καὶ ὀρῶν πλήρης, Τομάρου καὶ Πολυάνου καὶ ἄλλων πλειόνων, ὅμως εὐάνδρει ἥ τε Ἤπειρος πᾶσα καὶ ἡ Ἰλλυρίς; νῦνδὲ τὰ πολλὰ μὲν ἐρημία κατέχει, τὰ δ' οἰκούμενα κωμηδὸν καὶ ἐν ἐρειπίοις λείπεται. ἐκλέλοιπε δὲ πως καὶ τὸ μαντεῖον τὸ ἐν Δωδώνῃ καθάπερ τἆλλα. For the theme "past glory – present obscurity", see Alcock 1993, 26 ff. with reference to Gallo 1980.

NOTE 14
Cf. my bibliography. Among others the studies by van der Vliet 1984 and Thollard 1987 have been most useful to me.

NOTE 15
In the Strabonian vocabulary barbarian means not-civilized Cf. Van der Vliet 1984, 43-44 and Thollard 1987, 31: "En d'outre termes, le mot barbare n'a jamais désigné pour Strabon toute race qui n'était pas grecque mais tout peuple qui n'était pas civilisé.

NOTE 16
Cf. Van der Vliet 1984, 65-58; Thollard 1987, 9.

NOTE 17
Cf. Strabo 4. 1. 11 on the Allobroges:
    "Formerly the Allobroges kept up warfare with many myriads of men, whereas now they till the plains and the glens that are in the Alps, and all of them live in villages [κωμηδὸν ζῶσιν], except that the most notable of them, inhabitants of Vienna (formerly a village, but called, nevertheless, the "metropolis" of the tribe), have built it up into a city [...κατεσκευάκασι πόλιν.]

NOTE 18
Thollard 1987, 8.

NOTE 19
ἡ λυπρότης τῆς γῆς, ἡ τραχύτης τῶν τόπων, αἱ πάχναι, ἄκαρπος.

NOTE 20
ἡ εὐδαιμονία τῆς γῆς, ἡ ἀρετὴ τῶν τόπων, τὰ ἐμφύτα ἀγαθὰ οἷα κάρποι.

NOTE 21
ὁ συνεχὴς πόλεμος, τὸ πολεμεῖν, ληστεῖν, ἡ ὀλιγωρία τῶν ἀνθρώπων.

NOTE 22
ἡ εἰρήνη, ἡ σχολή, ἡ γεωργία.

NOTE 23
(unsociable, δυσεπίμικτος, lawless, ἡ ἀνομία, scattered living in villages, ἡ κώμη, κωμηδὸν ζῆν, κατὰ κώμας οἰκεῖν, own language or dialect, ἡ διάλεκτος, living from day to day, πρὸς ἀνάγκην ζῆν, with no rules and morality, μετὰ φαύλου

ἔθους/solidarity, τὸ κοινονικὸν, το φιλάνθρωπον, law-abiding, ἡ εὐνομία living in a city, ἡ πολιτεία, ἡ πόλις, or a settlement, ἡ κατοικία, in a colony, ἡ ἀποικία, the Roman/Italic way, ὁ τῶν Ρωμαίων τρόπος, ὁ Ἰταλικός τύπος, *togatus*, live orderly, πρὸς διαγωγήν ζῆν.)

NOTE 24
For this theme, see Van der Vliet 1984, 66-67.

NOTE 25
Cf. Van der Vliet 1984, 79, who quotes Strabo for stating that the people living around Dodone had been barbarians (7, 7, 10, where Strabo refers to the Iliad 16, 235):

"Ainsi, pou le public civilisé auquel Strabon destine sa Géographie, il n'est ni intéressant ni agreable d'être informé en detail de ce sujet."

NOTE 26
Gallo 1980, 1241-42.

NOTE 27
Strabo 9. 5. 12: ἐκλελοιπέναι δέ νῦν ἱστοροῦνται. τὴν δ'ἔκλειψιν διττῶς ἀκουστέον ἢ γὰρ ἀφανισθέντων τῶν ἀνθρώπων καὶ τῆς χώρας τελέως ἠρημωμένης ἢ τοῦ ὀνόματος τοῦ ἐθνικοῦ μηκέτι ὄντος, μηδὲ τοῦ συστήματος διαμένοντος τοιούτου. ὅταν οὖν ἄσημον τελέως ᾖ τό λειπόμενον νυνί

σύστημα, οὐκ ἄξιον μνήμης τίθεμεν οὔτ'αὐτὸ οὔτε τοὔνομα τὸ μεταληφθέν, ὅταν δ'ἔχῃ τοῦ μεμνῆσθαι δικαίαν πρόφασιν, λέγειν ἀναγκαῖον τὴν μεταβολήν. Cf. Alcock 1993, 147-49.

NOTE 28
Cf. 10. 2. 2: *perioikides poleis.*

NOTE 29
Cf. van der Vliet 1984, 75-77 and Thollard 1987, 40 ff.

NOTE 30
Cf. Funke 1991, 184-185, for Strabo's use of *eremia* in connection with Acharnania and Aetolia.

Bibliography

Alcock, S. E., 1993
Graecia Capta. The landscape of Roman Greece, Cambridge.

Aly, W., 1957
Strabon von Amasia. Untersuchungen über Text, Aufbau und quellen der Geographika. Bonn.

Antonetti, C., 1990
Les Étoliens, image et religions. Annales Littéraires de l'Université de Besancon, Centre d'Histoire Ancienne, Paris.

Baladié, R., 1978
Strabon, Géographie, Tome V. Ed. par R. B., Paris.

Baladié, R., 1980
Le Péloponnèse de Strabon. Paris.

Cabanes, P., 1979
Frontière et rencontre de civilisations dans la Grèce du Nord-Ouest, *Ktema* 4, 183-199.

Clarke, K., 1997
In search of the author of Strabo's Geography, *JRS* 87, 92-110.

Clavel-Lévêque, M., 1974
Les Gaules et les Gaulois: pour une analyse du fonctionnement de la Géographie de Strabon, *DHA* 1, 75-94.

Dauge, Y.-A., 1981
Le Barbare. Recerces sur la conception romaine de la barbarie et de la civilisation, Bruxelles.

Funke, P., 1991
Strabone, la geografia storica e la struttura etnica della Grecia occidentale, in: Prontera, F. (ed.), *Geografia storica della Grecia Antica,* Roma/Bari.

Gallo, L., 1980
Popolosità e scarsità, contributo allo studio di un topos, *Annali della Scuola Normale Superiore di Pisa,* S. III 10, 1233-1270.

Gehrke, H.-J., 1994
Strabon und Akarnanien, in: *Strabone e la Grecia,* a cura di A.M. Biraschi, Napoli, 93-118.

Hatzopoulos, M. B., 1997.
The Boundaries of Hellenism in Epirus during Antiquity. in: Sakellariou, M. B. (ed.), *Epirus,* Athens 1997, 140-145.

Lang, F., 1994
Veränderungen des Siedlungsbildes in Akarnanien von der klassisch-hellenistischen Zeit, *Klio* 76, 239-54.

Nicopolis I 1987
Nicopolis I. Proceedings of the first International Symposium on Nicopolis (23-29 September 1984). Edited by E. Chrysos. Preveza.

Pédech, P., 1971
La Géographie urbaine chez Strabon, *Anc. Soc.* 2, 234-253.

Pothecary, S., 1997
The expression "our times" in Strabo's Geography, *Class. Phil.* 92, 235-246.

Sakellariou, M. B. (ed.), 1997
Epirus, 4000 Years of Greek History and Civilization, Athens

Strauch, D., 1996
Römische Politik und griechische Tradition. Die Umgestaltung Nordwest-Griechenlands unter römischer Herrschaft, München.

Thollard, P., 1987
Barbare et civilisation chez Strabon. Etude critique des livres III et IV de la Geographie, Annales Littéraire de l'Université de Besancon, Centre d'Histoire ancienne, vol 77. Paris.

van der Vliet, E. Ch. L., 1984,
L'ethnographie de Strabon: ideologie ou tradition? in: F. Prontera (ed.), *Strabone. Contributi a lo studio della personalità e dell'opera,* I, Perugia, 27-87.

Zilkowski, A., 1986
The plundering of Epirus in 167 BC. Economic considerations. *PBSR* 54, 69-80.

Excavations at the Actian Tropaeum at Nikopolis

A preliminary report

Konstantinos Zachos

The Victory Monument founded by Octavian Augustus at Nikopolis in memory of the Actian naval battle was traced and partly excavated in 1913 by Alexandros Philadelpheus,[1] who interpreted his discoveries as the ruins of a Corinthian temple. In 1922 Konstantinos Romaios briefly noted that the architectural remains unearthed by Philadelpheus did not constitute a temple, but instead the Octavian Tropaeum, which was erected on the spot where, according to ancient writers, the Princeps had pitched his tent before the battle. Romaios regarded the memorial as a *temenos* or a sacred *peribolos*.[2] In 1924, Ioannis Miliadis resumed excavations on the lower terrace of the monument, but the only known result of this research was the detection of twelve blocks of the monumental inscription.[3] In 1936, Jean Gagé, in his article "Actiaca", proposed a reconstruction of the Latin inscription of the monument and analysed the background to and significance of the erection of the monument.[4] In 1974 Fotios Petsas excavated briefly on the upper terrace of the monument.[5] His results and all the previous partially known elements of the monument were brought together and published in a monograph in 1989 by him and William Murray, who also managed to explain the anchor-shaped cuttings on the facade of the monument ignored by previous research.[6]

Although this monument is of extreme importance, since its construction relates to one of the greatest historical events of the ancient world – the last major sea battle in antiquity – it remained little studied and poorly protected by the Greek Archaeological Service. Apart from that, the monument was plundered by the Italian army of occupation during World War II, when the locals were forced to smash many of its stone blocks in order to use them as material for the construction of three guard-houses on top of the Michalitsi hills.[7] During last year's excavations a limekiln was discovered in the south-west corner of the monument. We do not know either the exact date of the construction of the kiln or the extent of the destruction caused to the ruins. Also, there must have been extensive plundering in Antiquity, partly during the period of the barbarian invasions, when the monument's location outside the city walls made it extremely vulnerable, and partly during the early Christian period, when the pagan sanctuaries were demolished and new buildings were erected to glorify the Church.

The ongoing research, which started in 1995, aims to complete the excavation and

Fig. 1. Part of the Podium Façade with anchor – shaped cuttings.

conservation work.[8] Apart from the archaeological information to be gained, our project aims both to preserve the monument from further deterioration and to redesign the whole area in such a way that it can be visited by the public.

The Tropaeum is situated on the Michalitsi hills on the borders of the modern village of Nikopolis, north of the ancient city. The location of the monument is quite impressive and explains why it was chosen by Octavian for his camp.[9] From there one can observe the coastline of the Ionian sea and the shores of the Ambracian gulf, and, on a clear day, see the promontory of Actium and even the mountains of Acarnania and Leukas. At the foot of the hill towards the plain lie the ruins of buildings related to the Actian games,[10] the Stadium, the Gymnasium and the Theatre, described by Strabo as the Suburb (Προάστειον), situated in a grove.[11] Further south we come across the city of Nikopolis with its walls, cemeteries, and private and public buildings.

The monument was built on two terraces (Pl. 1). The visitor approaching the monument from the south sees on the first terrace a massive retaining wall of *opus caementicium*. Above this is the facade of a second pi-shaped retaining wall or podium, the side wings of which continue inside the hill. On the top of the podium there was a second terrace, along whose perimeter stood a pi-shaped stoa opening to the south. The main wing of the stoa defines the northern limit of the terrace, while its side wings reach the back of the podium. Thus an atrium is formed measuring 38 x 38 meters. The entire complex formed a kind of open-air sanctuary.

The subsoil of the hill is unsuitable for supporting the foundations of such massive constructions, a fact which demanded inventive solutions by the Roman architects. The erection of the monument in this specific location, and during a short period of time, must be connected with the ruler's political will and propaganda. The monument was built at the site where Octavian and his forces camped before the battle. It therefore sanctifies and

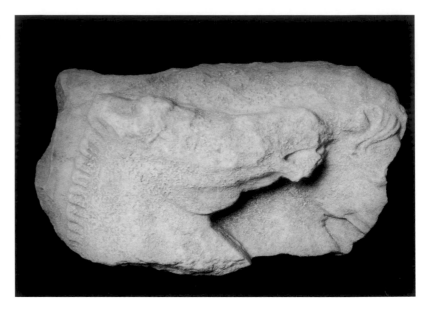

serves as a symbol of the New Order. Dio Cassius makes this clear when he mentions the location of the monument (51. 1. 3):

τὸ τε χωρίον ἐν ᾧ ἐσκήνησε, λίθοις τε τετραπέδοις ἐκρηπίδωσε καὶ τοῖς ἁλοῦσιν ἐμβόλοις ἐκόσμησεν, ἕδος τι ἐν αὐτῷ τοῦ Ἀπόλλωνος ὑπαίθριον ἱδρυσάμενος.
"On the spot where he had pitched his tent, he laid a foundation of square stones, adorned it with the captured ships' rams, and established on it a kind of open-air dwelling-place of Apollo" (Loeb edition of Cary).

Suetonius (*Aug.* 18, 2) is more specific as far as the symbolism of the Memorial is concerned:

Quoque Actiacae victoriae memoria celebratior et in posterum esset, urbem Nikopolim apud Actium condidit ludosque illic quinquennales constituit et ampliato vetere Apollinis templo locum castrorum, quibus fuerat usus, exornatum navalibus spoliis Neptuno ac Marti consecravit.

"To extend the fame of his victory at Actium and perpetuate its memory, he founded a city called Nikopolis near Actium, and provided for the celebration of games there every four years; enlarged the ancient temple of Apollo; and consecrated the site of the camp that he had used to

Fig. 2. Relief marble fragment with horse heads.

Fig. 3. Marble Gorgoneion from a cuirasse statue of an emperor or Mars Ultor.

Neptune and Mars, after adorning it with naval spoils" (Loeb edition of Rolfe).

According to the Greek and Roman tradition, trophies were usually erected on the battlefield. In this case, however, a site was chosen well away from the shores of Actium where the famous sea-battle took place, for reasons pointed out by Jean Gagé:[12]

"Mais le camp de Mikalitzi s'imposait à son choix; c'est à ses abords immédiates qu'avaient eu lieu les escarmouches de cavalerie [d'Antoine], suivis de l'entrée des transfuges; c'est là que dut se rendre, une semaine après la bataille navale, l'armée de terre d'Antoine, abandonnée par ses chefs – capitulation qui, quoiqu'elle fût facile à prévoir et obtenue sans combat, rendit seule la victoire définitive; c'est là surtout qu'Octave avait demeuré pendant toute la campagne, et la nuit même avant la bataille du 2 septembre; c'est donc là aussi qu'il en avait pris les auspices. Pour un *imperator* comme lui, superstitieux et particulièrement attaché aux rites auguraux que son nom même d'Auguste allait bientôt évoquer, ce *praetorium*, cet *augurale*, devait avoir une valeur sacrée, et, en effet, à coté des images divines qu'il y dressa, les fameuses statues de l'ânier Eutychios et de son âne Nicôn rappelait complaisamment les presages qui lui avaient annoncé sa victoire."

The area of the monument and the nearby hills consist of a clay substratum overlain by gravel. These two different formations cause a sliding effect, which is enforced by the underground waters emerging at the contact between these two layers. There are still springs in the area below and above the monument, and this was probably one reason why the area was chosen as a campsite. As we shall see below, the nature of the substratum has strongly affected the monument's stability.

The lower terrace

The retaining wall South side
The retaining wall is situated 3.50 metres from the podium facade. It is made of *opus caementicium*. In several places its surface was quite flat, but it was not possible to determine whether it was originally covered with stone slabs or other material or simply smoothed with plaster. On the top of its west and east sections two clay water-pipes were found running at right angles to the long axis of the wall. The facade of the wall was covered with small limestone blocks arranged according to the *opus quasi-reticulatum* system. Traces of plaster on some stones suggest that the facade of the wall was stuccoed. The wall is 2.80 metres in height, while its "stepped" foundation reaches 1.20 metres in height and 0.40 metres in width. The retaining wall is poorly preserved; its surface is mostly uneven, portions of the masonry have collapsed, and the entire structure from its foundations has slided southwards, especially in the eastern part. This last phenomenon is due not to pressure from material behind that shifted the retaining wall but to the slumping of the underlying layers. This also caused damage to the podium walls, which were found together with their foundations, pushed some meters south of their original position.

The podium facade
The podium is the best preserved and most impressive part of the monument. It is pi-shaped and is constructed of ashlar masonry. The original length of the facade

was ca. 62 meters long. The length of the side wings is unknown, since they are built into the slope of the hill. It is not clear yet if the side wings were visible in antiquity from the lower courses of limestone blocks to the top, or if they were partly covered with soil.

The foundations of the podium (1.20 m in height) were cut into the yellowish clay stratum, which is homogenous, compact and impermeable to water. The foundations are built of small sandstone slabs, mixed with small pieces of unworked limestone and a thin mortar. The sandstone blocks were most probably extracted from the nearby hills. On top of the foundation lies a line of roughly dressed limestone blocks, 0.50 m in height. These blocks form the *euthynteria* of the podium (Pl. 2).

The superstructure of the facade is constructed of ashlar masonry in an isodomic manner, with headers placed at irregular intervals. Each course consists of two rows of blocks (inner and outer). After the two rows of blocks of the *euthynteria* were laid on their concrete footing, additional concrete was poured behind them. The first course proper consisted only of the exterior blocks, while concrete was poured over the inner block up to the level of this first course. Thus limestone

blocks and concrete together constituted a massive structure. The blocks of limestone were clamped together with iron "double T" clamps. The presence of swallow-tail cuttings on several blocks at irregular positions is clear evidence that the blocks were reused and came from an older structure. The west part of the podium facade is the best preserved, with three courses of blocks above the *euthynteria*. In some instances blocks of the fourth course of the inner row are still in place. Neither

Fig. 4. Fragment of stamped roof tile.

Fig. 5. Fragment of sima with moulded depiction of the Lupa Romana and the twins.

the exact height of the podium, however, nor the way in which the whole monument was crowned, is as yet clear.

A long Latin inscription in capital letters decorated the upper part of the podium facade. Blocks with the inscription were discovered in front of the podium during the previous excavation's work. Twenty-eight blocks of the inscription were known up to 1995, nine of which are lost, I am afraid, forever. They were probably among those blocks smashed by the Italian army. Six new blocks, two of which are blank, were discovered during our investigation. The precise documentation of the position where the new fragments were recovered in combination with the complete clearing of the facade will hopefully help to restore this important Latin inscription.

Apart from the inscription, the podium facade preserves carved anchor-shaped sockets (Fig. 1), which originally held bronze rams from the captured battle ships of Antony and Cleopatra. The rams were displayed according to order of size, with the largest to the west and the smallest towards the east. The sockets of the largest rams rise up to the third course of the limestone blocks. A total of thirty-six to thirty-seven rams were displayed.

The rams were installed during the construction of the wall and not after its completion. Since the back of the rams is wider than the front, their placement after the construction of the wall would have compromised their stability. Therefore, after taking accurate measurement, the masons carefully carved the lower course of limestone blocks and placed the rams in position. Then the rest of the blocks were carved separately and carefully lowered into place. In this way each ram was locked into its individual socket and constituted part of the superstructure of the wall.

Besides the incorporation of the rams into the wall's masonry, their substantial weight demanded additional support. At a distance of about one-meter from the wall and just in front of each ram, rectangular sandstone foundations were uncovered.

Upon one of them a thick limestone slab is preserved. These foundations obviously constituted part of small supporting pedestals.

Water-drain behind the facade

Parallel to the podium's facade and 5.50 metres behind it, a water-drain made of clay bricks embedded in *opus caementicium* was uncovered, which extends deep into the ground. At the bottom of the drain there were roof tiles of the Corinthian type together with fallen clay bricks from the side walls. It is not clear as yet if the drain was covered by tiles.

The western wing of the podium

The podium's western wing displays the following characteristics: it was also constructed according to the isodomic masonry system, with headers at irregular intervals. The facade of the stone blocks was tooth-dressed and those of the superstructure were placed in a stepped manner, with the facade of the inner stones also tooth-dressed. Concrete was again poured here behind the outer row of blocks. "Double T" clamps and shift-holes were present on this part of the podium as well. Some blocks have an elongated cutting (up to 0.60 m. long) on their upper parts in order to secure the placement of the block above. Seven courses of limestone blocks have been attested above the *euthynteria*, but traces of concrete on the surface of the blocks of the seventh course, together with the presence of one block on top of it, probably in situ, suggest the existence of at least an eighth course.

The eastern wing of the podium

The same construction techniques were also used in the eastern wing. On the rear of the wall, in its southern part, we observed that a wall of sandstone slabs bonded with thin mortar had replaced the concrete and the second row of blocks. "Double T", "Pi-shaped" and swallow-tail clamps were also used here. The facade of the blocks is tooth-dressed, like that of the western wing. The uppermost stone preserved *in situ* in this part of the monu-

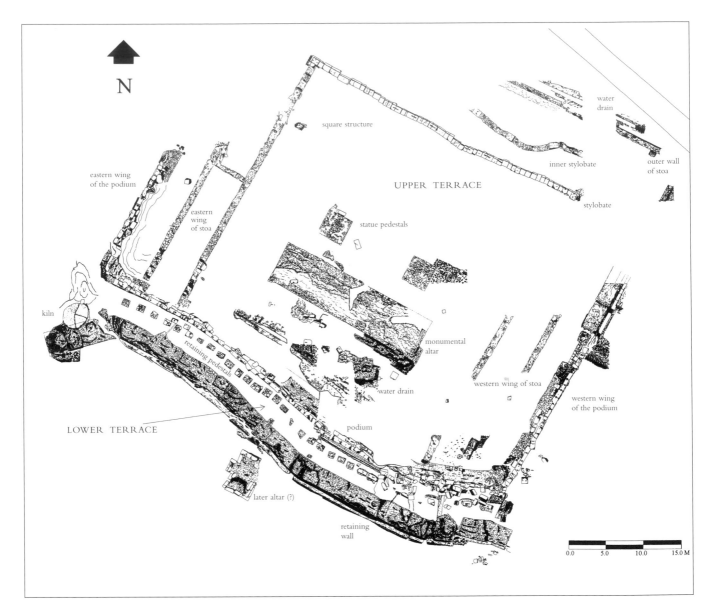

eastern wing
of the podium

eastern
wing
of stoa

kiln

retaining pedestals

LOWER TERRACE

later altar (?)

retaining
wall

square structure

UPPER TERRACE

statue pedestals

monumental
altar

water drain

podium

water
drain

inner stylobate

outer wall
of stoa

stylobate

western wing of stoa

western wing
of the podium

0.0   5.0   10.0   15.0 M

ment corresponds to the eighth stone course above the *euthynteria*, thus corresponding to the measurements of the visible stones on the west wing.

The structure in front of the podium

In the middle of the podium's facade and in front of the retaining wall, we found a rectangular structure with a square projection in the middle of its long west side. The structure is built of well-hewn limestone slabs, which form at least three steps. The stones are joined with Pi-shaped clamps, some of them still in situ, covered with lead. The interior of the structure was filled with stones and fragments of brick and roof tiles. The same filling is used for the foundation of the structure. Most probably the surviving elements belong to the lowest courses of the podium of an altar, which was erected after the completion of the main monument.

The excavation evidence given until this date shows that all the foundation walls of the monument on the lower and upper terrace are made of local soft yellowish sandstone slabs. The material of the foundation of the small edifice in front of the monument thus constitutes an exception. Furthermore, within the filling of the structure were found fragments of terracotta antefixes, which must originate from a roof belonging to the original building programme of the monument. Similar an-

Pl. 1. Plan of the Actian Trophaeum.

34

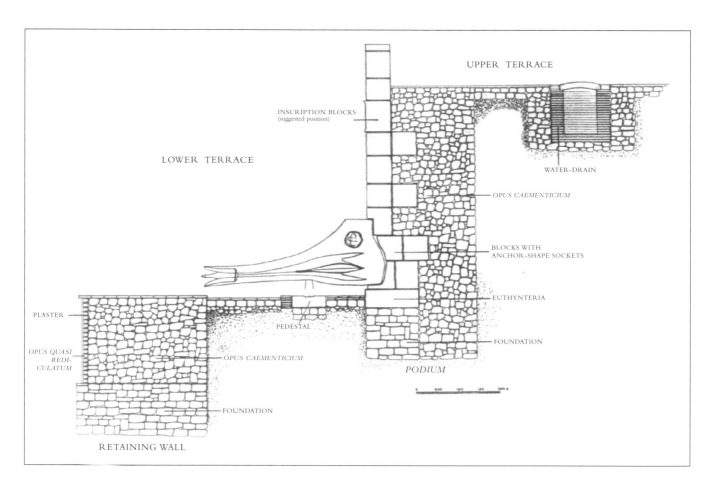

UPPER TERRACE

LOWER TERRACE

INSCRIPTION BLOCKS
(suggested position)

WATER-DRAIN

OPUS CAEMENTICIUM

BLOCKS WITH
ANCHOR-SHAPE SOCKETS

EUTHYNTERIA

FOUNDATION

PLASTER

*OPUS QUASI
REDI-
CULATUM*

PEDESTAL

OPUS CAEMENTICIUM

PODIUM

FOUNDATION

RETAINING WALL

Pl. 2. Reconstructed section of podium and retaining wall.

tefixes were found in other sectors of the excavations.

The upper terrace

The Stoa

The upper terrace measuring ca. 62 x 50m is enclosed on the north, east and west sides by a pi-shaped stoa, which has been partially excavated. The northern wing of the stoa preserves *in situ* limestone blocks of a 40.3 meters long stylobate[13] without steps (0.60-1.30 m long, 0.36 m thick). On the upper surface of the blocks are dowel sockets, shift-holes, lead channels, and setting lines. Also, in the space between the columns there are five long cuttings, possibly to hold metal tablets (in the 5th, 6th, 8th, 9th and 10th middle space). A swallow-tail cutting on the side of the third slab from the east of the stylobate indicates that the stones of this edifice were also transferred from elsewhere. The stylobate's foundation consists of small sand-

stone slabs bonded with thin mortar. About five meters north of the stylobate, the foundation of a second inner stylobate was found which has been excavated as far as 16 meters. Its construction was made of flat sandstones as well. Three limestone blocks (block dimensions: 1.10 x 0.90 x 0.45 meters) with sockets and setting lines were found up to present in the foundation wall. Their axial distance measures 5.60-5.80 meters from west to east. The wall has an elliptical distortion towards the south, due to the slumping of the substratum.

Further to the north, part of the outer wall of the stoa was found. It is made of *opus caementicium* resting on sandstone foundations. Near the wall, a destruction layer was found containing roof tiles. Along the outer wall of the stoa ran a drainage canal made of triangular bricks embedded in concrete. Its interior is covered with hydraulic mortar.

In the western wing of the stoa, parts of two long parallel foundation walls were found (0.95 m wide). They are made of roughly smoothed sandstone slabs with thin mortar as binding material. The easternmost wall meets on the north the western end of the outer stylobate of the north wing of the stoa. Likewise, the extension of the westernmost wall would meet the western end of the inner stylobate. The sandstone foundation in some parts reaches more than three meters in depth. Similar parallel foundation walls are partly preserved in the eastern wing of the pi-shaped stoa. It is not yet clear if the side wings of the stoa were double-aisled, like its north wing, or single-aisled. In the former case, the upper course of blocks of the perimeter of the podium would have served as a stylobate. The side wings of the stoa reached the rear of the south wall of the podium. This is verified by trial trenches at the south eastern corner of the terrace, where parts of the foundations of the eastern stoa wing were discovered. The western foundation wall towards the atrium, made of the usual sandstone slabs, was found detached from the podium's rear, due to the severe slumping in this part of the hill. The same phenomenon is also attested in connection with the next wall to the east, which is constructed in a different manner: upon the sandstone foundation a wall of *opus caementicium* dressed with triangular bricks *(opus testaceum)* was placed. This wall is preserved to a height of 1.50 m. On either side of the wall fallen column drums were found. This wall is connected with restoration and preservation works at the southeastern corner of the monument, which took place after a slippage that must have caused severe damage in that specific area. This hypothesis is supported by the different type of masonry attested in this part of the podium.

A section of about 17 meters of the eastern part of the podium's south wall has partly collapsed. In that part of the wall and behind the two rows of ashlar blocks, a two meter thick wall of *opus caementicium* constructed in a different manner is visible. Its southern face, which is in contact with the ashlar blocks, is dressed with square bricks bearing diagonal incisions, while on its outer face there are clear imprints of wooden framework.

Brick masonry *(opus testaceum)* is also attested in front of the ashlar blocks of the facade. The dating of this operation, obviously intended to retain the monument, it is not yet clear.

Among the various architectural elements, which have been attributed to the stoa, are four column drums, two Corinthian capitals and a column base, all made of limestone. According to the measurements of the column base, which correspond to the setting lines on the slabs of the stylobate, there was a total of fifteen columns in the northern wing of the stoa. The two surviving Corinthian capitals are, however, as has already been pointed out by other scholars, stylistically much later than the age of Augustus.[14] Do they belong to the restoration works mentioned above? And do these works have something to do with the activities at Nikopolis of the emperor Julian the Apostate? Claudius Mamertimus, prefect of Illyricum, who undertook the consulship on the 1st of January of 362 A.D., in his speech in honour of the emperor, mentions *(Paneg. Lat.* 11, 9) that Nikopolis was endowed by the emperor, who reorganized the Actian games and contributed to the repairs of the almost totally ruined private and public buildings of the city:[15] *Urbs Nikopolis, quam divus Augustus in monumentum Actiae victoriae trophaei instar exstruxerat, in ruinas lacrimabiles prope tota conciderat.*

Undoubtedly, the Trophy of Augustus must have been part of Julian's restoration programme, since it constituted the cornerstone of the religious activities during the Actian games and was the symbol of the city, commemorating the reason why it was founded by Octavian.

The area within the atrium

Statue pedestals
The foundations of two rectangular structures (3.60 x 3.55 m) were discovered in the central part of the atrium, 15 metres

from the stylobate of the stoa's north wing. They are made of sandstone slabs with a thin mortar as binding material. They must have served as pedestals for statues. From the western pedestal a large limestone block survives in situ. Various marble fragments with mouldings were collected from the area of the pedestals. A small bronze fragment with traces of drapery perhaps comes from one of the statues which stood on the pedestals.

Square structure
In the north eastern part of the atrium a small square structure was uncovered, sunk in the soil (0.90 x 0.60 meters), made of clay bricks (3-5 courses survive). A stone slab covers the bottom of its inner part. The soil inside and around the structure did not contain potsherds or other finds.

Monumental altar
South of the pedestals were found similar foundations, made of sandstone slabs, of a long rectangular structure, the excavation of which is still in progress. Its width measures 6 m, and its length is 22 meters. Although the topmost layer of the sandstone slabs of the foundation is missing, the layers of the surviving stones form a step along its long axis. The superstructure too was presumably stepped, because the excavation brought to light some limestone slabs south of it.

On the basis of the general characteristics of monumental altars, the central position of this structure on the upper terrace, and the plethora of marble architectural fragments found in the area of the structure and beyond, I suggest that the foundations belong to a monumental altar in the temenos. The altar like the main axis of the entire complex is oriented NE-SW, seventeenth degrees off the magnetic north.[16]

It is not clear as yet if this altar belongs to the pi-shaped with antis type of altar, like the altar from the Asklepieion on Kos[17], the altar of Nymphs at Knidos, the altar of Hera Epilimenia on Thasos and others, or to a oblong-shaped type.

Although Apollo's name is not present on the dedicatory inscription of the monument, where Neptune and Mars are mentioned, the hill itself, where the monument was erected, is referred to by Strabo as the holy hill of Apollo. The altar, as the central edifice for the cult rituals in the complex, must thus have been dedicated to Apollo, the princeps' patron god. The altar constituted the dwelling-place of Apollo, the ἕδος mentioned by Dio Cassius (51. 1. 3) ἕδος τι ἐν αὐτῷ τοῦ Ἀπόλλωνος ὑπαίθριον ἱδρυσάμενος. In addition, the pi-shaped altars have been connected with thrones, from which some scholars think that they were developed. Thus the famous altar of Apollo at Amyklae near Sparta was known as the Thronos of Apollo.[18]

On the thin earthen layers above and around the foundations were found marble architectural fragments with a variety of mouldings, which belong to the superstructure of the altar.

The marble relief fragments with various depictions in the Classicizing style, which were scattered all over the excavated area and especially in front of the collapsed part of the podium, must be assigned to a frieze or friezes adorning the altar. The fragmentary condition of the reliefs makes reconstruction difficult. The surviving fragments suggest battle scenes, and perhaps a triumphal procession and sacrifice. Fragments depicting spearheads, circular shields, horse heads (Fig. 2), and a chariot wheel, must come from a representation of a battle. A steering-paddle, representations of ships and human figures with short tunic perhaps come from a triumphal procession. This suggestion is confirmed by a fragment depicting a trophy. A fragment of a togatus and another of a woman perhaps belonged to a depiction of a procession with high officials. Similar scenes are known from other monuments of the Augustan period, such as the frieze on the temple of Apollo Sosianus[19] and the frieze on the Ara Pacis. However, the popular art motifs of the Augustan age, of ships and their attachments, with obvious reference to the Actian victory, have their origins in the Victory monument itself, which the princeps erected on the holy hill of Apollo. A marble fragment with relief gorgoneion seems to belong to a colossal statue of an emperor or Mars (Fig. 3).

In addition to the stoa, the monumental altar, and the statue pedestals, in the open space of the atrium various plants were grown. This suggestion is confirmed by the existence of small terracotta flowerpots, found in front of the stoa, which are similar to flowerpots from the garden of Hephaistos, in the Athenian Agora.[20]

Other finds

The amount of pottery discovered in excavation is exceptionally limited, in contrast to the great quantity of marble architectural fragments, terracotta roof tiles, bricks, and pieces of revetments, and about 15 coins, which await further study.

Roof tiles
Fragments of roof tiles of the Corinthian type were found all over the excavated area, both on the lower and upper terraces and especially within the destruction layer of the northern wing of the stoa. We propose that all these fragments come from the stoa, since there is no evidence that any of the other structures discovered to date was roofed. A considerable number of roof tiles were stamped. At least nine series with whole names or abbreviations, referring to builders, potters or persons who played an important role in the erection of a building, have been distinguished. The stamps, in descending order of frequency are:.
1. ΝΙΚΟΜΑΧΟΥ ΑΒΑ
2. ΣΩΤΗΡΙΧΟΥ
3. ΦΙΛΗΜΟΝΟΣ ΚΟΚ
4 ΝΙΚΗΦΟΡΟΥ
5 ΘΡΑCΩΝΟC
6. ΝΙΚΟΒΟΥΛΟΥ
7. ΑΝΔΡ
8 ΚΑΛΛΙΚΛΗ [Ι]
9 ΤΙΜΟΘ

On the basis of the letter forms the inscription ΝΙΚΟΜΑΧΟΥ should be dated to the 1st century B.C. The name is known in the Epirotic prosopography. It appears on the inscriptions in the theatre of Bouthroton[21] and on stamped tiles from Illyria.[22] The name ΣΩΤΗΡΙΧΟΥΣ (fig. 4) appears in the prosopography of Nikopolis.

The study of the stamps will certainly illuminate the history of the stoa's roof.

Terracotta revetments
A number of terracotta antefixes includes the following three types:
1. The first type is decorated with a moulded palmette. Nine wide leaves in low relief and ridged outline fan out from a gorgoneion.
2. The second type is also decorated with a moulded palmette. Four flame-shaped leaves with ridged outline flank on both sides a central dart shaped leaf. Below are two s-shaped volutes.
3. To the third type of antefix belong several fragments decorated also with palmettes. Nine leaves fan out from a heart. To this general type belong examples with minor variations.

Among the terracotta simas four types have been distinguished:
1. To the first type belong the lateral sima with a moulded depiction of the *Lupa Romana* and the twins (Fig. 5). On the right side of this fragmented wolf's-head water spout, the *Lupa Romana* is shown facing left with her head turned back towards the suckling twins below. Some other fragments come from the left side of the waterspout where the *Lupa Romana* is shown facing right. The motif of the *Lupa Romana* was very popular during the Empire and was represented on coins, gems, mosaics, funerary objects, military implements, lamps and items for personal use. The only representation on a terracotta revetment known to me is the example once in the Berlin Antiquarium, on which the shepherd Faustulus is also shown. The innocent charming scene with the she-wolf and the twins implies correlations between Romulus, the

founder of Rome and first Triumphator, and the victor Augustus, who on this hill dedicated the spolia of the enemy to Mars and Neptune.[23]

2. To the second type belongs the sima with a moulded decoration of dolphins. On either side of a dolphin's head water spout dolphins with raised tails are depicted swimming in opposite directions.

   Dolphins, like other marine creatures, are elements of the new iconographic repertoire which allude to the Victory at Actium and Neptune's assistance.

3. To the third and fourth type belong fragments of simas with relief floral decoration.

One of the most interesting finds in the excavations on the holy hill of Apollo is a massive six and a half kilo bronze fragment. It comes from a ram decorating the facade of the monument. This fragment is the only surviving element of the passionate lovers´ famous fleet. The detailed study and drawing of the fragment will perhaps help to locate its position among the displayed rams, while chemical analysis of the bronze will contribute to the study of technology of this important period.

Conclusions

The symmetry and axial planning of the monument on the holy hill of Apollo are evident. The pi-shaped stoa defines a regular space for a person inside the sanctuary. On the other hand, its location on a terrace with the impressive shining rams on the facade allowed the whole architectural complex to make its full impact when seen from a distance. The monument recalls the layout of the upper stoa of the Asklepieion on Kos of the late Hellenistic period, as well as several similar sanctuaries of this type built under the later Roman Republic, such as the sanctuaries of Juno at Gabii,[24] of Fortuna at Praeneste[25] and of Hercules at Tibur.[26] The main axes of the Tropaeum of Augustus correspond to the main axes of the city plan on the plain below. The orientation and planning of the monument most probably determined the orientation of the city plan. It seems that both monument and city were organized on a master plan initiatiated and authorized by the founder.

As to the construction date of the tropheum, the 16th of January 27 B.C. could be considered as *terminus ante quem* according to the words of the inscription: CONSVL SEPTIMUM. According to another point of view, the expression of the Latin inscription PACE PARTA TERRA MARIQUE should be considered as *terminus post quem*, correlating with the closing of the temple of Janus the 11th of January, 29 B.C. Thus, the summer of 29 B.C. is considered as the most acceptable date for the construction of the monument.[27]

Notes

I would like to express my acknowledgments to my colleagues: The archaeologists Hara Kappa, Mary Scandali, Anastasia Georgiou, the excellent designer Nicos Vagenas and the chief guard of the Nicopolis Museum George Nousias for their contribution to the whole progress of the excavations and the documentation of the Augustus Tropaeum which is deeply appreciated.

NOTE 1
Philadelpheus, A. 1913a, 85-91; Philadelpheus, A. 1913b, 235; Philadelpheus, A. 1921, 11-12, 44.

NOTE 2
Rhomaios, K. 1922, 515; Rhomaios, K. 1925, 1-4.

NOTE 3
The whole collection of 25 blocks, including the blocks located by Miliadis, was presented in an "epigraphic note" at the end of Gagé's article, see Gagé, J. 1936, 100.

NOTE 4
Ibid., 37-100.

NOTE 5
Petsas, F. 1974a, 50-53; Petsas, F. 1974b, 79-88, pls. 60-70.

NOTE 6
Murray, W.M. and Petsas, F.M. 1989.

NOTE 7
Ζημίαι των αρχαιοτήτων εκ του πολέμου και των στρατών κατοχής 1946, 66.

NOTE 8
Zachos, K. 1995 (in press); Zachos, K. 1996 (in press).

NOTE 9
Dio Cassius 51. 1. 3.

NOTE 10
Krinzinger, F. 1987, 109-120.

NOTE 11
Strabo 7. 7. 6: ἡ μὲν οὖν Νικόπολις εὐανδρεῖ καὶ λαμβάνει καθ' ἡμέραν ἐπίδοσιν, χώραν τε ἔχουσα πολλὴν καὶ τὸν ἐκ τῶν λαφύρων κόσμον, τό τε κατασκευασθὲν τέμενος ἐν τῷ προαστείῳ τὸ μὲν εἰς τὸν ἀγῶνα τὸν πενετετηρικὸν ἐν ἄλσει ἔχοντι γυμνάσιόν τε καὶ στάδιον, τὸ δ᾽ ἐν τῷ ὑπερκειμένῳ τοῦ ἄλσους ἱερῷ λόφῳ τοῦ Ἀπόλλωνος.

NOTE 12
Gagé, J. 1936, 75-76.

NOTE 13
Petsas, F. 1974b, 82; Murray and Petsas 1989, 84, figs. 6-7 and 52.

NOTE 14
Murray and Petsas 1989, 78, n. 91.

NOTE 15
Chrysos, E. 1981, 22, n. 1.

NOTE 16
In the present description of the various elements of the monument I use for simplicity a true north orientation in order to facilitate our communication.

NOTE 17
Coulton, J.J. 1976, 248, fig. 74.

NOTE 18
Papachatzis, N. 1976, fig. 396.

NOTE 19
La Rocca, Eug. 1985.

NOTE 20
Thompson-Burr, D. 1937, 396-425; Travlos, J. 1971, 273, fig. 350.

NOTE 21
Cabanes, P. 1974, 105-208.

NOTE 22
Ceka, N. 1982, 103-130.

NOTE 23
For the iconography of *lupa Romana*, see, *LIMC*, VI, 1, pp. 292-296.

NOTE 24
Ward-Perkins, J.B. 1977, 35, pl. 45.

NOTE 25
Ibid., 13. 35, 39, 99, pls. 46-51.

NOTE 26
Ibid., 34-35, pls. 36, 44.

NOTE 27
Schäfer, Th. 1993, 239-248.

Bibliography

Cabanes, P., 1974
Les inscriptions du théâtre de Bouthrôtos, *Actes du colloque 1972 sur l'esclavage*, Besançon 1974, 105-208.

Ceka, N., 1982
Timbres antiques trouvés dans la contrée entre Aoos et Genusus, *Iliria*, Vol.1, 103-130

Chrysos, E., 1981
Συμβολή στην Ιστορία της Ηπείρου, *Ηπειρωτικά Χρονικά* 23, 9-112.

Coulton, J. J., 1976
The Architectural Development of the Greek Stoa, Oxford

Gagé, J., 1936
Actiaca, *Mélanges d' archéologie et d' histoire* 53, 37-100.

Krinzinger, F., 1987
Nikopolis in der augusteischen Reichspropaganda, *Νικόπολις Α', Πρακτικά του πρώτου Διεθνούς για Νικόπολη (23-29/9/1984)*, Πρέβεζα.

La Rocca, E., 1985
Amazzonomachia. Le sculture frontonali del tempio di Apollo Sosiano, Roma

LIMC (Lexicon Iconographicum Mythologiae Classicae), 1992
Lupa Romana, VI, 1, 292-296.

Murray, W. M. and Petsas, F.M., 1989
Octavian's Campsite Memorial for the Actian War, *Transactions of the American Philosophical Society*, Vol. 79, Part 4, Philadelphia.

Papachatzis, N., 1976
Παυσανίου, "Ελλάδος περιήγησις", Vol. 2.

Petsas, F., 1974a
Νικόπολις (Ρωμαϊκή), *Το Έργον της Αρχαιολογικής Εταιρείας*, 50-53.

Petsas, F., 1974b
Ανασκαφή Ρωμαϊκής Νικοπόλεως, *Πρακτικά της εν Αθήναις Αρχαιολογικής Εταιρείας*, 79-88, pls. 60-70.

Philadelpheus, A., 1913a
Ανασκαφαί Νικοπόλεως, *Πρακτικά της εν Αθήναις Αρχαιολογικής Εταιρείας*, 1913, 85-91.

Philadelpheus, A., 1913b
Ανασκαφαί Νικοπόλεως, *Αρχαιολογικής Εταιρείας*, 1913, 235.

Philadelpheus, A., 1921
Ανασκαφαί Νικοπόλεως, *Πρακτικά της εν Αθήναις Αρχαιολογικής Εταιρείας*, 1921, 11-12, 44.

Rhomaios, K., 1922,
BCH 46, 515.

Rhomaios, K., 1925
Παράρτημα 1922-1925, *Αρχαιολογικόν Δελτίον* 9, 1-4.

Schäfer, Th., 1993
Zur Datierung des Siegesdenkmals von Actium, *AM* 108, 239-248

Thompson-Burr, D., 1937
The garden of Hephaistos, *Hesperia* 6, 396-425.

Travlos, J., 1971
Pictorial Dictionary of Ancient Athens, London.

Ward-Perkins, J. B., 1977
Roman Architecture, New York.

Zachos, K., 1995
Αρχαιολογικόν Δελτίον, Χρονικά (in press).

Zachos, K., 1996
Αρχαιολογικόν Δελτίον, Χρονικά (in press).

Ζημίαι των αρχαιοτήτων εκ του πολέμου και των στρατών κατοχής, Υπουργείον Θρησκευμάτων και Εθνικής Παιδείας, Διεύθυνοις Αρχαιοτήτων και Ιστορικών Μνημείων, 1946.

Landscape Archaeology in the Territory of Nikopolis

James Wiseman

Introduction★

The Nikopolis Project is an interdisciplinary archaeological investigation which has as its broad, general aim the explanation of the changing relationships between humans and the landscape they inhabited and exploited in southern Epirus, from Palaeolithic to Mediaeval times.[1] Specifically, the Project has employed intensive archaeological survey[2] and geological investigations[3] to determine patterns of human activity, and to reconstruct what the landscape was like in which those activities took place. This undertaking in landscape archaeology has led to new insights into the factors that underlie changes in human-land relationships, in some instances over a short time-span, but particularly over the long term.

There were annual field seasons during the summers of 1991-1994,[4] followed by

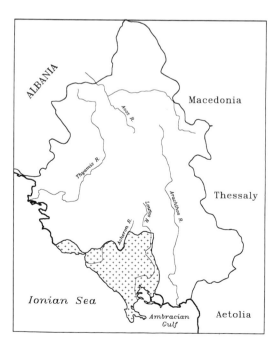

Fig. 1. Map of Epirus with adjacent regions; the survey zone is marked by crosses.

study seasons in Epirus in 1995 and 1996; research and analyses of the primary data have continued since that time, along with the writing of reports. The survey zone (Figs. 1, 2) extends from the straits of Actium at the entrance to the Ambracian Gulf north to Parga, and from the Louros river gorge to the Ionian seacoast, including the entire *nomos* (administrative district) of Preveza, a modern town on the Nikopolis peninsula. On the east the survey zone extended along the northern coast of the Ambracian Gulf into the *nomos* of Arta, so that the deltaic, lagoonal area of the Louros river was included, but not the city of Arta (the ancient Ambracia). Since the survey zone is about 1,200 square kilometers, far too large an area for a complete intensive survey, we chose to sample each of the different environmental zones: coastal plains, inland valleys, mountainous terrain, and upland valleys. We were guided in our selection of areas to survey by acquired knowledge of the region, ranging from geomorphology to direct observation of current conditions of the landscape. The advice of our geomorphologists, for example, enabled us to avoid surveying areas of recent alluviation where ancient remains (if any) would have been covered over and not detectable, although we did survey some areas to test negative indications from geomorphology or satellite imagery. We did not select for survey fields so densely covered with vegetation that ancient remains, if there, could not be detected, but we did return to survey some such fields in another year or season when the vegetation was less thick. The field work included both "siteless" and on-site survey, involving transects within large regions and intensive sam-

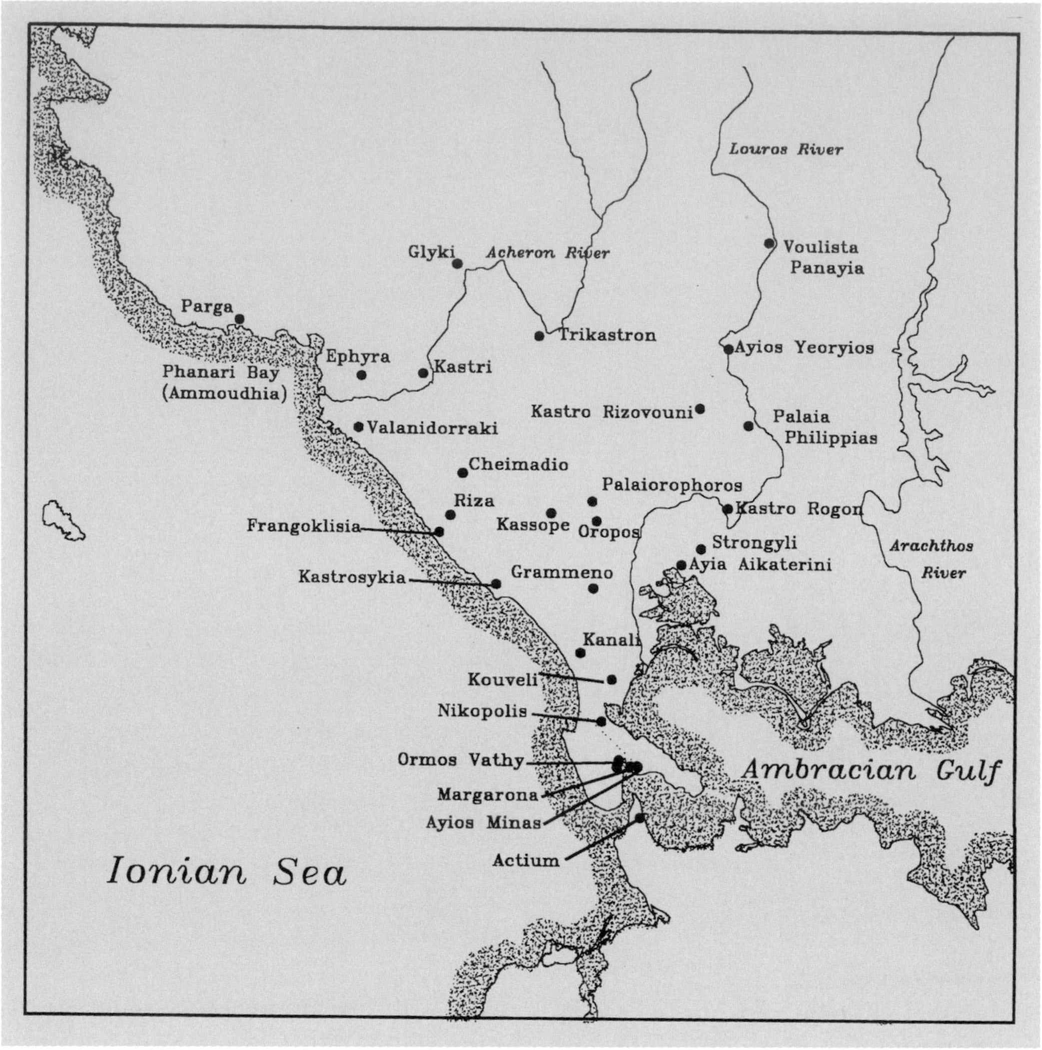

Fig. 2. Map of project area with selected sites discussed in text.

pling, or complete coverage, of human-activity areas ranging from small single-activity sites to extensive settlements. In addition, one fortified town site (Kastri, in the lower Acheron valley) was selected for complete, intensive urban survey.[5]

Multispectral (MSS) and panchromatic imagery of the survey zone, acquired from the French satellite company SPOT prior to field work in 1991, proved useful in a variety of ways. As a component-layer in some of the computer-aided maps we have generated as part of the Project's Geographic Information System (GIS), it adds details of current landcover and other features of the terrain (Fig. 3). The imagery was also helpful in defining zones for surface survey, but we had little success with it in developing spectral signatures[6] of archaeological features. A major prob-

lem was that the smallest detectable feature of the imagery (that is, its resolution) was 20 m in MSS and 10 m in panchromatic, too large for most archaeological features, although the resolution was at the smallest scale available for our research at the time. Because of the resolution and the inability of this type of sensor to penetrate dense vegetation, which covered much of our survey zone, we had not expected the imagery to be of significant value in the detection of ancient sites. The imagery was able, however, to detect eroded Pleistocene landscapes, which our field teams then located on the ground with the aid of Global Positioning System (GPS) units[7] and 1:5,000 topographic maps; prehistoric stone tools were found by ground-truthing teams at five areas visited in this manner (Stein and Cullen

Fig. 4. Kastro Rogon, the ancient Bouchetion. View from a tethered blimp at elevation of ca. 600 m. North is at the top of the photo. Photo by J. Wilson and Eleanor Emlen Myers.

Fig. 3. Northern SPOT satellite mage. The Acheron and the Louros, the two principal rivers of the project area, have been enhanced.

1994; Wiseman 1996). Other types of remote sensing, especially aerial photography and geophysical prospection, also were employed by the Project, and proved to be of significant value, as discussed below, for the study of all time periods.

The Nikopolis Project takes its name from the Roman imperial urban center of the region, a central concern of this conference. In this paper I focus on some of the results of the survey that contribute to an understanding of the changes that took place from Hellenistic and Roman times to the Mediaeval period, and on the methodologies and techniques employed by the Nikopolis Project.

North Coast of the Ambracian Gulf

A flat, partly deltaic plain extends south from the abrupt ends of Mt. Rokia and Mt. Stavros (west of Rokia) some 12 km to the swampy north shore of the Ambracian Gulf, which is separated from the main body of water by a series of lagoons. The plain stretches further northwest and west to Mt. Zalongo and the Nikopolis peninsula. The three mountains terminate a series of Mesozoic limestone ridges, separated by fertile basins, that served as natural corridors of varying convenience for traveling between north and south in Epirus and which were open both in prehistoric and historical times. The easternmost corridor within our survey zone is the gorge of the Louros river, which now, at its exit from the gorge, curves sharply to the northwest and follows the edge of Mt. Rokia for some four km before turning west and finally almost due south to empty at last into the gulf by the Tsokalio lagoon, less than four km northeast of the Mazoma, as the embayment by Nikopolis has been called since the early 9th century (Soustal 1981, 204). The plain now is widely cultivated, both drained and irrigated by a series of canals, some of which were dug as recently as the 1960s. The most imposing site in the region is Kastro Rogon (S/S91-1), the ancient Bouchetion, a fortified town on a low elevation

45

above the right bank of the Louros near the foot of Mt. Rokia. The earliest remains found date to the 6th century B.C., but the town may have existed earlier; it is one of four colonies founded in Epirus by the southern Greek city of Elis.[8] Its well preserved Classical fortifications were successively refurbished and expanded in Hellenistic and Medieval times, and have now been documented by the Project in aerial photographs at different elevations from a tethered blimp (Fig. 4).[9] Another important site, a Roman villa and Hellenistic farmstead, lies about 3.2 km to the southwest at the northern foot of Mt. Mavrovouni near the village of Strongyli (S/S91-10).[10] The Nikopolis Project conducted repeated surveys at, and in the vicinity of, both sites. The earlier site at Strongyli was probably a fortified farmstead of the 2nd century B.C.; the lower part of a tower with handsome trapezoidal masonry on the exterior and with interior rooms constitutes the principal visible remains of the farm. During the first three centuries of the Roman Imperial period, a large villa estate with mosaic floors in the main building, a bath house, and facilities for the production of olive oil (Fig. 5) covered the low elevation above the tower.[11]

A program of geologic coring and geomorphologic studies by Zhichun Jing and Rip Rapp in this region, coupled with archaeological survey, had some rather startling results. Jing and Rapp have shown that the period from about 2,500 B.C. until the 5th century A.D. was a time of maximum marine transgression in the Ambracian embayment, so that the north shore of the gulf lay at the foot of Mts. Stavros and Rokia, and there was no floodplain (Fig. 6). Mt. Mavrovouni, including the Hellenistic farmstead and early Roman villa at its foot, was the largest island in the bay, and even the hill of Bouchetion was a small island, 65-75 meters above sea level, separated from the mainland by a narrow stretch of water, which could have been bridged. A smaller island (elev. 54 masl) southwest of Strongyli, where there is a church of Ay.

Fig. 5. Olive mills at villa of Strongyli.

Aikaterini (S/S92-31), also was inhabited both in Roman times and in Late Antiquity. The Louros river during that period flowed directly into the sea northeast of the modern village of Nea Kerasous on a foothill of Mt. Rokia. The infilling of the embayment began by the 5th century when tectonic uplift of the Nikopolis peninsula, in progress for millennia, at last began to accelerate erosion already being caused by cultural factors along the western side of the gulf. At about the same time, as relative sea level had ceased to rise, the sediments carried by the Louros (perhaps in greater quantity) began to form a deltaic plain so that the mouth of the river moved progressively further to the south and southwest. Jing and Rapp have also shown that sometime between the 10th and the 15th century, after much of the northern and western part of the embayment had became swampy marshland and lagoons, the Louros was diverted by human means into its current channel, running north alongside Kastro Rogon (see Fig. 4) and following the course described in the preceding paragraph.[12]

The diversion of the river's course served two purposes: it drained part of the coastal swamp, thereby providing additional farmland, and it provided a canal, navigable by small ships, between the Ambracian Gulf and Rogoi, as Bouchetion was called by (at least) the late 9th century (Soustal 1981, 251-252). The new channel enabled Rogoi to become a harbor town as it had been during Greek and Roman times when, as Bouchetion, it lay on the edge of the open water of the bay. It served then as a commercial port, small though it was, linking sea-borne traffic

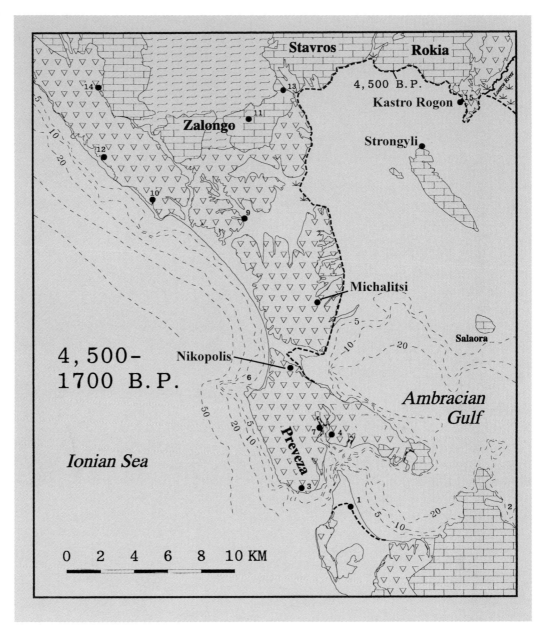

with the inhabitants scattered among the inland valleys and along the fringes of the flood plain. The town ranked above Arta in the 10th-12th centuries and remained a major city on the north shore of the gulf until Preveza, founded in the late 13th century and refounded by the Turks in the late 15th century,[13] superseded it as a seaport and administrative center, as Arta had as both an ecclesiastical and administrative center. Rogoi for awhile was the repository of celebrated holy relics. In 1436 Cyriacus of Ancona visited Rogoi, where he saw both the remains of St. Luke the Evangelist and the head of Anna, mother of the Virgin Mary, and on St. Luke's day (18 October) in 1448 he went from Arta to Rogoi expressly to pray to St. Luke.[14] The relics of St. Luke had been brought by ship to Rogoi by a French captain who had stolen them during the sack of Constantinople in 1204; they remained at Rogoi by orders of the Duke of Kephallenia who purchased them from the Crusader.[15] The occasional details provided by Cyriacus of his travels along the northern coast of the Ambracian Gulf reveal that the Louros (which he consistently called the Acheron) had been diverted before his first visit in 1436.[16] It seems likely, furthermore, that the new river channel was in place by 1204, inasmuch as the French captain sailed to Rogoi and (expressly) stopped "in the harbor."[17] Although there is no mention of the Louros river in the original Greek account, the French captain must have navigated his ship up the new channel to Rogoi because the bay around Rogoi had been filled in some centuries before, as Jing and Rapp have shown, and the Louros did not flow by Rogoi until after it was diverted.

The increasingly unhealthy, unpleasant living conditions on the north shore of the Ambracian Gulf that accompanied the infilling of the embayment beginning in the late 4th or 5th century, combined with the arrival of the Slavs in Epirus in the 6th century and a recurring pestilence (discussed below), were likely major factors in the sharp drop in the number of sites of all kinds in southern Epirus from Late Antiquity to Mediaeval times: and there is little evidence for occupation in the 7th and 8th centuries. Most of the new Mediaeval foundations were ecclesiastical communities, and often they were not placed in the older Roman towns. We might consider the possibility that some of them were founded as part of a policy of agricultural development in a largely abandoned landscape. In the coastal area of the Ambracian Gulf, Rogoi was revived, as we have seen, and was a bishopric by the late 9th century;[18] the monastery of Kozyle above the western edge of the new marshy plain was founded in the 10th or early 11th century;[19] the monastery of Ay. Varvara at the foot of Mt. Stavros near the modern town of Stephani, and close to the right bank of the Louros, was built in the 12th century above the ruins of a 6th-century church;[20] and the monastery at Pantanassa in the Louros river gorge near its mouth was founded in the 13th century.[21] It may be possible to view the diverting of the Louros river – perhaps in the late 9th or early 10th century, and no later than the end of the 12th century – as part of a larger, long-term effort, guided by the ecclesiastical communities, to bring eco-

Fig. 7. SPOT satellite image of the Nikopolis peninsula and the Straits of Actium.

nomic life back to the land by the establishment of fisheries in the lagoons;[22] by diverting and controlling the Louros and possibly constructing other canals to convert the coastal swamp into productive agricultural land; and by making Rogoi a river port. A similar role for ecclesiastical communities in a sparsely populated landscape has recently been noted in Anglo-Saxon Britain, in the Po Valley of Italy, and in other parts of western Europe (Balzaretti 1996; Wiseman 1997, 14). Indeed, the role of ecclesiastical communities in the revival of the countryside and the rise of urbanism in western Europe, is currently a topic of active scholarly debate. The results of our survey in southern Epirus suggest that Greece may make some contributions to that debate.

P. N. Doukellis (1990) found traces of centuriation in the orientation and size of fields in the plain of Arta and extending at least to the mouth of the Louros gorge; he associated the cadastral arrangements with the founding of Nikopolis.[23] Noting that some of the drainage canals in the central and western plain follow the same orientation as that of his proposed centuriation, he suggests that the Roman founders of Nikopolis also undertook the draining of swamps in the plain. Although he shows on his overall map of the plan (his Map 3) only scattered traces of the cadastral orientation in the western part of the plain, he seems inclined to extend the network at least to include the Roman villa at Strongyli (Doukellis 1990, 275). Since the geologists and archaeologists of the Nikopolis Project did not extend their investigations east of the survey zone, we cannot speak with authority about Doukellis's claims for the central and eastern plain. The Arachthos river, however, does have a much heavier discharge than the Louros,[24] so that alluviation in the eastern part of the north shore presumably began earlier and proceeded at a more rapid pace than in the west. If the southeastern part of the plain had formed by the late 1st century B.C., as Doukellis believes, the founding of Nikopolis would have provided a reasonable occasion for the centuriation. Intrigued by his hypothesis, and considering it possible that Roman surveyors might have extended centuriation lines across the water to include the island of Mavrovouni, we sought traces of the cadastral arrangement in radar imagery acquired in 1998 from Canadian RADARSAT. Using a variety of filtering techniques on the imagery, Cordula Robinson of Boston University's Center for Remote Sensing, in collaboration with Carol Stein and Wiseman, found that the orientation of field boundaries along Mt. Mavrovouni and in the area of Strongyli, as well as some roadways and canals in the area, do indeed follow the approximate orientation Doukellis noted (Wiseman, Robinson, and Stein 1998). The orientation, however, is about the same as the line of the ridge of Mavrovouni, the dominant topographic feature of the region, which should be expected to have influenced the orientation of field boundaries on its slopes and at its foot. What is more, the module of 710 m could not be found. The orientation of Mediaeval and modern field boundaries or other features in the reclaimed marshland of the

Louros delta could have been influenced by a pre-existing network in the plain of Arta, but further work is needed for confirmation. It would be particularly useful to have a geomorphologic study of the plain of Arta to determine its extent at different times from antiquity to the present. We did detect shadow lines in the radar imagery that appear to be the course of the Louros river before it was diverted, as well as the possible shoreline, but the latter certainly requires confirmation by a coring program extending into the plain of Arta.

The Nikopolis Peninsula

The Nikopolis peninsula (Fig. 7) is connected to the mainland by a low-lying isthmus, currently only 2.3 km wide, which was an open channel connecting the Ionian sea and the Ambracian Gulf during prehistoric periods of maximum marine transgression (before ca. 6000-7000 B.P), but by Roman times was narrower even than it is today. Continuous tectonic uplift of the peninsula and erosion of the hillsides to the north have combined to move the eastern shoreline further east; as a result, during Roman times the Mazoma embayment may have extended 500 meters or more inland (Jing and Rapp 2000, in press), and could have served Nikopolis as a small harbor close to its north wall. Ships coming from the Ionian Sea, however, after passing thorough the Actium Straits would have had to sail around the Ay. Thomas peninsula, which extends some 6.5 km eastwards into the gulf, before they could enter it. A far more important harbor for Nikopolis lay along the shores of Ormos Vathy (="Deep Harbor"), a two-pronged inlet on the south side of the Ay. Thomas peninsula at its juncture with the Nikopolis peninsula. Jing and Rapp (2000, in press) have shown that the western prong in Roman times extended further inland towards Nikopolis, and archaeological survey teams of the project have found extensive remains of settlement throughout the Roman period and Late Antiquity all along the shores of

Ormos Vathy. The Project has identified the main harbor town (SS93-8), whose ancient identity is unknown, on the west bank of Ormos Vathy, about 2.5 km south of Nikopolis, covering more than 16 ha. and probably extending under buildings of the northeastern suburb of Preveza. Special activity areas within the harbor town discovered by the Project include a locus for extracting purple dye[25] and storage facilities by the harbor. On the shore opposite the southern end of the harbor town stood a large Roman bath (SS93-24), perhaps drawing its water from a nearby spring that still supplies visitors to the area. The substantial ruins of the bath are around and under the Church of Zoodhochos Pygi and a taverna along the shore below a resort hotel; the region, called Margarona, is reached now by a bridge across the entrance to Ormos Vathy from the Preveza side. There is some architectural evidence for an earlier (Late Antique) church below the modern church, but excavation would be required to confirm this hypothesis.

The entire Ay. Thomas peninsula received much attention from the Project's survey teams and is discussed at length by Carol A. Stein in another paper presented at this conference. As an additional observation on the utility of remote sensing and GIS in survey, however, I note here that her plotting of some of the archaeological activity areas surveyed by the Project fall along lines that provide some supporting evidence for the centuriation of the Nikopolis peninsula, including Ay. Thomas, as proposed previously by scholars making use of aerial photography (Cladas 1975; Doukellis 1988).

Michalitsi and Areas North of the Nikopolis Peninsula

The largest Greek-period town discovered in the vicinity of Nikopolis lies north of the peninsula on Kouveli hill (SS93-12), reached by a major road that served travelers from at least Classical Greek times through the Turkish period. The road ascended from the region of the Mazoma and along the hill of the Augustan Victory Monument, to run along the north-south ridge known as Palaiosteno from which both the sea and the gulf are often visible; it is still used to provide access to farmlands, especially those on the slopes of the eroded hills, including Kouveli, that descend eastward to the plain of Grammeno and the north shore of the Ambracian gulf, to which the old road eventually led. The road, especially on Palaiosteno, was lined with ancient graves, many of which must have been for the inhabitants of the site at Kouveli; another major cemetery of Classical to Hellenistic times lies on the lower slopes to the southeast in a region known as Marathia (SS93-19) on the outskirts of the modern town of Michalitsi, where built tombs in family plots, one marked by a marble statue of a lion, were excavated in the 1960s and 1970s.[26] The town itself was centered on the upper slopes of Kouveli and was occupied at least from the Archaic period through Hellenistic; during the Roman period and Late Antiquity; Mediaeval and post-Mediaeval material (a Turkish-period pipe, diagnostic glazed sherds) was also found, especially on and near the peak. The region was intensively surveyed (Fig. 8),[27] and over 13,000 artifacts were counted.

Much work was focused on defining the nature and extent of the site, as the effects of erosion and slope wash, identifiable by visual examination, became evident in artifact densities, which were consistently lower downslope. From the site itself it is possible to see that the natural drainage of the entire Michalitsi area is towards the lagoonal area of the Ambracian Gulf, and there can be no doubt that much of the infilling of the western portion of the bay was from deposits of these hills that washed and slid down the slope. One memorable example that illustrates some aspects of the process is at a brick factory, abandoned some 15-20 years ago, located just off the main paved road from Preveza to Arta, about 500 meters west of the turnoff to Michalitsi. In the clay quarry behind the factory in 1995, I observed a landslide running west to east was carry-

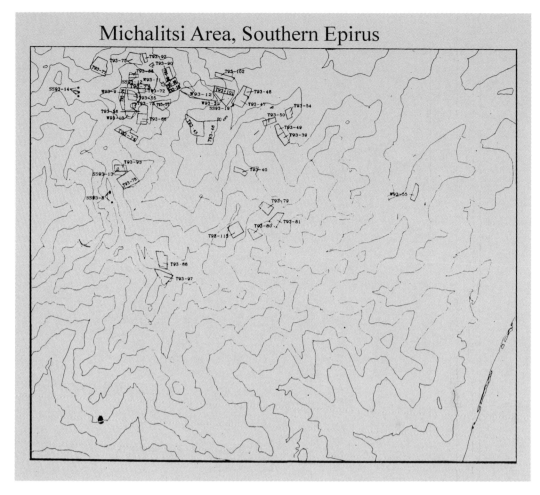

Fig. 8. Kouveli site near Michalitsi. AutoCAD drawing showing contour lines and locations of survey units.

ing shrubs and even olive trees with it, creating a new slope in the quarry on its way to the bay. On a visit to Kouveli itself with some of the senior staff in 1995 we noted that a farmer had recently brought earth (along with potsherds!) from some other place to create a small garden. Unfortunately, as Tjeerd van Andel pointed out to us, the farmer had placed his garden on the edge of an active gully, and within a few years the new earth, and the potsherds, will wash away down the gully to the lower slopes. In other areas terrace walls retain planted fields, and they will retard erosion, but only so long as someone tends the walls. These observations may serve as an example of how ancient material from one place gets transferred to another, and then by erosion to yet another place; the example also illustrates the problems of interpreting the significance of a limited amount of cultural material found on the surface of the ground any

place. It is critically important to try to understand the factors, whether geomorphologic or cultural or other, that may have influenced the location of cultural artifacts observed or collected in archaeological survey. The evidence from the site at Kouveli points to an area of about 6,125 square meters, which does not include outlying sites, such as a habitation area some 350 m to the south, or the cemeteries. Few remnants of structures were visible above ground, and there was no trace of a town wall.[28] Artifact distribution revealed little about special-activity areas. Magnetometer survey, on the other hand, was conducted in 1993 by John Weymouth (University of Nebraska) in two areas near the peak where some 40 pieces of iron slag had been collected on the surface. He detected in one field five significant anomalies, suggesting smelting activities and possibly an associated structure at depths of 2-3 m below the surface.

Geophysical prospection was also used at a number of other sites, and with a variety of instrumentation; the results were usually highly informative and useful. It helped to locate, for example, the walls of the predecessor, probably built in Late Antiquity, of the church of Ay. Minas on the Ay. Thomas peninsula, and resulted in the detection of buried cisterns, walls, and paths at Kastri (S/S94-20), the fortified townsite in the lower Acheron valley discussed below. Apostolos Sarris, staff geophysicist in 1994, now of the Institute of Mediterranean Studies on Crete, conducted geophysical prospection in selected areas not only of Kastri, but of all the fortified townsites surveyed by the Project.

Above the northern end of the long, sandy Nikopolis beach on the Ionian coast, a promontory with ancient remains by the modern town of Kastrosykia overlooks what may have been a small anchorage in Hellenistic and Roman times. The principal remains on the promontory are several architectural blocks, some of them reused in the church of Ay. Pelagia, which are mainly of Roman imperial date, as are the few graves noted nearby (Dakaris 1971, 95; Hammond 1967, 49). Further north along the coast a particularly interesting Roman site is that of Frangoklisia (SS93-27), west of modern Riza and overlooking the coast by the lovely little harbor known as Artolithia. Walls of brick and concrete have long been noted here (they are difficult to miss, since some are preserved to a height of 3 m!), and the remains had previously been identified as a nymphaeum (Chrysostomou 1982). The Project conducted a brief survey in the area in 1993, which was followed by cleaning, study, and drawing of the visible walls and floors by the Greek Ephoreia (Zachos 1993). The walls belong to an extensive architectural complex, including a bath, that must have served as the residence of a wealthy landowner during at least the Early Roman period; most of the pottery found during the Greek investigations dates from the 1st to the 3rd centuries A.D., and the Project recovered also material of Late Antiquity. Excavation

would be required to determine if Frangoklisia, like the villa at Strongyli, had a predecessor during the Hellenistic period.

The continued occupation, or eventual reoccupation, of earlier sites in Roman and Late Antique times was noted not only at Strongyli, Kouveli, and the fortified townsites, but also at sites in the interior highlands as, for example, in a small, fertile valley reached by crossing a ridge above the village of Cheimadhio, northeast of Riza. Along the lower northeastern slope of the valley dense accumulations of roof tiles, fine and coarse pottery, loom weights, and other debris of a settlement (SS94-15) were found indicating occupation from late Classical to early Roman times. The marble tombstone of Lysipolios,[29] presumably an inhabitant of the little town (its ancient name is not known) in the 3rd or 2nd century B.C., was found beside a little church of the Panayia, about 220 m northwest of the site, near a spring at the edge of the plain.

The Lower Acheron Valley

The Nikopolis Project developed a broad and intensive program of geologic and archaeological investigations of the lower Acheron river which has shown that the inhabitants of the region lived in a much different setting in Greek and Roman times (and earlier!) than at present. The region became a special focus of the Project because of its complex cultural and geologic history, which presented a number

Fig. 9. Wall of a fortified site (the Nekyomanteion, as identified by S. Dakaris) below the church of John the Baptist at Mesopotamon.

Fig. 10. Aerial photo of Ammoudhia Bay (top left) and coastal region. Part of the village of Mesopotamon is visible at edge of photo to right, and concentric relict beaches are visible in the plain north of the Acheron. Photo by Hellenic Army Mapping Service.

Acheron flows into its present coastal plain, and on the north it is connected by a rising saddle to the ridge of Ephyra (S/S92-33), an important site of the Late Bronze Age.[30] There is no archaeological evidence of occupation at Dakaris's site earlier than the Hellenistic period, and the polygonal walls, including a tower, are very similar to other fortifications in Epirus; for example, the walls of Kastri, some 4.5 km upstream on the Acheron. Skepticism has grown over the years, and alternative interpretations for the evidence adduced by Dakaris have been offered by other scholars (Baatz 1982, 1999; Haselberger 1980; Wiseman 1998). The overall complex, indeed, resembles fortified farmsteads or elite country residences known in various parts of Greece, including Epirus,[31] and the romantic designation of Nekyomanteion should probably now be abandoned in favor of Ephyra (as suggested in Baatz 1999), the larger ancient site on the nearby ridge, or perhaps Mesopotamon, the modern town with which it shares the hill of the Church of John the Baptist.

Mesopotamon and Ephyra look west across the fertile plain to the small Bay of Phanari, which is now often referred to as Ammoudhia Bay after the little resort town on the beach (Figs. 10, 11). The Acheron river empties into the bay on its south side, and its channel has recently been extended almost to the sea by a rock levee to provide maximum protection for the sandy beach. References in literature indicate the bay was much larger in antiquity than it is today, and the most critical topographic identifications are certain. The bay can only be the *Glykys Limen* ("Sweet Harbor") by the promontory of Cheimerion mentioned by Strabo (7.7.5), who comments that the Acheron river flows into it from the Acherousian Lake, and so sweetens the water of the bay. Although he does not mention the Glykys Limen, Thucydides (1.46) unites all the other topographic features in his description of the bay where the Corinthian fleet of 150 ships anchored before the Battle of Sybota in 433 B.C., an inconceivable

of unresolved problems, and because of the obvious significance of the bay, river, and valley in the economic and social evolution of Epirus.

The lower valley contains one of the most famous excavated sites in Epirus, identified by its excavator as the Nekyomanteion, the "Oracle of the Dead," mentioned both by Homer (*Odyssey* 10.487-574, 11) and Herodotos (5.92). This strongly fortified site with handsome polygonal masonry (Fig. 9), built over in part by a monastery and Church of John the Baptist at the edge of the town of Mesopotamon, was excavated by Sotirios Dakaris during the 1950s and 1960s (Dakaris 1993). On the south the hill overlooks the narrows through which the number for the present small and shallow bay. The Glykys Limen is specifically mentioned by Cassius Dio (50.12.2) as the harbor into which Octavian brought his fleet, perhaps 250 ships,[32] in the summer of 31 B.C. before proceeding to the Nikopolis peninsula and the Battle of Actium. As late as 1084 the harbor was still able to accommodate the large fleet of Robert Guiscard of Normandy (Anna Comnena, *Alex.* 4.33). A few small sailboats would now crowd the bay.

Concentric relict shorelines north of the Acheron between Ephyra and the present bay are visible in an aerial photograph (Fig. 10), and indeed can be seen from high vantage points around the bay. They provide further indications that there were significant changes in the shoreline of the bay over time. Dakaris had realized that there had been changes in this landscape over time, and his conclusions (Dakaris 1971, 62, 81-82, 170), based mainly on literary evidence and his own observations, were partly correct, but provided little geologic evidence and there was no chronological control.

As a part of the Nikopolis Project survey, 28 geologic cores were drilled at points throughout the lower and middle valley, from Ammoudhia to the narrows south of Ephyra and from there well to the north on both sides of the two principal rivers, the Acheron and the Vouvos (Fig. 12). The analysis of the cores and their context has resulted in an exemplary study of palaeogeographic change in the Acheron valley over the past four millennia (Besonen, Rapp, and Jing 2000, in press). In brief, by about 2100 B.C., Phanari Bay, with two entrances from the Ionian Sea,[33] was some six km across at its widest north-south distance and nearly as large from west to east, extending several hundreds of meters to the east of the valley constriction by Mesopotamon. The Acherousian Lake formed just east of the valley constriction, at the mouth of the Acheron, sometime after 800 B.C. and before Thucydides mentioned its existence in 433 B.C. By the time of Octavian's visit en route to the Battle of Actium, the low-

Fig. 11. View of Ammoudhia and the coastal plain from Ay. Eleni; the ridge of Ephyra is in the center in the distance.

er "Acheron" draining the lake had begun to spill into the bay just east of Mesopotamon. The infilling of the bay along the shorelines and at the mouth of the prograding Acheron proceeded gradually until about 1500 A.D. when the process began to accelerate; the southern entrance was closed and most of the successive relict beaches accumulated in the past five hundred years. The swamp of the Acherousian Lake continued to exist until it was drained earlier in this century.

Six transects across the relict beaches were walked by archaeological survey teams in 1993 to test the hypothesis of their recent origin; only 25 artifacts were found in all transects, and all were post-mediaeval with the exception of a single Roman-period handle. Bronze Age, Greek, Roman, and Late Antique sites were found on the island that once had closed the middle of the entrance to the bay (the Ay. Eleni ridge), on Ephyra ridge, and on elevations overlooking both the bay and the floodplain of the Acheron east of the valley constriction. The entire coastal plain seems clearly to be of recent origin.

The most important site east of Ephyra was Kastri,[34] which we have had occasion to mention before. The site is on a prominent hill 107 masl above the Acheron river, which now flows along its eastern and southern sides, but whose course in antiquity and in the Mediaeval period lay to the west below the steepest face of the hill. The entire site covers some 33 ha within a series of three fortification walls enclosing a lower town; an upper town; and an acropolis, where the encircling mediaeval walls rest in part on earlier walls. A

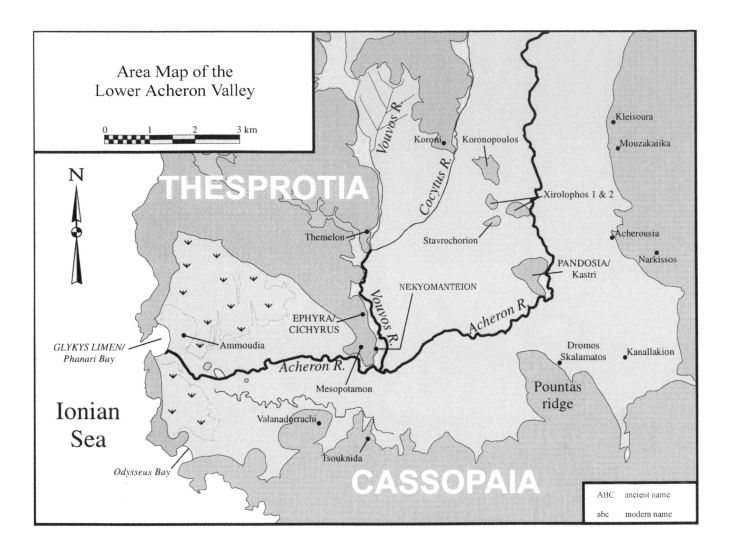

Area Map of the
Lower Acheron Valley

0   1   2   3 km

N

THESPROTIA

Vouvos R.

Cocytus R.

Koroni

Koronopoulos

Kleisoura

Mouzakaiika

Themelon

Stavrochorion

Xirolophos 1 & 2

Acherousia

Narkissos

NEKYOMANTEION

PANDOSIA/
Kastri

EPHYRA/
CICHYRUS

Vouvos R.

Acheron R.

GLYKYS LIMEN/
Phanari Bay

Ammoudia

Acheron R.

Dromos
Skalamatos

Kanallakion

Ionian
Sea

Mesopotamon

Pountas
ridge

Valanadorrachi

Odysseus Bay

Tsouknida

CASSOPAIA

ABC   ancient name

abc   modern name

Fig. 12. Valley of the lower Acheron River. Map by Mark Besonen.

post-Mediaeval church of John the Baptist on the highest part of the site is possibly the successor of an earlier church. The lower parts of numerous stone walls are preserved, some of which form the outlines of entire buildings, especially in the upper town, where they would have been used in Hellenistic and early Roman times. We selected the complex site of Kastri for special attention by the Nikopolis Project as the principal component of our program of interdisciplinary urban survey; other large townsites were only sampled.[35] Such intensive survey seemed warranted to complement the detailed study the Project was pursuing through the entire lower valley of the Acheron.

The methodology selected for the survey of Kastri required walking a series of consecutive tracts over the entire walkable area using a spacing interval of five meters (Fig. 13). In addition, artifact counts would be taken every thirty meters and a separate sample would be collected for the same area. In this way, we could acquire density counts and collect representative artifact assemblages for cells of thirty meters by fifteen to twenty meters (depending on the number of walkers on a team at a given time). This resolution makes it possible to generate detailed density maps for each period of occupation, and increases the likelihood that spatial functions may be recognized. A total of 119,487 square meters were walked as tracts at this site, comprising more than a third of the site (Fig. 13). About eighty-eight percent of the Upper Town was systematically explored; the remaining twelve percent was unwalkable because of prohibitively dense vegetation. In addition, three walkovers were completed at the site; one (W94-15) inside the upper acropolis, the other two (W94-29 and W94-30) in the Lower Town, adding more than 25,000 square meters to the area investigated by systematic survey. Several structures were discovered in the course of the survey and they were drawn on a new map of the town, which will be correlated with the density maps of artifacts.

Concluding Observations

Study of the pottery and other artifacts has only recently been completed, so that the analysis of site distribution by time periods is now being refined, including the preparation of maps to show the spread of artifacts across the landscape for indications of activity outside settlements. In this preliminary overview, I focus on larger habitation and special-activity sites, and offer three maps that provide a helpful visual impression of the locations of Roman sites (Fig. 14);[36] Late Antique sites (Fig. 15); and Mediaeval sites (Fig.16). The maps also cover rather long periods of time: 1st century B.C. through the 3rd century A.D. for the Roman period; Late Antiquity, 4th-6th centuries A.D.; and Mediaeval, 7th-15th centuries; not all sites shown were occupied continuously during the periods represented. Even if the 36 Roman-period sites, however, are thus over-represented, it is clear that there was no long-term deserted landscape in Roman times; within a century of the founding of Nikopolis earlier sites were being revived (e.g., Bouchetion and Kouveli) and new sites grew up, especially on the Ay. Thomas peninsula where we found little evidence of Classical and Hellenistic settlement. Islands close to the mainland attracted settlers: Strongyli and Ay. Aikaterina in the northern part of the Ambracian Gulf were occupied over several centuries and Kephalos opposite Anactorium at least by Late Antiquity, and Ay. Eleni at the entrance to the great bay at the mouth of the Acheron was occupied as early as the Bronze Age. The slight drop in numbers on the map, then, from Roman to

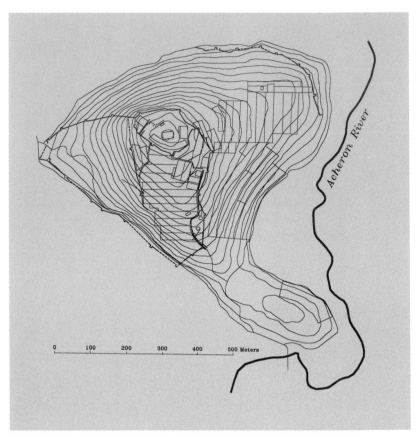

Fig. 13. Map of Kastri showing survey units. Map by Brenda Cullen.

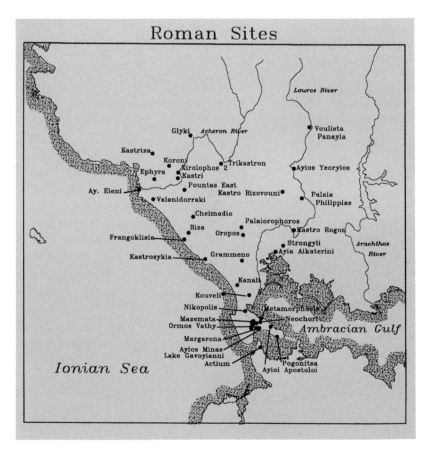

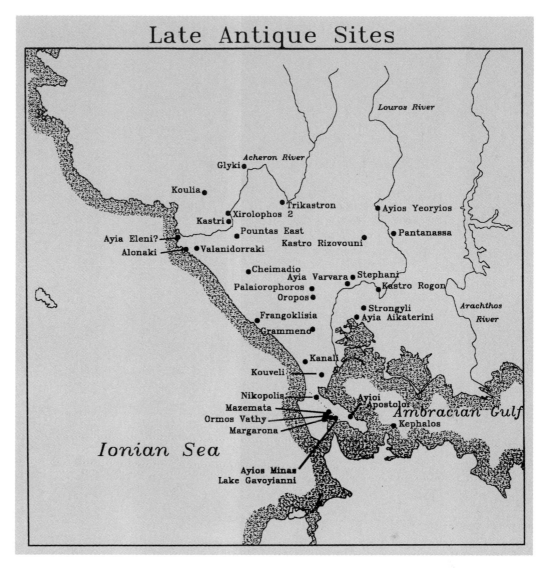

Fig. 15. Late Antique sites in the survey zone. Map by Brenda Cullen and Francisco Estrada-Belli.

Fig. 14. Roman sites in the survey zone. Map by Brenda Cullen and Franscisco Estrada-Belli.

Late Antique (30 sites) represents little or no change from Roman times. There may even have been a higher number of sites in the 4th century than either in the 3rd or 6th century; both possibilities are being investigated through our continuing analysis of artifact distribution. The sharp drop in sites seen on Fig. 16 may have been occasioned by a combination of factors, including the increasingly unpleasant environmental conditions along the north shore of the Ambracian Gulf and in the lower valley of Acheron, and the incursions of Slavs, as discussed in an earlier section. A drastic reduction of population is indicated, beginning in the 6th century and continuing until perhaps the 9th century; although emigration (forced or voluntary) doubtless played some role,[37] it is

unlikely to have been the sole factor; many Slavs, after all, settled in the land. A likely additional explanatory factor is the first plague pandemic of Europe, a virulent bubonic plague that reached the Mediterranean basin in 541-542 A.D. (Procopius, *BP* 2.22-23; *Secret History* 23.20).[38] The plague epidemics occurred in cycles of 10 to 24 years over the next two centuries, and are estimated to have reduced the population of Europe by 50-60 % (Gottfried 1983, 10-12). Epirus could hardly have escaped the consequences of such a repeated catastrophe that affected all of Europe, but especially the Mediterranean basin. The recovery from the decline in Epirus, beginning in the 9th century, seems to be associated with the establishment of ecclesiastical

Mediaeval Sites

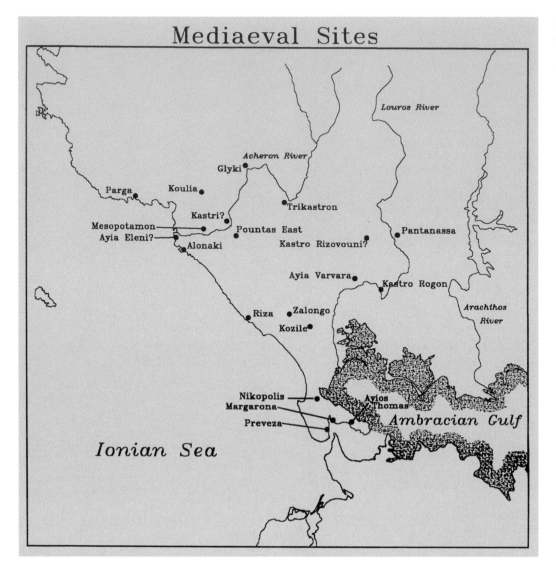

Fig. 16. Mediaeval sites in the survey zone. Map by Brenda Cullen and Francisco Estrada-Belli.

communities across the landscape, and was accompanied by efforts to drain marshes and to increase agricultural land, as in other parts of Europe, especially in the 11th–13th centuries.[39]

Finally, I want to emphasize that the results of the Nikopolis Project reflect the highly interdisciplinary nature of the research. The close cooperation between archaeologists and geologists has made possible a clearer understanding of how humans affected, and were affected by, the landscape and the environment in which they lived in southern Epirus.

Notes

NOTE 1

*It is a pleasure to extend sincere thanks to the Danish Institute in Athens, and in particular to its director Signe Isager and the conference organizer Jacob Isager, for initiating, organizing, and hosting the conference on northwestern Greece, and for undertaking the publication of the papers presented. I acknowledge with gratitude financial support for the Project from NASA, the National Geographic Society, the Institute for Aegean Prehistory, Apple Computer Corporation, Autodesk Inc., Trimble Navigation Company, and a number of private individuals, the FRIENDS OF THE NIKOPOLIS PROJECT, especially Dr. Martha Sharpe Joukowsky and Dr. Artemis A. W. Joukowsky, Mr. James H. Ottaway, Jr., and Mr. Malcolm Hewitt Wiener. I take this opportunity also to express my deep appreciation to the Greek nation in whose land I have had the privilege to study and carry out field work for some four decades.

The project is a joint undertaking of the Department of Archaeology, the Center for Archaeological Studies, and the Center for Remote Sensing of Boston University with two agencies of the Greek Archaeological Service: the 12th Ephoreia of Prehistoric and Classical Antiquities, directed by Angelika Douzougli, and the 8th Ephoreia of Byzantine Antiquities, directed by Frankiska Kephallonitou. The directors of the ephoreias are co-directors of the Project, along with Konstantinos Zachos of the 12th Ephoreia of Prehistoric and Classical Antiquities and the author of this paper. The Project is also sponsored by the American School of Classical Studies at Athens.

NOTE 2

The archaeological survey teams were led by senior staffmembers, primarily Thomas L. Tartaron, Carol Stein, and Brenda Cullen, with a varying number of fieldwalkers (5 to 10 per team), including students in Boston University Archaeological Field Schools (1992-1994), which were integrated into the work of the Nikopolis Project. Geologists often accompanied the surface-survey teams.

NOTE 3

The senior geologists of the Project were George (Rip) Rapp, Jr., Tjeerd van Andel, and Zhichun Jing, joined by an able and distinguished group of colleagues.

NOTE 4

The principal preliminary reports are in the Greek periodical, *Archaiologikon Deltion*: Wiseman, Zachos, and Kephallonitou 1991, 1992, and 1993; a report on the 1994 season is in press. Other reports appeared annually in *Context* and the *Nikopolis Newsletter*, publications of Boston University's Center for Archaeological Studies.

NOTE 5

A systematic, intensive survey unit was designated a Tract (=T) in survey terminology; extensive or scouting reconnaissance was termed Walkover (=W); a find-spot or activity area, large or small, was designated a Site/Scatter (i.e., a "site or a scatter," =S/S). The designations were followed by the year of discovery or entry into the survey archives and an accession number, sequential by year: e.g., Kastro Rogon, discussed in the next section, is S/S91-1. The principles and methodology of the surface survey and documentation are discussed in detail in Wiseman and Zachos 2000, in press, and Tartaron 2000, in press.

NOTE 6

That is, distinctive spectral responses, identifiable in the imagery.

NOTE 7

The Project used both Magellan and Trimble GPS units, which use signals from navigational satellites (21 at the time) constantly orbiting earth to obtain locational data; digital readouts provided UTM coordinates, among other types of information.

NOTE 8

The other three are Elateia or Elatreia, north of the village of Palaiorophoros (S/S91-9) at the eastern edge of Mt. Zalongo; Batiai, probably Kastro Rizovouni (S/S91-6) in the basin north of Mt. Rokia; and Pandosia, in the valley of the Acheron. See Hammond 1967, 57-63 (on Bouchetion), 427, 477-78 (Elean colonies); Dakaris 1971, 134-188 (on all the Elean colonies). Hammond places Pandosia at Trikastron (S/S95-3) in the upper Acheron, north of Palaiorophoros; Dakaris identifies Pandosia with Kastri (S/S94-20) in the lower Acheron valley.

NOTE 9

Similar documentation was made of the Roman aqueduct near its source at Ay. Yeoryios in the Louros River gorge and three other fortified sites: the hilltop site of Voulista Panayia, overlooking the narrows of the Louros gorge; Kastro Rizovouni; and the site near Palaiorophoros (see note 8). The blimp-photography team was headed in 1992 by J. Wilson and Eleanor Emlen Myers and in 1993 by Michael Hamilton, staff photographer in archaeology, Boston University.

NOTE 10

The ancient remains near Strongyli were first noted by Petsas 1950-51; see Hammond 1967, 61; Dakaris 1971, 72, 93, and notes 149 and 287.

NOTE 11

Excavations subsequently conducted by the 12th Ephoreia of Prehistoric and Classical Antiquities confirmed the identification as a Roman villa; see Douzougli 1998. Pottery and coins from the excavations date from Augustan times to the third century; the excavators date the mosaic floors to the late 2nd/early 3rd century.

NOTE 12

Jing and Rapp 2000, in press. I am indebted to Zhichun Jing and Rip Rapp for permission to refer to their results here, and to include their map in this publication as Fig. 6.

NOTE 13

We hear of ships putting in at Preveza in 1292. The Turkish refounding of Preveza probably occurred in 1477/78 or 1486/87, with a subsequent (in 1495) strengthening of the fortifications. The dates and sources are discussed by Soustal 1981, 242, and at greater length by Savvides 1992, 21-38. The fact that Cyriacus of Ancona, who made repeated visits to Nikopolis, Actium, and Rogoi in 1436 and 1448, makes no mention of Preveza may be an indication of the relatively minor significance of Preveza before its refounding by the Turks.

NOTE 14

Shortly afterwards the relics were removed on the advance of the Turks (Arta was annexed to the Ottoman state in 1449); they arrived in Smederevo in 1453. On the travels of Cyriacus of Ancona along the north coast of the Ambracian gulf, see Hammond 1967, 60-61 and App. II, 710-712, with comments on the letters of Cyriacus and their sources.

NOTE 15

The story of the relics of St. Luke is recounted by Hammond 1967, 60-61, based on an account in Greek, written in 1453-58 and edited in 1882.

NOTE 16

Cyriacus records in Epistula IV (11-12 January 1436) his plans to go in a dug-out boat by river (the Louros) setting out from Rogoi to visit Nikopolis. On a subsequent visit in the same year (Epistula V) he refers to crossing the Louros three times. Neither account would make sense unless the Louros had been diverted into its present channel by that time. The Epistulae follow the numbering in Mehus 1742; see the discussion in Hammond 1967, 710-711.

NOTE 17

Hammond 1967, 60-61, gives the Greek text: Τὸ πλοῖον ὁρμᾷ πρὸς τὴν πόλιν Ῥογὸς καί σταματᾷ εἰς τὸν λιμένα.

NOTE 18

Soustal 1981, 53-54, 251-52 suggests that Rogoi may have been resettled and its fortifications rebuilt at about the same time, all as part of the establishment of the Theme of Nikopolis (by which time the city of Nikopolis was presumably in ruins and largely abandoned) under the Byzantine Emperor Leo VI, which had its administrative and ecclesiastical center at Naupaktos.

NOTE 19

The monastery, which is located about 1 km north of the modern town of Nea Sampsous and 16 km north of Preveza, was mentioned as a bishopric for the first time in 1020; see Soustal 1981, 186-187.

NOTE 20

Personal communication from Varvara Papadopoulou, the excavator.

NOTE 21

Soustal 1981, 225. Excavations by P. L. Vokotopoulos have continued into the 1990s.

NOTE 22

Evlia Çelebi, setting out from Nikopolis for Rogoi in the early 17th century, passed a fishery not far along the coast; Ergolavos 1995, 37. It was probably located where one is still functioning at the edge of the Tsokalio lagoon; Hammond 1967, 61, 247; on fisheries in the harbors of Epirus, see Soustal 1981, 97. The Ambracian Gulf was famous in antiquity for its abundance of fish: Dakaris 1971, 17.

NOTE 23

Doukellis identifies an orientation of 27° west of north and field tracts of 710 m, corresponding to centuriated tracts of 20 by 20 Roman actus.

NOTE 24

Piper et al. 1988, 285, where the annual discharge of the Louros is given as 30m³/s compared with 80m³/s for the Arachthos.

NOTE 25

A large mound (ca. 4.5 high and over 16 m. in length) composed almost entirely of shells of murex brandaris was found. Dakaris 1971, 17, reports that shells remaining from the extraction of purple dye were found also at Kassope, Palaiorophoros, Rogoi, and Kastri (on the Acheron). There was even a Roman procurator who controlled the purple-dye industry in Achaia, Epirus, and Thessaly in the early 3rd century A.D.: CIL III 536, 1-7.

NOTE 26

Vocotopoulou 1970, 41-45; 1973, 220-222, 227. Dakaris 1971, 35, 51, 58, 78, 79, 75. The lion is displayed in the Archaeological Museum in Ioannina (Inv. No. 2594), along with other statuary, architecture, and artifacts from the graves.

NOTE 27

The archaeological survey included 23 tracts and five walkovers.

NOTE 28

The "very few traces of a wall around the settlement" mentioned by Dakaris (1971, 203, note 137) on the "oblong hill" are, I suspect, more of the terrace walls for grave plots near the cemetery at Marathia. Both Dakaris and Hammond (1967, 51) postulate a port of Michalitsi on the Ambracian Gulf, but offer no archaeological evidence and the Project survey found nothing to indicate one in the area.

NOTE 29

Inv. No. NI-94-1; the inscription is in raised Greek letters.

NOTE 30

The site, occupied also in Classical, Hellenistic, and Roman times, was excavated by Th. Papadopoulos in twelve seasons; preliminary reports appeared in Praktika, beginning in 1978. The western and southern slopes of the ridge were intensively surveyed by the Nikopolis Project in 1994.

NOTE 31
We have already noted the fortified farm-stead at Strongyli. A polygonal tower (SS93-25) studied by the Nikopolis Project near Oropos above the north coast of the Ambracian Gulf may also be part of a country estate.

NOTE 32
Orosius 6.19.8; see the discussion in Murray and Petsas 1989, 134.

NOTE 33
At the present entrance to Ammoudhia Bay and some 2 km to the south, at Kerentza Bay; the long ridge between the two was then an island at the entrance to the bay: see Figs. 10 and 12.

NOTE 34
Dakaris 1971, 164-170 provides a convenient summary of previous knowledge about the site, which he identifies as the Elean colony, Pandosia.

NOTE 35
The methodology described in the next paragraph was also employed in the shorter-term surveys at the other three fortified sites (Kastro Rogon, Palaiorophoros, and Kastro Rizovouni), so that the counts and samples by area may be compared with those from Kastri.

NOTE 36
Kassope, the most important city of the region in Classical and Hellenistic times, is not shown on the period maps; although it was still inhabited in the late 1st century B.C., it seems to have been largely aban-doned after the founding of Nikopolis; see Dakaris 1971, 101-133. Kassope was not included in the Project survey. I thank Francisco Estrada-Belli, a colleague at Boston University, for his help with these maps and other graphics for this paper.

NOTE [37]
In 603 the bishop and the inhabitants of Euroia (=Glyki on the Acheron) fled before the Slavs to Corfu, taking with them the relics of Ay. Donatos: Chrysos 1981, 74-77; Soustal 1981, 158.

NOTE 38
See also Cameron 1993, 111, 123-124, 164.

NOTE 39
See, e.g., Gottfried 1983, 18-20, and the discussion above of the Ambracian Gulf.

Bibliography

Audikos, O. G. (ed.), 1993
Η Ιστορία της Πρέβεζας.
Πρακτικά Α Διεθνούς Επιστημο-
νικού Συνεδρίου. Δήμος Πρέβεζας.

Baatz, D., 1982
Hellenistische Katapulte aus Ephyra
(Epirus), *Athenische Mittheilungen*
97, 211-233.

Baatz, D., 1999
Wehrhaftes Wohnen, *Antike Welt*
30:2, 151-155.

Balzaretti, R., 1996
Cities, Emporia and Monasteries:
Local Economies in the Po Valley, c.
AD 700-875, in: Christie and Lose-
by 1996, 213-234.

Cameron, A., 1993
*The Mediterranean World in Late An-
tiquity*, Routledge: London and
New York.

Christie, N. and Loseby S. T. eds.,
1996
*Towns in Transition. Urban Evolution
in Late Antiquity and the Early Middle Ages*, Scolar Press: Guildford.

Chrysos, E. K., 1981
Συμβολή στην ιστορία της
Ηπείρου κατά την πρωτοβυ-
ζαντινή εποχή (Δ'-ΣΤ'Αι.),
Ηπειρωτικα Χρονικά 23.

Cladas, C., 1975
La découverte de civilisations
anciennes à l'aide de la photogrammétrie, *Photogrammetria* 30, 213-218.

Chrysostomou, P., 1982
Το Νυμφαίο των Ριζών Πρεβέζης,
AAA 15, 10-20.

Dakaris, S., 1971
*Cassope and the Elean Colonies.
Ancient Greek Cities*, Vol. 4, Center
of Ekistics: Athens.

Dakaris, S., 1993
The Nekyomanteion of the Acheron,
Ministry of Culture: Athens

Doukellis, P. N., 1988
Cadastres romaines en Grece. Traces
d'un réseau rural a Actia Nicopolis,
in: *Dialogues d'histoire ancienne* 14,
159-166.

Doukellis, P. N., 1990
Ένα Δίκτυο Αγροτικών Ορίων
στην Πεδιάδα της Άρτας, in
Μελετήματα του ΚΕΡΑ 10, 269-
286.

Douzougli, A., 1998
Μια Ρωμαϊκή Αγροικία στις Ακτές
του Αμβρακικού Κόλπου,
Αρχαιολογία & Τέχνες 68, 74-78.

Ergolavos, S., 1995
Εβλία Τσελέπι, Ταξιδι Στην
Ήπειρο. Εκδόσεις Ήπειρος,
Ιοαννινα.

Gelzer, H., 1901
*Ungedruckte und ungenügend veröffent-
lichte Texte der Notitiae episcopatum,
ein Beitrag zur byzantinischen Kir-
chen- und Verwaltungsgeschichte.Abh.
Bayer. Ak.Wiss.*, I. Cl.21/3,
München.

Gottfried, R. S., 1983
The Black Death, The Free Press:
New York.

Hammond, N. G. L., 1967.
*Epirus: the geography, the ancient
remains, the history, and the topography
of Epirus and adjacent areas*. Oxford:
Clarendon Press.

Haselberger, L., 1980
Befestigte Turmgehöfte im Hel-
lenismus, in: *Wohnungsbau im
Alterutum. Diskussionen z. Arch.
Bauforsch.* 3, 147 ff.

Jing, Z. and Rapp, Jr. G. (Rip),
2000
Holocene Coastal Landscape Evolution of the Ambracian Embayment in Epirus, Western Greece,
and Its Relationships to Archaeological Settings (ms.), in: Wiseman
and Zachos (eds.) 2000.

Mehus, L., 1742
Kyriaci Anconitani Itinerarium,.
Florence

Murray, W. M. and Petsas, P. M.,
1989
*Octavian's Campsite Memorial for the
Actian War*. Transactions of the
American Philosophical Society
Vol. 79, Part 4. Philadelphia: Ameri-
can Philosophical Society.

Petsas, P. M., 1950-51
Ειδήσεις εκ της 10ης
Αρχαιολογικής Περιφερείας,
ArchEph, Χρονικά 40-41.

Piper, David J. W., Kontopoulos, N. and Panagos, A. G., 1988
Deltaic Sedimentation and Stratigraphic Sequences in Post-Orogenic Basins, Western Greece, *Sedimentary Geology* 55, 283-294.

Savvidis, A. G. K., 1993
Η Τουρκική Κατάληψη της Πρέβεζας Απο Τα Βραχέα Χρονικά, in: Audikos 1993, 25-38.

Soustal, P., 1981
Tabula Imperii Byzantini 3: Nikopolis und Kephallenia. Verlag der Österreichischen Akademie der Wissenschaften, Wien.

Stein, C. A. and Cullen, B. C., 1994
Satellite Imagery and Archaeology: A Case Study from Nikopolis, (Abstract), *AJA* 98, 316.

Mehus, L., 1742
Kyriaci Anconitani Itinerarium. Florence.

Tartaron, T. L., 2000, in press
Archaeological Survey: Sampling Strategies and Field Methods, in: Wiseman and Zachos (eds) 2000, in press.

Vocotopoulou, J., 1970
Νέα Ευρήματα εξ Ηπείρου, *AAA* 3, 39-45.

Vocotopoulou, J., 1973
Αρχαιολογικαί Ειδήσεις εξ Ηπείρου, *AAA* 6, 215-229.

Wiseman, J., 1996
Space Missions and Ground Truth, *Archaeology* 49:4 (July/August), 11-13.

Wiseman, J., 1997
The Post-Roman World, *Archaeology* 50:6 (November/December), 12-14, 16.

Wiseman, J., 1998
Rethinking the "Halls of Hades," *Archaeology* 51:3 (May/June), 12-16, 18.

Wiseman, J., Robinson, C. and Stein, C., 1998
Archaeological Applications of Radar Imagery In Northwestern Greece, paper presented at ADRO (Applications Development Research Opportunity) RADARSAT Conference, October 1998, Montreal.

Wiseman, J. and Zachos, K., 2000, in press
The Nikopolis Project: Concept, Aims, and Organization, in: Wiseman and Zachos (eds) 2000, in press.

Wiseman, J. and Zachos, K. (eds.), 2000, in press
Landscape Archaeology in Southern Epirus, Greece I.

Wiseman, J., Zachos, K. and Kephallonitou, F., 1991
Ελληνοαμερικανικό πρόγραμμα επιφανειακών ερευνών, *AD* 46 (1991; publ. Athens, 1996], *Chronika*, 247-251.

Wiseman, J., Zachos, K. and Kephallonitou, F., 1992
Συνεργατική Ελληνοαμερικανική Επιφανειακή Έρευνα στο Νομό Πρέβεζας, *AD* 47 (1992; publ. Athens, 1997), *Chronika*, pp. 293-298.

Wiseman, J., Zachos, K. and Kephallonitou, F., 1993
Ελληνοαμερικανικό Διεπιστημονικό Πρόγραμμα Επιφανειακών Ερευνών στη Νότια Ήπειρο," *AD* 47 (1993; publ. Athens, 1998), *Chronika*, pp. 309-314.

Zachos, K., 1993
Θέση Φραγκοκκλησιά κοινότητας Ριζών (αγροτεμάχιο αφών Αθανασιου), *AD* 48, Chronika, 301.

In the Shadow of Nikopolis: Patterns of Settlement on the Ayios Thomas Peninsula

Carol A. Stein

One of the stated themes of this symposium is to examine the effects of the foundation of Nikopolis on surrounding areas. That these effects were felt in regions quite removed from the city is attested to by both literary and archaeological evidence, and they have been described by several of the conference participants. In this paper, however, I present evidence from an area quite close to the city, the Ayios Thomas peninsula, which was the focus of intensive archaeological and geo-

logical investigations by the Nikopolis Project during the summers of 1993 and 1994 (Fig. 1).[1]

The Ayios Thomas peninsula extends eastward from modern Preveza into the Ambracian Gulf, and provides an excellent case study for examining the effects of imperial incorporation. Its proximity to Nikopolis all but ensured substantial changes in land use following the foundation of the urban center. Perhaps the most radical of these changes was the centuriation of the peninsula, previously detected by researchers using a combination of aerial photographs and topographic maps.[2] Equally important was the utilization of Ormos Vathy, an inlet at the western end of the peninsula, as one of two harbors for the newly founded city.[3] Multidisciplinary research by the Nikopolis Project has helped to clarify these changes and their effects on the peninsula's subsequent history.

A brief description of the landscape and our strategy for exploring it follows. The peninsula measures roughly 15 km[2], and, despite the rapid expansion of many of its coastal communities, there are still large areas covered by agricultural and grazing fields. The only elevations of note are a ridge along the north coast, and the elevations surrounding Ormos Pogonitsa at the eastern end of the peninsula. The surface of the peninsula is covered with a thin mantle of Pleistocene sediments and paleosols, which overlies a thick deposit of marine sands.[4] The great age of the surface (ca. 20–50,000 ya) indicates that sites of all periods may be found in the course of surface survey.

The sampling strategy employed on Ayios Thomas, and by the Project in gen-

Fig. 1. Map of the Ayios Thomas peninsula (after Murray and Petsas 1989, fig. 1).

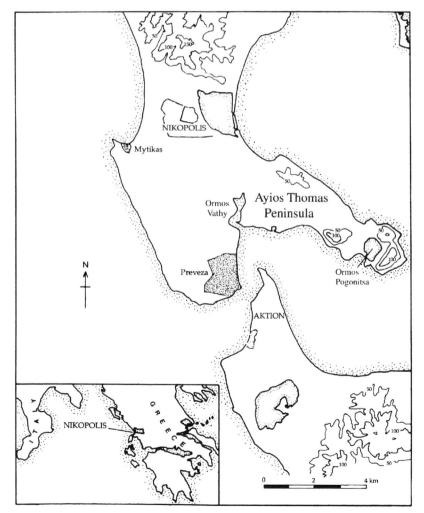

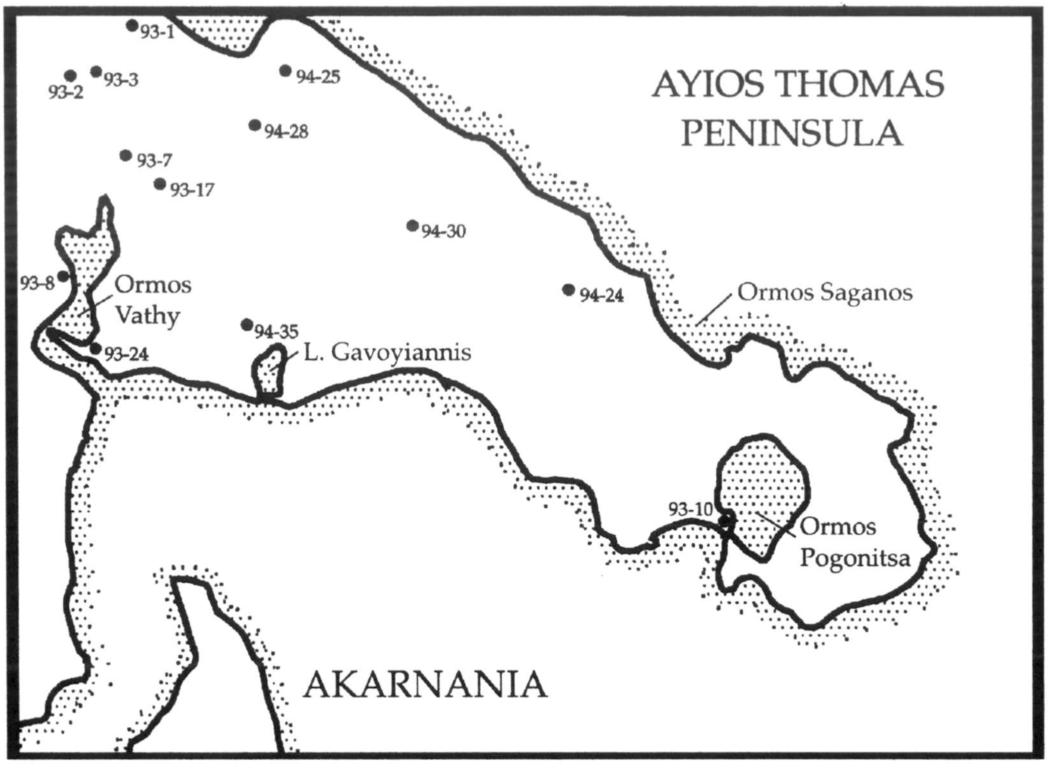

Fig. 2. Roman and Late Antique sites on the Ayios Thomas peninsula.

eral, used a combination of extensive and intensive survey across a variety of environmental zones. Three such zones were defined for this peninsula: a coastal zone, comprised of areas directly adjacent to the Ambracian Gulf; lowlands, defined as interior areas below 40 masl; and highlands, the upper slopes of the elevations mentioned previously. These divisions are somewhat arbitrary given the small size of the peninsula and the relative homogeneity of its landforms, but a sampling strategy based on such divisions increases the potential for locating sites of all types and periods. Special attention was also paid to areas of known archaeological or historical interest.

A total of 134 survey units were carried out on the peninsula, covering 1.3 km², or roughly 10% of the total surface area.[5] Evidence for human activity was found to range from the Lower Palaeolithic through Post-Medieval periods, providing a long, though not continuous, history of land use on the peninsula. One of the gaps in this land-use sequence occurs in the Archaic through Hellenistic period: of the thousands of artifacts counted and collected,

only about a dozen have been dated to Greek times, and most of these are likely Hellenistic. These Greek-period sherds were all found in the vicinity of either Ormos Vathy or Ormos Pogonitsa, not coincidentally where some of the best dated Early Roman material was found as well. At present, it appears that these two inlets, at opposite ends of the peninsula, may have been the only places to "witness" the transition to Roman rule.

In stark contrast to the underutilized Greek landscape, abundant evidence for activity in the Roman and Late Antique periods was found throughout the peninsula. Nine new sites were identified in the course of our investigations, and an additional four, previously known to the local Ephoreias, were systematically explored (Table 1; Fig. 2). I will discuss the finds at several of these sites in detail before considering their implications for Roman and Late Antique period land use. I must stress the preliminary nature of these findings, as the analysis of the data is ongoing.[6]

The Survey Results

The largest site on the peninsula, and the

Table 1. Roman–Late Antique Sites on the Ayios Thomas Peninsula

Site Name	Site Number	Size (ha)	Zone	Interpretation
Mazemata	SS93-1	0.21	lowlands	villa?
Analipsis 1	SS93-2	0.19	lowlands	farmstead
Analipsis 2	SS93-3	0.17	lowlands	farmstead
Kleopatra 1	SS93-7	0.25	lowlands	farmstead
Kleopatra 2	SS93-17	0.20	lowlands	farmstead
Ormos Vathy	SS93-8	22.50	coastal	harbor town
Margarona	SS93-24	0.10	coastal	bath
Metamorphosis	SS94-25	2.50	coastal	villa?
W. of Neochori	SS94-28	0.66	lowlands	farmstead
Ayios Minas	SS94-35	2.48	coastal	LA village, R. bath?
Ayia Triadha	SS94-30	0.01	lowlands	tile grave
Ayioi Apostoli	SS94-24	0.80	lowlands	farmstead
Ormos Pogonitsa	SS93-10	0.13	coastal	?

one that received the most detailed study, is located at Ormos Vathy, or "Deep Bay." The inlet was identified as the inner harbor of Nikopolis by Col. William Leake,[7] who used a passage in Strabo (7.7.5) and a complex of architectural remains at the inlet's southeast corner to support his theory. Despite such promise, the area had never been systematically explored.

The importance of Ormos Vathy was confirmed in 1993 when Nikopolis Project team members identified a harbor town (SS93-8) on its western shore. The locations of our survey units are indicated in Figure 3. The densest concentration of artifacts was noted within an area measuring 250 m (E–W) x 900 m (N–S). The northern and western limits of the site are fairly secure, but exploration of the southern boundary was limited by the presence of a military base and, further south, the buildings of Nikopolis's successor, modern Preveza. Over 39,000 artifacts were counted within the boundaries of the site, almost 2,000 of which were collected for further study, and the vast majority of this material (over 90%) dates to the Roman and Late Antique periods. The finds from

Ormos Vathy include large quantities of transport amphoras, fine wares, lamp and glass fragments, and coins, indicating that both commercial and domestic activities took place. In addition, several special activity areas were noted within the larger site.

The first activity area consists of a series of piers along the western edge of the inlet. The area is heavily overgrown, but portions of at least eight piers were identified, along a 100-m stretch, at the edge of the waterline. The piers are constructed of field stones and waterproof cement, with a brick-faced exterior, and they are clearly Roman in date (Fig. 4). Less clear is how the piers functioned. Despite their roughly linear orientation, the majority of the piers are not in situ, and for the time being they have been identified simply as harborworks.

A second activity area was identified 100 m north of the piers. Here a large midden of *Murex brandaris* shells was discovered, indicating that purple dye was produced somewhere in the vicinity.[8] At the time of survey, the midden was approximately 16 m long and several meters

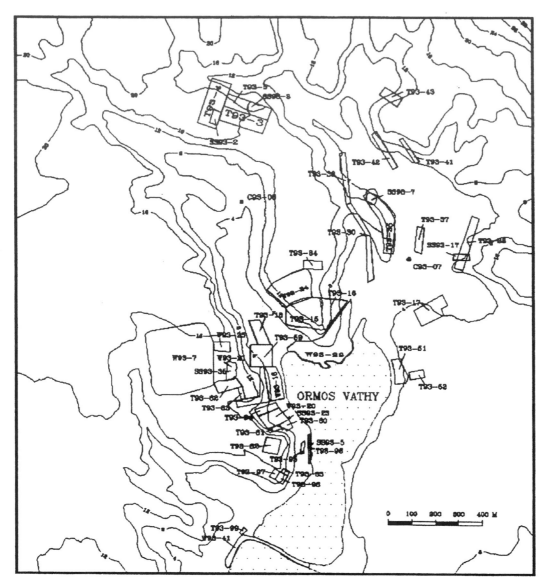

Fig. 3. Survey units at Ormos Vathy.

Fig. 4. Brick-faced pier at Ormos Vathy.

Fig. 5. Digital elevation model of Ormos Vathy. Lower elevations are indicated in yellow and green. Roman-Late Antique sites are outlined in red.

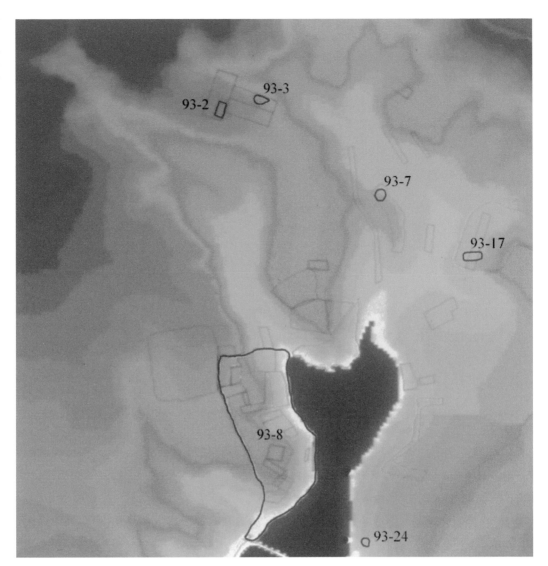

high, although it was partially obscured by the surrounding vegetation, and a portion of it had been cleared away by farmers. Artifacts collected in the vicinity of the midden, including fine wares, lamps, and a number of glass fragments, suggest that the activity in this area was not exclusively industrial.

A final activity area was designated near the northeast edge of the harbor town where two joining fragments of a marble inscription were found (NI 93-1a,b). The inscription, in well-cut Greek letters, preserves the first portion of someone's name, perhaps a freedman as the name is a combination of Roman and Greek forms:

KΛΑΥΛ – – –

ΦΡΟΣ – – –

The fragments may be part of a plaque

or grave stele and, if the latter, would be further evidence for the limit of the town in this direction. I should point out, however, that there was likely to have been almost continuous settlement between Nikopolis and the harbor town, with one or more roads connecting them as well.

In addition to the archaeological survey, limited geophysical survey was used to explore the remains within the harbor town.[9] In 1993, a magnetometer survey was carried out near the findspot of the inscription, but the presence of modern surface debris obscured any patterning in the data. In 1994, a second survey was carried out, this time in a small, fallow field on a terrace overlooking the piers. This field was selected for further study because of a particularly heavy concentration of

69

artifacts, as well as the presence of a threshold block, clearly not in situ, at the field's eastern end. Magnetometer survey in this location revealed the presence of a large structure, at least 20 m in length, with one internal cross wall. Some evidence for the date and/or function of this building may be obtained when the analysis of the artifacts has been completed.

The archaeological remains at Ormos Vathy cannot be understood without reference to the geomorphological study of the area, a project undertaken by Zhichun Jing and George Rapp.[10] That the configuration of the inlet has changed over time is suggested not only by the surrounding contours, but also by a map of the region drawn by Leake.[11] Leake's map, although clearly not to scale, shows the two arms at the north edge of Ormos Vathy projecting much further inland than they do today. He states that the western arm "touches a part of the site of Nikopolis" and that the eastern arm "approaches the coast of the Gulf of Arta."[12] The remnants of these two arms are seen clearly in a digital elevation model, where the lowest lying areas are indicated by yellows and greens (Fig. 5).

To investigate these probable shoreline changes, a series of four cores was taken at the northern end of Ormos Vathy. The geomorphological data indicate that the western arm of the bay did extend several hundred meters further inland during the Roman period, and Jing and Rapp suggest that the waterway would have been navigable for much of this distance. The data from the eastern arm, however, in apparent contradiction to Leake's description, indicates that much of the lowlying area was occupied by fringe marsh rather than bay water. This conclusion is based on the finds from a single core and should be tested further, but, in either case, whether covered by marsh or water, these lowlying areas would not have been habitable in the Roman period. The reconstruction of the Roman-period shoreline at Ormos Vathy has implications not only for our understanding of the harbor town, but also for a series of Roman–Late Antique

habitation sites located to the north of the inlet. These rural sites will be examined shortly.

Roman-period activity on the eastern shore of Ormos Vathy was more difficult to characterize. In general, the eastern side of the inlet is more heavily vegetated, and many areas were enclosed within modern house lots and not available for survey. Nevertheless, the substantial architectural remains at the southeast corner of the inlet do attest to a Roman presence on this side of the bay. These remains are located near the church of Zoodhochos Pygi, and probably once formed part of a Roman bath building (SS93-24). Among the surviving wall sections, constructed of *opus testaceum*, can be noted a vaulted corridor; a semi-circular and a rectangular niche; and two apsed areas, possibly for plunges. In addition, a fine black-and-white mosaic is reported to lie below the floor of the modern church.[13] Despite these impressive remains, our limited survey work on the eastern shore of Ormos Vathy did not reveal a level of activity comparable to that on the western shore. For the time being, therefore, the limits of the harbor town have not been extended in this direction.

Two other inlets on the south coast of the peninsula – Lake Gavoyiannis and Ormos Pogonitsa – were also the focus of activity in Roman and Late Antique times (Fig. 2). Lake Gavoyiannis is currently separated from the Ambracian Gulf by a narrow neck of land. As recently as the 19th century, however, the inlet was completely open to the sea and the locus of commercial fishing.[14] Although no cores were taken to determine the configuration of the inlet in the Roman period, the surrounding topography indicates that the lake may have extended several hundred meters further north. Some evidence for prehistoric activity (probably Bronze Age) was found on either side of the inlet, but, in general, the southern shores of the lake have been much disturbed by recent construction activities, and the historical-period remains are rather sparse. Roman-period occupation was identified near the northwest corner of the lake, in the vicinity of the church of Ayios Minas (SS94-35). The church is known to the Byzantine Ephoreia in Ioannina as the site of an Early Christian basilica,[15] and there are a number of reused architectural pieces within the church today. Archaeological and geophysical survey work in the environs of the church have helped to clarify the nature and limits of the activity there. The densest concentration of artifacts was found within a ca. 2.5-ha area south and west of the church. Although the bulk of the finds are, not surprisingly, Late Antique in date, ceramics from the first three centuries A.D. were also included in the assemblage. More intriguing is the discovery of a *tegula mammata* just south of the church, suggesting that there may have been a Roman bath building in the vicinity. Geophysical survey south of the church revealed possible structural remains, but whether these are related to the earlier church, the proposed bath building, or some other structure cannot be determined without excavation.

Ormos Pogonitsa was also once open to the sea, and must have been used as a harbor in Roman times. Nicholas Hammond identified it as such, and reported that large amphoras had been recovered from the waters there.[16] The lake is currently separated from the Ambracian Gulf by a causeway, almost certainly man-made, through which channels have been cut to supply water for a fish hatchery. Archaeological survey around the lake revealed concentrations of Roman material near its southern shore, both on the smaller of the two elevations incorporated within the causeway (SS93-10) and on the causeway itself.[17] The nature of the occupation here is still unclear, but an amphora waster included among the finds suggests that pottery production took place nearby. No kilns were identified during our survey, but the coastal location, with plenty of timber on the surrounding elevations, would have been ideal for such an activity.

One final coastal site was investigated, this one on the north coast of the peninsula in a locality known as Metamorphosis (SS94-25). The remains of this site are scattered over a large, low-lying area surrounding the church of Ayia Soteira. A spring to the northwest of the church has likely contributed to the extension of the coastline here, but no coring was done to confirm this hypothesis. Ca. 200 m east of the church, portions of an apsidal building were exposed and partially destroyed in a road cut. The apse of this building faces northeast, and thus the structure does not appear to be an early church. A second set of wall remains was located on a terrace to the south of the church, but its connection, if any, to the apsidal building is not clear. Surprisingly little ceramic material was found in the vicinity of these remains, but a large number of waterworn sherds was noted along the present shoreline. It is possible that a small harbor was located here, either for fishing or quick access to Nikopolis by sea; the architectural remains may form part of a small coastal community or perhaps even a villa. Identifying this site as a villa may seem overly optimistic, if not risky, given the meager ceramic evidence, but the architectural remains are suggestive and their location even more so. The site at Metamorphosis may form one of a string of coastal villas that have been identified along the north shore of the Ayios Thomas peninsula.[18]

Archaeological survey in the lowland zone identified a number of Roman–Late Antique sites that have been classified as rural farmsteads. Most of these sites are small in size, with assemblages typically spanning several centuries. A full range of domestic ceramics is usually present, and fragments of Roman rotary querns were a common find. Of the cluster of sites found north of Ormos Vathy (SS93-2, 93-3, 93-7, and 93-17), only one deserves further mention. This site (SS93-17), in a locality known as Kleopatra, was identified in an alfalfa field lying above what would have been the eastern arm of the bay. The long, thin shape of the artifact concentration at this site was unusual, and the presence of what appeared to be a buried limestone block north of the site aroused further suspicion. Geophysical survey of the main artifact concentration failed to reveal any subsurface architecture, however, and the site remains classified as a farmstead.

The two largest farmstead sites – one located west of the village of Neochori (SS94-28), the other near Ayioi Apostoli (SS94-24) – are each less than one hectare in size, and thus are unlikely to be second-order settlement sites, or villages. Still, the remains at these sites could easily belong to a few buildings rather than just one. More enigmatic is the small site that lies between them, near the village of Ayia Triadha (SS94-30). This site consisted of a small concentration of tiles with very little associated pottery, and a revisit to the site in 1995 failed to produce any diagnostic material. Some of the finds were identified as Roman on the basis of fabric, and the site was tentatively classified as a farmstead. An alternative interpretation of these remains will be presented below.

Fig. 6. SPOT panchromatic image of the Preveza peninsula.

Settlement Patterns

What can now be said of land-use patterns on the peninsula in the centuries following the foundation of Nikopolis? The coastal areas, particularly the inlets on the south coast, appear to have been heavily utilized, both for their access to marine resources and to seaborne travel and trade. Along several stretches of coastline, there is a fairly steep drop to the sea, and the absence of sites in these areas is not surprising. More perplexing is the absence of finds at Ormos Saganos (Fig. 2), northwest of Ormos Pogonitsa, which seemed to be a likely focus of activity in the past and was briefly surveyed in 1994; further investigation in this area might prove fruitful. The stretch of coastline between Lake Gavoyiannis and Ormos Pogonitsa was almost certainly exploited, but modern construction and heavy vegetation prevented survey in this location. We did, however, note probable ancient walls just offshore and midway between the two inlets, near the site of a modern jetty.

In the highland zone, not one site of the Roman or Late Antique period was identified. There are several possible expla-

nations for this, including poor visibility, a lack of walkable areas, or even the effects of increased erosion. But evidence for Post-Medieval habitation was plentiful in this zone, and erosion, at least, does not seem to be a major factor. In the Roman period, the highland areas may have been used for grazing and bee-keeping, activities less easily detected in the archaeological record. Comparative data from highland areas in other parts of the Project area may help clarify this issue.

In contrast, archaeological survey revealed substantial evidence for activity in the lowlying interior during the Roman–Late Antique period. Although it is unlikely that all of these sites were occupied simultaneously, preliminary phasing of the sites suggests that many of them were, and the pattern of rural habitation appears to have been fairly dense. This impression is strengthened when one considers that less than 10% of the lowlands was systematically surveyed. A higher density of rural sites closer to Ormos Vathy provides further evidence for the importance of this harbor, although there is some danger that the intensity of the survey work

72

6). I began by tracing some of the same ancient field boundaries used by Doukellis in his 1988 work, focusing on a fairly complete grid square just south of the city walls of Nikopolis. This square measures roughly 708 m on a side, quite close to the standard size for a 20 x 20 actus scheme. A grid pattern was then extrapolated from this square, and the locations of the survey sites were superimposed (Figs. 7–9).[22] On visual inspection, there appears to be a strong correlation between the two datasets. While the analysis of the patterning is still ongoing, some preliminary observations may be made.

Of the thirteen sites investigated by the Project, ten lie in close proximity to the projected *limites*, while three do not. Two of the three "anomalous" sites, Kleopatra 1 and 2 (SS93-7 and 93-17), are located on what would have been the eastern arm of Ormos Vathy, and their position was more likely influenced by this topographic feature than the rural network. The third site, at Metamorphosis (SS94-25), is exceptional both because of its coastal location and the fact that the remains are scattered over a wide area. Nevertheless, the location of Metamorphosis at the center of a grid cell may indicate a larger size for this landholding, providing possible support for its identification as a villa.

The close proximity of Analipsis 1 and 2 (SS93-2 and 93-3), part of the cluster of farmsteads north of Ormos Vathy, suggests an intriguing relationship that may be revealed with further study. A preliminary examination of the finds from these sites reveals a difference in the dates of their assemblages, raising the possibility that they may represent two (consecutive?) farmsteads working the same plot of land. The farmstead west of Neochori (SS94-28) is the best candidate for a single-period Early Roman site on the peninsula; its alignment with the rural network helps to confirm the Augustan date of the centuriation scheme. Ayioi Apostoli (SS94-24), the largest of the farmstead sites, is located at the intersection of two *limites*, a likely place for a higher-order settlement to grow. The position of Ayioi Apostoli with-

in this area has skewed the data. Were the remainder of the peninsula surveyed with equal intensity, a more even distribution of sites might be revealed.

Settlement and Centuriation

One further aspect of the settlement pattern remains to be explored: its relationship to the centuriation system identified south of Nikopolis.[19] Land division schemes are notoriously difficult to date, but Doukellis has convincingly argued that this scheme was laid out at the time Nikopolis was founded.[20] Surface survey data from a centuriated landscape are rare, and provide an opportunity to test various aspects of a field system, including its date, extent, and longevity.[21] In addition, as will be seen below, the position of a site within a centuriation scheme may aid in its interpretation.

To determine whether there was any correlation between the locations of the sites and the proposed centuriation scheme, I projected Doukellis's scheme onto the Ayios Thomas landscape using a combination of aerial photographs and SPOT panchromatic satellite imagery (Fig.

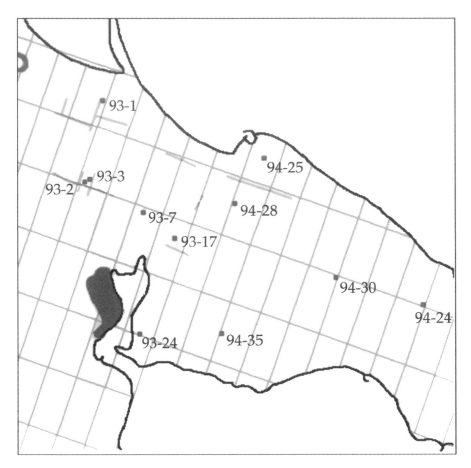

Fig. 8. Detail of Figure 7, western half of peninsula.

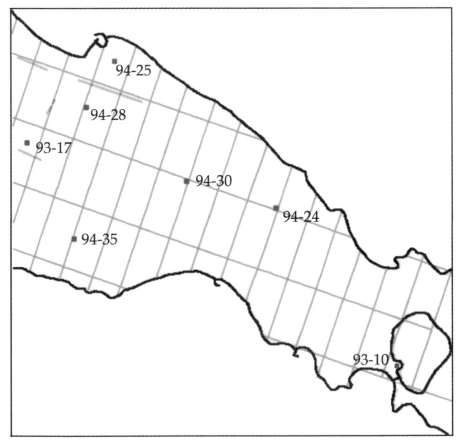

Fig. 9. Detail of Figure 7, eastern half of peninsula.

in the centuriation scheme and its relatively large size may indicate that it is better interpreted as a small village. Finally, it is now apparent that Ayia Triada (SS94-30), the enigmatic tile scatter, is also located at the intersection of two *limites*. In this case, the correlation provides some evidence, not found in the material record, that the scatter may best be interpreted as a tile grave.

Conclusion

Investigations by the Nikopolis Project have documented the profound changes in land use on the Ayios Thomas peninsula following the foundation of the city. This study presents only the initial stages in the analysis of the settlement patterns. The rural settlement typology on the peninsula will continue to be refined, and patterns of settlement and land use will be developed for each chronological period. The data from the Ayios Thomas peninsula will then be compared to the remainder of the Project area, in particular with the Acheron River valley, to the north, where investigations of similar intensity were carried out. The comparison of these two areas, at varying distances from the city of Nikopolis, will provide additional evidence for assessing the effects of the foundation. It is my firm belief that, with data from regional investigations such as these, we will be able to determine how far – and for how long – the shadow of Nikopolis was cast.

Notes

NOTE 1
The Nikopolis Project, directed by James R. Wiseman, Boston University; Angelika Douzougli and Konstantinos Zachos, 12th Ephoreia of Prehistoric and Classical Antiquities; and Frankiska Kephallonitou, 8th Ephoreia of Byzantine Antiquities, was carried out from 1991 to 1996 under the auspices of the American School of Classical Studies at Athens. An overview of the project and a listing of publications to date may be found in Wiseman (this volume).

NOTE 2
Cladas 1975; Doukellis 1988.

NOTE 3
Leake 1835, vol. 1, 196.

NOTE 4
Curtis Runnels, personal communication, 1993. See also Runnels et al. 1999.

NOTE 5
For an explanation of the terms used to designate survey units, see Wiseman (this volume) note 5. A fuller discussion may be found in Tartaron (in press).

NOTE 6
I am indebted to Melissa Moore for allowing me to incorporate her most recent thoughts on the ceramics from this area.

NOTE 7
Leake 1835, vol. 1, 196.

NOTE 8
For evidence of purple-dye production in Epirus during the Roman period, see Dakaris 1971, 17 (Cassope) and Dakaris 1986, 62 (Dodona). Cf. Wiseman, this volume, note 25.

NOTE 9
The geophysical surveys were carried out under the direction of John Weymouth and Apostolos Sarris, whose preliminary interpretations are presented here.

NOTE 10
Jing and Rapp, in press. For additional discussion of their findings, see also the article by Wiseman in this volume.

NOTE 11
Leake 1835, vol. 1, 187.

NOTE 12
Leake 1835, vol. 1, 181.

NOTE 13
K. Zachos, personal communication, 1992.

NOTE 14
Pouqueville 1826; see the map of the Preveza peninsula by J.G. Barbié du Bocage.

NOTE 15
Pallas 1959, 197–202; Soustal 1981: 270.

NOTE 16
Hammond 1967, 48.

NOTE 17
The material on the causeway appears to have been dredged up during a cleaning of the channels connecting the lake to the Ambracian Gulf.

NOTE 18
Cf. *Praktika* 1959, 98–113 [Phtelia]; another possible villa site (SS93-1) was identified by the survey ca. 400 m southeast of Phtelia. For other coastal villas in Epirus, see the article by Angeli and Katsadima in this volume [Riza, Frangoklessia]; and *ArchDelt* 48 (1993): 282–285 (with earlier references) [Strongyli].

NOTE 19
The system was first noted by Chevallier [Chevallier 1958] and published in more detail by Panagiotis Doukellis [Doukellis 1988], who incorrectly identified the module as 20 x 40 actus (707 x 1414 m). While the centuries may indeed be rectangular, the module corresponds to a 10 x 20 actus scheme; cf. Cladas 1975. See also note 14 below.

NOTE 20
Additional support for an Augustan-period date was presented by Kostas Zachos (this volume), who has determined that the temenos of Apollo, Augustus's victory monument, was aligned with the *cardo maximus* of the city.

NOTE 21
Survey data from centuriated land is available from other parts of the empire; see, e.g., Attolini et al. 1991 [Cosa]. At the time this paper was presented, however, the hinterland of Nikopolis was the only centuriated land in Greece to have been intensively surveyed. The project area of the Eastern Korinthia Archaeological Survey, which conducted its first season of fieldwork in 1999, also includes centuriated land; the results of this project should provide a valuable comparison to the data from Ayios Thomas.

NOTE 22
It is unclear whether the N–S limites that are visible south of Nikopolis at 10-actus intervals represent internal divisions of a 20 x 20 actus scheme or constitute evidence for a 10 x 20 actus scheme. Conservatively, I have reproduced Doukellis' 10 x 20 actus scheme. It should be noted that, aside from Nikopolis and Ormos Vathy, the remainder of the sites in Figures 7–9, regardless of size, are indicated with a single dot.

Bibliography

Attolini, I., Cambi, F., Castagna, M., Celuzza, M., Fentress, E., Perkins, P. and Regoli, E., 1991.
Political Geography and Productive Geography between the Valleys of the Albegna and the Fiora in Northern Etruria, in: Barker and Lloyd 1991, 142–52.

Bailey, G.N., Adam, E., Panagopoulou, E., Perlès, C. and Zachos, K. (eds.), 1999
The Palaeolithic Archaeology of Greece and Adjacent Areas: Proceedings of the ICOPAG Conference, Ioannina (British School at Athens Studies 3). London: British School at Athens.

Barker, G. and Lloyd, J. (eds.), 1991
Roman Landscapes: Archaeological Survey in the Mediterranean Area (Archaeological Monographs of the British School at Rome 2). London: British School at Rome.

Chevallier, R., 1958
Pour une interprétation archéologique de la couverture aérienne grecque: note sur les centuriations romaines de Grèce. *BCH* 82, 635-36.

Cladas, C., 1975
La découverte de civilisations anciennes à l'aide de la photogrammétrie. *Photogrammetria* 30, 213–18.

Dakaris, S., 1971
Cassopaia and the Elean Colonies (Ancient Greek Cities 4). Athens: Center of Ekistics.

Dakaris, S., 1986
Λωδώνη: Αρχαιολογικός Οδηγός. Ioannina: City of Ioannina.

Doukellis, P. N., 1988
Cadastres romains en Grèce: traces d'un réseau rural à Actia Nikopolis. *Dialogues d'histoire anciennes* 14, 159-66.

Hammond, N. G. L., 1967
Epirus: the Geography, the Ancient Remains, the History and the Topography of Epirus and Adjacent Areas. Oxford: Clarendon Press.

Jing, Z. and Rapp, Jr. G. (in press)
Holocene Coastal Landscape Evolution of the Ambracian Embayment in Epirus, Western Greece, and Its Relationship to Archaeological Settings. In Wiseman and Zachos (in press).

Leake, W. M., 1835
Travels in Northern Greece. 4 vols. London: J. Rodwell.

Murray, W. M. and Petsas, P. M., 1989.
Octavian's Campsite Memorial for the Actian War (TAPA 79.4). Philadelphia: American Philosophical Society.

Pallas, D. I., 1959
Scoperte archeologiche in Grecia negli anni 1956–1958. *Rivista di Archeologia Cristiana* 35, 187–223.

Pouqueville, F. C. H. L., 1826
Voyage dans la Grèce. 2nd ed. 3 vols. Paris: Firmin Didot.

Runnels, C., van Andel, T. H., Zachos, K. and Paschos, P., 1999.
Human Settlement and Landscape in the Preveza Region (Epirus) in the Pleistocene and Early Holocene, in: G.N. Bailey et al. 1999, 120–129.

Soustal, P,. 1981
Nikopolis und Kephallenia. (Tabula Imperii Byzantini 3.) Vienna: Verlag der Österreichischen Akademie der Wissenschaften.

Tartaron, T. F. (in press)
Archaeological Survey: Sampling Strategies and Field Methods. In Wiseman and Zachos (in press).

Wiseman, J. and Zachos, K. (eds.) (in press)
Landscape Archaeology in Southern Epirus, Greece I.

Roman and Late Antique Pottery of Southern Epirus: Some Results of the Nikopolis Survey Project*

*Melissa
G. Moore*

Two lines of inquiry will be presented here. First, this paper suggests some ways in which the Roman and Late Antique ceramic material collected in southern Epirus by the Nikopolis Project may be used to reconstruct southern Epirote trade with Italy and other parts of the Mediterranean after 31 BC. Second, evidence for change in the production technology of cooking vessels before and after the foun-

dation of Nikopolis is presented. Both lines of discussion relate to a central interpretive issue raised by several other participants at this conference: What was the extent of Roman cultural influence in southern Epirus following the foundation of Nikopolis?

Figure 1 indicates the areas in which the Nikopolis Project recovered the pottery discussed in this paper.[2] The most im-

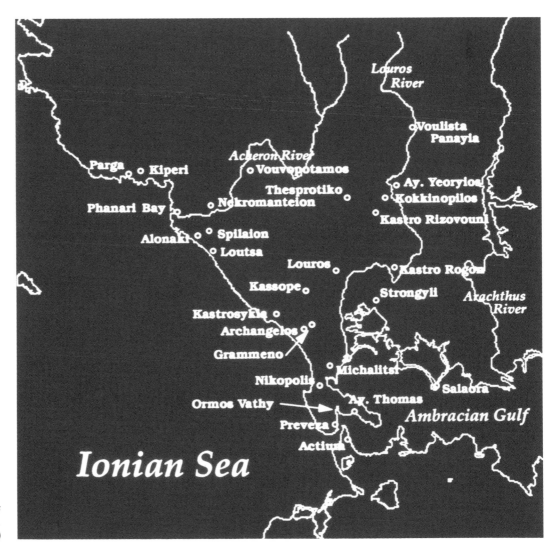

Fig. 1. Map of the Nikopolis Project survey region. (Nikopolis Project)

cooking vessels may be noted. Many of the Roman-period cookware fragments collected by the survey are from deep, round-bottomed vessels – used for stewing and boiling – with a distinctive deep grooving around the outer edge of a wide, flat rim (Fig. 6. 1-2). The distinctive rim bears a strong resemblance to published examples of cooking vessels from Roman levels at Butrint and other early Roman sites in the Balkans, rather than contemporary vessels from sites in Greece or Italy.[11] Other fragments do resemble, in shape, vessels found in Corinth, Isthmia, Athens, and other Roman sites in the Mediterranean (Fig. 6. 3).

All of the Roman-period cookware fragments belong to a different ware group than that of the Hellenistic-period cooking vessels. The new ware group is characterized by the presence of very large, sharp aplastic inclusions; like the Hellenistic wares, however, the Roman cookware was fired in an oxidizing atmosphere. Plate 3 illustrates the appearance of a Roman-period cooking vessel in thin-section. The clay is characterized by the presence of large, poorly sorted, angular chert, quartz, and feldspar grains, and is

easily distinguished in both thin-section and hand-specimen from the clay used the Hellenistic-period cooking vessels.[12] Plate 4 is a photomicrograph of a clay sample collected on the Ayios Thomas peninsula, fired in an oxidizing atmosphere to about 900° C; this type of clay is a good mineralogical match to the Roman-period cooking vessels. Clays of this general type are available throughout the survey region, and further study will be required in order to address the question of a specific production location (or the possibility of multiple production locations) for vessels made from this kind of clay.

A new set of firing practices had been adopted by the beginning of the Late Antique period. The Late Antique cooking vessels recovered by the survey are dark-gray to black in color, and contain large, sharp, aplastic inclusions. Plate 5 illustrates the appearance of the Late Antique cookware vessels in thin-section. The mineralogical composition and texture of these vessels is the same as that of the Roman-period vessels, but the fabric has been blackened throughout, possibly a result of firing in a reducing atmosphere. These cooking vessels probably resembled, in

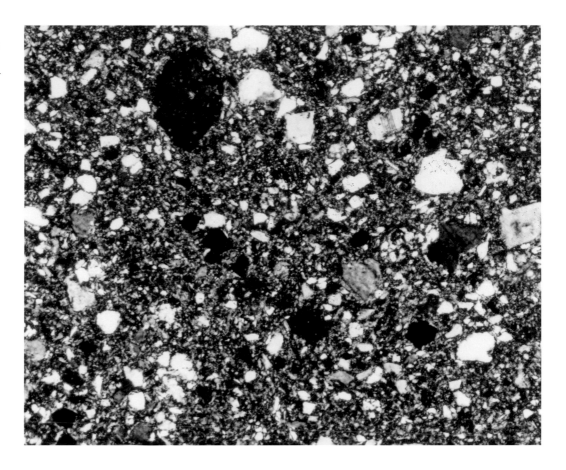

Plate 2. Photomicrograph of clay sample from the Koukos region, in thin-section. Magnification 25x. Crossed-polarized light.

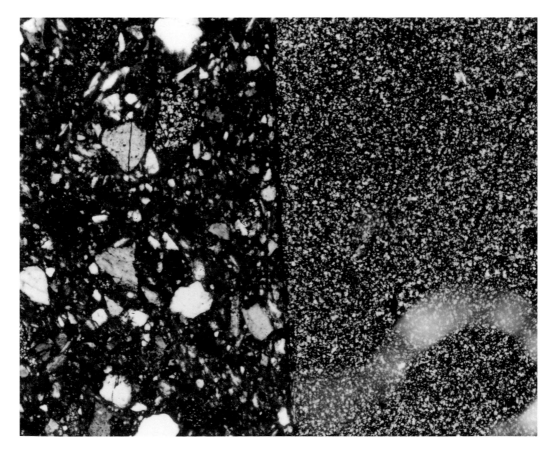

Plate 3. Photomicrograph of Roman-period cookware in thin-section. Magnification 25x. Crossed-polarized light.

shape, the deep, round-bottomed forms found on many sites in southern Greece in the same period (Fig. 7).

In summary, preliminary analyses of the coarsewares collected by the Nikopolis Project indicate that there were significant changes in the production of southern Epirote cooking-vessels during the Roman and Late Antique periods. The first such change took place shortly after the foundation of Nikopolis. New cookware forms were introduced, including forms common at southern Greek sites during this period as well as a different form found throughout Epirus and the southern Balkans. Shortly after the synoecism, new kinds of clay were used to produce southern Epirote cookware. A new firing practice for cookware was adopted by the early 4th century AD. During the Late Antique period, too, the shapes of the cooking vessels appear to have resembled contemporary southern Greek forms.

Conclusions

Some interesting conclusions emerge from this preliminary study of southern Epirote pottery. Southern Epirus maintained throughout its history a reliance on local production of coarse cooking-vessels, although the technology used to produce these vessels changed considerably during the Roman and Late Antique periods. Local production of tableware was important in both periods, but many local tablewares were produced as imitations of popular forms imported from Italy, Asia Minor, and North Africa. The survey recovered no evidence of amphora production in southern Epirus; all dateable amphorae fragments represent imported vessels that brought luxury foodstuffs such as wine and olive oil to Epirus from other parts of the Roman world, such as Italy and North Africa. The quantities of these amphorae in southern Epirus, though always rather small, did increase significantly from the 1st through 5th centuries AD, reflecting an increased participation in the pan-Mediterranean trade networks that developed over the course of this period.

The social impact of the Roman presence in southern Epirus is indicated to some extent by the uneven distribution of different vessel classes within the survey area. During both the Roman and Late Antique periods, the distribution pattern of imported amphorae and tablewares was significantly different from that of locally produced coarsewares, with the imported goods having a far more restricted distribution. The imported wares were recovered at large villa sites and an urban harbor area near Nikopolis itself, whereas the local cookware products are more evenly distributed across the landscape, even in areas (such as Michalitsi) where the primary period of occupation was previously thought to have ended with the Nikopolitan synoecism. Perhaps in the course of the 1st through 4th centuries AD there was a gradual resettlement of the land around the new Augustan city.

The social impact of the Roman presence in southern Epirus manifested itself in other ways as well. Disruptions of the regional social order, triggered perhaps by the synoecism process in the late first century BC, were severe enough to have caused change in the regional ceramic industry. Shifts in the selection of clay resources in the 1st century AD, for example, may have resulted from change in access to clay resources following the political reorganization of the region. The adoption of new firing processes by the 4th century AD may also reflect a reorganization of the ceramic industry in the aftermath of repeated invasions by Gothic and Slavic groups.

Further research will be necessary in order to address more fully the impact of the Roman conquest on ceramic usage in southern Epirus. Ongoing analyses of the material collected by the Nikopolis Survey Project will, it is hoped, refine these preliminary results. In the future, a full integration of survey and excavation data for this region would play an important role in the development of a more complete understanding of the Roman and Late Antique pottery of southern Epirus.

Plate 4. Photomicrograph of clay sample from the Ayios Thomas peninsula, in thin-section. Magnification 25x. Crossed-polarized light.

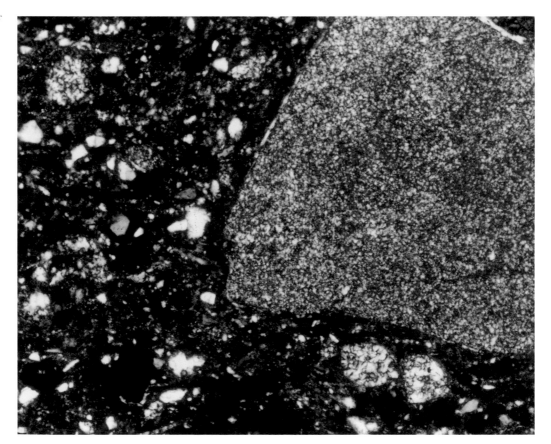

Plate 5. Photomicrograph of Late Antique cookware in thin-section. Magnification 25x. Crossed-polarized light.

Notes

NOTE 1*
I would like to acknowledge, with thanks, the assistance and kindness of the Danish Institute at Athens – especially of Drs. Signe and Jacob Isager – both during the conference at which this paper was first presented and in the subsequent preparation of the manuscript for publication. I am grateful to Virginia Anderson-Stojanović for generously sharing with me her expertise in the study of Roman pottery; any inaccuracies that appear in this paper are, of course, my own. William Morison provided invaluable editorial assistance and support. The assistance of the Greek Archaeological Service and the Wiener Laboratory of the American School of Classical Studies are also gratefully acknowledged.

NOTE 2
See J. Wiseman, this volume, and Wiseman and Zachos (in press) for a full discussion of survey methodology and the topography of the survey region.

NOTE 3
The Roman period is defined for the purposes of this paper as beginning in 31 BC and extending through the late 3rd century AD. The Late Antique period is here defined as the 4th to 6th centuries AD.

NOTE 4
I am grateful to Dr. K. Gravani for sharing with me her expert views on the identification of southern Epirote sigillatas.

NOTE 5
C. Stein, in this volume, presents the Ayios Thomas data in more detail.

NOTE 6
The most common forms represented are early "Africana Grande" and "Africana Piccolo" (Riley MR amphora 16, 17) and Riley MR amphora 14.

NOTE 7
See Williams 1989, 92-3 for discussion of this amphora type and its production in Cilicia.

NOTE 8
For a useful general discussion of Greek cooking practice, see Sparkes 1962; Bats 1988 is an important discussion of the differences between the Greek and Roman cookware assemblage. Berlin 1997, 121-122 is a useful summary of the Greek use of cooking struts and of the differences in Greek and Roman use of heat sources in cooking.

NOTE 9
It should be noted, of course, that typically "Italian" vessels do appear in ever increasing quantities in Greece following the consolidation of Roman hegemony in Greece after 146 BC. Even after the Roman conquest of Greece, however, most cookware forms were not *supplanted*, but were, rather, *supplemented* by the introduction of standard Roman cookware forms such as the flat baking dish (*patina/patella*). It is also interesting to note that *lopades* appear only very rarely in the Latin literary sources for cooking practices, in which baking vessels such as *patinae* and *patellae* and frying vessels such as the *patera* receive the greatest attention. Greek literature, on the other hand (specifically, Old and New Comedy), abounds in references to the use of *lopades*.

NOTE 10
The dating of cookware sherds based on clay fabric is a problematic practice. The same clay fabric appears to have been in use in southern Epirus at least as early as the Archaic period, and, therefore, cannot serve as the sole criterion for dating this material. The casserole sherds discussed here have been dated to the late Hellenistic period on the basis of shape rather than fabric class.

NOTE 11
See, for example, Baçe 1981. Like the Albanian vessels, the fragments collected by the survey have deeply grooved, broad horizontal rims and two vertical handles extending from either the upper or lower edge of the rim. Parallels to these vessels elsewhere in the Mediterranean are rare.

NOTE 12
Ongoing textural analyses suggest that these are differences in clay resource selection, and not in tempering practice.

Bibliography

Baçe, A., 1981
La forteresse de Paleokastra, *Iliria* 11, 165-235.

Bats, M., 1988
Vaisselle et Alimentation à Olbia de Provence (v. 350-v. 50 av. J.-C.). Modèles culturels et catégories céramiques, Revue Archéologique de Narbonnaise, Supplément 18, Paris.

Berlin, A., 1997
The Plain Wares, in: *Herbert 1997,* 1-246.

Herbert, S. (ed.), 1997
Tel Anafa II, i: The Hellenistic and Roman Pottery. Journal of Roman Archaeology Supplementary Series Number 10, Part II, i. Ann Arbor.

Sparkes, B. A., 1962
The Greek Kitchen, *JHS* 82, 121-137.

Williams, C., 1989
Anemurium: the Roman and early Byzantine pottery. Toronto.

Wiseman, J. and Zachos, K., In press.
Landscape Archaeology in Southern Epirus, Greece, I.

Chrysostomou gives the first account of the monument in a report, published in AAA, in 1982.[4] At that time the only visible part of the monument was the decagonal building, covered partly by the vegetation. In 1993, however, human intervention caused serious damage to the architectural remains. The local Ephoreia had subsequently to conduct a salvage excavation.[5] According to the first results of that brief investigation, the decagonal building (room A) forms part of a larger architectural complex, extending over an area of about 1800 sqm (Fig.1). During the excavations a new rectangular room (room B) was revealed at the south of the existing decagonal building. The room, measuring 7.40 x 6.90 m, is built on the same axis as its decagonal counterpart. No traces of doorways are visible, except for the one that leads to room A. The room's south wall continues to the east where it meets another wall forming a third room. Apart from a trial excavation farther east that revealed traces of a brick pavement and a fragment of a clay pipe in its northern section, this section was not farther investigated.

Similar investigations carried out to the west brought to light pieces of other brick and rubble walls, belonging probably to other rooms of the complex (rooms C, D, E). The façade of one of these walls gives evidence of the existence of at least two arched openings. Smaller rooms were also excavated in the southern part of the complex, where scattered remains of white tesserae indicate the existence of a mosaic pavement. Furthermore fragments of marble decoration, found in room C, give witness to a finely made construction.

The most impressive part of the whole architectural complex is room A. Situated in the north section of the complex, it dominates the whole area, as it is preserved to a height of over 4 meters (Fig. 2). It has a decagonal plan inscribed in a rectangular one. The rectangle measures 8 x 8.20 m, while the decagon's diameter is 7 m. Four doors open one on each side; the one on the south forms an opening of ca.5 m width. The three others are small-

er, with openings ranging from 1. 20 to 1. 25 m. Two niches, built in each one of the outer walls, flank the south entrance. The one on the left, surmounted by a horizontal band of vertical bricks, is preserved in good condition, while the one on the right is almost completely destroyed.

Double arches, opened on the top of each doorway carrying the vaulted roof are now gone. The only things that survive are the marks of the beginnings of these arches. Windows topped with arches are opened above each one of the other entrances. The interior is decorated with six niches (Fig. 3), two on the northwest corner, two on the northeast and one on each of the southern corners of the decagon.

Fig. 2. Riza. Decagon (RoomA). The west side.

Fig. 4. Riza. Decagon. Building technique (opus mixtum).

Fig. 3. Riza. Decagon.
Niche at the interior.

Decorative results are also provided by the specific technique for the construction of the walls. The walls are built with rectangular bricks (*opus testaceum*) combined with unworked stones mixed with mortar and enclosed in panels (*opus mixtum*) (Fig. 4).

Evidence for the superstructure of at least two adjacent rooms, one on the west and one on the south side respectively, can be traced on the two side walls that emerge from the southwest corner of the decagon.

It is difficult to determine the actual

function of the decagon. Chrysostomou interpreted it as a Nymphaeum with architectural particularities, comparing it with the Nymphaeum of Domus Augustana and the so-called Minerva Medica at Rome.[6] The Nymphaea in the form of polygonal rooms are very few, namely five, and they are all found in Italy.[7] Still in light of the findings of 1993, we think that we should look for another interpretation of the building.

It is quite obvious that the decagon follows in its basic lines the type of the octagon, enriching it by the addition of two more niches, in its northern part. As many examples from the Mediterranean region indicate, this type of architecture had a wide distribution under the late Roman Empire. Most of these examples belong to bath complexes. We should mention here for example the Hunting Baths at Lepcis Magna[8] and at Bulla Regia[9] in northern Africa, the South Baths at Bosra in southern Syria[10] or the Bath C at Antioch.[11] Even in the Greek mainland the same type is to be observed in the Olympeion Baths.[12] There is a similar bath complex located at Buthrotum in southern Albania as well.[13]

The examples cited above provide us with a relatively firm base for the identification of the function of room A. We contend that it is part of a bath complex. Adequate springs are near. The river, in spite of the fact that it is rather unimpressive with a very reduced flow in the summer, would have provided a steady base for the function of the bath complex. The existence of a fragment of a *hypokauston* collected from the area strengthens this interpretation.

According to the sequence of the usual rooms to be found in a bath building, namely *apodyterium*, *caldarium*, *tepidarium*, and *frigidarium*, the plan and the architectural features of this room correspond mainly to that of the *frigidarium*. The *frigidarium* could take many forms, but a common one, especially in late Antiquity, is the polygone. It was nearly always vaulted. Normally it had large windows and it was very rarely heated. It was the most decorated hall in the baths, with statues often placed in the niches.[14]

Chrysostomou objected to the building being baths, saying that a bath room could not have four entrances and windows and should have clay pipes in the walls to heat them with hot air. But, as has already been mentioned, it is obvious that these arguments cannot be accepted.

The building belongs to a special category of bathing accommodations identified as *balnea*. These relatively small (of an average size of c. 500 sqm.) non-monumental asymmetrical baths were quite common in the eastern provinces of the Roman Empire. They had a hygienic function and they could also serve social purposes. As Nielsen has pointed out, "the *balnea* were normally one of the smaller baths in a town which also had *thermae*, or could be placed in villages".[15] In the case of Strongyli near the Ambracian Gulf such a *balneum* belongs to a *villa rustica* that is placed 230 m north of it.[16] It is very possible that we are dealing with a similar case at Riza, where the rooms to the south seem to have had a residential character.

As far as the chronology of the complex is concerned, the pottery that comes from the excavation of 1993 indicates a dating from the 3rd to the 4th century AD.[17] Furthermore the construction technique using panels is very common during the 3rd and 4th centuries AD.[18]

Agia Pelagia

The Water reservoir

The remains of what in all probability might have been a water reservoir have been recorded 3 km south of Riza. The architectural complex was excavated by Chrysostomou in 1980 and has subsequently vanished due to the construction of the new Igoumenitsa – Preveza highway.[19]

What was partly revealed then was the substructure of a pi-shaped building measuring 5 x 4.90 m, facing towards the south (Fig. 5). The north side of the building was preserved to a height of 0. 40 m.

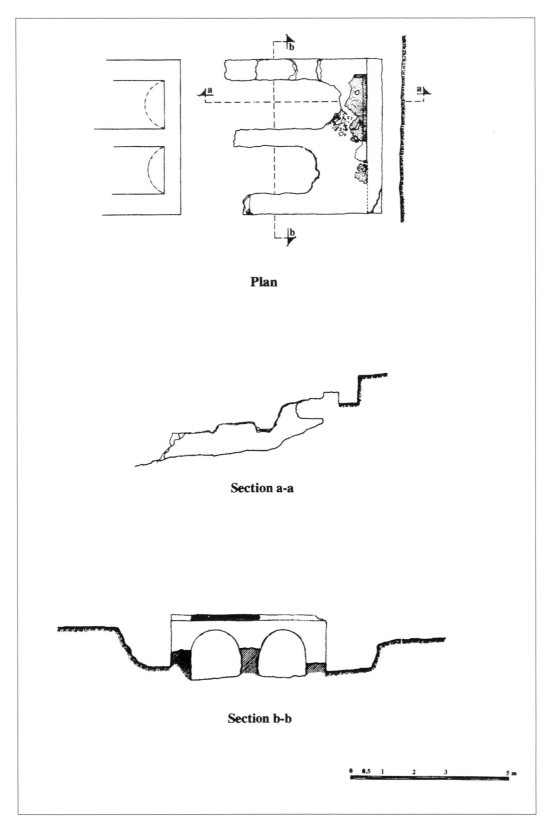

Fig. 5. Agia Pelagia.
The water-reservoir.
Plan and sections.

Plan

Section a-a

Section b-b

Three parallel walls emerged from there, carrying two arches. The walls were laid directly on the ground following its inclination. They had a rubble and mortar core with a substantial facing of very thin cement. Both arches bore traces of wooden scaffolding on their inner surface, which was used during their construction.

Parts of the upper structure survived to a height of 0. 10 m on the north side while on the west the indications were quite meager. A fragment of thick, two-layered concrete on the southwest corner indicate the existence of a pavement, coming from what might have been the water-tank. The lower layer was composed of coarse mortar with rubble and an aggregate of terracotta while the upper one was of well-compacted mortar. Traces of cement were found along the sidewalls as well. [20]

The pottery found in the construction indicates that the water reservoir was in use from the mid-first century AD to the Byzantine times.[20]

Another construction, whose ruins have been known to Ephoreia since 1980, lies less than 50 m south of the former water reservoir, on the west side of the precinct of the monastery of Agia Pelagia. The ruins belong to a wall, never recorded in the literature. The wall runs along the north-south axis with a total length of 6.25m but it is obvious that it continues in both directions (Fig. 6). It is preserved to a height of 1.30m and has three battlements on its west side, each at a distance of about 1. 60m. from the other. The south battlement has a length of 1. 03, a height of 1.17 and a depth of 1.05m. The one in the middle measures 1.03 x 1.02 x 1.06m. while the north measures 1.04 x 0.75 x 1.06m. Both the wall and the battlements are constructed of unworked stones and bricks, mixed with mortar and covered by thin cement.

Not far from the wall, south of the monastery there is a natural spring, where a destroyed Roman construction was recently detected. This construction together with the above mentioned wall and the water reservoir probably formed part of a

Fig. 6. Agia Pelagia. The wall on the west side of the monastery.

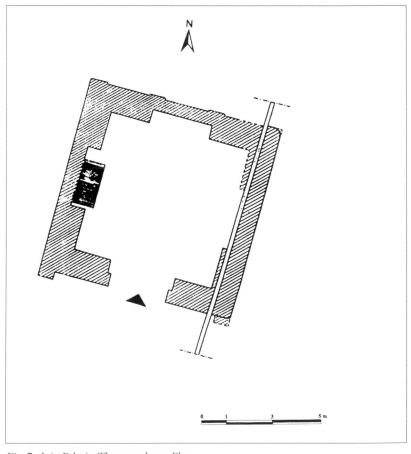

Fig. 7. Agia Pelagia. The mausoleum. Plan.

Fig. 8. Agia Pelagia. The mausoleum. General view from the NW corner.

system that supplied water to a garden presumably associated with the nearby *mausoleum*. These *cepotaphia* were common in the Greek-speaking provinces during the 2nd century AD. They were surrounded by an enclosure wall and they often served as places "for the eating of funerary meals, for keeping provisions and for other forms of social activities".[22] Furthermore a mortar for the crushing of the olives was found within the precinct of the monastery.

The Mausoleum

On the south side of the modern road that leads from Preveza to Igoumenitsa, another monument was partly excavated by Chrysostomou at about the same time as the water reservoir.[23] The monument is located within the precinct of the Monastery of Agia Pelagia, 80 m south of the village of Kastrosykia at an altitude of 85 m a.s.l. J. Vokotopoulou first recorded

the monument in 1969.[24] In 1971 during the renovations of the monastery the construction of the modern precinct destroyed part of the east niche and the pilasters on the southeast and northeast corners. Nine years later P. Chrysostomou conducted a short excavation. The construction measuring ca. 8.60 x 8.50m (Fig. 7), is comprised mainly of concrete (*opus caementicium*) faced by rectangular bricks (*opus testaceum*) (Fig. 8). The monument has a concrete podium, which on the south side has a total length of 2.58m while on the west side has been revealed to a length of 1.60m. Its façade has a doorway of 2.65m width, facing to the south and flanked by two flat brick pilasters. Two decorative pilasters are formed on the edges of the façade while four others decorate the outer surface of the north wall. The door must have had two leafs with jambs and a lintel, providing access to the almost square burial chamber (6.20

97

x 6.15m). Paved with concrete, the chamber has three rectangular niches built into the rear and the sidewalls (Fig. 9). Each of these had an arched recess, while the roof, which has now completely collapsed, consisted of a cross vault, as a part fallen into the chamber indicates. A few fragments of the stuccoed decoration of the interior remain in place on the walls, while traces of red vertical bands are to be found at the corners of the niches.

Furthermore, *tesserae* of blue glass found in the north niche indicate the existence of a mosaic decoration, that probably covered part of the arched recess. From the three niches, of which the one on the east side is partly destroyed, the niche at the west opens down to a cist grave (Fig. 10). The grave, measuring 1.92 L., 0.76 W. and 0.77m H., is paved with marble slabs and tiles. It contained five inhumations, but no grave offerings. No traces of graves were found in the other two niches, which probably contained sarcophagi.

This hypothesis is strengthened by the fact that at least four fragments of sarcophagi were found in the vicinity. Two of them were used as building material in the church of Agia Pelagia. The first one is part of a lid and bears a sculptured representation of a cupid holding garlands and ribbons.[25] (Fig. 11). The other two are smaller and are now embedded in the jambs of the two side doors that lead to the Holy Altar in the church.[26] They preserve part of a Lesbian cyma as well as garlands and ribbons. The fourth fragment, however, was recently found among the debris of the above-mentioned construction at the nearby spring.[27] It comes from the lower part of the sarcophagus and preserves part of the sculptured decoration, depicting the upper body of a dead male figure approached by a draped one (Fig. 12). The male figure is depicted lying on the ground, with the back of his head turned to the spectator, resting on his extended left arm. Just behind this figure the hoofs of a horse are discerned. The scene suggests iconography inspired by the Trojan circle, even though no exact parallels have been detected so far.[28] This kind of

Fig. 9. Agia Pelagia. The north niche of the mausoleum.

Fig. 10. Agia Pelagia. The cist grave.

Fig. 11. Agia Pelagia.
Coffer lid.

repertoire was favored by the Attic workshops from the late 2ⁿᵈ to the first half of
the 3ʳᵈ century AD.[29] A sarcophagus found
at Ladochori in Thesprotia, now at the
Ioannina Museum, belongs to the same
series. [30]

Sherds collected both from the interior
of the monument and the area around it
date from the mid-first to the 2ⁿᵈ century
AD,[31] but the architectural elements found
in the vicinity can be attributed to the 2ⁿᵈ
century AD. Most of them have been used
as building material for the construction
of the nearby church. For example, the
anta-capital found on the east side of the
church, could well have been dated on the
basis of typological and stylistic analysis to
the 2ⁿᵈ century AD.[32] (Fig. 13) As far as its
function and initial position are concerned, it has been suggested that it probably surmounted one of the pilasters that
flanked the doorway of the nearby monument.[33] This observation is confirmed by
the fact that the anta-capital has exactly

the same width as the pilasters. A fragment
of a second anta-capital is preserved embedded in the south wall of the church,
bearing the same characteristics as the first
one.[34] Furthermore, the cornice above the
main entrance of the church suggests possibly a similar use in the architectural decoration of the monument.[35] (Fig. 14) An
altar serving now as base for the Holy Altar of the church provides evidence for
the tomb furnishing.[36] The altar might
well have been placed in the burial chamber, as similar examples at Isola Sacra indicate.[37]

It is, however, very difficult to determine the position of two Corinthian capitals, one of which, together with a column
base, now forms part of the inner colon-
nade of the church.[38] (Fig. 15) Both are
dated to the 2ⁿᵈ century AD, but their size
and function do not seem to correspond
to the architectural decoration of the
monument.[39] It is very likely that they
were brought from the nearby Nikopolis

Fig. 12. Agia Pelagia. Fragment of a marble sarcophagus. Nikopolis Museum.

at the time when the church was built. [40]

Pilasters topped by anta-capitals are to be found on a series of Roman sepulchral monuments, such as the so-called tomb of Annia Regilla on the Via Appia at Rome,[41] the *Mausoleum* Psi in the St. Peter Necropolis[42] or similar tombs in the Isola Sacra cemetery dated to the 2nd century AD.[43] Furthermore, the stuccoed decoration of the chamber, despite its very poor state of preservation, finds parallels in two examples, one from Isola Sacra, [44]and the other from St. Peter's Necropolis,[45] both dated to the end of the 2nd century AD.

The existence of rectangular niches has been considered as a typical characteristic of the *columbarium* type of tomb.[46] Tombs of this type have long been known in Greece.[47] Still, the rectangular burial building with four rectangular niches, one on each side, is closely connected to the *mausoleum*, a type of monument well attested in the region. Similar *mausoleia* have been excavated in the area of the south cemetery of Nikopolis.[48] Monuments of this type have been recorded in the district of Troizen, too.[49] Furthermore, the niches of *columbaria* in most cases contained cremations in funerary urns, and in only a very few cases inhumations in graves and certainly never in sarcophagi. [50]

Conclusions

The above mentioned monuments should be examined within the scope of the historic situation in Epirus in the Roman period.

At the end of the 1st century BC Epirus presented a picture of complete deterioration. The Epirotic mainland experienced a population decline caused by a series of dramatic events, i.e. the destruction of seventy towns by Aemilius Paullus in 167 BC, the Civil Wars of the 1st century BC and the synoecism of Nikopolis after the naval battle at Actium in 31 BC. Still the importance of Epirus with its westward position, which indicated a greater emphasis upon communications and contacts with Italy, demanded stabilization of this region. These circumstances favored the interference of Rome.[51] Of major importance was the colonial foundation of Julius Caesar at Buthrotum.[52] A few years later, according to Strabo, Octavian established Roman settlers (*epoikoi*), veteran warriors, at several points in Epirus.[53] Furthermore the region's plenti-

ful supply of livestock attracted the attention of financially successful Romans to the coast of Epirus. These were the *Synipirotae*, the *Epirotici homines* of Cicero's correspondence[54] and the second book of Varro's *De re rustica*,[55] men such as Cicero's friend Titus Pomponius Atticus, who kept herds of oxen at Buthrotum and at the mouth of river Thyamis. According to Dakaris similar enterprises had been established by the outlets of the rivers Acheron and Louros.[56] After the settlement of these Romans in Epirus in the 1st century BC,[57] from the reign of Augustus to the Gothic invasion of 250 AD, Epirus as well as the rest of the Greece, enjoyed the *Pax Romana*, experiencing the benefits of long term peaceful coexistence.

The architectural remains in Riza and Agia Pelagia should be considered as signposts of the rural presence of wealthy and important individuals. Whether these individuals were descendants of the above-mentioned Romans or of the pre-roman aristocracy whose status was enhanced by the adoptions of Italian upper class customs, is a matter that demands further investigation. Still, the appearance of distinctively Roman buildings in the countryside, such as the bath complex at Riza or the *mausoleum* at Agia Pelagia, need not indicate Roman owners. Epigraphic testimonies stemming mainly from funerary inscriptions found at nearby Nikopolis might indicate that the residents of Riza and Agia Pelagia were in fact Greeks.[58] If this is true, then the architecture and the everyday life of those Greeks were clearly affected by Roman customs.

The ornate sepulchral monument at Agia Pelagia was undoubtedly the family burial place of a landowner, whose residence would not have been far away. The monument might have stood out in the landscape as a visible claim to ownership and prestige. At Riza the impressive size of

Fig. 14. Agia Pelagia. Cornice. On site.

Fig. 15. Agia Pelagia. Corinthian capital. Nikopolis Museum.

the complex, its favorable location, the presence of baths, marble decoration and mosaics might indicate a villa of a well-to-do landowner and an affluent lifestyle.[59] Although, it should be noticed that these observations have a preliminary character and only the completion of the excavation will provide us with final answers about the actual function of the complex. The "villa" testifies to the existence of a sizable landed estate and represents a strong élite presence in the countryside.

Were these villas permanent or part-time residences? The examples from other Roman provinces show that owners would be at least part time absentee land-lords, who would move on a regular basis. It is possible that the landlord of the villa at Riza had his permanent residence in Nikopolis, which lies only a few kilometers to the South.

The architectural assemblages at Riza and Agia Pelagia may reflect the prosperity of the inhabitants but do not yet reveal the basis of that wealth. The excavations at the villa at Strongyli might give an answer to this question. Located at the mouth of the Ambrakian Gulf, the villa had access to land suitable for intensive oil cultivation and for cereals as well as for the possibility of grazing livestock.[60] An olive oil production unit was found there with two presses and three mills.

Olive oil together with grain and wine were the three most important agricultural products traded in the Roman world.[61] The demands of a growing population from the 1st to the middle of the 3rd century AD[62] led to exploitation of tree and wine crops, which in turn led to the development of oecistic models like the case of the villa at Strongyli.

The Strongyli case can provide us with the most vivid picture of land exploitation near our place of interest. The study of the villa as well as the completion of the excavation at Riza and Agia Pelagia, will contribute to the understanding of the economic background to the social and political history of the examined area.

Notes

NOTE 1*
Our thanks are due to Dr. K. Zachos, Director of the IB Ephoreia of Prehistoric and Classical Antiquites, and P. Chrysosto-mou of the IZ Ephoreia of Prehistoric and Classical Antiquities, for giving us the permission to study the two monuments and publish the plans of the water-reservoir and the mausoleum at Agia Pelagia, and Professor L. Marangou, of the University of Ioannina, for reading the manuscript.

NOTE 2
Strabo 7. 7. 5.

NOTE 3
Cunliffe 1978, 216-225.

NOTE 4
Chrysostomou 1982, 10-21. Alcock 1993, 70-71, fig. 24.

NOTE 5
Zachos 1993, 301.

NOTE 6
Chrysostomou 1982, 16.

NOTE 7
Letzner 1990, 135.

NOTE 8
Ward–Perkins & Toynbee 1949, 191-195, pl. XLVII, XLVIII.

NOTE 9
Hanoune et al. 1983, 87-91, fig. 3, 34, 35.

NOTE 10
Krencker et al. 1929, 297, fig. 437.

NOTE 11
Antioch on- the-Orontes I, 19-31, pl. V.

NOTE 12
Travlos 1949, fig. 2.

NOTE 13
Bace 1980, 51-87, fig. 15. Nielsen 1990, fig. 245.

NOTE 14
Nielsen 1990, 153-154.

NOTE 15
Nielsen 1990, 114.

NOTE 16
Douzougli 1993, 282-285. Douzougli 1998 with bibliography, 74-78.

NOTE 17
Hayes 1972, 218. Hayes 1983, 132, fig.15: 187. Agora V, 68, pl. 14: K106.

NOTE 18
Aupert 1990, 626, fig. 14b.

NOTE 19
Chrysostomou 1980, 320-321.

NOTE 20
Hodge 1992, 124, fig. 77. Radt 1979, 331, fig. 21.

NOTE 21
Corinth XVIII, part II, 65, pl. 9: 141. Agora V, 88, pl. 18: M39, M40.

NOTE 22
Toynbee 1971, 94-100.

NOTE 23
Chrysostomou 1980, 321.

NOTE 24
Vokotopoulou 1969, 253-254.

NOTE 25
The fragment has been recorded by Hammond as well: Hammond 1967, 49. For dimensions see: Chrysostomou 1980, 322, no. 4. This type of decoration is strikingly similar to that of several sarcophagi from Athens: Koch 1993, 106, 108, 109, fig. 62. However, the decoration from the Agia Pelagia fragment differs from the Attic series because it is restricted to the lid and not to the chest as in most of those cases.

NOTE 26
Dim: max. L 0.80, H 0.10 m.

NOTE 27
Dim: max. L 1.15, H 0.22, W 0.37 m.

NOTE 28
The motif of the reclining figure might be a lively adaptation from similar scenes on Attic Amazonomachy sarcophagi; for the latest discussion of their dating: Kintrup 1998, 206-215.

NOTE 29
For the Attic workshops in general: Koch-Sichtermann 1982, 366-475. Koch 1993, 97-112. Rogge 1993, 111-139.

NOTE 30
Rogge 1995, 129, no 12, pl. 1,2.

NOTE 31
Hayes 1983, 118, fig. 3: 27. Corinth XVIII, part II, 54, fig. 8: 108, 88, fig. 21: 190, 122, fig. 31: 266, 120, pl. 17: C-62-3.

NOTE 32
Pergamon, Asklepieion, North Stoa (156 AD): Heilmeyer 1970, 93-95, pl. 28, 3.4. Mylasa, City Gate, Pilaster Capital: Vanderput 1997, pl. 98.1 (Hadrianic). Afrodisias, Hadrianic Bath, Cornice: Vanderput 1997, pl. 75.3.

NOTE 33
Dim: Chrysostomou 1980, 322, no.1.

NOTE 34
Dim: Chrysostomou 1980, 322, no. 2.

NOTE 35
Dim: Chrysostomou 1980, 322, no.3. The exact dating of the fragment seems problematic. The structure of the acanthus leaves lies closer to the Athenian tradition represented by examples such as the capitals of the Hadrian's Library, dating in the middle of the 2nd century AD. Heilmeyer goes even further and wishes to see in such works the influence of the School of Asia Minor,

namely Ephesos and Pergamon: Heilmeyer 1970, 74-76, pl. 29,1.2. Still one cannot overlook a certain dryness in the rendering, which is alien to the above mentioned examples.

NOTE 36
Chrysostomou 1980, 322, no. 9. Dim. H 0.98, max. W 0.70 m.

NOTE 37
Calza 1940, 110-111,grave no 3, fig. 45. See also Boschung 1987, 37-41.

NOTE 38
Chrysostomou 1980, 322, no. 5, 7, 8. Dimensions are given only for no. 5.

NOTE 39
The capital bears a strong resemblance, especially in the rendering of the acanthus leaves, to a capital from the Frigidarium of the Forum thermae in Ostia dating from 160 AD. This "Akanthusblatt" had been considered by Heilmeyer typical of the School of Aphrodisias, but according to Freyberger the capitals from Ostia reveal an Athenian craftmanship, enriched in minor details, e.g. acanthus leaves, by the tradition of the big cultural centers of Asia Minor: Heilmeyer 1970, 168-171, pl. 31, 3.4. Freyberger 1990, 132, no 314, pl. 48b, 49c. Furthermore the arrangement of the acanthus on the calathos finds parallels on a capital from Euromos in Caria, dating to the 2nd century AD (Heilmeyer 1970, 172, pl. 38.1) as well as on capitals from Hirbet Amrit in Palestine: Fisher 1990, 59, no 223a, pl. 40.

NOTE 40
The date 1776 is written with relief letters on the east side of the church.

NOTE 41
Toynbee 1971, 133, pl. 40. Colvin 1991, 79-80, fig. 70. For other sepulchral monuments on Via Appia, carrying brick pilasters on the façade and on the rear wall: Rausa 1997, 104, no. 22 and 135, no. 31.

NOTE 42
Mielsch –Hesberg 1995, 250, 252, pl. 29-31, 39.

NOTE 43
Calza 1940, 85-87, graves nos 20, 21 (Hadrian -Antonine period), grave no 29, fig. 18, 26 (2rd cent. AD).

NOTE 44
Calza 1940, 140, grave no 57, fig. 66, 69 (200 AD).

NOTE 45
Mielsch- Hesberg 1995, Mausoleum I, 212, 221, figs. 255, 257 (160 AD).

NOTE 46
Morris 1994, 44-47 with bibliography.

NOTE 47
Patrai: Dekoulakou 1980, 556-575. Corinth: Morgan 1936, 484, fig. 25. Morgan 1938, 370, fig. 12. Wiseman 1978, 69, fig. 85-87.

NOTE 48
Zachos 1989, 268, fig. 10-12.

NOTE 49
Welter 1941, 41, pl.2, RG2, pl.23, 25a and b, 42, pl. 2, RG 5, pl. 26b.

NOTE 50
During recent renovations in the nearby cells of the monastery, another building was partly revealed. It will be investigated by the Ephoreia in the near future.

NOTE 51
Alcock 1993, 132–145.

NOTE 52
Alcock 1993, 133. Dakaris 1987, 21.

NOTE 53
Strabo 7. 7. 3.

NOTE 54
Cicero Ad Atticum 1. 5. 7, 7. 2 .3-4, 7. 5. 21, 14. 20. 2.

NOTE 55
Varro De re rustica 2. 15. 18 and 2. 3. 7.

NOTE 56
Dakaris 1971, 93. See also Reginos 1992, 347-348.

NOTE 57
Apart from the colonists and the Synipirotae, it is known that foreign negotiatores came to Greece as well. Alcock 1993, 75-77.

NOTE 58
Sarikakis 1970, 68.

NOTE 59
Another interpretation might be that the complex was an inn that provided accommodation and other facilities to people travelling from Apollonia to Nikopolis: Casson 1974. For an inn in Albania see Ceka 1976.

NOTE 60
Signs of a centuriated pattern have been detected in the territory as well. Doukellis 1988, 159-166. Doukellis 1990, 269-283. Alcock 1993, 139-140.

NOTE 61
Because of their ubiquity around the Mediterranean today, the plants that produced them are known as the " Mediterranean Triad " and the farming as " polyculture". Green 1990, 72.

NOTE 62
Alcock 1993, 158.

Bibliography

Agora, V., 1959
Robinson H.S., *The Athenian Agora. Pottery of the Roman Period.* Volume V. Princeton.

Alcock, S. E., 1993
Graecia Capta. The Landscapes of Roman Greece. Cambridge.

Antioch on-the-Orontes I., 1934
Elderkin G. W. (ed.). *Antioch on-the-Orontes. The Excavations of 1932.* Princeton.

Aupert, P., 1990
Évolution des appareils en Grèce a l' époque imperiale, *BCH* 114, 593-637.

Bace, A., 1980
Les Bains en Albanie pendant les premiers siècles de notre ère, *Monumentet* 19, 51-87.

Boethius A. & Ward-Perkins, J. B., 1970
Etruscan and Roman Architecture. London.

Boschung, D., 1987
Antike Grabaltare aus den Nekropolen Roms. Bern.

Casson, L., 1974
Travel in the Ancient World. London.

Calza, G., 1940
La Necropoli del Porto di Roma nell' Isola Sacra. Roma.

Ceka, N., 1976
Ad Quintum, *Iliria* VI, 287-312.

Chrysostomou, P., 1980/35
ADelt 35, *Chronika*, 316-323.

Chrysostomou, P., 1982/15
Το Νυμφαίο των Ριζών Πρεβέζης, *AAA* 15, 10-21.

Colvin, H., 1991
Architecture and the After-Life. London.

Corinth XVIII, part II., 1990
Warner Slane K. *Corinth. The Sanctuary of Demeter and Kore. The Roman Pottery and Lamps.* Volume XVIII. Part II. Princeton.

Cunliffe, B. W. (1978), 1994
Rome and her Empire. London.

Doukellis, P. N., 1988/14
Cadastres romains en Grèce: traces d' un reseau rural a Actia Nicopolis, *Dialogues d' histoire anciennes* 14, 159-166.

Doukellis, P. N., 1990/10
Ένα δίκτυο αγροτικών ορίων στην πεδιάδα της Άρτας, *Meletemata* 10, 269-283.

Dakaris, S., 1971
Cassopaia and the Elean Colonies. Athens.

Dakaris, S., 1987
Η ρωμαϊκή πολιτική στην Ήπειρο, in: Chrysos Ev. (ed.), *Nikopolis I. Proceedings of the First International Symposium on Nikopolis (23-29 September 1984).* Preveza, 1-21.

Dekoulakou, I., 1980
Ρωμαϊκό Μαυσωλείο στην Πάτρα in *Στήλη, εις μνήμη Ν. Κοντολέοντος.* Αθήνα, 556-575.

Douzougli, A., 1993/48
ADelt 48, Chronika, 282-285.

Douzougli, A., 1998/68
Μιά ρωμαϊκή αγροικία στις ακτές του Αμβρακικού Κόλτου, *Αρχαιολογία* 68, 74-78.

Fischer, M. L., 1990
Das korinthische Kapitell im Alten Israel in der hellenistischen und römischen Periode. Mainz am Rhein.

Freyberger, K. S., 1990
Stadtrömische Kapitelle aus der Zeit von Domitian bis Alexander Severus: Zur Arbeitsweise und Organisation stadtrömischer Werkstätten der Kaiserzeit. Mainz am Rhein.

Ginouvès, R., 1962
Balaneutiké. Paris.

Greene, K., 1990
The Archaeology of the Roman Economy. Los Angeles.

Hammond, N. G. L., 1967
Epirus. The geography, the ancient remains, the history and the topography of Epirus and adjacent areas. Oxford.

Hanoune, R., et al., 1983
Les Thermes au nord-ouest du Theatre, in: *Recherches Archeologiques Franco-Tunisiennes a Bulla Regia I. Miscellanea 1.* 63-92. Rome.

Hayes, J. W., 1972
Late Roman Pottery, London.

Hayes, J. W., 1983/78
The villa Dionysos excavations, Knossos: the pottery, *BSA* 78, 97-169.

Heilmeyer, W. D., 1970
Korinthische Normalkapitelle. *RM Erg.*16.

Hodge, A.T., 1992
Roman Aqueducts and Water Supply. London.

Kintrup, C., 1998
Chronologie der attischen Amazonomachie–Sarkophage, in: *Koch, G.(ed.) Akten des Symposiums "125 Jahre Sarkophag-Corpus" Marburg, 4.-7. Oktober 1995.* Mainz, 206-215

Koch, G., 1993
Sarkophage der römischen Kaiserzeit. Darmstadt.

Koch, G. -Sichtermann H., 1982
Römische Sarkophage, München.

Krencker, D. et al., 1929
Die Trierer Kaiserthermen, Ausgrabungsbericht und grundsätzliche Untersuchungen römischer Thermen, Abt.1. Augsburg.

Letzner, W,. 1990
Römische Brunnen und Nymphaea in der westlichen Reichshalfte. Münster.

Mielsch, H. -Hesberg, von H., 1995
Die heidnische Nekropole unter St. Peter in Rom. Die Mausoleen E-I und Z-Psi. Memorie XVI, 2. Roma.

Morgan II, C. H., 1936/40
Excavations at Corinth, 1935-1936, *AJA* 40, 466-484.

Morgan II, C. H., 1938/42
Excavations at Corinth, 1937-1938, *AJA* 42, 362-370.

Morris, I., 1994
Death-Ritual and Social Structure in Classical Antiquity. Cambridge.

Nielsen, I., 1990
Thermae et Balnea. Arhus.

Radt, W., 1979/94
Pergamon. Vorbericht über die Kampagne 1978. *AA* 94, 306-337.

Rausa, F., 1997
Pirro Ligorio, Tombe e Mausolei dei Romani. Roma

Reginos, 1992/47
ADelt 47, Chronika, 347-348.

Rogge, S., 1993
Tektonik und Ornamentik attischer Sarkophage. Studien zur Chronologie dieser Denkmalergattung, in: Koch, G. (ed), *Grabeskunst der römischen Kaiserzeit.* Mainz am Rhein.

Rogge, S., 1995
Die attischen Sarkophage. Achill und Hippolytos, ASR IX 1.1. Berlin.

Sarikakis, Th., 1970
Προσωπογραφία της Ακτίας Νικόπολεως, *AEphem* 1970, 66-85.

Travlos J., 1949 (1951)
Ἀνασκαφικαὶ ἔρευναι παρὰ τὸ Ὀλυμπιεῖον, *Prakt.*, 25-43.

Toynbee, J. M. C., (1971) 1996
Death and Burial in the Roman World. London.

Vokotopoulou, I., 1969/24
ADelt 24, Chronika, 253-254.

Ward-Perkins, J. B. & Toynbee J. M.C., 1949/93
The Hunting Baths at Lepcis Magna, *Archaeologia* 93, 165-195.

Welter, G., 1941
Troizen und Kalaureia. Berlin.

Wiseman, J., 1978
The Land of the Ancient Corinthians. Göteborg.

Vanderput, L., 1997
The architectural Decoration in Roman Asia Minor. Sagalassos: a Case Study, Leuven.

Zachos, K., 1993/48
ADelt48, Chronika, 301.

Zachos, K., 1989/44
ADelt 44, Chronika, 268.

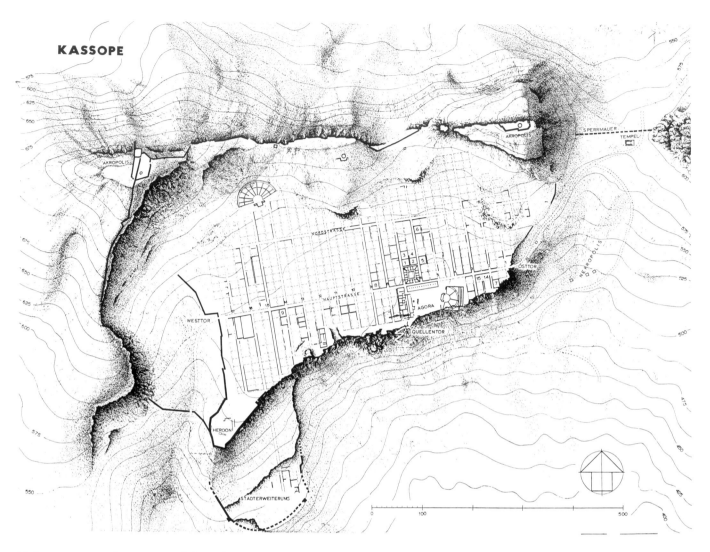

Fig. 1. Kassope, plan of the city, founded in c. 370/60 BC.

Zalongon pass, the preserved foundations of the temple lie 300 m to the northeast, outside the city walls.

The plan of the city was evidently not oriented towards a division into insulae and city districts, as is known from Hippodamos in Piraeus, but more likely was according to the plan of colonial coastal cities in southern Italy and Sicily. This is quite understandable, in view of the intensive trade relations of Kassope on the west coast of the Greek mainland with the cities on the Adriatic and in lower Italy. Yet, we also find a regional peculiarity in the originally uniform house plans, that obviously were already established before the city's founding.

Town-houses with a hearth room (*Herdraum-Häuser*) were erected on lots 14.40 m long and 15.60 m wide, all following the same scheme (Fig. 3). The courtyard was entered from the street through a two-winged entrance with a stone threshold; this was adjoined to the right and the left by the one-storied Andron as well as by workrooms. Towards the back stood the two-storied Oikos. From the courtyard one entered the central hearth room, which reached two-stories in height to the roof. The hearth was located in the middle of the room, and the steep wooden stairs led from a stone base to the upper story, whose rooms in turn formed a wooden gallery encircling the hearth room. The sleeping quarters were most likely on this level, since only rooms for weaving and storage (i.e. household activities) and baths were found on the lower level next to the hearth. As a rule, the baths were always located on the outer

Fig. 2. Aaerial view of Kasso-pe from the east (1980). Left: area of the Agora; centre: "Katagogion"; right: residential area.

walls of the house near the drainage channel. The floor of the baths was covered with baked brick-sized tiles; a bathtub was slightly sunken into the floor near the outer wall; thereby surplus water could run off through an opening in the wall into the channel.

Since the inner and outer walls of the house were built with air-dried bricks upon a low stone foundation, during the excavation it could be confirmed by the stair-threshold in the hearth room that the two-storied part of the house was in the back. However, the plan of the sleeping quarters could not be comprehended at first. Again, thanks to a joint excavation with Sotiris Dakaris in ancient Orraon, near the village Ammotopos, a house from the classical period was investigated, whose ashlar walls were completely pre-

served as high as the roof. It corresponded with the ground-floor plan of houses in Kassope; but more importantly, in Orraon holes for the beams were preserved in the walls of the two-storied hearth room, thus enabling a complete reconstruction of the stairs and the gallery to the upper sleeping rooms.

In the course of the almost three and a half centuries of the city's history neither the original land allotments nor the uniform type of house plans remained the same in Kassope. Nevertheless, house no. 5 demonstrates that even after several renovations and its change from a place of residence to economic purposes and then again a residence, by the first century BC the traditional hearth room had not been removed; in the final building phase the time-honoured floor plan was used again.

The excavations revealed that two decisive breaks must have occurred during the city's history. S. Dakaris presumed that the Kassopaeans were allied with the neighbouring Molossens from 170-168 BC, thus on the side of the Macedonian king Perseus. This would imply that following the disastrous defeat of the Macedonians and their allies by the Roman army under Aemilius Paullus by Pydna in 168, the Kassopaeans were also subject to the terrible sentence on the Epirotes. The ensuing destruction of cities, the massacre or abduction into slavery[5] of 150,000 inhabitants could not have taken place without leaving its traces in Kassope as well. Yet, no destruction level was recognizable in the city's private houses. By contrast it could be proven that the municipal Katagogion and the Prytaneion were destroyed by fire at this time. Hence, had the city not fallen under the sentence of the Romans (indeed, the Kassopaeans stemmed from the Thesprotoi, who allegedly supported the Romans (turbulences in the neighbouring regions and the embittered struggles for power would nonetheless have shaken political stability.

Based on the stratigraphy and research on the pottery, Konstantina Gravani can prove in the following paper that an abrupt decline occurred in Kassope after 167 BC. Not only was there a reduction in productive enterprises, but a distinct decrease in the population can also be assumed. The remaining residents were able to expand their houses onto neighbouring lots, and everywhere poor-quality renovations can be observed. A functional community could not have continued for years after the conflagration of the municipal buildings in the Agora. As late as the 40s of the 2nd century BC did the situation become stable enough again for the city to flourish for over one hundred years. This ended when, following his victory at sea near Actium in 31 BC, Augustus founded the „victory city" of Nikopolis on the territory of the Kassopaeans, within view to the south of the late classical city of Kassope. The Kassopaeans were forced to leave their traditional home and resettle in the new metropolis.

The fact that not only the population, but the statues of their heroes and honourable citizens were relocated to Nikopolis as well, including presumably the temple of the city goddess Aphrodite, can be deduced from the total absence of any fragments of statues from the more than 40-odd preserved anathema bases in the Agora and even the smallest of fragments from the superstructure of the temple of Aphrodite. A single house of the 12 excavated revealed remains indicating its further use during the first century AD, and is contemporary with the Roman tile construction (facade for a spring ?) in the modern village of Kamarina.[6] Kassope remained abandoned, and only in the late Medieval period was the area to the west of the ancient Agora used for crop cultivation and vineyards, recognisable through the heaps of stones and the stone wall encircling the fields. The fields were laid out and cultivated by the members of the nearby Zalongon monastery, situated at the foot of the towering Zalongon cliff, that played such a prominent role in the history of Greece in the 19th century.

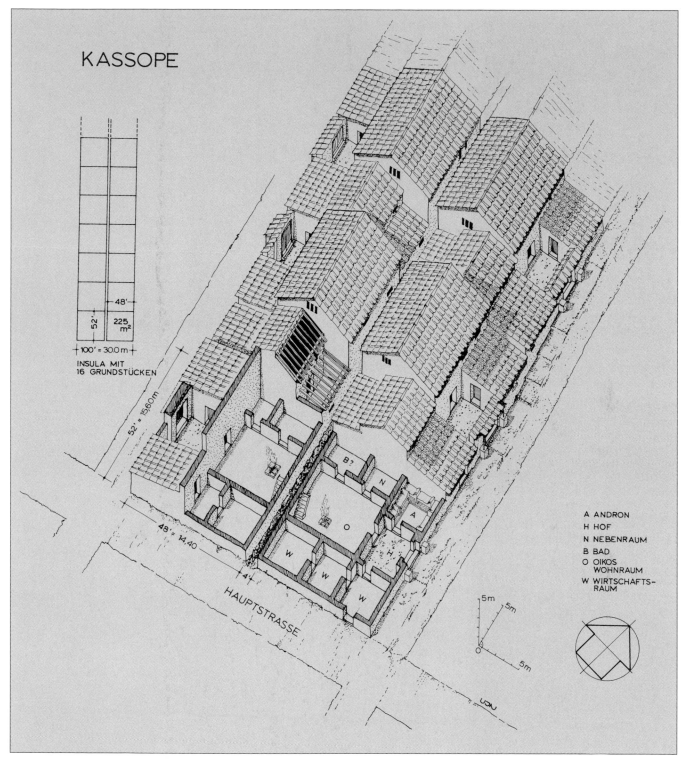

KASSOPE

48'
52'
225 m²
⊢ 100' = 30.0 m ⊣
INSULA MIT
16 GRUNDSTÜCKEN

52' = 15.60 m

48' = 14.40

4'

HAUPTSTRASSE

B?
N
O
A
H
W
W
W

5m
5m
O
5m

A ANDRON
H HOF
N NEBENRAUM
B BAD
O OIKOS
    WOHNRAUM
W WIRTSCHAFTS-
    RAUM

*Fig. 3. Kassope, reconstruction
of the insulae in the 4th century BC, with floorplan of
two typical houses.*

Notes

NOTE 1

This paper relates to the publications about the excavations in Kassope, which have already appeared:
S. I. Dakaris, Kassope, Neoteres Anaskaphes 1977–1983, University of Ioannina 1984; W. Hoepfner/E. L. Schwandner, Haus und Stadt im klassischen Griechenland, Wohnen in der klassischen Polis I, 75 ff. (München 1986); renewed issue (München 1994) 114 ff. Reference to these original publications is highly recommended when using the information and results presented in this paper. Lengthy quotations from the studies were avoided here, in order not to overburden the contents.

NOTE 2

For the meaning *kata komas*, cp. the paper of Jacob Isager in this publication.

NOTE 3

Pseudo-Skylax 31 f.; for the dating cp. N. G. L. Hammond, Epirus, The Geography, the Ancient Remains, the History and the Topography of Epirus and Adjacent Areas (Oxford 1967) 517-18.

NOTE 4

Cp. F. Noack, AA 1916, 218-221 ("Zwei-Kuppen-Stadt").

NOTE 5

Polybios 30. 15; Strabon 7. 7. 3; Livius 45. 34; Plinius *NH* 4. 39; Plutarch, *Aemilius Paullus* 29.

NOTE 6

The remaining section of the Roman tile wall, which was originally located near the modern spring, was no longer present in 1997.

Archaeological Evidence from Cassope. The Local Workshops of Mouldmade Bowls

Konstantina Gravani

The first excavations of the Archaeological Society at Athens in Cassope were carried out by Professor S. Dakaris between 1951 and 1955. During this period, the large building in the centre of the city, identified as the public inn (Katagogion), as well as part of the North Stoa of the Agora were excavated (Fig. 1)[1]

From 1977 to 1983, excavations on a larger scale were carried out under the direction of S. Dakaris, in co-operation with W. Hoepfner and E.L.Schwandner, architects at the German Archaeological Institute-Berlin, and myself, on behalf of the University of Ioanina. During this most recent period of excavation, attention was focused mainly on private houses, ten of which were excavated, most of them near the centre of the city (houses 1-9 and 14).

At the same time, research in the Katagogion and the North Stoa was completed, bringing to light even older buildings under their foundations. Furthermore, excavations were carried out in the civic Agora, with the Prytaneum and the West Stoa, as well as in the roads surrounding the relevant building blocks[2]. (Fig. 1).

Conclusions reached on the basis of both periods of excavations[3] can be summarized as follows: The city was founded and settled before the middle of the 4th century BC, probably in the second quarter; great building activity and economic prosperity followed in the Middle Hellenistic Period, especially during the time of the Epirotic League (234/3 – 168 BC); there was a decline in the Late Hellenistic Period and finally the city was

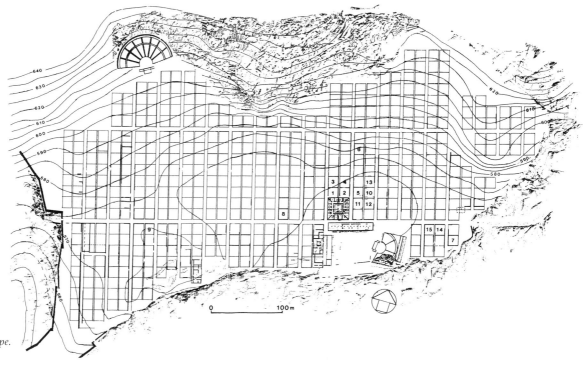

Fig. 1. Townplan of Cassope.

abandoned around the end of the 1st century BC.

The results of these excavations show that the following historical events played a decisive role in the rise and fall of Cassope during the Hellenistic period: the participation of the Cassopeans in the Epirotic League and their autonomy at the end of the 3rd, beginning of the 2nd century BC, the Roman conquest of Epirus in 168 BC, the re-establishment of the Epirotic League after 148 BC and finally the founding of Roman Nikopolis by synoecism in 31 BC.

Thanks to systematic excavations, we have at our disposal reliable stratigraphical indications for the study of the numerous archaeological finds[4] brought to light, particularly, during the recent excavations. Among the mass of ceramics[5] found at Cassope, one distinct category consists of mouldmade relief bowls, most of which came from private houses. After conservation and restoration work, this rich collection of finds comprises 1981 recorded fragments and pieces of relief bowls, as well as a few whole vases. Nine fragments and parts of moulds were also recorded and together with the relief bowls were made the subject of a special study.[6]

Stratigraphy was studied first[7], so as to obtain a reliable basis for the study of the chronology of the archaeological finds. For the purposes of stratigraphy, the evidence of all datable finds, primarily 1.500 coins and a large number of ceramics, was considered. Their examination in the context of the historical events, led to a chronological sequence of excavation layers in each particular place and the recognition of specific construction phases, despite the disturbed stratigraphy in certain buildings. From a study of the geological and geomorphological aspects of the area, the formation of this stratigraphy was found to be due mainly to external reasons (inclination and erosion of the ground), as well as to the action of endogenous factors (earthquakes and landslides). There was also human intervention in the area (foundations laid on the rock – transfer of debris).

As we have also discovered, the stratigraphy is not particularly enlightening in the case of buildings on sloping ground, usually in the higher part of the city. Houses 3, 6, 7 and 9, although placed on two or three different terraced levels, artificially formed by chiselling the rock, have suffered the consequences of erosion, which has not only carried away most of the later layers but in certain cases has damaged even the surface of the local limestone (houses 6 and 9). Even in those cases, however, where the rocky substratum has not come to the surface, very few traces of earlier construction phases remain. Most of the phases were destroyed by the deep foundations of later walls and the clearing of the natural rock, which in many places, due to difference in elevation, was used as a floor over a long period of time (houses 3 and 7). The latter practice, together with continuous habitation over three or more centuries, is the main reason that certain buildings, even those built on relatively even ground, do not show the expected stratigraphy (houses 2 and 4). At the same time, there is a group of buildings from which only a few layers survive, mainly because, even though they were inhabited for a long period of time, they were completely rebuilt (houses 8 and 14).

For the same reason, the public buildings in the Agora have a poor stratigraphy even though their foundations are on level ground in the lower part of the city (Prytaneum, West and North Stoa). On the contrary, the Katagogion presents an unexpected sequence of layers due to the sloping ground on its southern and eastern sides which was raised and levelled for the construction of the later building.

Buildings constructed on natural cavities (houses 1, 2 and 5), mainly in the lower parts of the city, present the best stratigraphy because they hold fast the various construction layers (artificial landfill – rubble) or those layers created either by the use of the area as a living space (living levels – floors) or by the destruction of previous construction phases. The lowest layers, however, even in these buildings

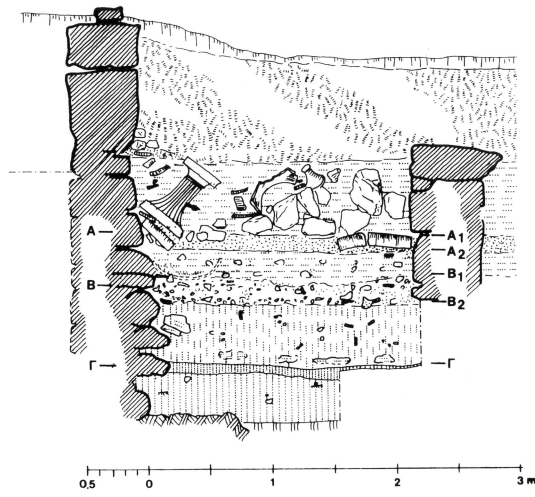

Fig. 2. House 5. Room e. Stratigraphy of the north side.

0,5   0   1   2   3 m

have sometimes been seriously damaged by the deep foundations and repairs of later times (house 1). This repeated practice probably reflects the desire of the Cassopeans for structural stability in case of earthquakes, which as shown by the stratigraphy of the Katagogion and central road (Figs. 4 – 5), were common in the area due to its endogenous mobility and Karst phenomena. The upper layers are also not always unmixed, mainly because the layers of houses on higher levels have been swept down by erosion. Finally, another characteristic of this group of buildings is the raising of the floors and doorsills in later construction phases in line with the raising of the road levels and drainage passageways.

The best example of the buildings that provide a clear, continuous stratigraphy is house 5, which was built on a natural cav-

ity, in one of the lowest parts of the city. The building retains its layers and shows all its phases of construction, from its foundation in the 4th century BC until its abandonment in the 1st century BC. The study of its stratigraphy has proved that it has undergone three changes of use during its six construction phases[8] (Fig. 2). The three main stages in its life are shown clearly in stratigraphical sections, as well as the interim changes made to its interior layout, which play an important role in determining the buildings chronology due to their short duration. Of great importance for the study of ceramics is the fourth construction phase, which dates from the beginning of the second quarter of the 2nd century BC and is connected with the extension of the existing ceramic workshop into the surrounding rooms (floor B1). After 167 BC, during the fifth

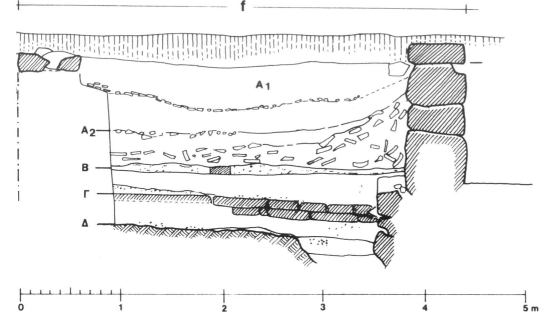

Fig. 3. House 2. Room f. Stratigraphy of the south side.

construction phase, house 5 stopped functioning as a workshop, as evidenced by the construction of a large room with a hearth in the centre (floor A2). The house remained as such, with some small changes in the layout (floor A1), until its abandonment in the 1st century BC.

The neighbouring house 2 gives a different picture, maintaining the same layout after 167 BC. Floor B (Fig. 3) was constructed at the end of the 3rd century BC and was in use after 148 BC, when the house was radically altered by the construction of a large peristyle court, probably at the end of the 2nd century BC.

Only later construction phases remain

in the case of private houses built on sloping ground, whose floors, in constant use from their foundation in the 4th century BC until their abandonment in the 1st century BC, are on different levels artificially formed by chiselling the rock, as previously mentioned.

Typical of this phenomenon is the stratigraphy of house 6, where only the floor of later repairs, dated after 167 BC, remains. Equally characteristic is the stratigraphy of house 3, which extends to the property on the north side, and was probably abandoned after the Roman invasion. The floor laid during re-building after 148 BC survives in part, however,

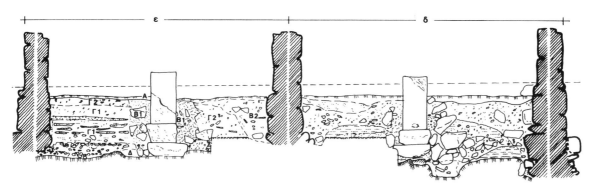

Fig. 4. Katagogion. Rooms e and d. Stratigraphy of the west side.

120

Fig. 5. Central road. Stratigraphy of the west side.

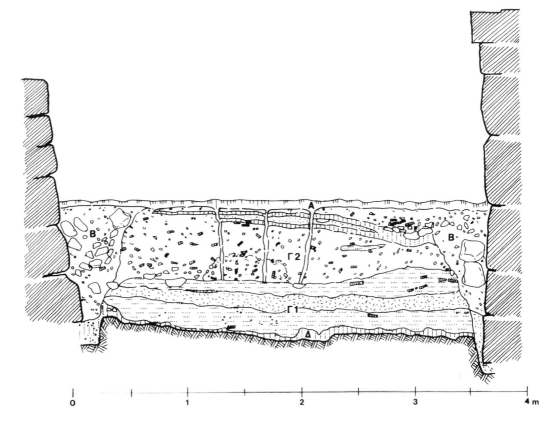

mainly under the contemporary peristyle.[9] In the other rooms the later layer was carried away by erosion, resulting in the exposure of natural rock under the surface layer (humus).

Of the public buildings in the Agora, only the Katagogion shows a continuous stratigraphy (Fig. 4). The archaeological layers, however, were disrupted by the strengthening of the internal walls and the central pilasters with materials and block-stones removed from elsewhere, at the end of the 2nd century BC. This was probably due to landslides, as it is attested by a crack, which was detected under the building during the excavations. The external walls of the Katagogion and the neighbouring northern stoa were also strengthened as is shown by the stratigraphy of the intervening main road (Fig. 5). Moreover, we can distinguish fissures in the road surfase due to earthquakes, which occurred after the final abandonment of the city by its inhabitants at the end of the 1st century BC, when they were forced to resettle in neighbouring Nikopolis.

From the study of the stratigraphy, it has been observed that most of the relief bowls were found within the layers of construction phases associated with the period of the Epirotic League (234/33–168 BC), whether dating form the beginning (house 3), from the middle (houses 1 and 2) or from the end of this period (house 5). During later phases of habitation, these layers were removed or mixed up with newer construction materials. This is indicated, in the case of the buildings rebuilt after 167 BC, by the discovery of sherds from the same vases in different rooms of the same house (house 5). As observed in the stratigraphy, more extensive interventions occurred during the rebuilding of the city after 148 BC. Rubble from the various layers must have been transferred from one building to another as attested by potsherds of different origins (houses 8 and 14), which fit together. This also explains, to a great extent, the poor condition of the material. So we are deprived – in stratigraphical terms – of the most valuable chronological terminus, i.e.

Pl. 1.

the destruction of Epirus by the Romans in 167 BC, an historical event attested by written sources[10]. The conquest of Epirus by the Romans and the subsequent Roman policies are documented archaeologically in the case of Cassope by the construction phases after 167 BC, the decline of the city during the later Hellenistic period and its partial rebuilding after 148 BC, which affected ownership, when the Epirotic League was re-established[11] under Roman control.

The study of ceramics sheds light on the nature of the changes mentioned above. Our knowledge of local relief bowl workshops in particularly sheds light on political, economic and social aspects of the history of Cassope during Hellenistic times and helps us to trace the cultural identity of the city as a production center.

Locally produced bowls represent approximately 80% of the total of this category of vases. The majority of them have an almost hemispherical or parabolic shape and an inwardly curved rim. The decorative layout on the bowls is uniform and usually occupies 3/4 of their height, up to the horizontal band(s) under the rim. The clay for the bowls comes from local deposits and is the same as that of their moulds (Pl. 18). As a rule it is yellowish – rose in colour and usually covered by black glaze. The surfaces of most of the bowls are worn. Many of the relief decorations look noticeable worn, an indication that a great many of them are produced in worn moulds. Apart from the use of worn moulds, the heavy wear observable on the surfaces of the bowls is due to the disturbance of the archaeological strata during the levelling of the ground for the construction of later buildings. In addition, as previously mentioned, a large number of bowls were not found in their original site, but in later layers together with rubble brought from elsewhere. This, among other factors, explains the poor condition of the bowls.

According to the exact or near similarity of the main decorative themes, the following categories of bowls (Pls.1-18)[12] were produced in local workshops:

1 Bowls with circular nodules, which are the most characteristic of local production and often have relief supports (Pls. 1-4).
2 Bowls with overlapping decoration, usually leaves and petals, which also have relief supports (Pl.5).
3 Bowls with a floral calyx, usually lotus, fern or acanthus, which are the most common. The floral calyx is either composed of leaves of the same type or of a combination of different leaves in several variations. (Pls. 6-13, 17, nos. 187, 344).
4 The fourth category also includes bowls with a floral calyx, in which the floral patterns alternate equally with figures (Pls.14-15). In a very few bowls, figures in the shape of calyx are the only decoration of the wall (Pl.16).
5 The fifth category consists of a small number of bowls which are decorated with animal and human figures usually above a short floral calyx (Pl.17, nos. 410, 188).
6 Here are included a few bowls, which are decorated with long petals (Pl.17, nos. 416 α-γ).
7 One single potsherd hints at a seventh category, on which is barely recognizable the decoration of the type "Macedonian shield" (Pl.17, no. 415).

The results of a comparative study of the finds from a typological and iconographical point of view, on the basis of which we traced the influences and detected variations and deviations of local character, cannot be set out here due to publication limits. For the same reason imported bowls are not presented although many of them can be assigned to large geographical areas, some even to local workshops. Therefore, we are, in fact, restricted to conclusions gained from examining the technique and style in the context of local workshops and their chronology.

On the basis of stratigraphical data and historical events, it is possible to put in chronological order locally produced bowls from Cassope.

Only the Katagogion provides evidence

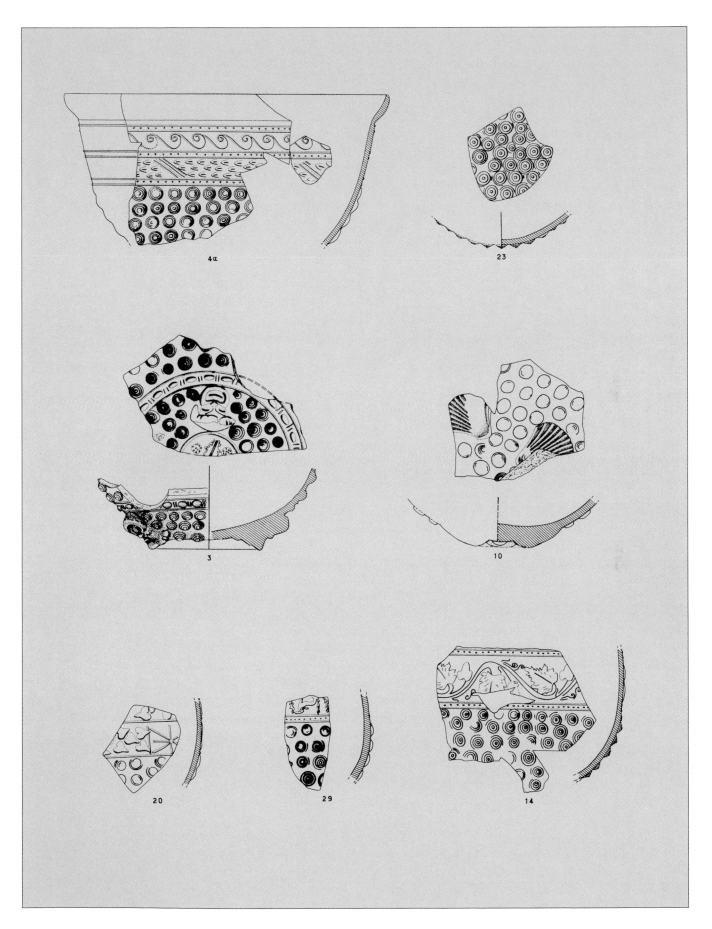

4a

23

3

10

20

29

14

for the appearance of relief bowls in Cassope and the beginning of their production in local workshops. The presence of fragments of moulds in the destruction layer of the oldest building (Γ1) and the presence of potsherds in the rubble (Γ2) used to construct the later Katagogion (Fig. 4) prove that relief bowls were known in Cassope before the end of the 3rd century BC. For the early phase of the production of relief bowls, evidence comes from the construction layers of floor B[13] in houses 1 and 2 (Fig. 3) which was built in conjunction with the widening of the paved side road north of the Katogogion at the end of the 3rd century BC. The diffusion of these vases during the 2nd century BC, before 167 BC, is shown by their presence in the construction layers as well as in those used for flooring B1 in house 5 (Fig. 2), which dates from the beginning of the second quarter of the 2nd century BC.

Relief bowls continued to be used after 167 BC as shown by their presence on floor A in house 5 (Fig. 2) and in the last building phase of house 6, which is dated to the first years of the Roman conquest of Epirus. Their significant diffusion in the first half of the 2nd century BC is evidenced by the large number of relief bowls found on floor B of house 2 (Fig. 3), which was not destroyed in 167 BC but instead sometime after 148 BC, possibly at the end of the 2nd century BC. A terminus ante quem is provided by their presence in the debris used to construct floor A in house 1, which dates from immediately after the reestablishment of the Epirotic League in 148 BC. Moreover, relief bowls are the main drinking vessels in Cassope as shown by the lack of cups in the layers of the first half of the 2nd century BC.

The presence of relief bowls under the later floor of houses 3 and 4, the Prytaneum and under the pavement of the roads, dating from the end of the 2nd century BC, provides very little evidence of their diffusion in the second half of the 2nd century BC, since these were built on the layers of the previous construction

phase. Also of no significance is the finding of relief bowls in the later construction layers of the Katogogion (Fig. 4) and the North Stoa, because they contain mainly older finds originating from the foundation ditches of the walls when they were strengthened later.

There is also a lack of accurate stratigraphical data for the 1st century BC, because most of the later floor levels with their derelict layer have been carried away by erosion. We can conclude indirectly, however, that relief bowls were not in fashion during this period. The presence of cups and bowls of local and imported red and gray ware[14] in the layers of the later Hellenistic period show that after the middle of the 2nd century BC the steady replacement of relief bowls with other drinking vessels had begun. The decline of the local workshops is also evidenced by the increase in the importation of relief bowls to Cassope from other areas during the later Hellenistic period.

It is possible to attain a relative chronology for the local workshops and workshop-groups of Cassope by comparing excavation data with the results of the stylistic analysis, the study of technique and workshop classification. We run into difficulties obtaining an absolute chronology for relief bowls as isolated vases, which are related to the general problems of dating Hellenistic ceramics, but also to more specific problems associated with their mechanical reproduction using moulds and stamps[15]. In Cassope, the large number of bowls which came from the same moulds compels us to accept a narrower time limit for the life of the moulds than that of 25 to 30 years already estimated, from the data of antiquity.[16] However, the heavy wear shown by the bowls is consistent with the long-term use of the moulds, which could last a quarter of a century or more. Although we do not know the average rate of wear on the moulds and stamps, or the tempo of production in the workshops, the conclusions reached from the study of the stratigraphy confirm the above estimates resulting from the chronological classification of the

Pl. 2.

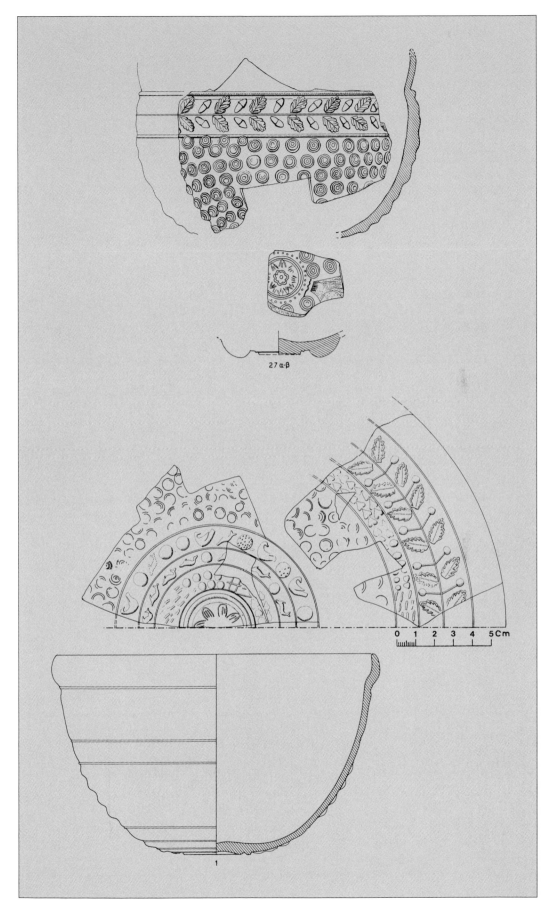

27 α-β

1

workshops and workshop-groups of Cassope.

Despite the difficulties arising from the lack of signatures on the vases, the fragmentary condition of the finds, their poor state of preservation and the derivation of the majority of them from worn moulds, it is possible to distinguish six groups[17] of relief bowls thanks to the detection of characteristic decorative patterns. Three of them point to the possible existence of three different workshops (A, B, C). The other three, because they do not represent the total production of one workshop, can be described as workshop-groups (1, 2, 3). It is possible that the bowls assigned to these groups were produced in workshops A and B.

Workshops A and B and workshop groups 1,2,3 draw their decorations from a common repertoire, formed initially in workshop A, enriched in workshop B and imitated by workshop groups 1, 2 and 3. Stylistic analysis has shown that workshop groups 1 and 3 copy the bowls of workshop A, while group 2 copy those of workshop B. The main decorative ornaments, encountered in bowls of the three groups, are created by mechanical stamping from the initials of workshops A and B, so we are in a position to distinguish three generations of stampings. The secondary ornaments, which are found in the band under the rim, the filling ornaments and the medallions are made with new stamps.

None of the stamps, which were used for decorating the moulds of local workshops (Pl. 18) has been found in the excavations. Thus, for types and range of stamps the only information we have is from their imprints on the bowls. All imprints of the stamps, which are on the fragments of seven of the moulds found, are recognized on locally produced bowls, except the bowls from workshop C. Two fragments of moulds, stamped with a natural pine-cone (Pl. 18, nos. 649-650) probably represent an experimental stage in the production of relief bowls, considering that no bowls were found in Cassope decorated with pine-cone scales.

Most probably, bowls with circular nodules from local workshops copied this natural decoration.

As established by the stratigraphy and the study of the material, the production in workshop A began at the end of the 3rd century BC. Bowls with round, conelike nodules (Pls. 1-2, 3, no 38), which often have masks and shells as relief supports, but occasionally have no medallions on their bases, are characteristic of Workshop A. Favourite decorations in the band under the rim are oak wreaths, scrolls with vine leaves and grapes, and rows of palmettes or leaves alternating with dolphins or birds. On those bowls decorated with floral decoration a preference is shown for large pleated acanthus leaves, straight and with their tops bent to one side (Pl.8), for the pointed lotus leaves, incised on the mould (Pl. 6, nos. 173-174), and for triangular fern leaves with eyelet shaped holes (Pl. 7, nos. 189, 197). Probably the pattern of floral motifs alternating with figures was introduced by Workshop A.

Research has also shown that Workshop B produced bowls from the beginning of the 2nd century BC. Typical of its production are bowls with disclike nodules on the wall, occasionally with relief support (Pl. 3, nos. 45, 52 α-β). The most popular of the decorations in the band under the rim are scrolls and wreaths of ivy. A large number of bowls are decorated with overlapping leaves on some of which relief supports are preserved (Pl. 5, nos. 109, 119). On a small number of bowls the overlapping leaves are combined with hanging semicircles (Pl. 5, nos. 128 α-β). In Workshop B there is a tendency towards the use of stamped oval lotus leaves (Pl. 6, nos. 160, 150 α - β) rather than incised as in Workshop A, where however fern leaves (Pl. 7, no. 230) and acanthus with their tops bent to one side (Pl. 9, no. 286 α-γ) are freely copied. Also very popular are triangular tufted acanthus leaves (Pl. 11), as well as elongated tufted acanthus (Pl.15), alternating with female figures, and there are also distinctive medallions.

The appearance of relief bowls in Cas-

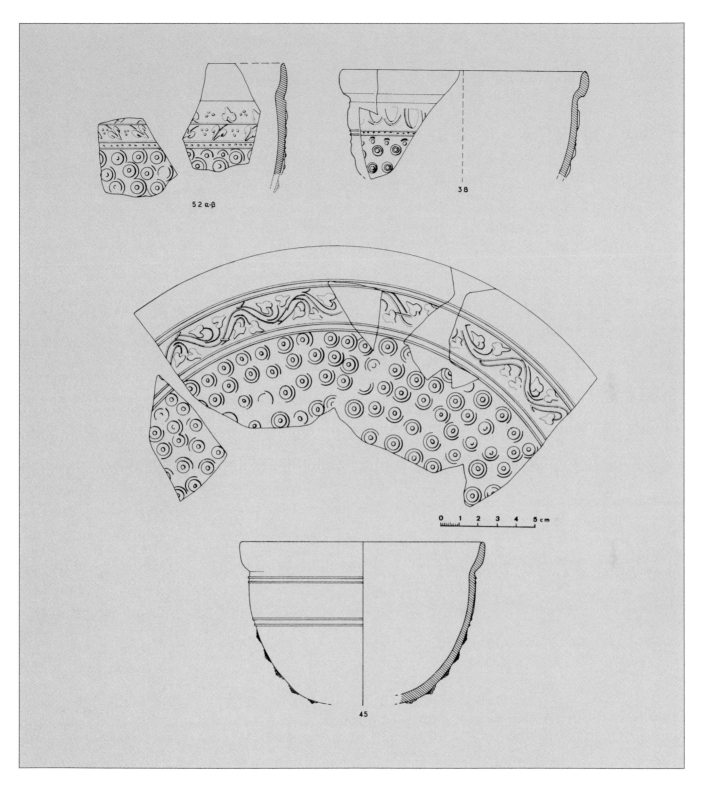

0 1 2 3 4 5 cm

Pl. 3.

sope, in the last quarter of the 3rd century BC, coincides with their diffusion throughout the most important centres of the Hellenistic period, something to be expected, given Cassope's traditional relations with Attica and its contacts with Alexandria and Tarent.[18]

The best parallels to the moulds decorated with pine-cone scales are found in the earliest workshops of Attica.[19] To the influence of common prototypes are owed probably the decorations of circular nodules, overlapping leaves, calyx of lotus leaves, as well as certain decorative pat-

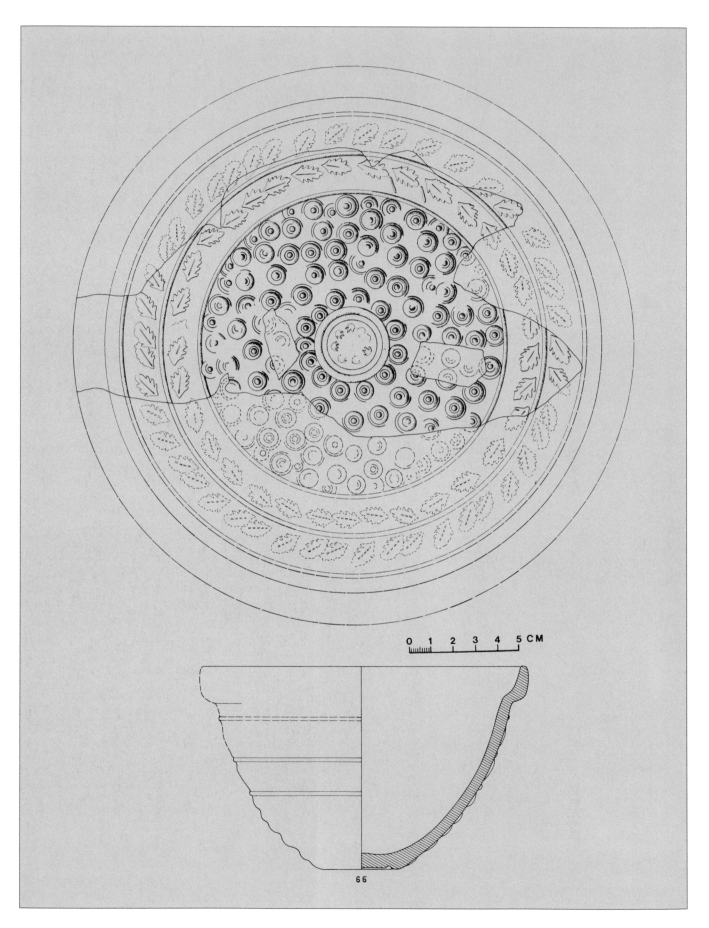

66

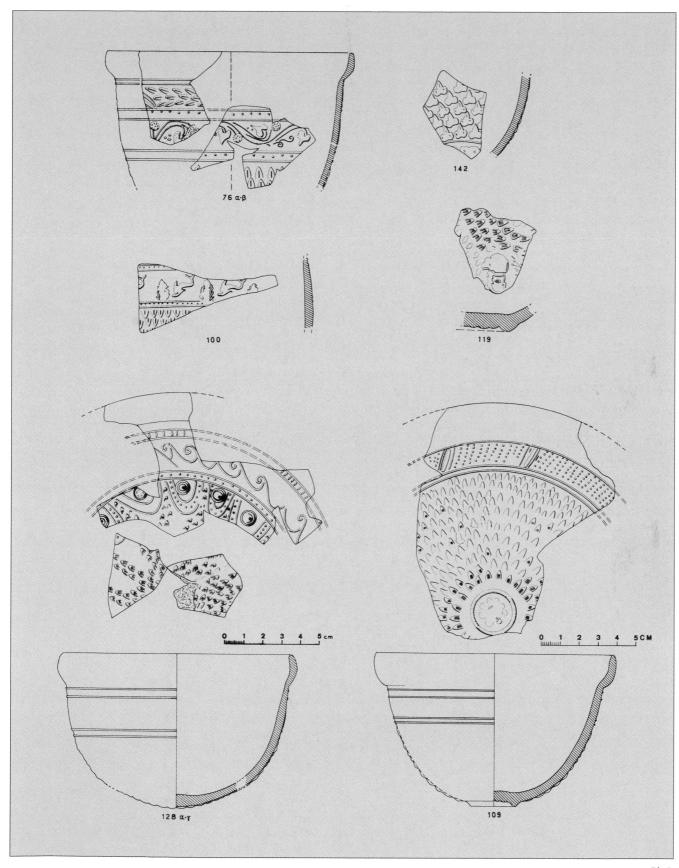

76 α-β

142

100

119

128 α-γ

109

0 1 2 3 4 5 cm

0 1 2 3 4 5 CM

Pl. 4.

Pl. 5.

Pl. 6.

terns on the bands under the rims of bowls of workshop A.[20]

The shape of locally produced bowls points to Tarent.[21] Analogous shaping of the rim in bowls from Macedonia[22] indicates, up to a point, the cultural unity of northwestern Greece. At the same time, there is a difference in the layout of decoration in calyx between the bowls of Cassope and similar products from the Ionian workshops, with their familar layout of decoration in bands.[23] Bowls with floral decoration and figures from the two first workshops seem to have common prototypes with bowls from local workshops in the Peloponnese, which probably derive their art from Magna Grecia.[24]

Bowls with a decoration of acanthus leaves from the same workshops point to works of art from Macedonia and Thessaly, where metal vessels with similar decoration were found.[25] This similarity strengthens the hypothesis that there existed unknown centres of metalwork in the northwestern wider area. Among them, in the region of ancient Epirus can be included Ambracia, originally a colony of Corinth, in whose art similar decorative compositions occur.[26] Apart from that, the Epirotic school of copperworking was located in Ambracia during the ancient and classical periods,[27] and the city is known to have flourished during the Hellenistic period, especially after it was established as the capital of Epirus by Pyrrhos.[28] Unfortunately, its destruction by the Romans did not allow the survival of its most important works of art, which were seized and taken to Rome.[29] It is possible that certain sculptural figures on the bowls of Cassope reflect its monumental art. The view has already been expressed that Ambracia was the centre where on ornate type of grave stele, common all over northwestern Greece and in Cassope,[30] was created. Many of the decorations on the grave stele are recognized on locally produced relief bowls and bear witness to local tradition.[31] Probably, this strong tradition in northwestern Greece is also the reason for the presence of equivalent decorations on relief bowls in Italy.[32]

The beginning of the production of relief bowls in Cassope in workshops A and B, at the end of the 3rd and at the beginning of the 2nd century BC respectively, reflects the desire of a large part of the population to use decorated vessels with an 'air' of luxury, given that they are substitutes for bowls made of precious metal or glass.[33] Their appearance and diffusion coincides with the period when the Cassopeans were independent of the Epirotic League, an era[34] when the city was in its heyday. Cassope as an autonomous city minted silver coins and at the same time put into circulation a type of coin related to the Roman denaria in order to facilitate sea trade, which reached its peak at the time of the 2nd Punic war via already Roman-occupied Corfu.[35] At the same time it maintained relations with the Hellenistic centres in the East, as is shown by its participation in the games in honour of the goddess Artemis held in Magnesia of Maiandros in 206 BC.[36]

Bowls from both workshops were found outside Cassope,[37] which allows us to assume that their production covered not only local needs but was also intended for export. The location of the city near the most important natural passes of Epirus and the unified monetary policy[38] of the Epirotic League favoured the development of regional trade, as the bowls imported from Cassope to the Dodona sanctuary show clearly.[39]

Relief bowls from the workshops of Cassope have not been found outside Epirus. However, the attempt to standarize their form and the existence of a series of vases with small variations show the rationalization of the workshops' industry, aimed at constant production, responding to the conditions of a wider market. Moreover in this era, apart from the circulation of Italian coins in Epirus and in Cassope,[40] there was movement of people and distribution of goods within the areas of the Adriatic basin.[41] In the context of these relations, we can explain the decorations common to Italian bowls and those of Cassope, which are typical of the latter.[42]

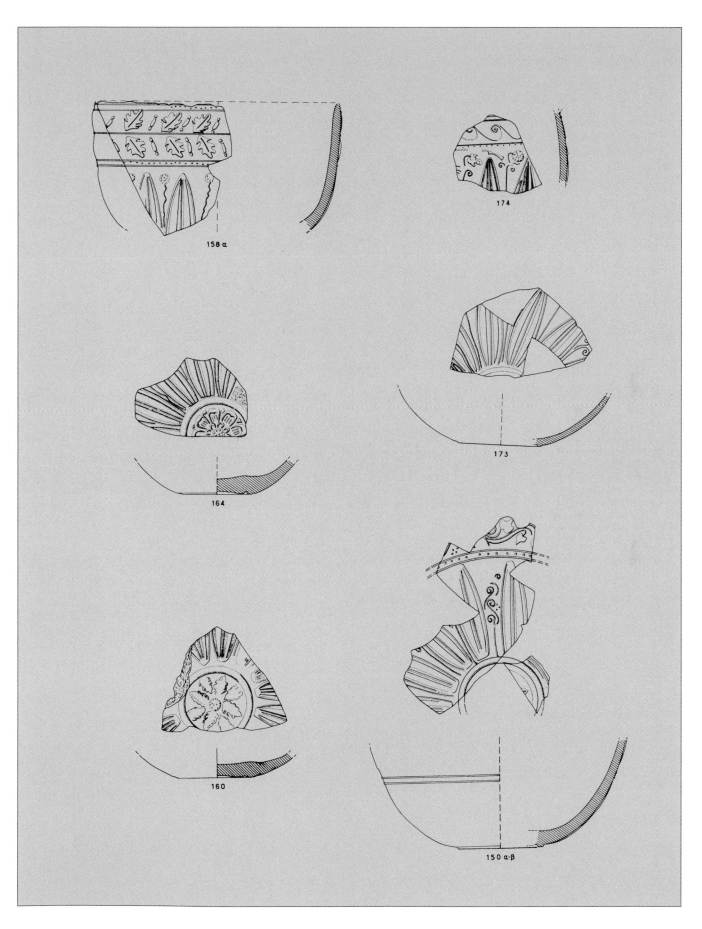

158 α

174

164

173

160

150 α-β

Pl. 7.

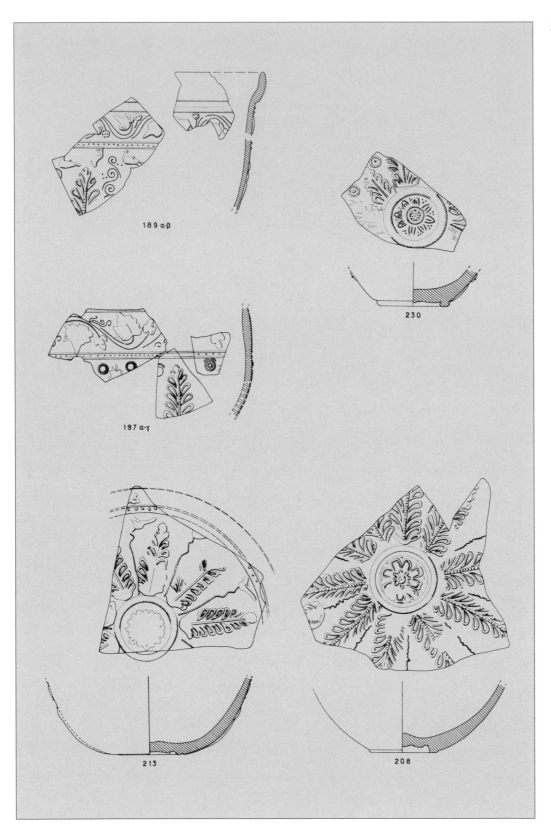

189 α-β

230

197 α-γ

213

208

As established by the stratigraphy and the study of the material, the production peak of workshops A and B is dated before the Roman destruction of 167 BC. In the first quarter of the 2nd century BC, workshop-groups 1, 2, and 3 began their production, which continued until about the middle of the century. Relief bowls of

Pl. 8.

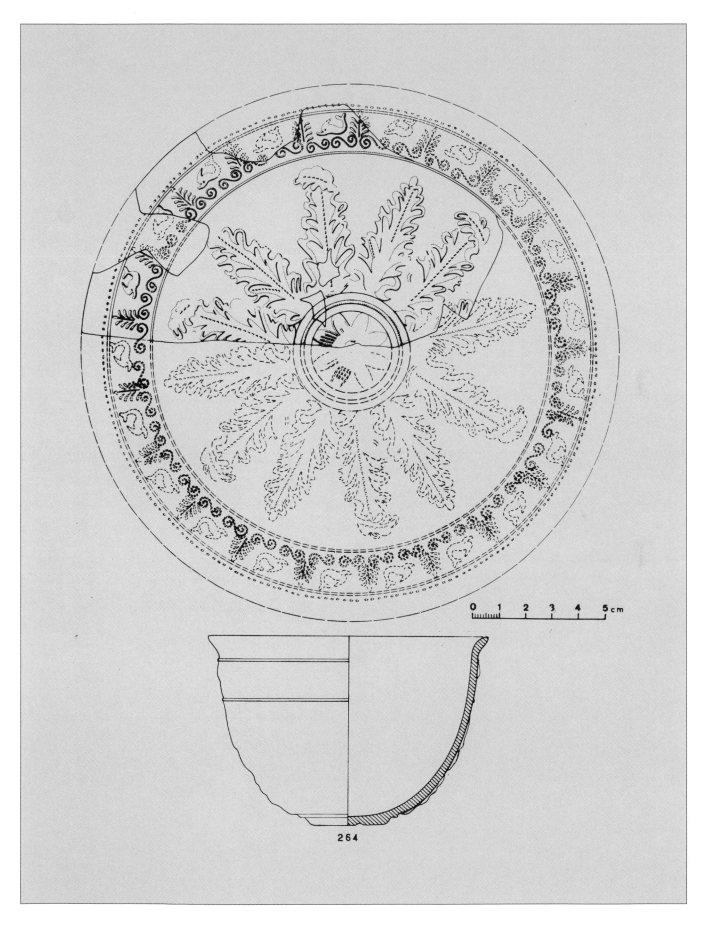

264

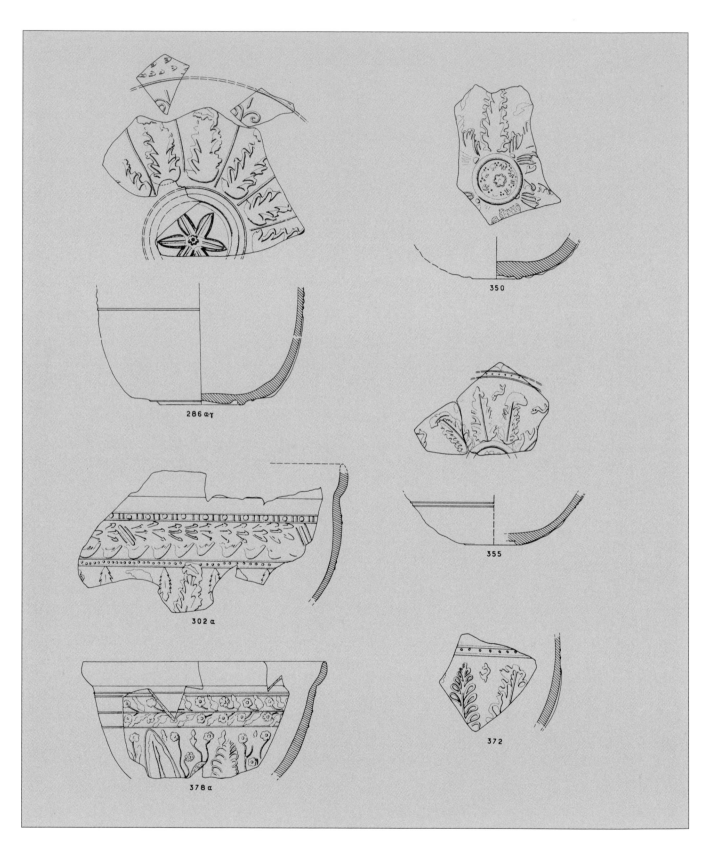

350

286 αγ

302 α

355

378 α

372

workshop A are badly copied by workshop group 1, as can be seen mainly on
bowls with shield-shaped circular nodules
(Pl. 4), as well as on bowls with various

floral decorations from the same group
(Pl. 13). On these bowls characteristic
decorations of workshop A can be recognized also on the band under the rim, for

Pl. 9.

Pl. 10.

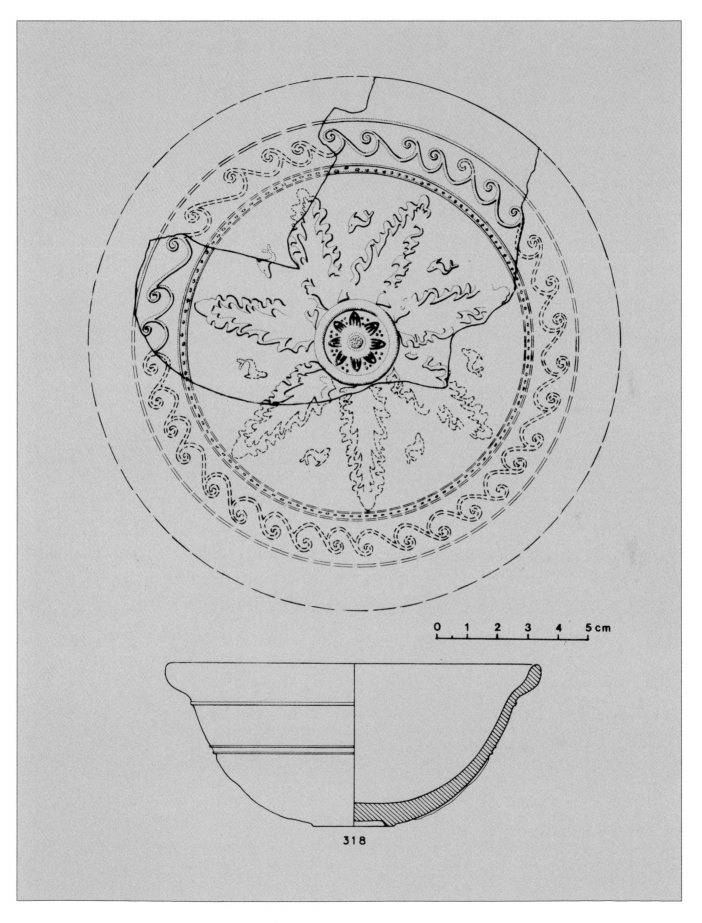

0   1   2   3   4   5 cm

318

Pl. 11.

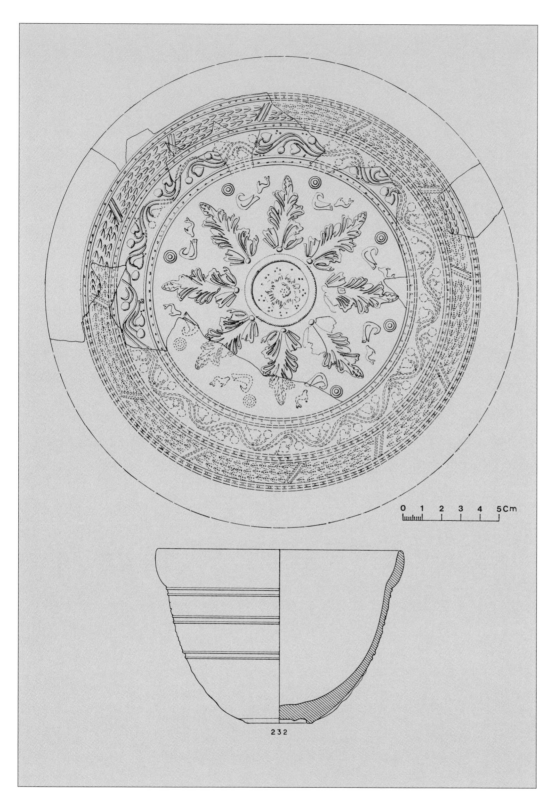

232

example the oak wreath and dolphins alternating with leaves.

In the case of the relief bowls from
workshop-group 3, the triangular fern
leaves with eyelet shaped holes were de-
rived by stamping the original decorations
of workshop A onto the vase. That is why
these decorative patterns are smaller in
size and less lively than the originals (Pl. 7,
no. 213). The same method was used for
the pleated acanthus, with straight and
bent tops (Pl.9, no. 302α, Pl. 10) as well as

136

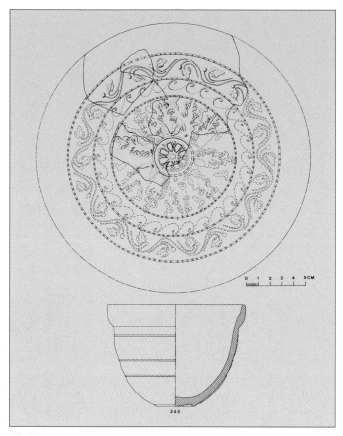

Pl. 12.

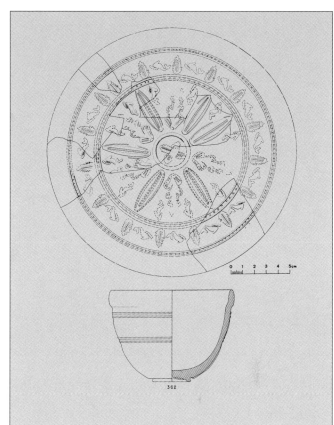

Pl. 13.

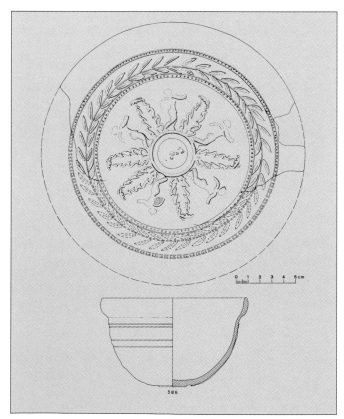

Pl. 14.

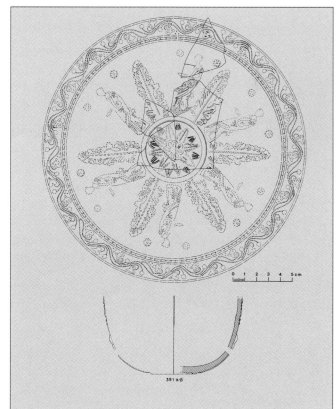

Pl. 15.

Pl. 16.

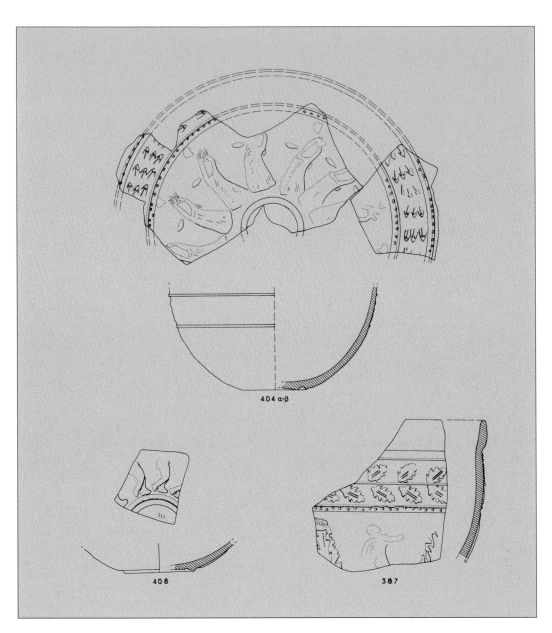

404 α-β

408

387

for the figures on the walls of the bowls (Pl.14), while the minor decorations under the rim are made from new stamps.

The floral decorations on the walls of the bowls of workshop-group 2 are even smaller in size and hardly discernible, because they were made with the same method of stamping from already worn stamps from workshop B, while the medallions and the decorations under the rim are made from new stamps (Pls. 12, 16, nos. 404 α-β).

As observed, the outcome of this process is that gradually the decorations on the bowls reflect the trivialization of the prototypes and the ineptitude of the arti-

sans. The beginning of activity by workshop-groups 1,2, and 3 is associated with an increase in production of bowls, but at the same time a decline in their quality. Undoubtedly, the difference in quality of the bowls corresponds with their market value and reflects the social distinction between poor and well-off users. This phenomenon can be interpreted better, however, if we associate it with historical events in Epirus before the Roman conquest of 168 BC. During the 3rd Macedonian war, with the break-up of the Epirotic League,[43] 170 - 168 BC, it is reasonable that inhabitants of unwalled settlements in Cassopaia should seek refuge in fortified

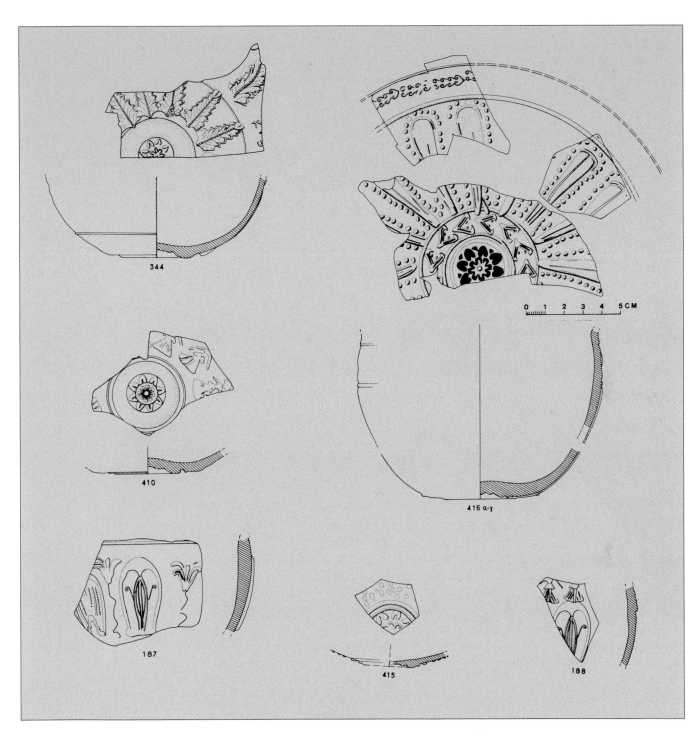

Cassope for protection against the Roman advance. The result of this increase in the population of Cassope was the enlargement of the market for ceramic products.

The enlargement of the ceramic workshop in house 5 during its fourth construction phase, dated at the beginning of the second quarter of the 2nd century BC, reveals the increase in demand for storage vessels, needed to safeguard goods in case of siege or blockade. This is indicated as well by the discovery of quite a few amphorae and large jars (Fig. 2) on floor B1. At the same time, during this period, production of relief bowls was increased at the expense of quality in order to meet the demands of new consumers.

The Roman conquest of 167 BC[44] proved to be a determining factor in the activity of local workshops. Workshop A ceases to be active, while workshop B and workshop-groups 1, 2, and 3 continue to make relief bowls after 167 BC from already worn moulds, which explains the heavy wear on the bowls. From then on workshops declined, since they renew neither their equipment nor their repertoire and reproduced the same themes to the point of satiety.

The beginning of the activity of workshop C is dated after 167 BC. Workshop C has a different repertoire. It manufactures floral bowls in which we do not recognize any of the decorations of the previous workshops. Moreover, it produces categories of bowls, which are not part of the repertoire of the previous workshops, such as relief bowls with short calyx and figures, with figures and living creatures, with 'Macedonian' decoration and long petals (Pl. 17). The decorations of workshop C are not copied or stamped, which indicates the mediocre quality of the workshop and the short duration of its production, which does not seem to extend beyond the end of the 2nd century BC. From the stratigraphy and decorations on the bowls of workshop C it is clear that its production is contemporary with later series of bowls from workshop B. Based on the available evidence, we can interpret the activity of workshop C as an attempt at the re-establishing of workshop B by renewing its repertoire.

The new decorative repertoire of the relief bowls from workshop C allows us to assume that its activity is probably connected with the settling of new inhabitants in Cassope after 167 BC. Evidence which strengthens this assumption is the privileged treatment given by the Romans to those of the indigenous population friendly to them and to the former colonists, a policy[45] which became official with the re-establishment of the Epirotic League in 148 BC under Roman control. Apart from the change in the makeup of the population, Roman policy in Epirus after 167 BC probably is associated with the change in ownership status, which we discovered in some of the houses in Cassope, as well as with repairs in the public buildings.

The production of most of the relief bowls of workshop C from new moulds allows us to conclude that its activity was of short duration and that this activity was suddenly interrupted. The mobilization of the Cassopeans by the Romans to suppress the revolution of Aristonikos in Asia Minor, 133 - 129 BC, is an event[46] which can explain significant social and economic upheavals in Cassope and its surrounding area at the end of the 2nd and the 1st century BC.

The greatest number of imported relief bowls date from this period. Their presence in Cassope is not only an indication that production of relief bowls in local workshops ceased but also that the local economy was too weak to protect itself from expensive imports. These vases were probably meant for the privileged few, to whom the house with the peristyle court, built on the site of the original houses with a living room and courtyard in the centre, must have belonged. Moreover, the construction of large houses with peristyle courts, next to abandoned properties and poorly repaired houses which are of the original type of house,[47] provides an example of social inequality and shows the decline of Cassope in the late Hellenistic period.

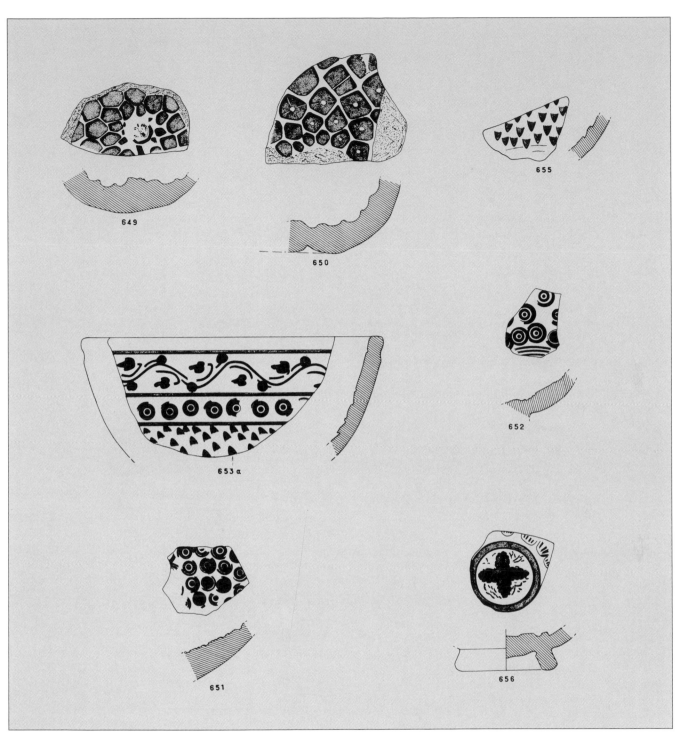

649

650

655

653 α

652

651

656

Pl. 18.

Notes

NOTE 1
S. Dakaris, *ΠΑΕ* 1952, σ. 326-362; 1953, 164-174; 1954, 201-209; 1955, 181-186.

NOTE 2
S. Dakaris, *ΠΑΕ* 1977, 141-148; 1978, 96-106; 1979, 114-118; 1980, 21-32; 1981, 72-77; 1982, 97-84; 1983, 87-80.

NOTE 3
See Dakaris 1971, Dakaris 1989, Hoepfner, Schwandner, Dakaris, Gravani, Tsingas 1994, 114-161. See also Hoepfner, Dakaris, Gravani, Schwandner 1999, 368-383.

NOTE 4
For examples, see Gravani 1994, 162-172, Oikonomidou – Karamesini 1994, 172-174, Boessneck 1994, 175-179.

NOTE 5
For examples, see Gravani 1988/89, 89-132, Gravani, 1994.

NOTE 6
Gravani 1996, with catalogue of 657 finds.

NOTE 7
Gravani 1996.

NOTE 8
For the various construction phases of house 5, see. Hoepfner, Schwandner, Dakaris, Gravani, Tsingas 1994, 157, fig. 151.

NOTE 9
For the extension of house 3, see Hoepfner, Schwandner, Dakaris, Gravani, Tsingas 1994, 159, fig.155.

NOTE 10
Strab. 7. 7. 3, Polyb. 30. 15. 1, Liv. 45. 34, 1-6. Plut., *Aem.Paul.* 29, 1-3, *App.Illyr.* IX 10,9. Plin. *HN*, IV. 39.

NOTE 11
See Franke 1961, 218-237, Dakaris 1971, 97-98, 157-161.

NOTE 12
The drawings of vases (Pls. 1-17) and moulds (Pl. 18) are the work of Mr. I. Diamandopoulos, designer of the University of Ioannina.

NOTE 13
For the plan of house 1, to which belongs floor B, see Hoepfner, Schwandner, Dakaris, Gravani, Tsingas 1994 151, fig. 141.

NOTE 14
See Gravani 1994, 172, Gravani 1988/89, 124.

NOTE 15
See in general, Drougou 1983, 7-12. Gravani, 1989, 3-18. See especially Siebert 1980, 55-83.

NOTE 16
Rotroff 1982, 32.

NOTE 17
For the method of assigning relief bowls to workshops (on theoretical and technical ground), see Siebert 1980, A. Laumonier, 1977, Rotroff 1982, Akamatis 1994.

NOTE 18
See Dakaris 1971, 35, 128-129. Gravani 1988/89, 127-129, Gravani 1997, 81-93.

NOTE 19
Cf. e.g. Rotroff 1982, 16, pl. 1-3.

NOTE 20
Cf. e.g. Rotroff 1982, pl.12, no. 68, pl.3, no. 18, pl. 50, nos. 248, 252, pl. 9, nos. 55-56, pl. 98.

NOTE 21
See Wuilleumier 1932, pl. XXII.

NOTE 22
See e.g. Drougou – Touratsoglou 1980, 149-150, pl. 51, no. Π 1438, Π 1438, Ελληνιστική Κεραμική από τη Μακεδονία, Θεσσαλονίκη 1991, 127, 133, 167.

NOTE 23
See e.g. Laumonier, 1977.

NOTE 24
See Siebert 1978, 138, pls. 19, 56.

NOTE 25
See e.g. Arvanitopoulos 1912, 73-118, πίν. I-VII, Kakavogiannis 1980, 282, Andronikos 1984, fig. 135-136, 156, 157, Pfrommer 1987, 263, Kbk 114, pl. 28b-e, 102, 104, 123, 177, note 744, 1264,

NOTE 26
See e.g. Fraser – Ronne 1971, 64-67, 74, pl. 70, fig. 27, Ambr. 11

NOTE 27
See Vokotopoulou 1975, Walter-Karydi, 1981, 14-48.

NOTE 28
See Leveque 1957, 228-232, Tzouvara-Souli 1992, 45-50.

NOTE 29
Polyb. 21. 27. 30. 35-36. Plin. *HN*, 34. 66. For the written sources see Tzouvara-Souli 1992.

NOTE 30
Frazer – Ronne 1957, 111 ff., Frazer – Ronne 1971, note 26.

NOTE 31
Gravani 1994, 170.

NOTE 32
Gravani 1994, 170 and Hausmann, 1994, 275-282.

NOTE 33
For the origins of mouldmade bowls, see Rotroff 1982, 6-13.

NOTE 34
See Hammond 1967, 646-648. Dakaris 1971, 66.

NOTE 35
See Franke 1961, 63, Dakaris 1989, 65.

NOTE 36
See Franke 1961, 53-54. Hammond 1967, 656.

NOTE 37
See Gravani, 1997a, 336-337, pls.239-241, 243-245.

NOTE 38
See Oikonomidou-Karamesini 1990, 264-272.

NOTE 39
Gravani, *art.cit.* in note 37.

NOTE 40
See Dakaris 1989, 66-67. Hoepfner, Schwandner, Dakaris, Gravani, Tsingas 1994, 118, fig. 93.

NOTE 41
See Lamboley 1987, 195-202.

NOTE 42
Cf. Marabini-Moevs 1980, 146-225.

NOTE 43
See Franke 1961, 81-84. Hammond 1967, 641-642. Dakaris 1971, 67, 87, Dakaris 1989, 65-66

NOTE 44
See *supra* (note 10).

NOTE 45
See Dakaris 1987, 11-21.

NOTE 46
Dakaris 1987, 16-18, Dakaris 1989, 25-27.

NOTE 47
For the type of houses, see Dakaris 1989, 38-58. Hoepfner, Schwandner, Dakaris, Gravani, Tsingas 1994, 145-158.

Bibliography

Akamatis, I., 1994
Πήλινες μήτρες αγγείων από την Πέλλα, Αθήνα (2nd ed.).

Andronikos, M., 1984
Βεργίνα, Οι βασιλικοί τάφοι, Αθήνα

Arvanitopoulos, A. S., 1912
Ein Thessalischer Gold – und Silberfund, *AM* 37, 73-118.

Boessneck, J., 1994
Zooarchäologische Ergebnisse an der Tierknochen-und Molluskenfunde, in: W. Hoepfner – E. L. Schwandner, *Haus und Stadt im klassichen Griechenland, Wohnen in der klassichen Polis I,* München (2nd ed.) 175-179.

Dakaris, S., 1971
Cassopaia and the Elean Colonies, Ancient Greek Cities 4, Athens.

Dakaris, S., 1987
Η ρωμαϊκή πολιτική στην Ήπειρο, *Πρακτικά Α' Διεθνούς Συμποσίου για τη Νικόπολη,* Πρέβεζα 1984, 11-21.

Dakaris, S., 1989
Κασσώπη, Νεότερες ανασκαφές 1977-1983, Ιωάννινα (2nd ed.).

Drougou, St., – Touratsoglou, G., 1980
Ελληνιστικοί λαξευτοί τάφοι Βεροίας, Αθήνα.

Drougou, S., 1983
Ελληνιστική κεραμική. Μέθοδος και στόχοι, *Ανθρωπολογικά* 4, 7-12.

Ελληνιστική κεραμική από τη Μακεδονία, 1991
Θεσσαλονίκη.

Franke, P. R., 1961
Die antiken Münzen von Epirus, Wiesbaden.

Frazer P. M. and Ronne, T., 1957
Boeotian and West Greek Tombstones, *Skifter utg. av. Svenska Inst.i Athen* 4, VI.

Fraser, P. M. and Ronne, T., 1971
Some More Boeotian and West Greek Tombstones, *OpAth* X, 53-83.

Gravani, K., 1988/1989
Κεραμική των ελληνιστικών χρόνων από την Ήπειρο, *ΗπειρΧρον* 29, 89-132.

Gravani, K., 1989
Προβλήματα στην έρευνα της ελληνιστικής κεραμικής, *Α'ΕλλΚερ,* 3-18.

Gravani, K., 1994
Die Keramik von Kassope, Ein vorläufiger Überblick, in: W. Hoepfner – E. L. Schwandner, *Haus und Stadt im klassichen Griechenland, Wohnen in der klassichen Polis I,* München (2nd ed.), 162-172.

Gravani, K., 1996
Ανάγλυφοι σκύφοι από την Κασσώπη, Συμβολή στη μελέτη της ελληνιστικής κεραμικής από την Ήπειρο και στην ανασκαφική στρωματογραφία της Κασσώπης (Diss.), Ιωάννινα.

Gravani, K., 1997a
Ανάγλυφοι σκύφοι από το ιερό της Δωδώνης, *Α'ΕλλΚερ,* 329-344.

Gravani, K., 1997b
Τοπογραφικά Κασσωπαίας, Πρακτικά Συμποσίου προς τιμήν N. G. L. Hammond, Θεσσαλονίκη, 79-93.

Hammond, N. G. L., 1967
Epirus, The Geography, the ancient Remains, the History and the Topography of Epirus and Adjacent Areas, Oxford.

Hausmann, U., 1994
Phasen und Werkstätten mittelitalischer Reliefbecher, *Γ'ΕλλΚερ,* 275-282.

Hoepfner, W., Dakaris, S., Gravani, K. und Schwandner, E. L., 1999
Kassope. Eine spätklassische Streifenstadt in Nordwestgriechenland, in: W. Hoepfner (edit.), *Geschichte des Wohnens* I: *5000 v.Chr.-500 n.Chr., Vorgeschichte-Frühgeschichte-Antike,* Stuttgart 1999, 368-383.

Hoepfner, W., Schwandner, E. L., Dakaris S., Gravani, K, und Tsingas, A., 1994
Kassope. Bericht über die Ausgrabungen einer spätklassischen Streifenstadt in Nordwestgriechenland, in: W. Hoepfner – E. L. Schwandner, *Haus und Stadt im klassichen Griechenland, Wohnen in der klassichen Polis I*, München 1994 (2nd ed.), 114-161.

Kakavogiannis, E., 1980
Ομηρικοί σκύφοι Φερρών Θεσσαλίας, *AAA XIII*, 262-284.

Lamboley, J. L., 1987
Le canal d Otrante et les relations entre les deux rives de l Adriatique, *L' Illyrie méridionale et l' Épire dans l' Antiquitè, Actes du Colloque International de Clermont – Ferrand 1984*, 195-202.

Laumonier, A., 1977
La céramique hellénistique a reliefs, 1. Ateliers "ioniens", *Délos XXXI*, Paris.

Levèque, P., 1957
Pyrrhos, Paris.

Marabini-Moevs, M. T., 1980
Italomegarian Ware at Cosa, *MAAR XXXIV*, 146-225.

Oikonomidou-Karamesini, M., 1990
Epire, Relations politiques et économiques au IIIe et au Ier siècle jusqu' à 146 av. J.-C., *RevNum*, XXXII, 264-272.

Oikonomidou – Karamesini, M., 1994
Die Münzen der Ausgrabung von Kassope, in: W. Hoepfner – E. L. Schwandner, *Haus und Stadt im klassichen Griechenland, Wohnen in der klassichen Polis I*, München (2nd ed.), 172-174.

Pfrommer, M., 1987
Studien zu alexandrinischen und grossgriechischer Toreutik frühhellenistischer Zeit, *AF 16*, Berlin.

Rotroff, S. I., 1982
Hellenistic Pottery, Athenian and imported Moldmade Bowls, *The Athenian Agora XXII*, Princeton.

Siebert, G., 1978
Recherches sur les ateliers de bols à reliefs du Pèloponnése a l' époque hellénistique, Paris.

Siebert, G., 1980
Les bols à reliefs. Une industrie d' art de l époque hellénistique, *Céramiques hellénistiques et romaines*, Annales Littéraires Université Besançon, Paris, 55-83.

Tzouvara-Souli, Chr., 1992
Αμβρακία, Άρτα.

Vokotopoulou, I., 1975
Χαλκαί κορινθιουργείς πρόχοι, Αθήνα.

Walter-Karydi, H., 1981
Bronzen aus Dodona – eine epirotische Bildhauerschule, *JbBerlMus* 23, 14-48.

Wuilleumier, P,. 1932
Bol mégarien de Tarent, *BCH* 56 399-402.

Apart from the scattered architectural remains, numerous Roman tile graves[39] were also investigated not only in the same area south of the tombs, but also in the position of building P, where – according to the excavator – a Mycenaean palace must have been located. Roman burials were also excavated above graves R8[40] and R26.[41] Between the graves, a wall of the same period[42] passes through. The Roman graves of "Steno", which werc of a maximum length 1.80 m. and width 0.40 m., were directed from East to West and in some cases included 2 burials, even though their majority did not contain any funeral items. Only Roman bronze coins and fragments of lamps from the 4th - 5th centuries[43] AC are included among the few finds.

Similar graves were excavated in the northern part of the plain, on the slopes of mountain Skaros. One of the graves contained coins depicting the emperor Lucius Verus and a clay lamp signed by KARPOS.[44] Based on the potter's signature, the pot has been identified as the creation of a workshop in Roman Patras, which apparently exported its products to Leukas[45] in the 2nd century AD. The rest of the graves contained bronze coins, including a coin of the emperor Marcus Aurelius and clay lamps of the 3rd century AD.[46] Finally, a group of 5 cist graves was traced and investigated during the more recent research conducted by the Archaeological Service on the plain's western edge in the torrent Dimossari.[47] The better-preserved grave, as derives from its archaeological contents, dates to the time of Augustus.

Apart from the excavated evidence, Roman appearance on this site is fairly suggested by a large group of coins found during Dörpfeld's investigations on the island, currently held at the Archaeological Museum of Ioannina. Some of these coins date to the Republic, the time of Augustus and other Emperors and to subsequent periods. Even though there is little evidence about their origin, it is assumed that a significant sample of the coins originates from the plain of Nydri, since this was the

Fig. 10. Roman farmhouse: glass unguentarium.

site where the German archaeologist focused his investigation.

All the data stated above, indicate that the fertile plain of Nydri, inhabited ever since the Early Bronze Age due to its advantageous location, is also inhabited during the Roman period. Presently, there is no trace of extensive architectural remains, thus the investigation of the settlement's structure during the Roman period appears to be difficult. Nevertheless, the arrangement of grave groups leads to the assumption that detached building complexes of a rural character are also developed in this area.

Indications of the Roman period have also been traced in other locations of Leukas and the adjacent islands. In the area of the village Vournika, the excavation of the ancient temple, which still exists under the foundations of the church of St.

Fig. 11. Meganisi, area of Spartochori: glass vessel from the Roman cist grave.

Ioannis Rodakis,[48] revealed a few Roman finds, while at the edge of the plain of Vasiliki, a tombstone was found bearing the inscription: ΠΟΜΠΗΙΟΣ ΝΕΙΚΙΑΛΑΣ.[49]

During the Roman period, it is evident that apart from the sanctuary of Aphrodite Aineias, the sanctuary of Apollo Leukatas also survives, built on the remote cape of Leukatas at the far south end of the island. The depiction of Apollo Leukatas on a rare coin of Nikopolis dated to the time of Traian, mirrors the spreading of the Apollonian worship from the settlement[50] to Nikopolis. It may also suggest the continuation of the sanctuary's use in Leukas in the beginning of the 2nd century AD, since pottery and coins of the Roman period were found in the area of the sanctuary.[51]

Finally, in a small rural sanctuary at the village of Chortata, among the finds from the geometric period, a clay lamp dated to the 2nd century AD was found with a depiction of gladiators on its discus.[52]

Finds of the Roman period were also traced outside the island, on the neighboring islands of Meganisi, Kastos and Kalamos, situated in the sea area between Leukas and Akarnania. At the cape of Kefali in Meganisi, tile fragments were found[53], whereas on the NW side of the island, in the location Paliolakos near Spartochori, a cist Roman grave was investigated (Fig. 11).[54] On the other two islands, architectural remains of brick masonry were detected dating to the Roman or early Christian period.[55] The Roman presence on these sites should be associated with their location in the main sea passage linking Nikopolis with Patras.

The significance of the sea passage along the coasts of the Adriatic and the Ionian Sea during the period of the Ro-

NOTE 35
Dörpfeld 1965, 160-161.

NOTE 36
Dörpfeld 1965, 193 Abb 7, 194.

NOTE 37
Dörpfeld 1965, 163, II Taf. 10.

NOTE 38
Dörpfeld 1965, 177, 195 Abb 8.

NOTE 39
Drpfeld 1965, 250, II Taf. 12, 255.

NOTE 40
Dörpfeld 1965, 229, 249, 255.

NOTE 41
Dörpfeld 1965, 244 Abb 20, 245 Abb 21,
247, 249, 255.

NOTE 42
Dörpfeld 1965, 250 Abb 19.

NOTE 43
IG 10.1, 596. Stamatelos 1868, 1671.

NOTE 44
Dörpfeld 1965, 255.

NOTE 45
Petropoulos 1994, 150,163, pl. 75b.

NOTE 46
Dörpfeld 1965, 322.

NOTE 47
Touloupa 1973-73, 590, pl. 404c.

NOTE 48
Dörpfeld 1965, 325.

NOTE 49
Dörpfeld 1965, 325.

NOTE 50
Souli-Tzouvara 1987, 176. Oeconomidou
1975, 47.

NOTE 51
Dörpfeld 1965, 325.

NOTE 52
Dörpfeld 1965, 328.

NOTE 53
Dörpfeld 1965, 328.

NOTE 54
In 1989, a Roman cist grave was found in
the location Paliolakos near Spartochori
village, containing glass and clay vessels.

NOTE 55
Andreou 1979, 269.

NOTE 56
Axioti 1980, 187-205.

Bibliography

Andreou, H., 1979/34
A Delt. 34 Chronika, 269.

Axioti, K., 1980/35
Ρωμαϊκοί δρόμοι της Αιτωλοακαρνανίας, A Delt. 35 Meletes,
186-205.

Dakaris, S., 1987
Η ρωμαϊκή πολιτική στην
Ήπειρο, in Νικόπολις Α', Πρα-
κτικά Α' Διεθνούς Συμποσίου

για τη Νικόπολη (23-29 Σεπτεμβρίου 1984), 11-21. Preveza.

Dörpfeld, W., 1965
Alt-Ithaka I. Ein Beitrag zur Homer-
Frage, (1927) Osnabrück

Dodwell, E., 1819
A Classical and Topographical tour
through Greece during the years 1801,
1805, 1806 vol.I. London.

Douzougli, A., 1993a/48
A Delt. 48 Chronika, 290-293.
1993b/48
A Delt. 48 Chronika, 293-300.
1993c/48
A Delt. 48 Chronika, 287.

Douzougli, A., 1994/49
A Delt. 49 Chronika, in press.

Douzougli, A., 1998
Μια ρωμαϊκή αγροικία στις

ακτές του Αμβρακικού Κόλπου, *ΑΡΧΑΙΟΛΟΓΙΑ* 68, 74-78.

Fiedler, M., 1999
Leukas. Wohn und Altagskultur in einer nordwestgriechischen Stadt, in Hoepfler, W. (ed.), *Geschichte des Wohnens in 5000 v. Chr. - 500 n. Chr. Vorgeschichte Fruhgeschichte – Antike*, 412-416. Stuttgart.

Karatzeni, V., 1999
Ambracia during the Roman era, in Pierre Cabanes (ed.) *L' Illyrie, méridionale et l' Épire dans l' antiquité. Actes du 3ème colloque International de Chantilly (16-19 Octobre 1996)*, 241-247. Paris.

Murray, W. M., 1982
The Coastal Sites of Western Akarnania: a topographical- historical survey. University of Pensylvania.

Oberhummer, E., 1887
Akarnanien, Ambrakia, Amphilochien, Leukas in Altertum. München.

Oeconomidou - Karamessini, M., 1975
Η Νομισματοκοπία της Νικοπόλεως. Athens.

Petropoulos, M., 1991
Η Αιτωλοακαρνανία κατά τη ρωμαϊκή περίοδο, in *Α' Αρχαιολογικό και Ιστορικό Συνέδριο Αιτωλοακαρνανίας (21-23 Οκτωβρίου 1988)*, 93-125. Agrinion.

Petropoulos, M., 1994
Τα εργαστήρια των ρωμαϊκών λυχναριών της Πάτρας και το Λυχνομαντείο. University of Ioannina.

Pliakou, G., 1997-1998/51-52
A Delt. 51-52 Chronika, in press.

Rondogiannis, P., 1980
Ιστορία της νήσου Λευκάδας, Εταιρία Λευκαδικών Μελετών, vol. A. Athens.

Rondogiannis, P., 1988
Οι πρωτεύουσες της Λευκάδας, ΕΠΕΤΗΡΙΣ Εταιρείας Λευκαδικών Μελετών vol. Z', 42-291. Athens.

Sarikakis, Th., 1964
Συμβολή εις την ιστορίαν της Ηπείρου κατά τους χρόνους της ρωμαϊκής κυριαρχίας (167-31 π.Χ.), *AE* 1964, 105-119.

Souli –Tzouvara, Ch., 1987
Λατρείες στη Νικόπολη, in *Νικόπολις Α', Πρακτικά Α'Διεθνούς Συμποσίου για τη Νικόπολη (23-29 Σεπτεμβρίου 1984)*, 176. Preveza.

Stanmatelos, I., 1868
Συλλογή των Λευκαδίων Επιγραφών, *Εφημερίς των Φιλομαθών* 1868, 1649 ff.

Strauch, D., 1996
Romische Politik und Griechische Tradition. Munchen.

Strauch, D., 1997
Aus der Arbeit am Inschriften. Corpus der Ionschen Inseln: IG IX 1.4, *Chiron* 27, 209-254.

Touloupa, E., 1973-74a/29
A Delt. 29 Chronika, 589.

Touloupa, E., 1973-74b/29
A Delt. 29 Chronika, 590.

Zachos, K 1992/47
A Delt. 47 Chronika, 281-285.

Epirus in the Roman Era

Vivi Karatzeni

The knowledge available about the history of Epirus during the Roman period, that is from the 2nd century BC until the years of Late Antiquity, based on limited literary testimonies is quite meagre. Nevertheless, in recent years, archaeological research and historical studies have started filling the gaps, thus, the image of Epirus in the period under investigation becomes much clearer.

The present study aims at presenting the archaeological data in Epirus and particularly in the southern part of Epirus, which is today within the boundaries of the Greek State. These data lead to certain conclusions, the confirmation of which will depend on the findings of future excavations.

A. Historical data[1]

Roman presence in Epirus dates from as early as the end of the 3rd century BC, when the Romans – after defeating the Carchedonians – set towards the East in order to conquer the eastern part of the Mediterranean. After the 2nd and 3rd Macedonian wars, the Macedonian kingdom was abolished. The defeat of Perseus at Pydna in 168 BC had devastating consequences for Epirus and especially for its southern part, which had allied with the Macedonians. In 167 BC, 70 cities in Epirus were destroyed and 150,000 people were sold as slaves by the Romans[2]. After the revolution of Philip Andriscos was put down in 148 BC, Macedonia lost its independence and became a Roman province which included Epirus and Illyria.

In the beginning of the 1st century BC, Epirus suffered from a new disaster caused by the Thracian incursions. The subsequent civil wars among the Roman commanders as well as the arbitrary acts of the Roman regional governors deteriorated even more the condition in the area[3]. And yet, as indicated by the archaeological research, the cities seem to have survived even under these circumstances. Excavations in Kassopi, Ammotopos, Gardiki and Kastritsa have shown that the cities suffering from the destruction of 167 BC, continue to be inhabited until the end of the 1st century BC[4]. As is after all known, the *koina* continue to exist, Ambracia and Charadros maintain – at least typically – their independence and in general, it appears that each political community maintains – even under the power of the Roman commander in the Macedonian province – its political institutions[5]. Therefore, the gloomy description of total abandonment, which Strabo gives to Epirus slightly before the founding of Nicopolis, should probably be considered overstated.[6] Undoubtedly, the constant wars, disasters, seizures and the inhabitants' captivation had caused a demographic reduction of the city's population and a more general regress both in economic and cultural terms. It appears that the foundation of Nicopolis at the coasts of S. Epirus towards the end of the 1st century BC, apart from representing the desire to perpetuate the memory of the historical victory at Actium, aimed at the reconstruction and revival of the area by creating a new urban centre that served expediencies both of an economic and strategic character.[7]

All the cities of Epirus and Akarnania located around the Ambracian gulf, as well as some cities of Aetolia[8] were forced to participate in the settlement. Because of their dominant position, some of these cities were not totally abandoned; on the contrary, they survived as *perioikides* of Nicopolis for a few more centuries. This category mainly includes the coastal cities of Akarnania and Ambracia.[9]

The interval between the foundation of Nicopolis and the middle of the 3rd century AD is a period of recovery for Epirus. Especially during the early 2nd century – a period of prosperity for the empire – the emperors showed particular merit to this area. In the beginning of the 2nd century, between the years 103-114 AD, Trajan detached Epirus from the province of Achaia (where it was initially submitted by Augustus in 27 BC) and established it as an independent province, appointing Nicopolis as its seat.[10] The constant minting of coins at Nicopolis in the age of Trajan, indicates the prosperity of the city that declared the emperor as a "Saviour".[11] Hadrian who appears to have visited Nicopolis in 128 AD[12] also showed special merit to Epirus.

The revival and prosperity of the area will not last. In the 3rd century AD, the empire is threatened by internal misrule. The barbaric peoples take advantage of the situation and begin to invade the empire from the west and the east. In 267 AD, the Herouli invade Epirus. The hiding of coinage treasures has been related to this invasion and shows the turmoil caused in the area.[13]

In the end of the 3rd century AD, the rise of the Illyrian dynasty eliminated temporarily the danger of the empire's abolition. The administrative reforms effected by Diocletian and Constantine, as well as the policies adapted towards the barbaric peoples, restored the internal serenity until around the end of the 4th century. Most likely in the period of Diocletian, Epirus was divided into two administrative provinces, Old Epirus (*Epirus Vetus*) consisting of the area from the Kerauneia Mountains to the mouth of Acheloos with Nicopolis as its seat and New Epirus (*Epirus Nova*) further north, with Dyrrachium as its seat.[14]

Julian also showed interest in the area and saw to the execution of building works in several cities of Epirus and especially to the restoration of the public buildings in Nicopolis which were collapsing.[15] Furthermore, he took a series of economic measures in order to release the inhabitants of Epirus from heavy taxation.

After the death of Julian in 363 AD, Christianity prevailed. The oracle at Dodona stops functioning at the end of the 4th century (possibly in the age of Theodosius I), while slightly later, Dodona is mentioned – according to sources – as an episcopate seat.[16]

From the end of the 4th century and for a long period, Epirus suffers Gothic invasions.[17] These invasions will disturb Europe for two centuries. Especially in connection with southern Epirus, there are references to two invasions by Visigoths in 380 and 395 AD, and two invasions from sea by Vandals in 467 and 474 AD.

During the invasion in 474 AD, Nicopolis was ferociously plundered. Old Epirus was conquered by Getes in 517 AD and by Ostrogoths in 551 AD. The final stroke was given by the Slavic invasions, which – according to historical sources – forced the inhabitants to seek refuge in other areas, probably in the neighbouring islands of the Ionian Sea and in the mountainous areas.[18]

B. Sites in Epirus with Roman remains

This chapter will refer to the sites of each prefecture where archaeological remains of the Roman period have been traced. More emphasis will be given to the prefectures of Ioannina and Arta, since reference to the prefectures of Thesprotia and Preveza is given in the studies of S. Dakaris "Thesprotia" and "Cassopaia". His chapters on the Roman period refer analytically to every site traced until the beginning of the 1970's. It should also be clarified that in most cases, the archaeological finds mentioned has not been systematically published. Nevertheless, the picture given by references to the traced sites facilitates the better comprehension of the area's history during this particular

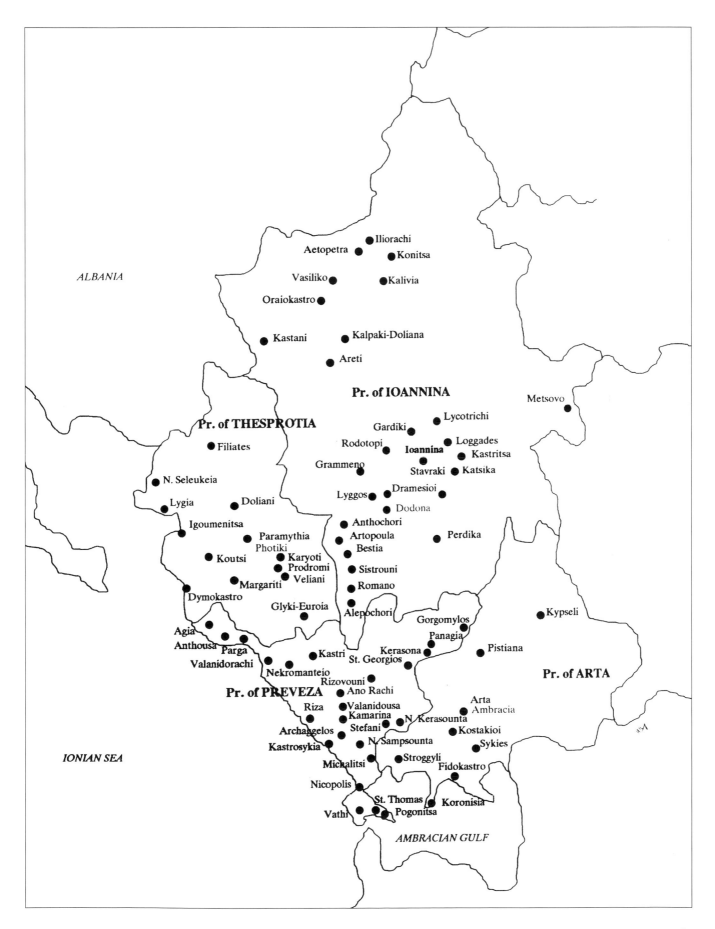

ALBANIA

Iliorachi

Aetopetra ●

Konitsa

Vasiliko ●

Kalivia

Oraiokastro ●

Kastani ●

Kalpaki-Doliana

Areti ●

Pr. of IOANNINA

Metsovo ●

Pr. of THESPROTIA

Lycotrichi

Gardiki

Filiates ●

Rodotopi

Loggades

Ioannina

Kastritsa

Grammeno ●

Stavraki

Katsika

N. Seleukeia ●

Dramesioi

Lyggos

Dodona

Lygia ●

Doliani ●

Anthochori

Igoumenitsa ●

Artopoula

Perdika

Paramythia ●

Bestia

Photiki

Koutsi ●

Karyoti ●

Sistrouni

Prodromi ●

Margariti ●

Veliani

Romano

Dymokastro ●

Glyki-Euroia

Alepochori

Gorgomylos

Kypseli ●

Panagia

Agia ●

Anthousa ●

Parga ●

Kastri ●

Kerasona

Pistiana ●

Valanidorachi ●

St. Georgios

Pr. of ARTA

Nekromanteio ●

Rizovouni ●

Pr. of PREVEZA

Ano Rachi

Arta

Ambracia

Riza ●

Valanidousa

Kamarina ●

N. Kerasounta

Stefani ●

Kostakioi

Archaggelos ●

N. Sampsounta

Sykies

Kastrosykia ●

Stroggyli

Michalitsi ●

Fidokastro

Nicopolis ●

St. Thomas

Koronisia

Vathi ●

Pogonitsa

IONIAN SEA

AMBRACIAN GULF

period. After all, during the recent years, the excavations conducted in some of these locations, despite their confined extent, provided a considerable amount of new data giving light to this historical period.

B1. Prefecture of Ioannina

Area of Lakka Souli

Sites with Roman-early Christian finds have been located along the plain of Lakka Souli, which was one of the main roads linking the area of Ambracian Gulf with the inland of Epirus since the earlier periods.[19] More specifically, building remains dating to the early Christian times have been traced in the area between Polistafylo and Alepochori.[20] In Alepochori two cist graves were found dating to the 2nd century AD,[21] while in Romano two graves were found dating to the 1st –2nd centuries AD.[22] Remains of a Roman bath with a mosaic floor and an early Christian basilica were discovered in Sistrouni.[23] Finally, a grave of the 3rd to 4th century AD was found in Bestia[24] and Roman coins were found in Artopoula[25] and Anthochori.[26]

Area of Dodona-Grammeno

Apart from the early Christian basilica found in the area of the sanctuary at Dodona,[27] extended remains from a late Roman – early Christian settlement and a basilica were found in the neighbouring Dramesioi.[28]

Slightly northern, in Lyggos (Mospina) two tombstones were found dating to the Roman period.[29] In Grammeno, in the small plain north of the Kastri hill where the surviving remains of a Hellenistic acropolis are located, a temple-like building has been excavated in which, a Roman phase has also been identified.[30]

Area of the Ioannina basin

In the citadel "Its Kale", inside the castle of Ioannina, a tombstone, most likely moved over from another area, was found.[31] Outside the castle, on the lakeshore, a small head of Dionysus was found made of limestone, dating to the Roman times.[32] It is estimated that it had been moved over from another location, due to the fact that it was found in debris.

Foundations of a Roman building have been traced in Katsika[33] and a Roman grave in Loggades.[34]

Architectural remains as well as a sarcophagus of the 3rd century AD were found in the area between Kranoula and Lycotrichi.[35] Two Roman graves were also found in Stavraki.[36] Further north, in Rodotopi, a Roman construction phase[37] has been recognised in the remains of the Hellenistic temple of Areios Zeus. Two Roman inscriptions and a headless statue of a Roman emperor dating to the 2nd century AD also come from Rodotopi.[38] Alongside Rodotopi, on the hill of Gardiki where a fortified Hellenistic city, the ancient Passaron, is located, the excavation of a confined area conducted in 1992 uncovered two Hellenistic buildings, the one of which remains in use during the early Roman period (1st century BC- 1st century AD).[39]

Of a great interest are the results of the excavation research conducted in 1994 on the hill of Kastritsa, by the southern edge of the lake of Ioannina, where the remains of another fortified Molossian city, probably Tekmon, are preserved.[40] The excavation uncovered the foundations of two Hellenistic buildings which present an additional second construction phase, in use from the 4th century to the 6th century AD[41]. It should be noted that on the northern and southern part of the ancient fortification, repairs have been recognised, which, according to S. Dakaris, date from the years of the Roman ruling, immediately after 167 BC. However, according to F. Wozniak, these restorations should be dated to the late Roman period.[42] The results of the aforementioned excavation seem to verify the above view.

Area of Parakalamos

Remains of a fort and potsherds of the Roman period have been reported in the site of Petrovouni, at the village Areti (former Gribiani).[43]

Area of Kalpaki-Doliana

Graves dating to the Roman period and remains of at least two early Christian basilicas have been found in the plain of the Kalpaki-Doliana area.[44]

Area of Pogoni

Roman finds and remains of an early Christian basilica have been traced at the valley of Gormos in Oraiokastro (or Lachanocastro).[45] Additionally, a tombstone dating to the 2nd - 1st century BC was found in Kastani,[46] while a late Roman grave has been found in Vasiliko.[47]

Area of Konitsa

Around the plain of Konitsa through which the river Aoos flows, many sites have been traced with remains from the period under investigation.[48] A building complex of the early Christian times and a cist grave dating to the 1st - 2nd centuries AD was found in Aetopetra. A small pillar of the late Roman period was found in Iliorrachi, while architectural remains dating to the early Christian period were found in the site of Kalivia at Kleidonia.

Nevertheless, most remains are traced in the area of Konitsa. Eight Roman coins and architectural remains were found westwards of the Agricultural School. Architectural remains probably of a Roman farmhouse were discovered on the hill of Palaiogoritsa, on top of which the remains of a large building were also found dating to the early Christian period (probably a basilica). A double cist grave dating to the late Roman times was found between Palaiogoritsa and Konitsa in the site of Elia. The ruins of a fort probably dating to the Justinian age remain on top of a remote rocky hill, above Konitsa.[49]

The density of the remains in the area of Konitsa suggests the existence at this location of an important settlement dating from the Roman years to the early Christian period. As indicated by the archaeological remains, the wider area had always been very favourable for human settlements, as it consisted of a vast plain, a continuous flow of ample water from the river Aoos and its tributaries in combina-tion with sites suitable for the construction of defence fortification. Additionally, of great importance is the fact that it lies in the beginning of a natural passage, which follows the flow of the river Aoos extending to the area of Apollonia. Apparently, this is the passage Philip V followed in 198 BC on his way to Macedonia when retrieving after his defeat by Flamininus to the narrows of Aoos.[50] The same passage was a main communication route between Epirus and Albania in recent years. Thus, this passage should probably be identified with the Roman route presented on the map of the 4th century AD (known as Tabula Peutingeriana) as the parallel route to a larger river flowing to Apollonia.[51] This river is probably Aoos, since Genousos is shown on its northern side and the mouth of the river Apsos is shown further down.

On the right edge of the river, right next to a big mountain chain, the site Ilio is set as a station. Anyone who has visited Konitsa must have admired the mountains of Pindos, Smolikas and Tymfi, which rise above the city. Thus, Ilio, which is not mentioned in any other source, may be identified with the remains of the Roman – early Christian settlement in Konitsa. Nevertheless, such an assumption may only be confirmed by archaeological research.[52]

In the interior uplands of the prefecture of Ioannina, only a few remains of this period have been found: Roman coins, as well as the remains of a fortification, which according to Leake's interpretation must have been a Roman outpost, have been found in Metsovo.[53] Roman coins have also been found in Perdika (Moulesi).[54]

B.2 Prefecture of Arta

A Roman building with 4 aligned rooms, probably a storage place for agricultural goods, was discovered near the southwestern cemetery of ancient Ambracia, during the excavations conducted in one section of Arta, where only recently, constructions

Very few sites with finds of the Roman period have been traced in the mountainous areas of the prefecture. Potsherds and coins were found in Trikastro[97] and a Roman tombstone in Ano Rachi.[98] A Latin funeral inscription carved on a small column comes from Valanidousa.[99]

B.4 Prefecture of Thesprotia

As is mentioned in the introduction of chapter B, the sites with finds of the Roman period at the prefecture of Thesprotia, are analysed in the study of S. Dakaris "Thesprotia". Thus, the present paper will be limited to the reference of the basic sites and those that have been traced after the publication of the aforementioned study.

Photiki is undoubtedly the most important site during the period of the Roman domination in Thesprotia, in significance the second Roman City in southern Epirus after Nicopolis. It was founded in the 1st century BC.[100] The extended remains of Photiki are preserved near Paramythia, in the site of Limboni (St. Donatos). Due to the fact that the city was built on a plain and its soil was unsuitable for establishing fortification, Justinian built on the hill above Paramythia a castle serving as a refuge for the city's inhabitants in case of an emergency. The size of the remains, the architectural sections, the inscriptions, the marble sarcophagi, indicate the wealth and prosperity of the city which after the 6th century AD begins to decline, probably due to barbaric invasions.

Evidence of a settlement, graves and remains of an early Christian church are also preserved in Glyki, at the northern bank of Acheron, where the river flows from the gorge of Souli. This site has been identified with Euroia, one of the four cities of southern Epirus known by the literary sources.[101]

Archaeological remains of the Roman-early Christian period have also been traced in the valley of Kokytos, between Glyki and Paramythia: in Karioti, there are remains of a unfortified settlement. Remains of an early Christian basilica, inscriptions and coins were found in Veliani, whereas Roman graves were discovered at Prodromi.[102]

Latin inscriptions have been found in the small plain of Margariti.[103] In the site of Koutsi, between the plain of Margariti and the coastal plain of Plataria, on the mountains of Parga, in the north western angle of an ancient fortification, a more recent fort is built in the inner side, probably dating to the Roman or late Roman period.[104] This fort was used for controlling the Plataria bay. Signs of a construction phase of this period also exist in the fortification of ancient Elina, at the coastal site of Dymokastro.[105]

In the area of Igoumenitsa, at the sites of Ladochori and Xenia, a settlement and cemeteries of the Roman-early Christian period have been traced, while on the hill where a Turkish castle is located, fortification traces of this era exist.[106] Restorations of the Roman or late Roman period also exist in the ancient fort at Lygia, at the entrance of the Igoumenitsa bay.[107] In New Seleukeia, near the city of Igoumenitsa, the remains of a building that is probably part of a Roman farmhouse were discovered in 1992.[108]

In the area of Filiates, north of the Myloi village, a fort exists (known as Kasnetsi) on a remote hill, which was used for controlling the plain of Goumani from the north. According to Dakaris' estimations, this fort probably dates to the Roman period.[109] He also claims that the more recent restorations to be observed in the fortification of the ancient settlement at Doliani,[110] which he identifies with ancient Fanoti, date to the Roman period.

C. Conclusions

From the aforementioned sites, it is ascertained that during the period of the Roman domination, the mountainous areas are abandoned and the settlements are gathered at the coasts and the vast plains (like the plains of Arta and Acheron), in smaller plains (such as Konitsa, Kalpaki, basin of Ioannina), the river basins and across the main roads.[111] Unfortunately, the lack of archaeological research does not allow the acquisition of further knowledge about these settlements and their development. They must be small unwalled villages of a rural character. The number of urban centres is small. The *Synekdemos* of Hierokles that presents the conditions during the 5th century, even though it was not completed until the years of Justinian, numbers only four cities in the area of South Epirus: Nicopolis, Photiki, Euroia and Dodona, which used to be episcopate seats.[112] The earlier urban centers, that is the walled cities of the classical and Hellenistic years built on fortified sites, have been abandoned. Only Ambracia appears to survive until around the 4th century AD. Although it initially maintained a legal status as a city until the 2nd century, as indicated by the two aforementioned inscriptions, it later appeared to suffer total decline, since in Tabula Peutigeriana there is no indication of Ambracia on the road leading from Nicopolis to Thessaly.[113]

Apart from the cities and the rural settlements, farmhouses appear to be another form of inhabitancy during the Roman period. It is known that from the beginning of the 1st century BC, wealthy Romans settled in Epirus, became owners of large estates especially in coastal areas and undertook agricultural activities.[114] The banker Titus Pomponius Atticus was one of these wealthy Romans; he owned properties in the area of Bouthrotum (and a luxurious villa called Amaltheia) and on the mouth of the river Thyamis (Kalamas). As aforementioned, this type of installation has been found in Strongyli near the mouth of Louros, in the area of Konitsa, in Nea Seleukeia of Thesprotia and possibly in Riza of Preveza. Thus, it appears that in Epirus, the economy of which in this period becomes a purely agricultural one, owners of large properties undertake the exploitation of agricultural production.[115] The regime of large ownership (*latifundia*) is valid until the 4th century AD, as becomes known by the historical sources referring to the senator Rogatus, a landowner in the area of Nicopolis.[116]

The socio-economic structures, which did not change with the prevalence of Christianity, as the higher ranks of the clergy were taken over by wealthy landowners,[117] undergo transformation under the pressure of the barbaric invasions, which were about to cause a turmoil in the area for more than two centuries. The great losses in human lives, the damage in the countryside, the settlements, the road network and other community projects such as aqueducts, draining channels etc. must have created a sense of uncertainty and terror.[118] Under these circumstances, the lack of security in the unfortified settlements of the plain area became apparent. The abandonment of the villa in Strongyli at the end of the 3rd century, which is possibly connected with the first invasions and particularly with the invasion by Herouli in 267 AD, reflects the ruling of insecurity in the area which will reach its peak within the subsequent centuries. New fortifications are constructed for protection, in areas like Nicopolis and Photiki, while at the same time, many previously abandoned fortifications of the classical-Hellenistic age are restored and used as a refuge for the inhabitants of the surrounding areas.[119] As already shown, repairs can be observed in the fortification of the ancient Vatia in Rizovouni, of Vouchetion (castle of Rogoi), of Pandosia in Kastri of Acheron, as well as in the ancient fortifications at Koutsi, Dymokastro, Lygia, Doliani (Fanoti), Phidokastro and Kastritsa. According to several postulations, these restorations are dated from the years immediately after 167 BC to the period of the Turkish domination. Undoubtedly, the archaeological research will provide the final answer, however, it is most likely that the repairs date to the years of the barbaric invasions.[120] The results of the excavation conducted in Kastritsa agree with this point of view, since it has been proven that after a period of abandonment this site was re-inhabited from the 4th century AD to the end of the 6th century AD, i.e. during the invasion period. Thus, it seems that throughout this troublesome period, a fortified site is used as a refuge for the inhabitants living in unwalled settlements in every small or large plain. This is the reason why, either new fortifications are built, like in Nicopolis, in the area of Photiki, in Igoumenitsa and in Konitsa, or fortifications dating to the classical-Hellenistic period are used after being restored, like the ones aforementioned.

The repairs of the ancient fortification at the port of Ambracia, in Phidokastro, possibly relate to barbaric invasions and particularly the invasions from sea by Vandals in 467 and 474 AD.

All attempts relating to the area's defensive armouring failed to contain the invaders' fury. The inhabitants were often forced to abandon their homes in order to seek refuge in other safer areas. According to historical sources, the inhabitants of Euroia had to move, in the age of Justinian, to a safer location, which they named after their old homeland.[121] A massive movement of the population possibly occurred in the case of Ambracia, which – according to archaeological evidence – was already abandoned in the 5th century AD. Its inhabitants most likely settled in the area near the modern city of Amfilochia, where in the 9th century AD a town called Amvrakia is mentioned and which later is presented as Amvrakià.[122] With the exception of Nicopolis, which survives for four more centuries, the settlements and cities are abandoned in the 6th century. The Slavs, the last invaders, settle in the area as indicated by the numerous Slavic place-names replacing the now forgotten old ones.[123]

Notes

NOTE 1
For the history of Epirus during the Roman period see Oost 1954. Sarikakis 1964. Sarikakis 1966. Hammond 1967, 594 ff. Dakaris 1972, 192-198, Dakaris 1987. Chrysos 1981. Cabanes 1997. Chrysos 1997.

NOTE 2
Polyb. 30. 15; Strab. 7. 7. 3; Liv. 45. 34. 5-6; Plut. *Aem*. 29. 4-5; Plin. *HN* 4. 39. Hammond 1967, 629-635. Dakaris 1972, 192-194.
Ziolkowski 1986, 69-80.

NOTE 3
Sarikakis 1964, 110-112 and 114 ff.

NOTE 4
Dakaris 1971, 95. Dakaris 1986. Dakaris 1989. *A. Delt*. 48 (1993) 262-267. *A. Delt*. 1994, in press.

NOTE 5
Cabanes-Andreou 1985. Dakaris 1987. Cabanes 1997, 120-122.

NOTE 6
Strab. 7.7.6 and 7.7.9

NOTE 7
Purcell 1987. Doukellis-Dufaure-Fouache 1995, 229.

NOTE 8
Strab. 7.7.6 and 10.2.2.; Paus. 5.23.3 and 7.18.8-9
Anth. Pal. 9.553; Dio 51.1.3. For the settlement of Nicopolis, see Hoepfner 1987. Kirsten 1987. Purcell 1987.

NOTE 9
Petropoulos 1991. Karatzeni 1999.

NOTE 10
Sarikakis 1966, 195 ff.

NOTE 11
Karamesini-Oikonomidou 1975, 79-80

NOTE 12
Sarikakis 1967, 180.Cabanes 1987.

NOTE 13
Karamesini-Oikonomidou 1967. Karamesini-Oikonomidou 1971.

NOTE 14
Sarikakis 1966, 194, 213-214. Chrysos 1981, 12-13

NOTE 15
Chrysos 1981, 22-27

NOTE 16
Dakaris 1972, 198.

NOTE 17
Dakaris 1972, 197-198. Chrysos 1981, 37 ff.Wozniak 1987, 264 ff.

NOTE 18
Chrysos 1981, 68 ff. Koder 1982, 9 ff.

NOTE 19
For the roads of Epirus during the Roman period, Hammond 1967, 699 ff. Dakaris 1971, 97-98.

NOTE 20
Konstantios 1984, 123

NOTE 21
A.Delt. 17 (1961-2) B', 197. *A. Delt*. 23 (1968) B2, 286 ff. Dakaris 1971, 96.

NOTE 22
A.Delt. 16 (1960), 200-201. Dakaris 1971, 96.

NOTE 23
A. Delt. 23 (1968) B2, 292. Dakaris 1971, 96, *A. Delt*. 34 (1979) B1, 260. Konstantios 1984, 142.

NOTE 24
Dakaris 1971, 96.

NOTE 25
A. Delt. 42 (1987) B1, 321.

NOTE 26
A. Delt. 48 (1993) B1, 303.

NOTE 27
Dakaris 1993, 35.

NOTE 28
A. Delt 34 (1979) B1, 260.Konstantios 1984, 118-123.

NOTE 29
BCH 1953, 223-4. Hammond 1967, 183.

NOTE 30
A. Delt. 27 (1972) B2, 446-8.

NOTE 31
A. Delt. 41 (1986) Chron., 100.

NOTE 32
Vokotopoulou 1973, 95.

NOTE 33
From the Ephorate's archives.

NOTE 34
A. Delt. 40 (1985) Chron. 224.

NOTE 35
BCH 1959, 673.

NOTE 36
BCH 1954 I, 135.

NOTE 37
Evangelidis 1952. Dakaris 1954, 1059-1061.

NOTE 38
Evangelidis 1935, 261.

NOTE 39
A. Delt. 48 (1993) B1, 262-267.

NOTE 40
Dakaris 1951. Dakaris 1956. Hammond 1967, 173-175.

NOTE 41
A Delt. 1994, in press.

NOTE 42
Dakaris 1951, 174. Dakaris 1952, 540.
Hammond 1967, 174. Wozniak 1984, 35.

NOTE 43
From the Ephorate's archives.

NOTE 44
A. Delt. 19 (1964) B3, 313. A.Delt. 23
(1968) B2, 294. Douzougli 1994, 15.

NOTE 45
Chalkia 1997, 168. Hammond (1967, 270-
271) dates the fortification to the Byzantine period.

NOTE 46
A. Delt. 17 (1961-62) B', 197-198.

NOTE 47
From the Ephorate's archives.

NOTE 48
Douzougli 1996, 26 ff. Papadopoulou
1996, 75 ff.

NOTE 49
Hammond 1967, 273.

NOTE 50
Hammond 1966. Hammond 1967, 617-
619.

NOTE 51
Hammond 1967, Map 17.

NOTE 52
Hammond identifies the river with Kalamas and places Ilium at Despotiko
(Hammnod 1967,696) where, however, no
traces of a Roman settlement have been
confirmed. After all, the river cannot be in
any case Kalamas, as Kalamas flows further
south in Thesprotia. Miller (Hammond
1967, 696 notes 1, 2) locates Ilium near
Kalpaki, although there is no relation between Kalpaki and the river Aoos that
flows to Apollonia.

NOTE 53
Hammond 1967, 265. A. Delt. 41 (1986)
Chron., 114.

NOTE 54
Hammond 1967, 156.

NOTE 55
A. Delt. 47 (1992) B1, 243-247.

NOTE 56
Plot Papanikolaou, A. Delt. 1999, in press.

NOTE 57
A. Delt. 1999, in press.

NOTE 58
A. Delt. 47 (1992) B1, 262-264.

NOTE 59
From the Ephorate's archives.

NOTE 60
Karatzeni 1999.

NOTE 61
Papadopoulou 1997, 344

NOTE 62
Dakaris, HE 1955, 455. Hammond 1967,
140. A. Delt 45 (1990) B1, 265-266. Papadopoulou 1997, 344.

NOTE 63
Hammond 1967, 137 ff. Soustal 1981, 720.
Soustal-Koder, 233.

NOTE 64
Hammond 1967, 137 n.2.

NOTE 65
A. Delt. 30 (1975), 218. A. Delt. 45 (1990)
B1, 265. H.X. 1926, 116.

NOTE 66
AE 1950-51, Chron. 40-41, Hammond
1967, 71, Dakaris 1971, 59, 95. A. Delt. 47
(1992) B1, 294-295. A. Delt. 48 (1993) B1,
282-285. Douzougli 1998, 74-78.

NOTE 67
A. Delt. 44 (1989) B2, 285. A. Delt. 47
(1992) B1, 295. A. Delt. 48 (1993) B1, 303.

NOTE 68
Dakaris HE 1955, 451-453.

NOTE 69
Hammond 1967, 152. A. Delt. 29 (1973-
74) B2, 595-6.

NOTE 70
For Nicopolis, see Soustal-Koder 1981,
213-14 where all the relevant bibliography
until 1981. See also Νικόπολη Α',
Πρακτικά του Πρώτου για τη
Νικόπολη, 23-29 Σεπτεμβρίου 1984,
Πρέβεζα 1987. Zachos 1994.

NOTE 71
In the larger section of the prefecture of
Preveza, a Greek-American Project was
conducted from 1991 to 1995 by the University of Boston, the 12th and the 8th
Ephorates of Antiquities; see A. Delt. 46
(1991) B1, 245-251. A. Delt. 47 (1992) B1,
293 ff. A. Delt. 48 (1993) B1, 309 ff. A.
Delt. 1994, in press. A. Delt. 1995, in press.

NOTE 72
A. Delt. 34 (1979) B1, 246. A. Delt. 48
(1993) B1, 309.

NOTE 73
Soustal-Koder 1981, 270 entry St. Thomas.

NOTE 74
A. Delt. 48 (1993) B1, 310.

NOTE 75
A. Delt. 42 (1987) B1, 334.

NOTE 76
A. Delt. 47 (1992) B1, 295.

NOTE 77
BCH 118 (1994), 728.

NOTE 78
A. Delt. 31 (1976) B2, 203-204.

NOTE 79
A. Delt. 17 (1961–62) B, 194. *A. Delt* 30 (1975) B2, 219-220

NOTE 80
Papadopoulou 1997, 342-344.

NOTE 81
Hammond 1967, 57-61. Dakaris 1971, 179 ff. Dakaris 1977, 201ff.

NOTE 82
Hammond 1967, 55-56. Dakaris 1971, 183-187.

NOTE 83
Hammond 1967, 56. Dakaris 1971, 190. Wozniak 1984, 73.

NOTE 84
Wozniak 1984, 73. Papadopoulou 1997, 340.

NOTE 85
A. Delt 19 (1964) B3, 309. Konstantios 1984, 148. Papadopoulou 1997, 342.

NOTE 86
Vokotopoulou *AAA* 1971, 3, 336-337. Dakaris 1971, 97-98.

NOTE 87
Chrysos 1981, 24. Doukellis-Defaure-Fouache 1995, 232-233.

NOTE 88
For the course of the aqueduct see *A. Delt.* 17 (1961-62) B', 188 plan 1, 194. Doukellis-Defaure-Fouache 1995.

NOTE 89
A. Delt. 24 (1969) B2, 253-254. Dakaris 1971, 95. *A.Delt.* 35 (1980) B1, 320-321.

NOTE 90
Chrysostomou 1982. *A. Delt* 47 (1992) B1, 313. *A. Delt.* 48 (1993) B1, 301

NOTE 91
Dakaris 1972, 199.

NOTE 92
A. Delt. 48 (1993) B1, 312.

NOTE 93
Hammond 1967, 67-68. Dakaris 1971, 95. Wozniak dates the repairs to the years after the 12th - 13th century (Wozniak 1984, 73-74).

NOTE 94
Dakaris 1972, 135, 200.

NOTE 95
Dakaris 1972, 100, 136. *A. Delt* 34 (1979) B1, 246-247.

NOTE 96
Dakaris 1972, 136, 200.

NOTE 97
Dakaris 1971, 96.

NOTE 98
Dakaris 1971, 96.

NOTE 99
Dakaris 1971, 96, 216 n. 287.

NOTE 100
Dakaris 1972, 201-202. Soustal-Koder 1981, 236-237. Triantafyllopoulos 1984.

NOTE 101
Dakaris 1972, 136-137, 200-201. Soustal-Koder 1981, 158. Pallas, 1983.

NOTE 102
Dakaris 1972, 201. *A. Delt.* 47 (1992) B1, 349.

NOTE 103
Dakaris 1972, 142, 202.

NOTE 104
Dakaris 1972, 100-101, 203.

NOTE 105
Dakaris 1972, 146, 203.

NOTE 106
Dakaris 1972, 204. *A.Delt.* 48 (1993) B1, 318-319.

NOTE 107
Dakaris 1972, 105-107.

NOTE 108
A. Delt. 48 (1992) B1, 347-348.

NOTE 109
Dakaris 1972, 205.

NOTE 110
Dakaris 1972, 39 ff., 154-155, 206.

NOTE 111
Dakaris 1972, 207. This is also observed in the neighboring Aetoloakarnania. See Petropoulos 1991, 119.

NOTE 112
Dakaris 1952, 542-543. Chrysos 1981, 13-14.

NOTE 113
Hammond 1967, Map 17. For the passing of this route through Arta see Hammond 1967, 695-696 and map18.

NOTE 114
Cicero, *Ad Atticum* 1.5, 1.13.1, 1.16. Sarikakis 1964, 112 ff. Sarikakis 1966, 204. Dakaris 1971, 93. Dakaris 1972, 196.

NOTE 115
For the farmhouses traced in the neighboring Akarnania, which in this era was part of Epirus, see Petropoulos 1991, 119-121.

NOTE 116
Chrysos 1981, 91-93.

NOTE 117
Chrysos 1981, 27-30, 91-99.

NOTE 118
Chrysos 1981, 37 ff.

NOTE 119

It is known that Justinian particularly provided for the defence of the provinces by restoring old fortifications and by making fewer new constructions. (Procopius, *De Aed.* 4.4).Besides, according to more recent studies, many of these fortifications which Procopius attributes to Justinian, are projects by his predecessors (see Wozniak 1987, 265-266) like for example the early Christian fortification of Nicopolis which, according to Chrysos, was built immediately after the city's seizure by the Vandals in474 AD (Chrysos 1981, 53).This view is also accepted by other researchers. See Gregory 1987, 253 ff. Hellenkemper 1987, 243 ff.

NOTE 120

For the late Roman fortifications in Epirus see Wozniak 1984 and Wozniak 1987, even though only few of the surviving fortifications dating to this era are investigated and thus, it is assumed that Epirote fortifications of the late Roman period were few.

NOTE 121

According to Procopius (*De Aed.* 4.1. 37-41) Justinian moved the inhabitants of Euroia to a safer site where a new city was founded (Nea Euroia) in order to protect them. Dakaris (1952) identifies the Nea Euroia with the Castle of Ioannina, whereas Pallas (1983) locates it in the ancient Pandosia.

In the beginning of the 7th century the inhabitants of Euroia left their houses once again so as to get away from the Slavs and sought refuge to Kassiope in northern Corfu, see Chrysos 1981, 74-77. Koder 1982, 19.

NOTE 122
Soustal - Koder 1981, 104-113.

NOTE 123
Hammond 1967, 27 n.2. Chrysos 1981, 78. Koder 1982.Wozniak 1987, 267.

Bibliography

Cabanes, P., 1976
L' Épire, de la mort de Pyrrhos a la conquête romaine (272-167 av.J.C.) Paris.

Cabanes, P.-Andréou, I., 1985
Le règlement frontalier entre les cités d' Ambracie et de Charadros, *BCH* 109, 499-544.

Cabanes, P., 1987.
L' Empereur Hadrien à Nicopolis, in *Νικόπολις Α'. Πρακτικά του Πρώτου Διεθνούς Συμποσίου για τη Νικόπολη, 23-29 Σεπτ. 1984*, 153-167. Πρέβεζα.

Cabanes, P., 1997.
Από τη Ρωμαϊκή κατάκτηση ως τη μεγάλη κρίση του 3ου αι. μ.Χ. in: *Ήπειρος-4000 χρόνια ελληνικής ιστορίας και πολιτισμού*, 114-139. Αθήνα.

Chalkia, E., 1997
Παλαιοχριστιανική τέχνη, in: *Ήπειρος, 4000 χρόνια ελληνικής ιστορίας και πολιτισμού*, 168. Αθήνα.

Chrysos, E., 1981
Συμβολή στην ιστορία της Ηπείρου κατά την πρωτοβυζαντινή εποχή (Δ'-ΣΤ αι.), *Η.Χ.* 23 (1981), 6-11.

Chrysos, E., 1997.
Πρωτοβυζαντινή περίοδος (4ος-6ος αι.), in: *Ήπειρος 4000 χρόνια ελληνικής ιστορίας και πολιτισμού*, 148-165. Αθήνα.

Chrysostomou, P., 1982.
Το Νυμφαίο των Ριζών Πρεβέζης, *AAA* 1982, 10-21.

Dakaris, S., 1951
Ανασκαφή εις Καστρίτσαν Ιωαννίνων, *Prakt.* 1951, 173-183.

Dakaris, S., 1952
Ιωάννινα, η νεώτερη Εύροια, *HE* 1 (1952), 537-554.

Dakaris, S., 1954
Η αρχαιολογική έρευνα στην Ήπειρο, *HE* 3 (1954), 1059-1066.

Dakaris, S., 1956.
Αρχαιολογιές έρευνες στο λεκανοπέδιο των Ιωαννίνων, in: *Αφιέρωμα εις την Ήπειρον, εις μνήμην Χρ. Σούλη*, 46-80. Αθήναι.

Dakaris, S., 1971
Cassopaia and the Elean colonies. Ancient Greek cities 4. Athens.

Dakaris, S., 1972.
Θεσπρωτία. Αρχαίες Ελληνικές πόλεις. 15. Αθήναι.

Dakaris, S., 1977
Το κάστρο των Ρωγών, *Δωδώνη. Επιστημονική Επετηρίδα Φιλοσοφικής Σχολής Πανεπιστημίου Ιωαννίνων. Τόμος* 6ος, 201-234.

Dakaris, S., 1986
Το Όρραον. Το σπίτι στην αρχαία Ήπειρο, *AE* 1986, 108-146.

Dakaris, S., 1987
Η Ρωμαϊκή πολιτική στην Ήπειρο, in: *Νικόπολις Α' Πρακτικά του Πρώτου Διεθνούς Συμποσίου για τη Νικόπολη, 23-29 Σεπτ. 1984*, 11-21 Πρέβεζα.

Dakaris, S., 1989
Κασσώπη. Νεότερες ανασκαφες 1977-1983. Ιωάννινα.

Dakaris, S., 1993
Δωδώνη. (Οδηγός αρχαιολογικού χώρου). Αθήνα.

Doukellis, P.-Dufaure J.-J.-Fouache, É., 1995
Le contexte géomorphologique et historique de l' Aqueduc de Nicopolis. *BCH* 119 (1995), 209-233.

Douzougli, A. -Zachos, K., 1994
Αρχαιολογικές έρευνες στην Ήπειρο και τη Λευκάδα: 1989-1990, *H.X* 31 (1994), 11-50.

Douzougli, A., 1996.
Η κοιλάδα του Αώου: Αρχαιολογικές μαρτυρίες για την ανθρώπινη δραστηριότητα από την προϊστορική εποχή ως την ύστερη αρχαιότητα, in: *Η επαρχία Κόνιτσας στον χώρο και το χρόνο Α' Επιστημονικό Συμπόσιο*, 11-61. Κόνιτσα.

Douzougli, A., 1998.
Μία ρωμαϊκή αγροικία στις
ακτές του Αμβρακικού κόλπου,
Αρχαιολογία ΙΧ 68. Σεπτ. 1998,
74-78.

Evangelidis, D., 1935
Ανασκαφή Ραδοτοβίου, *ΗΧ*10,
1935, 260-264.

Evangelidis, D., 1952
Η ανασκαφή εις Ροδοτόπι,
Prakt. 1952, 306-325.

Gregory, T., 1987
The early Byzantine fortifications
of Nikopolis in comparative perspective, in: *Νικόπολις Α'. Πρακτικά του Πρώτου Διεθνούς
Συμποσίου για τη Νικόπολη 23-
29 Σεπτ. 1984*, 253-261. Πρέβεζα.

Hammond, N. G. L., 1966
The opening campaigns and the
battle of the Aoi Stena in the Second Macedonian War, *JRS* 1966,
39-54.

Hammond, N. G. L., 1967
*Epirus. The geography, the ancient re-
mains, the history and the topography
of Epirus and adjacent areas.* Oxford.

Hellenkemper, H., 1987.
Die byzantinische Stadtmauer von
Nikopolis in Epeiros. Ein Kaiser-
licher Bauauftrag des 5.oder 6.
Jahrhunderts?, in: *Νικόπολις Α.
Πρακτικά του Πρώτου
Διεθνούς Συμποσίου για τη
Νικόπολη, 23-29 Σεπτ. 1984*,
243-251. Πρέβεζα.

Hoepfner, W., 1987
Nikopolis-Zur Stadtgrundung des
Augustus, in: *Νικόπολις Α.
Πρακτικά του Πρώτου
Διεθνούς Συμποσίου για τη
Νικόπολη, 23-29 Σεπτ. 1984*,
129-133.

Karamesini-Oikonomidou, M.,
1967.
Συμβολή εις την Μελέτην της
Νομισματοκοπίας της
Νικοπόλεως. Περιγραφή δύο
θησαυρών, *ΑΕ* 1967, 91-114.

Karamesini-Oikonomidou, M.,
1971.
Εύρημα Νικοπόλεως, *ΑΕ* 1971,
Chron., 42-51.

Karamesini-Oikonomidou, M.,
1975.
*Η νομισματοκοπία της
Νικοπόλεως.* Αθήναι.

Karatzeni, V., 1999
Ambracia during the Roman era,
in: *L' Illyrie méridionale et l' Épire
dans l' Antiquité-III. Actes du III colloque international de Chantilly (16-
19 Oct. 1996) réunis par P. Cabanes*,
241-247. Paris.

Kirsten, E., 1987
The origins of the first inhabitants
of Nikopolis, in: *Νικόπολις Α.
Πρακτικά του Πρώτου
Διεθνούς Συμποσίου για τη
Νικόπολη, 23-29 Σεπτ. 1984*, 91-
97. Πρέβεζα.

Koder, J., 1982.
Προβλήματα της σλαβικής
εποίκησης και τοπωνυμίας στη
μεσαιωνική Ήπειρο, *ΗΧ*24
(1982), 9-35.

Konstantios, D., 1984
Επιφανειακές και σκαφικές
έρευνες στη ΒΔ Ελλάδα
(Παλαιοχριστιανική περίοδος),
*ΗΧ*26 (1984), 117-145.

Oost, St. I., 1954
*Roman policy in Epirus and Acarnania
in the age of the roman conquest of
Greece.* Dallas.

Pallas, D., 1983
Εύροια-Γλυκή, *Παρνασσός* 25
(1983), 547-566.

Papadopoulou, B., 1996
Η Κόνιτσα και η ευρύτερη
περιοχή της κατά την βυζαντινή
περίοδο in: *Η Επαρχία
Κόνιτσας στο χώρο και το
χρόνο" Α' Επιστημονικό
Συμπόσιο*, 75-85, Κόνιτσα.

Papadopoulou, B., 1997
Η ευρύτερη περιοχή του
Αμβρακικού κόλπου κατά την
Παλαιοχριστιανική περίοδο, in:
*Αφιέρωμα στον N.G.L.
Hammond*, 335-348. Θεσσαλονίκη.

Petropoulos, M., 1991
Η Αιτωλοακαρνανία κατά τη
Ρωμαϊκή περίοδο, in: *Α'
Αρχαιολογικό και Ιστορικό
Συνέδριο Αιτωλοακαρνανίας,
Αγρίνιο Οκτωβρ. 1988*, 93-125.

Purcell, N., 1987
The Nicopolitan Synoecism and
Roman Urban policy, in:
*Νικόπολις Α'. Πρακτικά του
πρώτου διεθνούς Συμποσίου για
τη Νικόπολη, 23-29 Σεπτ. 1984,*
71-90. Πρέβεζα.

Sarikakis, Th., 1964
Συμβολή εις την ιστορίαν της
Ηπείρου κατά τους χρόνους της
ρωμαϊκής κυριαρχίας (167-
31π.Χ.), *Α.Ε.* 1964, 105-119.

Sarikakis, Th., 1966
Συμβολή εις την ιστορίαν της
Ηπείρου κατά τους ρωμαϊκής
χρόνους, *Ελληνικά* 19 (1966),
193-215.

Sarikakis, Th., 1967
Ανέκδοτοι Ελληνικαί και
λατινικαί επιγραφαί της Ακτίας
Νικοπόλεως, *ΑΕ* 1967, 178-186.

Soustal, P., 1981
Bompliana und das "Phidokastron".
Zwei mittelalterliche Festungen in
der Umgebung von Arta (Epirus),
in: *Actes du XVe Congrès International d' Études Byzantines. Athènes Sept.
1976. IIB,* 715-720. Athènes.

Soustal, P.-Koder, J., 1981
Nikopolis und Kephallenia. T.I.B3.
Wien.

Theophylactos, Th., 1984
Παρατηρήσεις για τη Νικόπολη
της Ηπείρου. *10º Διεθνές
Συνέδριο Χριστιανικής
Αρχαιοογίας, Θεσσαλονίκη
1980, Τόμος Β,* 563-574.
Θεσσαλονίκη-Citta del
Vaticano.

Triantafyllopoulos, D., 1984
Η μεσαιωνική Φωτική και η
θέση της στην παλαιά Ήπειρο,
in: *Πρακτικά του 10ου Διεθνούς
Συνεδρίου Χριστιανικής
Αρχαιολογίας, Θεσσαλονίκη
1980, Τόμος Β,* 577-584.
Θεσσαλονίκη-Citta del Vaticano.

Vokotopoulou, I., 1973
Οδηγός Μουσείου Ιωαννίνων,
95 n. 339. Αθήναι.

Wozniak, F., 1984
Late Roman fortifications in
Epirus, *HX* 26 (1984), 71-77.

Wozniak, F., 1987
Nikopolis and the Roman Defense
of Epirus, in: *Νικόπολις Α'.
Πρακτικά του πρώτου διεθνούς
Συμποσίου για τη Νικόπολη, 23-
29 Σεπτ. 1984,* 263-267. Πρέβεζα.

Zachos, K., 1994
Αρχαιολογικές έρευνες στο
Γυμνάσιο της Ακτίας Νικο-
πόλεως, in: *Φηγός. Τιμητικός
τόμος για τον καθηγητή Σωτήρη
Δάκαρη,* 443-453. Ιωάννινα.

Ziolkowski, A., 1986.
The plundering of Epirus in 167
BC. Economic considerations.
PBSR 54 (1986), 69-80.

Die Umwandlung Butrints von einem Koinonzentrum zu einer römischen Kolonie

Neritan Ceka

Ich muss Ihnen schon am Anfang erklären, dass noch keine unmittelbare Beziehung zwischen Nikopolis und Butrint bewiesen ist und dass mein Vortrag als Ziel die Darstellung eines "Parallellebens" hat, ein anderes Beispiel für die Veränderungsprozesse, die in der städtischen Struktur des Epirus in den Anfängen des Prinzipats des Augustus in den letzten dreissig Jahren des 1. Jahrhunderts v. Chr. stattfanden. Butrint (*Bouthroton, Butrintum)* ist eins der malerischten und best bewahrten Zentren der Antike Albaniens, eine Art kleines Pompei, welches der Zerstörung durch die menschliche Hand, viel katastrophaler als die der Vulkane, entkommen ist, aufgrund seiner isolierten Lage und der Entfernung von den Stadtzentren des 20. Jahrhunderts. Es ist diese besondere Lage gewesen, hauptsächlich verbunden mit dem Pelodes-See und mit dem relativ kleinen Tal von Vrina, aber beiseite gelassen von den grossen Bewegungen, die von Korkyra ausgesaugt wurden, welche Butrint zu cinem sehr wenig bekannten Zentrum der antiken Zeit machte, falls wir hier den Briefwechsel zwischen Cicero und Pomponius Attikus bezüglich des Einbaus einer Kolonie für Caesar-Veteranen auf dem Lande der Butroter als Quelle benutzen. Was Butrint darstellte bevor er die Aufmerksamkeit der römischen Kolonisten auf sich zog, können nur die archäologischen Daten aufklären, weil die vorrömische Geschichte der Stadt sich in den Legenden über ihre troianische Herkunft zusammenfasst, erzählt durch Dionysos von Halikarnassos und Virgil, als auch durch die Erwähnung des Namens in Hekatäus "Europa", Stephan von Byzanz nach.

Die durch eine italienische Expedition vor und während des 2. Weltkriegs, als auch durch eine albanisch-griechische Expedition im letzten Jahrzehnt in der Akropolis von Butrint durchgeführten archäologischen Grabungen haben bewiesen, dass die Legenden über die troianische Herkunft Butrints keine Grundlagen haben. Das Butrint des mykenischen und geometrischen Zeitraums zeigt sich als ein gewöhnliches Dorf einheimischer Fischer, zu denen die Leistungen der damaligen

Plan von Butrint und Umgebungen (Ceka 1999).

griechischen Welt noch nicht angekommen waren. Erst in der zweiten Hälfte des 7.Jh. v.Chr.bildete sich ein urbanisiertes Zentrum, welches sich innerhalb einer Befestigung ca.0,7 Hektar ausbreitete, gebaut mit einer relativ primitiven Technik, aber mit einem Plan in Einklang mit den poliorketischen Kenntnissen der Zeit. Das Verschwinden der handgearbeiteten lokalen Keramik und die Vielfältigkeit der spätkorinthischen Keramik zeugen von einer hellenischen Gründung. Diese Annahme wird bestärkt durch die Tätigkeit eines archaischen Heiligtums, welches im höchsten Teil des Hügels durch den Fund von frühkorinthischen Fragmenten mit Graffiti lokalisiert wird. Es ist sehr möglich, dass von diesem Heiligtum auch das archaische Relief mit der Darstellung des einen Stierkopf fressenden Löwen seine Herkunft hat, welches als Architrav in einem späten Wiederaufbau eines der Tore der antiken Stadt benutzt ist.

Die Anwesenheit der Keramik aus Kerkyra in beträchtlichem Masse in den archaischen Schichten Butrints zeigen, dass die Bauer der Akropolis von Butrint von der Insel gegenüber gekommen sind und somit ein Emporion in der Gegend der barbarischen Chaonen begründet haben. In den folgenden zwei Jahrhunderten veränderte Butrint weder seine Grösse noch seinen Charakter. Erst in der 2.Hälfte des 5.Jh.v.Chr. wurde die Befestigungsmauer der Akropolis mit einer polygonalen Technik wiedergebaut.

In derselben Zeit und mit derselben Technik wurde auch eine Festung auf dem Kalivo-Hügel gebaut, welcher trotz seiner beträchtlichen Oberfläche von 18 ha. nie bewohnt wurde; sie scheint für eine kurze Zeit als eine militärische Stütze für Butrint gedient zu haben gegen eine Gefahr, die vom Lande kam. Dies wird auch durch die Tatsache unterstützt, dass Kalivo nur von der Bodenseite befestigt war, während die Seeseite offenblieb. Butrints Verteidigung wurde danach mit dem Bau der Dema-Mauer verstärkt, welche, indem sie von der Küste quer zum Ufer der See lief, die ganze Ksamil-Halbinsel durchtrennte, weil Butrint und die Umgebung gleichzeitig der Peireia von Kerkyra zugehörte.

Das Schaffen eines solchen Verteidigungssystems lässt sich erklären durch den Druck der Ereignisse in Zusammenhang mit dem Peloponnesischen Krieg auf dem Festland gegenüber von Korkyra. Thukydides (I, 46 und 47; II, 68) erzählt, dass im Jahre 431 v.Chr. während deren Feldzug gegen Korkyra die Korinther ihr Lager auf dem Kap von Himera, zwischen den Flüssen Acheron und Thyamis aufschlugen, also nicht so weit von Butrint entfernt. Mit den Korinthern und deren Verbündeten, den Ambrakern, waren auch die Chaonen,und es gibt keinen Zweifel, dass Butrint ein Angriffsziel im Theater der Kämpfe ausmachte, die in den folgenden Jahren andauerten. Thukydides informiert uns auch darüber, dass anders als die Molosen, die durch Könige beherrscht wurden,die Chaonen *abasileutoi* waren und durch zwei jährlich aus den bedeutendsten Familien gewählten Prostaten regiert wurden. Die Rolle dieser Familien durchläuft die ganze vorrömische Geschichte Chaoniens und es scheint, dass deren frühe Form als politische Einheiten durch Pseudo-Skylax mit dem Begriff *kata komas* ausgedrückt worden ist. Von nun an wird nicht von Dörfern geredet, das bestätigt eine ganze Kette von Städten die Ende des 5. und während der 1.Hälfte des 4.Jhs. entstanden waren, eine Zeit, die in seinem *Periplus* widerspiegelt wird.

Das Butrint des Anfangs des 4.Jhs vertritt, insofern es die Befestigungen betrifft, einen Bau *ex novo*. Die innerhalb der Mauern erfasste Fläche war verfünffacht, und das alte Siedlung war in der Form einer Akropolis geblieben. Die grosse Zahl der Eingänge, mindestens fünf, deutet auf eine dichte Bevölkerung. Drei davon waren auf die Seeseite des Sees gestellt,wo der Haffen gewesen zu sein scheint. Das interessanteste Auftreten war das Existenz einer gesellschaftlichen Zone auf der südwestlichen Seite, wo sich eine heilige Quelle befand, eine Tatsache, die für einen städtischen Charakter spricht. Diese Zone wurde durch ein *diateichisma* vom andern Teil der Stadt getrennt und kommunizierte mit ihr durch einen Eingang, während ein zweiter Eingang gegenüber der Quelle ihn mit einem zweiten möglichen Hafen am Rande von Vivar verband. Die Bautechnik, mit dem trapeizodal-poygonalen Mauerwerk und der häufigen Verwendung von eckigen Wänden und Bastionen anstatt der Türme, ist dieselbe wie diejenige der inneren chaonischen Zentren wie Phoinike und Çuka Aitojt. Als Folge war das Butrint des 4.Jhs. von Kerkyra getrennt worden und gehörte zu Chaonien. In der Abwesenheit der historischen Daten helfen uns die archäologischen Daten auch um eine Vorstellung davon zu bilden, was das vorrömische Butrint von der Hälfte des 3.Jhs. v.Chr. an darstellte. Während der 2.Hälfte dieses Jahrhunderts würde anfangs ein an Asklepios gewidmetes Prostil-Tempel in der Nähe der heiligen Quelle gebaut, sowie eine einstöckige Stoa, welche dem Beherbergen der Pilger diente. Ein Teil dieser Stoa wird zerstört, um an der Seite des Tempels ein Theater mit ca.700 Plätzen zu bauen, ein Modelle, das demjenigen von Dodona nahekommt (die Cavea mit einem fast viereckigen Plan durch Stutzpfeiler verstärkte Seitenmauern und Analemmata in einer fast geraden Linie).

Zur selben architektonischen Formulierung der Agora gehörte auch ein viereckiges Monument mit einem Peristyl-Hof, eine Monumentalstrasse, so wie auch ein Heiligtum neben einer zweiten Quelle südlich der Stoa gebaut. Architektonische Elemente, die während der Grabungen in den römischen Monumenten gefunden wurden, bezeugen, dass die Agora sich Richtung Süden durch eine in der zweiten Hälfte des 3.Jhs.v.Chr. gebaute Erweiterung erstreckte. Gleichzeitig ist auch eine Erweiterung der Befestigungen durchgeführt worden, in welcher ein in der alten Linie der Mauer einbezogenes Tor mit zwei Türmen auffällt.

Die Ursachen, die eine Verstärkung der Befestigungen angeregt haben, können mit dem Angriff der Illyrer gegen Chaonien und dessen Hauptstadt Phoinike im Jahre 230 v. Chr. zusammenhängen, ein Ereignis, das von dem ersten Auftauchen der Römer in Chaonien gefolgt wird. Dank der Entdeckung von zwei grossen epigraphischen Komplexen, dem ersten in dem Analemma des westlichen Parodos des Theaters und dem anderen in einem mit Spolien gebauten öffentlichen Monument des 2. bis 1.Jhs.v.Chr., erkennen wir in genügendem Masse den politischen Status von Butrint in diesem Zeitraum. Die zwei frühesten Inschriften, datiert in den letzten dreissig Jahren des 3.Jhs.v. Chr., zeigen noch die Abhängigkeitslage Butrints durch das Epirotische Koinon mit Phoinike als Zentrum, weil in denjenigen der Prostat der Chaonen als Eponymos bewertet wird. Der andere Teil der Inschriften widerspiegelt eine statische Lage, die ca.40 Jahre dauerte, nach der Auflösung des Epirotischen Koinon im Jahre 170 v.Chr., oder genauer nach dem Jahr 157, auf welcher Zeit die früheste Inschrift dieser Gruppe datiert wird. Dies war die Zeit, in der die Römer Epirus unterwarfen, indem sie Molosien und Atintanien zerstörten, also die ganzen Gegenden im Osten Chaoniens. Selbst Chaonien, die seine prorömische Stellung gehalten hatte, wurde zwar durch die römische Wut nicht berührt, bewahrte aber auch nicht ihre Selbständigkeit. Dessen Zentralteil wurde als *to koinon ton Epiroton ton peri Phoiniken* erkannt, und hatte als Ausdehnung die heutige Vurgu-Ebene und natürlich den Hafen von Onkesmos (Saranda). Butrint wird als das Zentrum einer anderen autonomen Einheit anerkannt, und in den Inschriften als *koinon ton Prasaibon* eingeschätzt. Seine politische Struktur war fast eine treue Kopie des Epirotischen Koinons, als Folge der Kontinuität der aus der Zeit der Abhängigkeit von der koinonischen Struktur vererbten Organe. Die Eklesia vertrat das höchste Organ und, zusammen mit dem Bule als gesetzgebendem Körper, drückte sie auch die Souveraenität der Prasaiben aus, indem sie solche Rechte wie die Proxenia oder Ateleia zuteilte. Ein dritter gesetzgebender Körper, die Synarkontes, machte eine Art Senat aus, in dem die administrativen Einheiten des Koinon vertreten waren. In den ausführenden Ämtern des eponymischen

Magistrats befindet sich der Stratege, gefolgt von seinem Prostat, nach dem bekannten epirotischen Model. Es ergibt sich aus den Inschriften, dass es fast eine Übungsregel in der Diarkie dieser Funktionen war, einer Tradition nach, der man schon in dem Chaonien des 5.Jhs.v. Chr. begegnet. Eine andere Funktion, mit grossem Ansehen, war der Priester von Asklepios,mit dessen Kult das Hauptheiligtum von Butrint verbunden war.

Das Koinon der Prasaiben hatte eine begrenzte Ausdehnung, die ausser der Ksamil-Halbinsel und der Umgebung vom Pelodes-See auch die Vrina-Ebene mit einem städtischen Zentrum bei Çuka Ajtoit umfasste. Dessen Namen kennen wir noch nicht, aber es ist sehr möglich, dass er sich hinter einem der vierzig Ethnikonen versteckt, welche die verschiedenen Magistraten in den ca.150 Inschriften des Koinon der Prasaiben begleiten. Eine so grosse Zahl von Ethnikonen auf einem relativ begrenzten Gebiet bezeugt, dass sie mehr als die Demoi die Familien mit bürgerlichen Rechten vertraten, die von anderen Regionen des Epiros gekommenen auch miteinbezogen, die aber das Recht der Politeia gewonnen hatten.

Die Erhaltung der alten politischen Strukturen, indem man sie in die provinziale Verwaltung integrierte, war eine Praktik, die funktionierte, insofern das auf der regionalen Autarchie beruhende wirtschaftliche Modelle bewahrt wurde. Um die Mitte des 1.Jhs.v. Chr. gab es deutliche Zeichen, dass dieses Modelle der "goldenen Zeiten" im Rahmen einer gewissen Globalisierung der Wirtschaft des römischen Reiches und der Expansion der römischen Grossbesitzer nicht mehr funktionieren konnte. Das Beispiel von L.Calpurnius Piso, Prokonsul Mazedoniens zwischen 57-55 v.Chr., der von Cicero unter anderem auch wegen der Zerstörung von Epirus angeklagt wurde, bezeugt, dass die Funktion solcher Organismen wie die der Prasaiben hauptsächlich der Erleichterung der Steuereinnahmen durch die provinziale Verwaltung diente und nicht einer liberalen Politik des Senats. Diese führte gleichzeitig auch zum Mechanismus der

Zerstörung der autarchischen Wirtschaft, welche gegen die Plünderung und den Missbrauch der hohen römischen Beamten empfindlicher war. Cicero stellt sich diesem dramatischen Prozess entgegen mit derselben Überzeugung, mit der er die republikanischen Institutionen verteidigt, indem er die römischen Unternehmer als "schlechte" und "gute" behandelt. Cicero beweist uns, dass seit Zeiten in dieser Art archaischer Wirtschaft auch "römische Buerger, die in diesen Gegenden Handel treiben "integriert" waren, aber auch Besitzer wie Pomponius Atticus, der um das Jahr 68 v.Chr bei Butrint Land gekauft hatte. Ein Teil dieser römischen Geschäftsmänner hatten als Ziel ihrer Tätigkeit genau die Übernahme der Steuern von den alten Gemeinschaften koinonischen Typus. Das Koinon der Prasaiben stellt sich als ein Opfer dieser Praktik dar, da es als Kreditgeber für dessen fischalischen Verpflichtungen Caesar hatte, und er suchte, durch die Beschlagnahme der Länder der Butroter und die Unterbringung der Veteranen, auf diesen ausgeglichen zu werden. Die Angelegenheit der Butroter, die bei Atticus und Cicero mächtige Verteidiger findet, wird nur formal als eine Angelegenheit des Geschäfts gelöst, bei der nur wenig Zeit vor dem Mord Caesars Atticus den Kauf der Schulden der Butroter übernimmt. In der Tat wurde diese Vereinbarung nicht verwirklicht und um die Hälfte des Jahres 44 trotz des Widerstandes der Butroter hat es eine erste Installation der Veteranen gegeben, wie die *Colonia Iulia Buthrotum*. Dies hat Butrint die Möglichkeit gegeben, am Ende des Jahres 44 die Rolle einer militärischen Basis zu spielen, als Gaius Antonius mit den ihm treugebliebenen Truppen hier beherbergt wurde.

Ebenso bot Butrint eine sichere Stütze auf dem Wege Octavians von den Akrokeraunen,wo er im Frühling des Jahres 31 landete, nach Aktium. Die Kolonisten stellten sich auf die Seite Oktavians und bauten die Befestigungen in dem meist beschädigten Teil der unteren Stadt wieder auf, indem sie Steine der Agora der Prasaiben verwendeten.Ein Turm, wo auch 105 Inschriften als Spolien verwendet worden

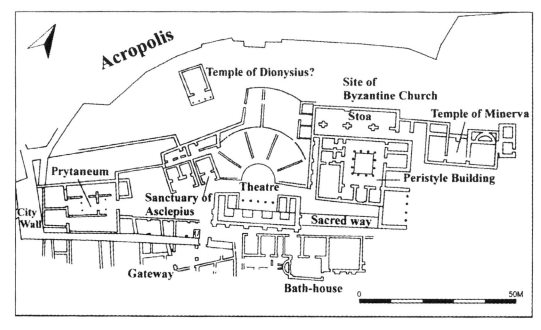

waren, die bis zur ersten Hälfte des 1.Jhs.v.Chr. hinaufreichen, hängt sicherlich mit diesem Ereignis zusammen. Gleich nach dem Sieg in Aktium sendet Oktavian eine zweite Kolonistengruppe nach Butrint. Mit diesem Ereignis hängt die Bewertung Butrints als auch die Wahl L. Domitius Ahenobarbus, des Adoptivonkels des Augustus, zum *patronus coloniae* zusammen. Schon mit der ersten Unterbringung der Kolonisten löste sich das Koinon der Prasaiben auf, und an die Stelle der traditionellen Institutionen traten die kolonialen. Die prasaibische Stadt bei Çuka Ajtojt wurde verlassen, während die befestigte Villa der einheimischen Besitzer bei Malathre durch die neuen Besitzer in eine gewöhnliche Farm verwandelt wurde. Die römische Stadt von Butrint breitete sich auf die südöstliche Seite aus, wo sich der Hafen seit der Bauzeit des Tores mit Türmen im 2.Jh.v.Chr.befand. Es war diese Seite, die kurz vor der Schlacht von Aktium mit aus den prasaibischen Monumenten genommenen Materialien gebaut wurde. Durch die zweite Ansiedlung der Kolonisten bekam Butrint stufenweise die Aussehen einer römischen Stadt. In der Zeit von August wurde die Wasserleitung gebaut, die über eine Brücke den Kanal von Vivari überspannte, sodass die Möglichkeit der Entstehung eines neuen

Wohnbezirks jenseits dieses Kanals bestand. Temenos erfährt die erste Veränderung durch den Wiederaufbau des Prytaneion in der Technik *opus reticulatum*. Eine vor dem Eingang ins Gebäude montierte Inschrift mit grossen bronzenen Buchstaben bezeugt, dass da die koloniale Verwaltung untergebracht wurde. Trotzdem wurde der heilige Komplex um den Tempel von Asklep in der Originalkomposition bis zum Zeitabschnitt der Antoninen bewahrt. Das Theater wurde bewahrt und nicht für Gladiatorenkämpfe adoptiert. Die wichtigsten Bauten wurden in der alten Agora aufgeführt, woher auch die lateinischen Inschriften der frühen Kaiserzeit stammen, wie z.B. die an L. Domitius Ahenobarbus, oder an Germanikus gewidmete Inschrift. In diesem frühen Zeitabschnitt prägte Butrint auch die Kolonialmünzen, auf denen wir ebenfalls den von Augustus gebauten Aquädukt finden.

Die archäologischen Daten bezeugen, dass die Ansiedlung der römischen Kolonisten in Butrint und im Gebiet der Prasaiben von keiner vollständigen Aussiedlung der Einheimischen und der Auslöschung der kulturellen Tradition gefolgt wurde. Eine Inschrift auf griechisch aus Ende des 1.Jhs. n. Chr. den Nymphen gewidmet, spricht für die Aufbewahrung dieser Tradition.

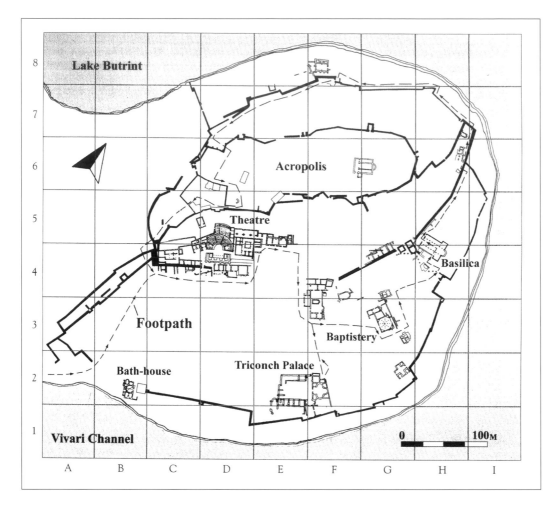

Plan von Butrint (Ceka 1999).

Während des 2.Jhs.n.Chr. erfuhr Butrint einen intensiven Fortschritt, wie es die in der öffentlichen Zone gebauten Monumente bezeugen. In der Zeit von Hadrian wurde auf gründliche Weise das Theater wiedergebaut, dem ein Gebäude mit Peristyl hinzugefügt wurde. Das Tempel von Asklepios wurde neu gebaut, während in Richtung der Agora eine Reihe von Gebäuden öffentlichen Charakters errichtet wurden. Es scheint, dass auch der Strassenbau, der von Butrint nach Nikopolis führt, dieser Zeit zugehört. Es ist genau dieser Zeitabschnitt, noch wenig studiert wie in Butrint, so auch in Nikopolis, der die Möglichkeit eines Parallelstudiums auf dem Gebiet der Architektur, aber auch auf den anderen von der Archäologie bezeugten Feldern anbietet.

Literaturverzeichnis

Ugolini, L. M., 1942
L'Albania Antica. L'Acropoli di Butrinto. Roma.

Cabanes, P., 1974
Les inscriptions du théâtre de Butrôtos, *Annales litteraires de l'Université de Besançon,* 105-209.

Ceka, N., 1976
Fortifikimi antik i Butrintit dhe i territorit te prasaibeve, *Monumentet* 12, 27-48. Tirana.

Bace, A., 1980
Banjat e shekujve te pare te eres sone, *Monumentet,* 19, 51-87. Tirana.

Drini, F., 1984
Sur la chronologie et les frontiéres du koinon des Prasaiboi à la lumière des nouvelles donnés, *Iliria* 2, 101-108. Tirana.

Cabanes, P., 1985
Le koinon des Prasaiboi: institutions et societé d'après les inscriptions de Bouthrôtos, *Symposion in Santander 1-4 Septembre 1982,* 147-183. Valenzia.

Freis, H., 1985
Zwei Lateinische Inschriften aus Albanien, *ZPE,* 61, 224-228.

Cabanes, P., 1986
Nouvelles inscriptions d'Albanie (Bouthrotos et Apollonie), *ZPE,* 63, 137-155.

Deniaux, E., 1987
Atticus et l'Epire. *L'Illyrie méridional et l'Épire dans l'Antiquité,* 1, 245-254, Clermont-Ferrand.

Deniaux, E., 1988
Cicéron et la protection des cités de l'Illyrie du Sud et de l'Epire, *Iliria,* 2, 143-164, Tirana.

Deniaux, E., 1990
Cicéron et les hommes d'affaire romains d'Illyrie et d'Épire. *L'Illyrie méridionale et l'Épire dans l'Antiquité,* 2, 263-270, Clermont-Ferrand.

Budina, D., 1988
Butrinti pararomak, *Butrinti,* 6-114, Tirana.

Pollo, G., 1988.
Fillimet e kolonise romake ne Butrint, *Butrinti,* 157-178, Tirana.

Pollo, G., 1989
Colonia Buthrotum: themelues dhe patrone ne kohen e Augustit, *Iliria,* 2, 125-132. Tirana.

Pollo, G., 1990
Quelques aspects de la numismatique coloniale de Buthrote. *L'Illyrie du Sud et l'Épire dans l'Antiquité,* 2, 257-261, Clermont-Ferrand.

Ceka, N., 1999
Butrint. A Guide to the City and its Monuments. The Butrint Foundation, London.

Acheloos´ Homeland.

New Historical–Archaeological Research on the Ancient Polis Stratos*

In memoriam Friedrich Sauerwein († 5th Oct. 1997)

Peter Funke

The northwestern Greek regions Aitolia and Akarnania are among the least studied areas, archeologically and historically, in Greece. Only recently have these areas which in antiquity too (at least up until Hellenistic time) lay in the lee of historical events, found attention in scholarly study of the ancient past.[2] This circumstance is due not least to the fact that the western parts of central Greece, until only a few years ago, lay outside of all important transportation networks, and were opened to modern vehicular traffic only with great difficulty.

It is for this reason also that only a few of the explorers and topographers who travelled Greece in every direction in the past centuries reached this area,[3] even though it abounds in ancient monumental remains. The most important archaeological-historical survey of this area remains that of the English traveler William Martin Leake who, at the beginning of the 19th century, made an extraordinarily precise and still essential inventory of the most important find spots.[4] A few decades later the French scholar Léon Heuzey travelled the region and published his studies on Akarnania. Together with Leake´s works, and those of a few other scholars such as Henri Bazin, Eugen Oberhummer and William Woodhouse, these laid the foundation for all further investigations.[5]

At the end of the 19th century the German Archaeological Institute (DAI) commissioned the archaeologist Friedrich Noack to take a complete archaeological und topographical inventory of all ancient sites and fortifications in Northwestern Greece. In an extraordinarily short time he drew up extensive maps and plans. But he was able to publish his results only in two preliminary reports.[6]

More than twenty years ago now, Lazaros Kolonas, the director of the 6th Ephorate of Prehistoric and Classical Antiquities, which is responsible for this area, beginning with Noack´s results, initiated a research programme which aimed at a systematic recording of all ancient urban sites of Akarnania and Aitolia. It was his inten-

Fig. 1. Ancient cities in Akarnania (E.-L. Schwandner).

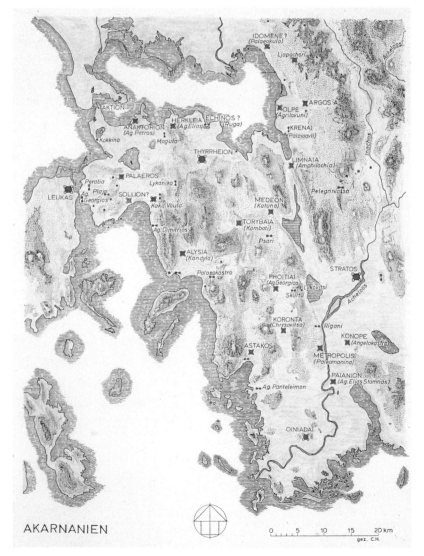

189

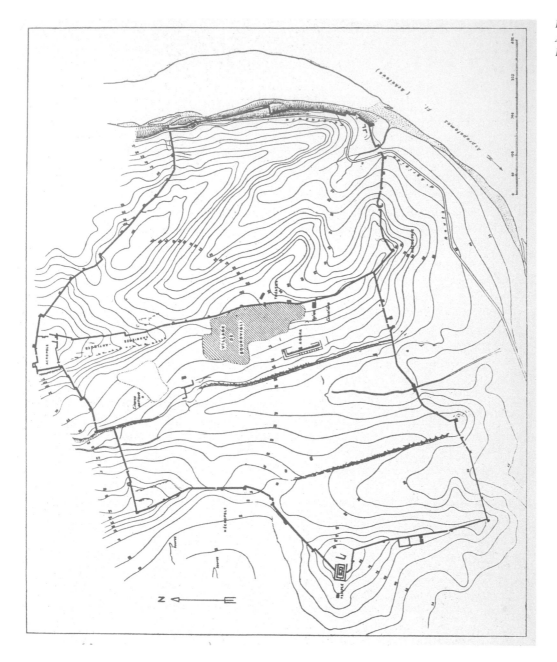

Fig. 2. Stratos. Plan of the Ancient city (Courby & Picard 1924, fig. 58).

tion to get a clearer picture of the history of human settlement and a better insight into the historical development of this area. Such a recording is all the more urgently needed as the archaeological remains are irrevocably destroyed by the building of new roads and reservoirs, as well as by intensive agricultural exploitation and a growing urban development of the area.

On the map (Fig. 1) the most important ancient sites in Akarnania known today are marked. They are among the best preserved in all of Greece. To the present

day none of these sites has been completely explored; often Noack's plans[7] are still the only working basis. During the last decade, archaeological research has concentrated on the ancient harbour city, Oiniadai,[8] and the city of Stratos. Investigations in the West-Akarnanian peninsula Plagia[9] with the ancient city Palairos in its centre are to follow in the coming years.

The research work in and around Stratos will be the main topic of what follows here. At the end of the eighties Lazaros Kolonas had decided to start a systematic

Fig. 3. Stratos. Temple of Zeus.

excavation of this important ancient city which was the centre of the Akarnanian League until Stratos was integrated into the Aitolian League in the middle of the 3rd century. The construction of a new dam immediately east of the ancient city wall of Stratos, which turned the Acheloos to a gigantic lake of more than 6 kilometres in lenght, brought about momentous changes in the whole landscape that made a rescue excavation indispensable. And so the research work in Stratos, that had been started in 1892 and continued between 1910 and 1921 (with some interruptions due to the war) by French archaeologists, was taken up again in some parts of the ancient city.[10] The new excavations were carried out by the 6th Ephorate of Prehistoric and Classical Antiquities in cooperation with Ernst-Ludwig Schwandner, the director of the Department of Architecture of the German Archaeological Institute (DAI).

In 1990 the plan was developed to investigate the entire territory of ancient Stratos, the so-called Stratiké, by a systematic field survey at the same time as and in close relationship with the excavations. I undertook this task together with Hans-Joachim Gehrke, my collegue from Freiburg, in a Greek-German *synergasia*. Constant cooperation with collegues from the fields of archaeology and architectural history (Lazaros Kolonas, Franziska Lang, Ernst-Ludwig Schwandner), geography (Friedrich Sauerwein (†)), palynology (Eberhard Grüger) and geophysics (Norbert Blindow) offered us a singular opportunity to draw a more accurate picture of the history of human settlement in a Greek area that up to now has hardly been known. The period of Greco-Roman antiquity was the focus of our interest, but we also looked at previous eras as well as post-antique times through the present. The following overview, however,

tions in this area, however, could only be carried out after the inhabitants of the old village had been resettled. After a promising trial excavation in 1991 the whole theatre area was excavated during the following years. Under a layer of earth, in some places more than 4 metres thick, generally very well preserved remains of an orchestra, of a stage-building, flanked by two ramps and of the cavea with a complete prohedria were found (Fig. 5). The theatre shows three construction phases: the first belongs still to the last third of the 4th century, the other two to the 3rd century BC. After the final publication of the excavation results, the exact determination of the chronological sequence of the reconstructions, especially of the stage-building will offer important information about the development of the Greek theatre and also about staging practices in early Hellenistic times.

After this short outline of the recent excavations within the ancient municipal area, some preliminary results of the field research that was carried out simultaneous to these excavations in the Stratiké, the territory of the polis Stratos outside its city walls, will now be presented. The close cooperation with the excavators was an extremely important prerequisite for a successful survey. Only by a constant comparison with the finds of the excavation within the city was it possible to classify the surface finds of the survey in a chronological pattern, and thus draw conclusions as to the date of these finds. The data of the excavation in the city provided the missing stratigraphy for the surface survey.

The determination of the survey area was based on the geographical and geomorphological conditions of the landscape, which probably had defined the territory of the polis Stratos already in antiquity. The river-bed of the Acheloos und the lake Ozeros formed the natural limits to the East and the South, whereas in the North and the West the watersheds and passes of the southern and, respectively, eastern foothills of the Pindos mountains

and the Akarnanian mountains delimited the survey region, which covered a total area of about 100 square kilometers.[21]

In order to eliminate all random results the so-called method of a intensive "Raster-survey" was used to prospect the area. Not only were single selected zones investigated, but the whole surface of the survey area was inspected by small groups, usually 3 – 4 of "walkers" under the direction of a leader responsible for organisation and documentation. Franziska Lang has described the methods of the recording and evaluation of the data in detail in her contribution so that a closer description can be dispensed with here.[22] A total of 215 find spots and more than 40.000 significant single finds (mainly tiles and pottery) have been collected and documented. The chronological range extends from late neolithic age to the Ottoman era. More than half of the discovery places (133) date from the Classical and Hellenistic as well as the Roman periods. Another focal point is the middle Byzantine period with 65 find spots.[23]

There are rather few and disparate prehistoric finds. They start with the late Neolithic/early Helladic age, increase somewhat during middle Helladic times and decline significantly in the late Helladic period. Within the boundaries of Spathari 4 kilometers east of Stratos a high density of very early finds could be observed. The excavations that were started by the Ephorate as a result of these finds discovered the foundations of houses of a middle Helladic settlement. In late Geometric times these were covered by a sanctuary. The continuity of this cult can be demonstrated up until the Roman period (see below). In the Geometric and Archaic periods the number of find spots increases constantly. The densest settlement of the Stratiké dates, however, from Classical and Hellenistic times. During these periods, many small settlements and a great number of single farms existed outside the fortified city especially in the western part of the polis territory. Moreover many remains of dwellings could be found west of

Fig. 5. Stratos. Theatre.

the city obviously belonging to a kind of suburb immediately adjacent to the city walls. North and south of these suburbs extended large necropoleis from Classical and Hellenistic times. The spatial extent of the southern necropolis, which is largely covered by the present village, and of the western necropolis, could largely be settled. Especially remarkable is the discovery of a hitherto unknown necropolis north of the city where there were not only graves with stone slabs and sarcophagi, many of which can be found in the other necropoleis as well, but also grave-terraces, as those above all else, are typical for Attica. There are also many examples of grave steles in a form typical for Western Greece, which can be assigned to these grave-terraces now. Up until now we had only little knowledge of their positioning.

In Roman times the great plain southwest of Stratos developed apparently into the preferred settlement area. In the present state of excavations, it is impossible to decide whether the area within the ancient city walls of Stratos was settled in Roman times as well.[24] At any rate, the center of the settlement seems to have shifted to an unfortified place with a bath complex west of the modern village of Ochthia (about 3 kilometres southwest of Stratos). Although the number of finds from Roman times is considerably smaller in comparison to previous periods, it shows that the habitation of the region in the Roman era was greater than presumed. Since even finds from early Imperial times were discovered, the continuity of habitation apparently was not completely disrupted by the founding of Nikopolis and the Roman colony at Patras. A clearly visible decline in this area must be noted for the first phase, when the Roman Empire established its power, but in Imperial times settlement activities – at least outside the old city of Stratos – revived considerably.

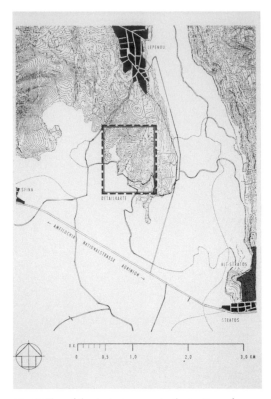

Fig. 6. Plan of the Ancient quarry in the territory of Stratos.

I wish also to mention some especially important ancient finds separately. About 4 kilometers northwest of Stratos and one kilometre south of the village of Lepenou in an impassable area a quarry was discovered that had been used in Classical and Hellenistic times. Its high-quality shining white limestone was used especially for the construction of public buildings in the city (Fig. 6). Some of the many raw capital, column and architrave components, that lie strewn across the site, were designed for the temple of Zeus in Stratos and other buildings. Previously, it had been common opinion that the stone material for representative buildings in the city had to be transported from the Akarnanian coast more than 50 kilometres away. Now, it has been proved that the quarries were located in the immediate neighbourhood of the city.

Within the boundaries of Spathari at the southern verge of this quarry area on a hill above the plain of Stratos a significant concentration of ancient pottery and tiles

of different periods and traces of settlement could already be observed during the first survey campaign in 1991. When the documentation of the find spot started in autumn 1993 with a cleaning of the surface, the foundations of a 17 x 11,5 meter rectangular building were discovered immediately under the sward. On the north side, parts of the wall with the orthostates were even preserved on which, originally, a wall of sun-dried mud bricks had stood. The Ephorate began immediately upon excavations which are still continuing. The building proved to be an oikos temple or temple in antis that had already been constructed in the middle of

Fig. 7. Spathari. Temple (photo taken from balloon).

196

Fig. 8. Spathari. Temple (N and W sides).

the 6th century BC and lasted up to the 1st / 2nd century AD (Figs. 7, 8 and 10).[25] In a collapse layer not only the greater part of the roof from late Hellenistic times (2nd / 1st century BC) was found, but also many structural components of a roof from Archaic times (about 550/40 B.C.) with, in parts, still well preserved painting. The examination of the Archaic roof construction (Fig. 9) carried out by Ernst-Ludwig Schwandner and Jörg Denkinger led to the conclusion that this is to now the "wohl früheste Kombination von Traufsima und Anthemien-Antefixabschluss der Kalyptere ('Reiterantefixe') für das griechische Mutterland".[26] The origins of the temple, however, reach back far beyond Archaic times. Northeast of the temple foundations of a house of a middle Helladic settlement were found; south of the temenos wall, the foundations of an apsidal building from late the Geometric or early Archaic period were discovered. Its function has not been definitely clarified up but it might be a sort of hestiato-

rion, according to the interpretation of the excavators.

In the plain east of Spathari and about 3,5 kilometers northwest of Stratos, a second hitherto unknown sanctuary has been discovered. An examination of a recently ploughed field led to the recovery of hundreds of terracotta fragments, mostly of female statuettes dating from the late Archaic to the late Classical period (Fig. 11).[27] In the ensuing rescue excavation the Ephorate uncovered the remains of a sacrificial pit (*bothros*) of stone construction that, apart from remains of coal and ashes, contained a large number of further votive statuettes. Corinthian and Lakonian roof tile fragments of superior quality, as well as two large well hewn limestone blocks on the edge of the field that obviously served as threshold of an ancient house, gave eloquent testimony of larger buildings that must have belonged to this sanctuary. In spite of intensive archaeological and geophysical investigations, a corresponding

197

Fig. 9. Spathari. Roof of temple (reconstruction of the Archaic eaves, drawing by E.-L. Schwandner).

Fig. 11. Stratiké. Votive statuettes.

site could not be discovered. Probably the buildings we were looking for are located at a site where recently a small farm house with stables had been erected.

This preliminary overview of the most recent archaeological and historical-geographical research in the ancient city of Stratos and the surrounding territory of the Stratiké ought only to give a first impression of the aims, methods and results of this joint Greek-German research project. An extensive and complete evaluation is left to the final publications, which are now in process, of the survey and the excavations.[28]

STRATIKE - SPATHARI
STEINPLAN — M.1:100

(rot = Tempel; gelb = Hausmauern)

Notes

NOTE 1*
The following text is based on a paper that I read at the symposium and on the final report that I wrote together with K. Freitag (Münster) and F. Lang (Rostock) for the German Research Community (DFG) which sponsored this research project on a large scale. Since the field work was finished only in 1998 and the archaeological excavations are still going on, only a very general summary of the first preliminary results can be offered here. The final presentation of the results will be published by Franziska Lang in an extensive evaluation of all data. For the time being I refer to the preliminary reports by L. Kolonas in *AD* 46, 1991 (1991), 163; 47, 1992 (1997), 147f.; 48, 1993 (1998), 140f; 49, 1994 (1999), 242 and E.-L. Schwandner in *AA* 1992, 66f.; 1993, 677ff.; 1994, 605ff.; 1995, 783ff.; 1996, 555ff.; 1997, 509f. My special thanks go to L. Kolonas, the director of the 6th Ephorate of Prehistoric an Classical Antiquities, who supported the examination of the polis territory of ancient Stratos from the beginning. Without his help this joint Greek-German research project would never have been realized; he allowed me to report also about the Greek excavations in the city area. I would also like to thank H.-J.Gehrke (Freiburg), F. Lang (Rostock), E.-L. Schwandner and F. Sauerwein (†) (Heidelberg), who directed the field work in cooperation with me, and all the co-workers whose untiring labour was essential for the success of the survey campaigns. E.-L. Schwandner made fig. 1, 4, 6, 7, 9, 10, 11 and L. Kolonas fig. 3 and 5 available.

NOTE 2
Only during the last ten years has the research work on the ancient history of this area been intensified; cf. (with further literature) Bommeljé et al 1987; Antonetti 1990; Pritchett 1991, passim; Pritchett 1992, passim; Pritchett 1994a; Gehrke 1995; Freitag 1996; Strauch 1996; Funke 1997; Beck 1997, esp. 31-54; Dietz et al. 1998; Corsten 1999, esp. 94-159; Grainger 1999; Dany 1999; Wacker 1999; Scholten 2000.

NOTE 3
Cf. Dietz et al. 1998, 244-252.

NOTE 4
Leake 1835.

NOTE 5
Heuzey 1860; Bazin 1864; Oberhummer 1887; Woodhouse 1897.

NOTE 6
Noack 1894; Noack 1916. Noack's nearly finished manuscript, which had been entrusted to Ernst Kirsten for publication since 1938, was destroyed during the turmoil of the war at the occupation of Berlin (Kirsten 1951, 253). Extensive notes and many plans remained in Noack's scholarly bequest that is kept in the archive of the German Archaeological Institute (DAI) at Berlin. The section on Akarnania was screened and evaluated by Ernst-Ludwig Schwandner, the part on Aitolia by me. Kirsten had already based his RE-articles on Oiniadai, Paianion, Palairos, Phoitiai, Phythaion and Pleuron on some of Noack's plans as well as his topographical and archaeological descriptions.

NOTE 7
Cf. footnote 5.

NOTE 8
Kolonas et al. 1989/90; Gogos & Kolonas 1995/96; cf. also Freitag 1994.

NOTE 9
Cf. for the time being Wacker 1999.

NOTE 10
Courby & Picard 1924.

NOTE 11
The discovery of an up to now totally unknown Byzantine phase of settlement is to be considered one of the most important results of the exploration of the Stratiké.

Koder & Hild 1976 listed this region as an area still without the slightest remains from Byzantine times. The results of the field survey as well as of the excavations in the city fundamentally changed this picture. In addition to the remains of several churches, some villages were also discovered that were densely populated especially in middle Byzantine times; cf. Schwandner 1994. The very productive results of research on the history of human settlement in Akarnania in late medieval and early modern times, which had been carried out by Friedrich Sauerwein on the basis of the Ottoman land-register from the 16th to the 18th century, that had been analysed by Machiel Kiel, must left aside here; cf. for the time being Sauerwein 2000.

NOTE 12
Weigand 1895, esp. 187-192.

NOTE 13
Cf. Thuk. 2.80.8.

NOTE 14
Cf. footnote 6.

NOTE 15
The surveying was carried out by J. Barthel, A. Preiss and Th. Tsingas under the direction of E.-L. Schwandner.

NOTE 16
Schwandner & Kolonas 1996.

NOTE 17
Cf. for the historical background Strauch 1996 (with further literature).

NOTE 18
Heuzey 1860, 332 (fig. 2); Courby & Picard 1924, esp. 96-99.

NOTE 19
Courby & Picard 1924, 96ff.

NOTE 20
Courby & Picard 1924, 99 and pl. 1; cf. Heuzey 1860, 332 (fig. 2).

NOTE 21
Cf. the maps of the survey area in Franziska Lang´s contribution to this volume (p. 205ff.). Most recent palynological investigations show that Lake Ozeros emerged only in post-antique times and therefore today covers part of the polis area of Stratos.

NOTE 22
Cf. p. 211ff.

NOTE 23
Cf. the contribution of Franziska Lang and the corresponding maps of the diachronic and regional distribution of the finds in the survey area (p. 209ff.); cf. also Lang 1994.

NOTE 24
No monumental remains from Roman times were found at the excavations in the agora area except for the altar mentioned above, whereas there is rich evidence for the Byzantine phase of settlement; cf. Schwandner 1994.

NOTE 25
Cf. for the construction finds for the time being Schwandner 1996; Nirmaier 2000.

NOTE 26
Schwandner 1996, 52.

NOTE 27
Schwandner 1995, 783f.

NOTE 28
Cf. footnote 1★.

Bibliography

Antonetti, C., 1990
Les Étoliens. Image et religion. Paris.

Bazin, H., 1864
Mémoires sur l'Étolie, *Archives des missions scientifiques et littéraries. Choix de rapports et instructions publié sous les auspices du Ministère de l'Instruction Publique et des Beaux Arts,* vol. I 2,1. Paris.

Beck, H., 1997
Polis und Koinon. Untersuchungen zur Geschichte und Struktur der griechischen Bundesstaaten im 4. Jahrhundert v. Chr. Stuttgart.

Berktold, P. et al., 1996
Akarnanien. Eine Landschaft im antiken Griechenland. München.

Bommeljé, S. et al., 1987
Aetolia and the Aitolians. Towards the Interdisciplinary Study of a Greek Region. Utrecht.

Corsten, Th., 1999
Vom Stamm zum Bund: Gründung und territoriale Organisation griechischer Bundesstaaten. München.

Courby, F. & Picard, Chr., 1924
Recherches archéologiques à Stratos d'Acarnanie. Paris.

Dany. O., 1999
Akarnanien im Hellenismus. Geschichte und Völkerrecht in Nordwestgriechenland. München.

Dietz, S. et al., 1998
Surveys and Excavations in Chalkis, Aetolias 1995-1996. First Preliminary Report, *Proceedings of the Danish Institute at Athens 2,* 234-317.

Freitag, K., 1994
Oiniadai als Hafenstadt. Einige historisch-topographische Überlegungen, *Klio 92,* 212-238.

Freitag, K., 1996
Der Akarnanische Bund im 5. Jh. v. Chr., in: Berktold et al. 1996, 75-86.

Funke, P., 1997
Polisgenese und Urbanisierung in Aitolien im 5. und 4. Jh. v. Chr., in: Hansen 1997, 145-188

Gehrke, H.-J., 1994/95
Die kulturelle und politische Entwicklung Akarnaniens vom 6. bis zum 4. Jahrhundert v. Chr., *Geographia Antiqua 3-4,* 41-48.

Gogos, S. & Kolonas L., 1995/96
Peri tou theatrou ton Oiniadon, *Archaiognosia 9,* 167-176.

Grainger, J. D., 1999
The League of the Aitolians. Leiden etc.

Hansen, M. H. (ed.), 1997
The Polis as an Urban Centre and as a Political Community. Copenhagen.

Heuzey, L., 1860
The Mont Olympe et l'Acarnanie. Explotation de ces deux regions, avec l'étude de leurs antiquités, de leurs populations anciennes et modernes, de leur géographie et de leur histoire. Paris

Kirsten, E., 1951
Pleuron, *RE 21,2,* 239-268.

Koder, J. & Hild, F., 1976
Tabula Imperii Byzantini I: Hellas und Thessalien. Wien.

Kolonas, L. et al., 1989/90
Anaskaphe Oiniadon, *Archaiognosia 6,* 153-176.

Lang, F., 1994
Veränderungen des Siedlungsbildes in Akarnanien von der klassisch-hellenistischen zur römischen Zeit, *Klio 76,* 239-254.

Leake, W. M., 1835
Travels in Northern Greece, 4 vols. London.

Nirmaier, P., 2000
Manganschwarz und Hämatitrot. Farbige Gestaltung der Dachterrakotten eines griechischen Tempels, *Restauro 3,* 188-192.

Noack, F., 1897
Untersuchungen und Aufnahmen griechischer Stadt- und Burgruinen im westlichen Lokris, Aetolien und Akarnanien, *AA,* 80-83.

Noack, F., 1916
Befestigte griechische Städte in Aitolien und Akarnanien, *AA*, 215-239.

Oberhummer, E., 1887
Akarnanien, Ambrakia, Amphilochien, Leukas im Altertum. München.

Pritchett, W. K., 1991
Studies in Ancient Greek Topography VII. Amsterdam.

Pritchett, W. K., 1993
Studies in Ancient Greek Topography VIII. Amsterdam.

Pritchett, W. K., 1994a
Roads of Akarnania, in: *Pritchett 1994b*, 179-242.

Pritchett, W. K., 1994b
Essays in Greek History. Amsterdam.

Sauerwein, F., 1998
Wegeverbindungen in Aitolo-Akarnania, *MDAI (Athen)* 113, (in press)

Scholten, J. B., 2000
The Politics of Plunder. Aitolians and their Koinon in the Early Hellenistic Era, 279-217 B.C., Berkeley etc.

Schwandner, E.-L., 1994
Stratos am Acheloos, he polis phántasma?, in: *Phegos. Festschrift S. Dakaris*, Ioannina, 459-465.

Schwandner, E.-L., 1995
Arbeitsbericht, *AA*, 783-784

Schwandner, E.-L., 1996
Spáthari – Tempel ohne Säule und Gebälk?, in: *Schwandner (Ed.) 1996*, 48-54.

Schwandner, E.-L. (Ed.), 1996
Säule und Gebälk. Zu Struktur und Wandlungsprozeß griechisch-römischer Architektur. Mainz.

Strauch, D., 1996
Römische Politik und griechische Tradition. Die Umgestaltung Nordwest-Griechenlands unter römischer Herrschaft. München.

Wacker, Chr., 1999
Palairos: eine historische Landeskunde der Halbinsel Plagia in Akarnanien. München.

Weigand, G., 1895
Die Aromunen. Ethnographisch-philologisch-historische Untersuchungen über das Volk der sogenannten Makedo-Romanen oder Zinzaren, vol. 1, Leipzig.

Woodhouse, W. J., 1897
Aetolia. Its Geography, Topography and Antiquities. Oxford.

The Dimensions of the Material Topography

Franziska Lang

It will be presented some considerations about the organisation of landscape as observed in the Stratiké Surface Survey Project (SSSP) carried out around the ancient town of Stratos in Western Greece (Fig. 1).[1] The discussion will be concerned with specific details, such as the different uses of the landscape and sites at various times. The SSSP is concerned not only with the recovery of unknown sites from the earliest period down to the present day, but also with determining the extent of the chora of the city of Stratos, the reconstruction of its settlement patterns and the history of the Stratiké.

Introduction

Geology, topography and natural resources mould the natural environment and influence the use of space and the installations necessary for living within a certain area.[2] Whether and how these resources are exploited and the topography and the built environment are shaped depends upon the inhabitants.[3]

One generally distinguishes between nature and landscape.[4] The natural environment is defined as something without any human impact, the physical growth of the animals and plants. When a person

Fig. 1. Stratiké: distribution of sites by chronology (scale 1: 500).

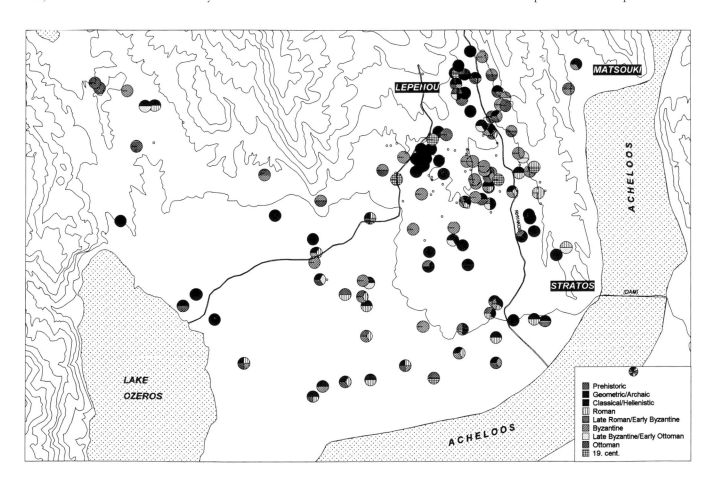

LEPENOU

MATSOUKI

ACHELOOS

RHYNON

STRATOS

[DAM]

LAKE OZEROS

ACHELOOS

Prehistoric
Geometric/Archaic
Classical/Hellenistic
Roman
Late Roman/Early Byzantine
Byzantine
Late Byzantine/Early Ottoman
Ottoman
19. cent.

thinks of nature he or she frequently imagines places without any visible human impact upon them: no houses, no industrialisation, but only trees, bushes and so forth. The present state of the environment, in fact, shapes the perception of what nature is or what nature ought to be. The more-or-less treeless northern part of England, for example, is seen by many people there as their natural environment, and any attempt at reforestation provokes resistance. Opponents argue that it would be an intrusion on nature. Despite the fact that the treeless countryside was created by a massive deforestation in the last 200 years, the present perception of this region is that this is original, unspoilt nature.[5] Even the national parks devoted to nature are carefully set up and structured, and so-called, "unspoilt nature" no longer exists in them.

As nature dictated the constraints or advantages of the geographical situation, so generation after generation of humans shaped this geography they transformed nature and the result might be called landscape.[6] Therefore "every landscape bears traces of this continuous and cumulative labour".[7] The most impressive sort of human impact on nature is certainly the carving of statues into mountains – a desire since the time of Alexander (Vitruvius 2. 2) – , like the oversize Buddhas on Sri Lanka or the heads of US presidents carved into Mount Rushmore. A very subtle form of landscape 'shaping' is the hidden organisation of the often cited song-lines of the Australian Aborigines.[8] Flora and fauna and landmarks form a system of signs and the basis of the "dream tracks" created by their ancestors. This sort of "totemic geography" is almost invisible and thus almost undetectable by archaeological methods and should remind us of other forms of landscape organisation and also of the fact that the unoccupied space between sites can be the result of a conscious 'leaving blank'. Therefore the formation of landscape is anything but a uniform process; the shaping and perception of landscape differ from period to period, from region to region, and from person to person.

The dimensions of topography

The interdependence of people and nature involves a complex system of spheres and concepts[9] the political, social, economic, artistic and religious-symbolic are mirrored in the landscape's 'style' This complex system of landscaping follows various rules in different chronological periods. Therefore dissimilar settlement patterns and economic systems, for instance, can form the same landscape. Since the influence on the organisation and structure of space are so manifold, it seems useful to distinguish them through different kinds of topography.

The *natural and physical topography* provides the fundamental conditions for life: water, quality of soil, vegetation, climate, natural resources.[10] This natural topography determines the possible settlement patterns and access to wider communication networks. The natural resources, such as rock, provide the material for construction. The climate influences the use of material in the construction of building as well as the kinds of clothing worn. In our case, Stratos is situated on the largest river in Greece, the Acheloos, in a wide, fertile plain – called Stratiké by Polybius (5. 96. 3) – surrounded by hills and mountains. This plain is the largest in Acarnania and permits intensive agriculture. Fords and passes allowed for access to this area (Fig. 2). The local rock – a specific kind of sandstone, called flysch – was used for building. This brownish, very soft and easily crumbled sandstone was not used for more elaborate and representative constructions. For anything which should be constructed in a more sophisticated manner, for example the orchestra or the ramps of the theatre in Stratos, a white limestone extracted from a proper nearby quarry was used.

Natural factors influence politics, economy, social organisation, and human behaviour, which leads to the second kind of topography: the *material topography*. The material topography informs how people shape their environment. Most changes in

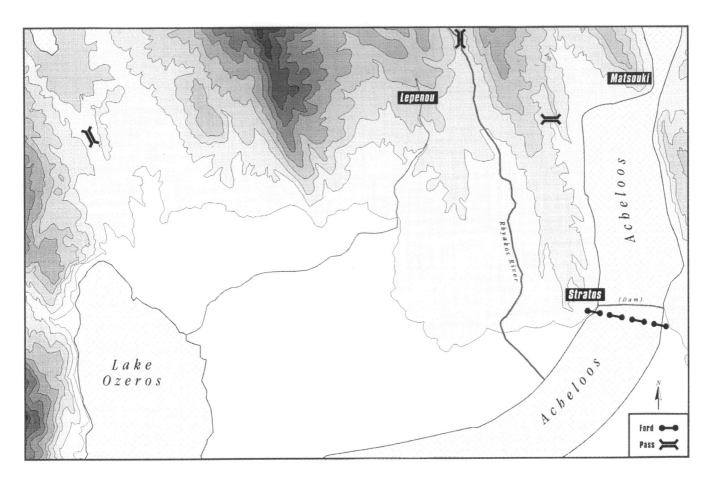

Fig. 2. Stratiké: ford and passes (scale 1: 750).

nature and landscape caused by human beings may be identified by the material culture. Material culture on a very broad definition, stands for all man-made objects, regardless of size or material (e.g. architecture as well as ceramics, art objects). The 'production' of these artefacts is influenced by several factors. The *political* and *socio-economic* conditions affects how people form their living areas. The most visible expression is the architecture: the layout of a big or small city, the construction of city walls, farmsteads, and villas. The largest settlements of the Stratiké is Stratos itself.[11] As a last bulwark against the Aetolians, Stratos, the only fortified town in the Stratiké, was set up in the far east of Acarnania on the border with Aetolia, its site overlooking the plain. The establishment of city walls clearly reflects a political decision, since the building of a city wall must be financed by the community, and land must be provided for its construction.

The distribution and features of settlements and their houses varies with time and the social organisation of a community. The arrival of the Romans marked a decided change in the use of landscape, both for Acarnania in general and for the Stratiké in particular. Acarnania in the pre-Roman period, for example, was characterised by its fortified settlements, while in the Roman era settlements were not fortified. In the Classical-Hellenistic period the settlements were built in the mountains and on the plain, while the most of Roman era settlements were situated on lower elevations.[12] The northern part of the Stratiké apparently no longer attracted settlers (Fig. 8) and people now preferred to live on the plain. Some places already settled endured, but others were abandoned as yet others were newly founded. It is very striking that in the Roman period the land use in the Stratiké differs from previous and later periods. It must be investigated how and to what extent the different economic and administrative strategies of the Roman Empire led to the obvious change of use of space in

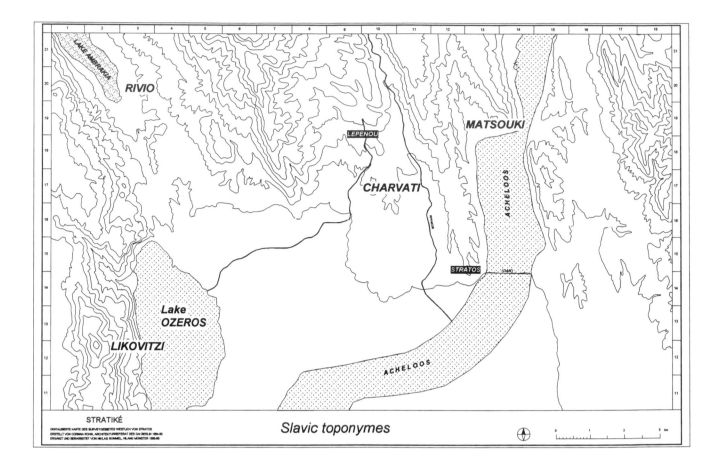

Fig. 3. Stratiké: slavic toponymes.

Acarnania, and how this affected the Greeks – certainly still living in this area.[13] Furthermore the possibilities for the use of space within and outside a settlement are manifold, and consideration of this fact can provide hints about the organisation of a society: in ancient times, for instance, cemeteries were normally placed outside the settlement, while in the Medieval period cemeteries began to be incorporated within it.[14]

Different *ecological* factors bring about different nutrition strategies and these affect the economy and architectural features of an area as well. In regions with larger plains and good soil, extensive agriculture may be expected, while settlers in hilly and mountainous regions prefer pastoralism. Different facilities are required in each region. In an agricultural area, like the Stratiké, farmers need shelters in the fields for the harvested grain. Also, farmers may live in their fields, especially in the work-intensive summer months, and we may see houses there as well as granaries.

Pastoralism uses landscape differently, e.g. whether it relies on summer-transhumance with seasonal long-distance walks, or the daily moving of flocks around a village. The latter requires folds or stables within the village or close by it, whereas transhumance is characterised by semi-permanent settled areas with special facilities like fences, huts, milk pens and animal folds, where the animals may be watered and fed. Such features are usually ephemeral in nature.[15] Both forms of pastoralism have occurred in the Stratiké. In the last century the Vlachs, a Balkan tribe, regularly visited the area in the course of seasonal transhumance, while present-day shepherds daily move their flocks in and out of the villages.

Information about various ethnic groups provides a good idea of what may be expected in landscape use and material culture and one might call it the '*ethnic' environment*. In late Roman and early Byzantine times there was an obvious decline in settlement in the Stratiké, and

208

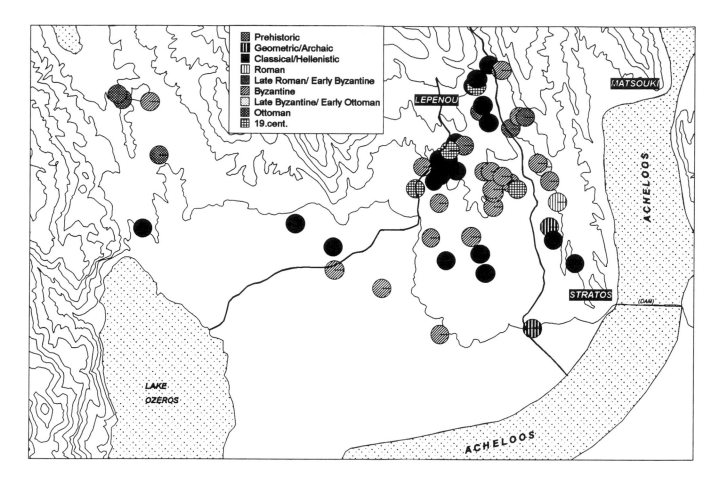

Legend:
- Prehistoric
- Geometric/Archaic
- Classical/Hellenistic
- Roman
- Late Roman/ Early Byzantine
- Byzantine
- Late Byzantine/ Early Ottoman
- Ottoman
- 19.cent.

MATSOUKI

LEPENOU

ACHELOOS

STRATOS

(OAN)

LAKE OZEROS

ACHELOOS

Fig. 4. Stratiké: sites with one-phase occupation (scale 1: 750).

Slavic invasions of Greece left their traces with toponymes like Charvati, Matsouki, Ozeros and Rivio (Fig. 3). Other groups followed. Benjamin of Tudela,[16] for example, tells us that in the 12th century there was a small Jewish community in Stratos. From the 15th century on, the Ottomans controlled all of the Stratiké. In the 19th century the Vlachs came regularly to the Stratiké and lived in temporary huts, as Heuzey mentioned in his book.[17] And in 1924 Greek refugees from Asia Minor were settled in the Stratiké.

A further kind of environment is the *symbolic-religious*. Emotional experiences could be expressed by religious-ritual acts. Trees or odd landmarks were perceived as magical, received a symbolic meaning and were worshipped. The installation of cult-places at certain locations, and the cosmology of the Greek gods, are closely tied to landscape. A nature deity like Pan symbolises both nature and culture. In myth, human beings may work out an attempt to rule nature as well as to conceal their

fear of nature. The struggle between Heracles and Acheloos, the biggest river in Greece, might among other thing be read as the mythical conversion of the theme of "human being conquers nature", that is, the transformation of a wild, powerful stream into a navigable river. Symbolic-religious topography is easiest to comprehend when there are architectural remains, such as temples, churches or mosques, but finds like votives are also helpful.[18] The hidden secret of the "dream tracks" mentioned at the beginning of this paper might be an another example, but one which is forever lost and undetectable by archaeologist. A further example might be the conversion of a public into a sacred place by simply joining the city wall to a column of the Artemis temple at Ephesos with a rope (Herodotus, 1, 26), an act which leaves no trace. Even if one cannot give a definite answer as to why a religious structure was established at a specific location, its very existence suggests that people living within the area assigned a

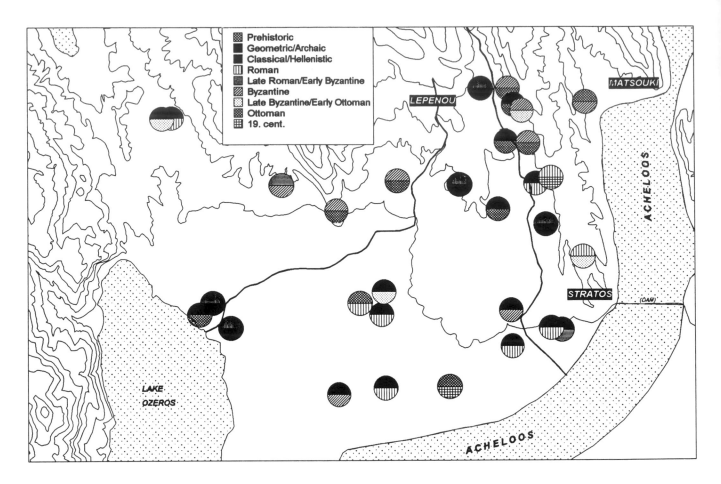

Legend:
- Prehistoric
- Geometric/Archaic
- Classical/Hellenistic
- Roman
- Late Roman/Early Byzantine
- Byzantine
- Late Byzantine/Early Ottoman
- Ottoman
- 19. cent.

Fig. 5. Stratiké: sites with two-phases occupation (scale 1: 750).

symbolic meaning to the place and the location adds this evidence to our understanding of its function and of its symbolic meaning. One should not forget that religious structures have a metaphysical as well as economic aspects. Whether in ancient times or in the mediaeval period, sanctuaries owned real estate which they leased out, and from the cultivation of which they received income.

Finally, one could add a further form of topography which is not physically linked with landscape: the *artistic*. Artists are probably influenced by their environment and can express their feelings about and perceptions of the environment in sculpture, vase-painting etc.[19] Often styles differ from region to region. In archaeology these regional styles are often the basis for identifying so-called ethnic groups, which is problematic.[20]

Besides the natural and material topographies there is the *perceived topography*. Especially in the symbolic-religious environment certain experiences which will not be expressed in artefacts. It is therefore more difficult to reconstruct the perception of people than the natural and material topography. More precisely this varies for different periods: the chance to understand prehistoric perceptions of the environment is fairly small[21], while the chances are better for periods in which written sources are known. Even if we have just distinguished these different topographies and environments in order to point out the diverse levels of concepts, one should not forget that this is an artificial construct. These remarks should remind us of the manifold influences upon a landscape, as well as of the difficulties encountered in recognising their impact upon the material culture.

Continuity and discontinuity

The relationship between human beings and nature are expressed through the *natural* and *material topography*. This complex system involves, to sum up, the natural-

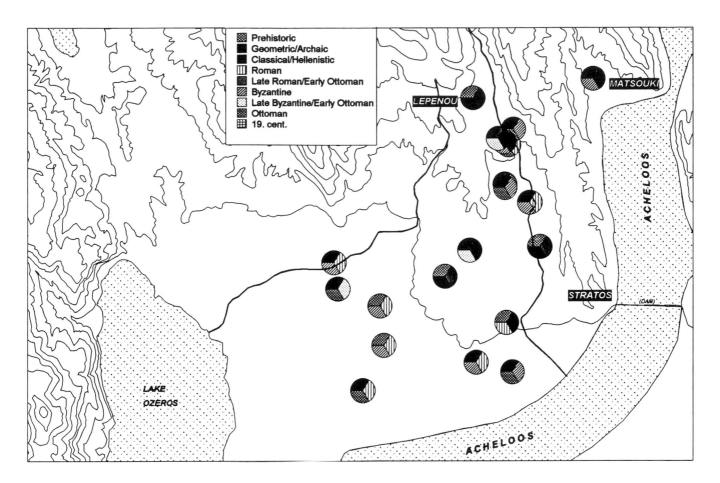

Legend:
- Prehistoric
- Geometric/Archaic
- Classical/Hellenistic
- Roman
- Late Roman/Early Ottoman
- Byzantine
- Late Byzantine/Early Ottoman
- Ottoman
- 19. cent.

Fig. 6. Stratiké: sites with three-phases occupation (scale 1: 750).

physical, political, socio-economic, 'ethnic', symbolic-religious and artistic environment. This means that landscape reflects the organisation, thinking and perception of a society in a given area and these are further more mirrored in the archaeological finds. The archaeological method of survey[22] is an appropriate means of collecting data which offers interpretations of "rules" and patterns across wider areas in a diachronic perspective. Based on this data the analysis of a landscape allows us to recognise the phenomena such as persistence, more generally continuity, or changes of land use through our time. The shifting of sites represents very clearly the modification of landscape use and reflects social changes such as nucleation, migration, and more generally: discontinuity.[23] The continuous and discontinuous use of location is affected by time and function and concerns population, institutions, religion and religious practices. If one analyses sites and their material culture in relation to time and

function, the specific features of both that location and the settlement pattern of a entire region may be reconstructed in a more precise way. If one considers continuity and discontinuity, it can be perceived in a region as a whole – at the intersite level – as well as in the site itself – at the intrasite level.

Continuity and discontinuity at intersite level

The analysis of settlement patterns is based on the distribution of sites through several periods.

The examination of a site can provide us with an indication of the preferred utilisation of certain parts of the region in different periods and of the importance of single sites within the area in various periods. The abandonment of a place may show us that it was not highly regarded or that it lacked resources. A site which remained occupied through successive periods indicates a particular interest in that location. The abandonment of sites means

211

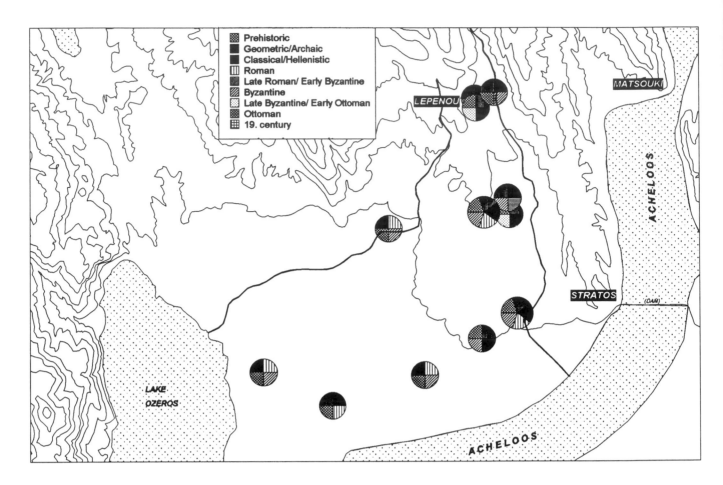

Fig. 7. Stratiké: sites with
four- and five-phases occupation (scale 1: 750).

discontinuity and implies a drop in site
numbers. This, however, does not necessarily testify to depopulation at the same
time. Lower site numbers can attest to migration to other regions, or to the movement of inhabitants into fewer but bigger
settlements in the same area; for instance,
of families who follow relatives who had
made the move earlier.[24] By observing
where, when and for how long sites were
established, it is possible to reconstruct
land use and the importance of sites.

The majority of sites – Stratos occupied
through all periods, will be excluded in
the following – in the Stratiké were occupied only once (Fig. 4). The sites are
mostly situated in the northern and western part of the Stratiké. A concentration is
fairly be identified in the area between the
two modern villages of Stratos and Lepenou. The southern and especially the
south-western part is almost unoccupied.
Sites inhabited during two phases are
quite common too (Fig. 5). These sites are
distributed more or less equally in the

whole Stratiké and now even the Southwest is inhabited. Occupation with three
phases at each site occurs in the north and
south, but does not occur in the western
part (Fig. 6). Most sites are now situated in
the plain. Multi-period sites are less common (Fig. 7). Four-phase sites exist in the
area between Stratos and Lepenou and in
the south, the western part is not inhabited. The few five-phase sites are all located
in the eastern plain. Through all periods
the eastern region was inhabited and this
fact emphasises the importance of that
area. Also, the northern area, around the
modern village of Lepenou, was almost
consistently inhabited, indicating its significance throughout a long period of time.
From here, one might travel through a pass
to the interior or continue on to the Ambracian Gulf. All the more exciting, therefore, is the fact that in Roman times this
region was not very popular, as the drop
in the number of places in this region indicates (Fig. 8). It might imply that the
pass to the north was no longer of interest.

212

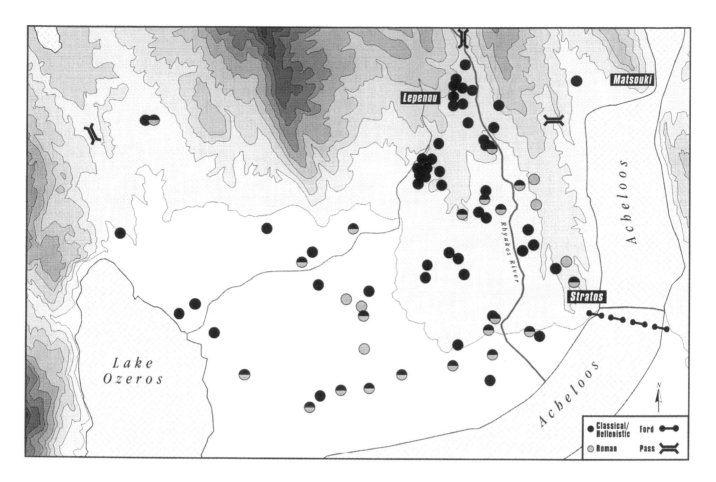

Fig. 8. Stratiké: distribution of Classical/ Hellenistic and Roman sites (scale 1: 500).

The far south of the Stratiké (Figs. 4-8) along the river Acheloos was settled again and again. Remarkable is the fact that all sites exist more or less in the same locations creating a line parallel to the river, although not all sites were continually occupied. The permanent existence of settlements in this area indicates its importance and it seems likely that a road ran through the region, running south from Stratos and its ford on the Acheloos

Continuity and discontinuity at intra-site level

Within a site there are various possibilities of continuity and discontinuity in use. One might have a permanent occupation with the same function like the settlement Stratos; or are might have a short-lived site. A third possibility is temporal continuity but for different periods in limited sections of the site. One might recognise continuity or discontinuity on a temporal as well as a functional level.

Temporal level

Different types of continuity and discontinuity may be perceived in the following ways. A site existed within a certain period, but modifications of the occupation of the site may be detected through time. In site 084 (ca. 0,65ha), for instance, the Classical-Hellenistic pottery is concentrated in the eastern part, while the density of Byzantine finds is greater in the western part (F ig. 9). This means that the settlement of the Classical-Hellenistic period was located in the eastern part and was moved to the western part by the Byzantine period. Thus one can ascertain the chronological continuity of the whole site, although different parts of the site were occupied at various times.[25]

Functional level

There may be continuity or discontinuity of function as well. A site such as a cemetery may keep its function over time. Discontinuity of function means that a site continues to exist but its function

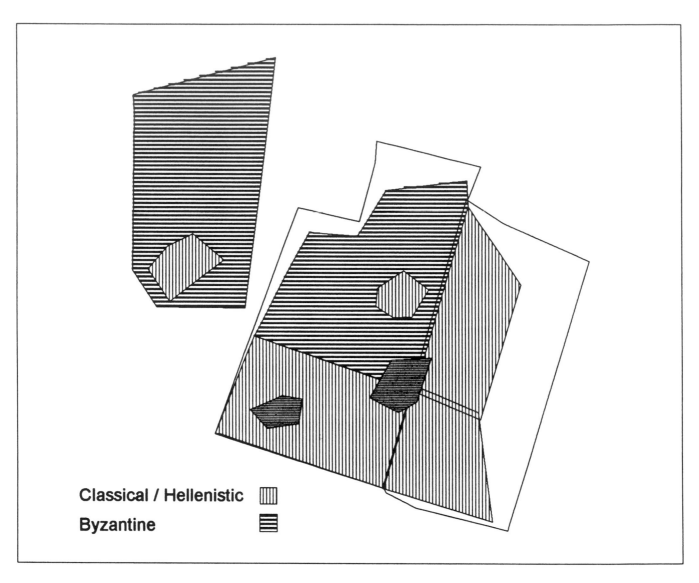

Classical / Hellenistic ▥

Byzantine ▤

Fig. 9. Stratiké: Classical/ Hellenistic and Byzantine periods in site 084.

changes. A site can show religious continuity even if the religion changes over the centuries – the Hephaisteion in Athens has served, during its existence, both as a temple to Hephaestus and as Christian church. At Spathari, a middle Helladic settlement was discovered by the Stratiké-Survey (Fig. 10). From the Geometric to the Roman period this place was turned into a sanctuary. At Agios Georghios, another location in the Stratiké, there was a bath in Roman times, but in the mediaeval period a chapel was built on the site. In both cases the site as a whole was occupied continuously but it shows discontinuity of function. Discontinuity of function might also indicate a conscious break with older tradition, as does the relocation of churches in Late Antiquity away from

public areas of Roman times. This relocation may indicate the political intention of the Church to underline its break, not only with the pagan tradition, but with the Roman Empire in general.[26]

Finally, continuity or discontinuity may apply not only to the material culture of a settlement, but also to the settlement's name. Stratos, for example, has changed from Stratos to Gerovigla and Sorovigli and back to Stratos again from Classical period to the modern.

Analysis of site function
A study of surface material concerns to the chronological and functional assessment of sites and should provide an interpretation of land use in a synchronic and diachronic perspective. The identification

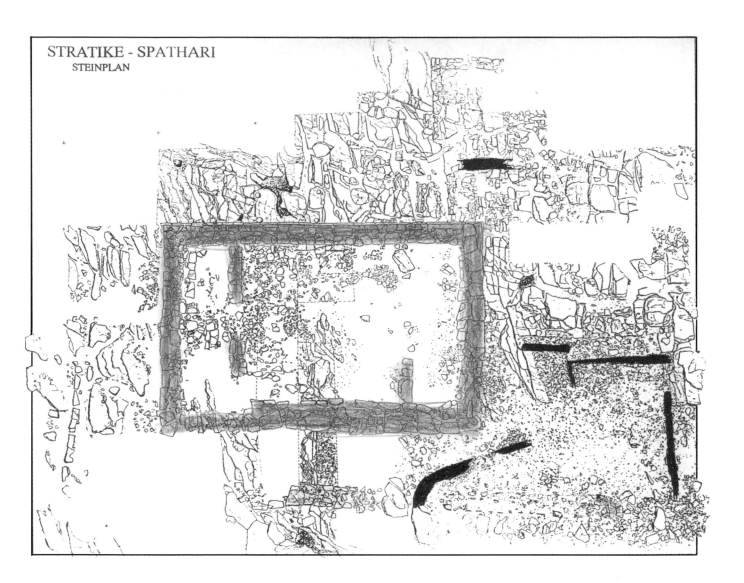

STRATIKE - SPATHARI
STEINPLAN

Fig. 10. Stratiké: Spathari – Middle Helladic period (black) and Archaic temple (grey).

of the sites is the basis for further discussions, especially the analysis of settlement patterns. Unless there are obvious hints of different use as in the case of graves, sites are mostly defined as settlements in these discussions. This identification is often *ex silentio*, since most sites have only pottery. These artefacts have lost their original context, which makes it more difficult to interpret them and makes the sites more difficult to evaluate. Definition *ex silentio* is particularly problematic for studies of the central place theory or size-rank-rule theory[27], because definition *ex silentio* does not consider the whole range of possibilities in land use.[28] For that purpose one needs a more sophisticated analysis. For the reconstruction of site use, the two main aspects to be considered are: its

chronology and its function. The first step, of course, will be to date the sites.[29] For this, the one-phase sites are most important for establishing a regional chronology. Such places offer the possibility of dating previously undated sherds, since the material is more or less homogenous and is datable to one epoch. One can determine by comparing the shape and fabric of the datable sherds with the undatable ones if the same chronological period pertains for the undated pots.[30]

To assess the function of sites, a specific method of site-function-analysis has been developed during the SSSP (Lang, in press) This is based chiefly upon a detailed examination of pottery, since ceramics are the largest group of finds. Although this tool cannot be used to reconstruct each

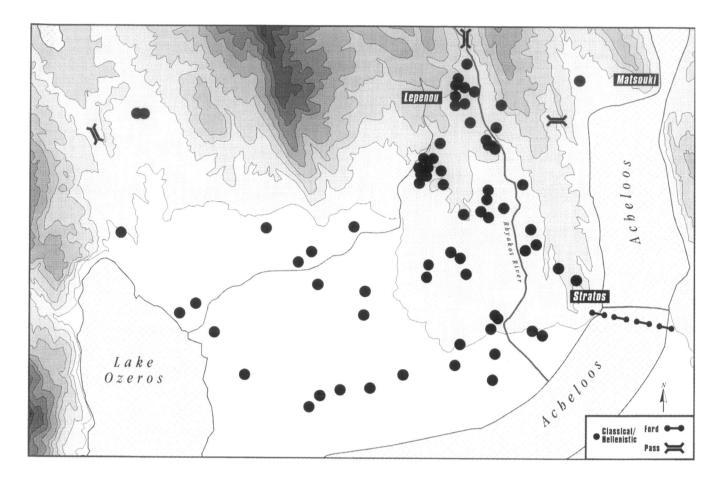

Fig. 11. Stratiké: distribution
of Classical sites
(scale 1: 500)

specific site function, at least three main categories of functions can be distinguished, concerning human living conditions and behaviour: living areas (like settlements, farmsteads, field shelters, industrial installations, etc.), religious structures, and cemeteries. Each of these categories yield a specific assemblage of material culture: e.g. vessels for food production, storage etc. in the living area; votive offerings in sanctuaries; and particular items might be put in graves if burial customs required it. This *site-function-analysis* assumes that sites with the same function produce a similar set of ceramics. Therefore the vessels at each site must be examined. Single pots – distinguished by periods – are grouped by shape (e.g. jugs, cups) and fabric (e.g. decorated, coarse). These groups and the composition of vessel assemblages at sites with a function explicitly defined by unambiguous indicators such as foundation walls constitute the references for further comparisons. In the next step the ceramics of sites with unknown function

are compared with the reference-group. The more similar the assemblage the more likely it is that the sites had the same function.[31] This analogous-comparative model offers the opportunity to define the function of more sites – especially of those delivering only pottery – and helps to form a more detailed view of the area surveyed.

The interpretation and reconstruction of the political, socio-economic and cultural organisation of a landscape and of human behaviour within it could be made more precise by putting together all information available and considering the functions of individual sites. What might be gained through detailed site-function-analysis is illustrated in Figure 11. Here Classical/Hellenistic sites have been plotted by location. Dots are distributed over the whole map. In some places concentrations are visible, but what the single dot actually means is not recognisable. A discussion of this map could not be very detailed. In Figure 12 the sites whose func-

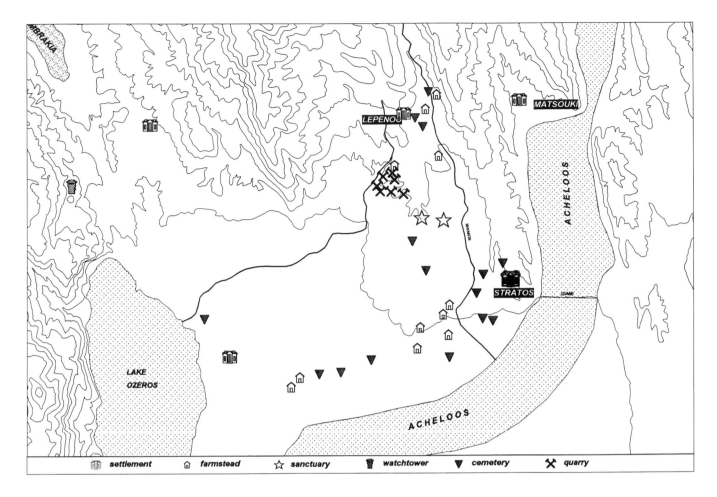

| | settlement | 🏠 farmstead | ☆ sanctuary | 🏛 watchtower | ▼ cemetery | ✕ quarry |

Fig. 12. Stratiké: distribution of Classical sites plotted by function (scale 1: 500)

tion are known are plotted again, this time by function. It is fairly obvious that an interpretation is now easier to give. The distribution of the settlements, sanctuaries and cemeteries and the interrelations are discernible. In this way the material topography offers to write the biography of a landscape more easily. Of course, I do not maintain that, with this, or any, method one can discover every secret of a landscape, but it can increase one's understanding of a region.

Notes

NOTE 1
For a more detailed description of the Stratiké Survey Project cf. P. Funke in this volume.

NOTE 2
For a long time the aspect 'space' was neglected in historical science and the aspect 'time' was not important in geographical science (Rapoport 1994: 465; Peet 1998: 158-160).

NOTE 3
Rapoport 1990, 9-20, Mahler 1998: 162ff.

NOTE 4
Mitchell 1991, 5 21.

NOTE 5
In the perception of nature the aspect of time is certainly meaningful, since the definition of 'nature' depends on contemporary experience. That is to say for the people who lived in this area 200 years ago, nature was certainly differently defined. I thank A. Möller reminding me of this problem. A reconstruction of this perception at a certain time would be essential for any analysis of the environment, even if I do not believe that we will able to reconstruct that perception for each time period.

NOTE 6
Clarkson 1998, 120.

NOTE 7
Braudel, 1993, 9.

NOTE 8
Strehlow 1970.

NOTE 9
Harvey 1996, 207-208.

NOTE 10
Rackham 1996, 16-43.

NOTE 11
Until the second century Stratos was the largest city in Acarnania.

NOTE 12
Cf. Lang 1994, 241-254, fig. 4-5, Strauch 1996, 104-108.

NOTE 13
Alcock 1993, Strauch 1996, 47-75.

NOTE 14
The spatial relation between graves and religious structures changed through time. While in the ancient Greek and pre-Christian Roman world cemeteries, without temples, were situated outside the settlement, the cemeteries of Christian societies were normally established around churches.

NOTE 15
Chang 1992, 65-89.

NOTE 16
Asher 1840, 46.

NOTE 17
Cf. the city map of Stratos: Heuzey (1846: 332) mentioned in the location of the ancient agora "cantonnement de Valacque"

NOTE 18
Cf. site 08850 in the Stratiké, where a sanctuary could be detected, since hundreds of terracotta were found on the surface. A following rescue excavation brought a bothros to light (Schwandner 1995: 783-784).

NOTE 19
In the literature – for instance, the bucolic poetry of Vergil – nature played a rôle too.

NOTE 20
Raeder 1990, 634, Alcock 1993, 6, Hall 1997, 132-134.

NOTE 21
As e.g. it is presented by Tilley 1994.

NOTE 22
Kardulias 1994, 10-17, Bintliff 1996, 246-255, Shipley 1996, 7-8.

NOTE 23
Schlanger 1992, 91-112, Kunow 1994, 338-352.

NOTE 24
Greenwood 1985, 521-544.

NOTE 25
In order to understand this shift in occupation, in the Stratiké Project, the single sites were divided into several sections and the finds from each section were collected and documented separately.

NOTE 26
Why and to what extent churches were built outside or inside settlements is much discussed. The intentional break is one theory, the other is that the church did not have real estate at its disposal within the settlement, where the governmental/municipal institution, still existed albeit on a lower level.

NOTE 27
Haggett, Cliff, Frey 1977, 111-115; 146-153, Peet 1998, 19-21.

NOTE 28
Lang, in press.

NOTE 29
Gregory – Kardulias 1990, 488.

NOTE 30
I have constructed a model for this purpose which cannot be described in detail here.

NOTE 31
A detailed explanation and the application of this model will be presented in the forthcoming Stratiké publication.

Acknowledgement: For the draft reading I thank very much to T. Boyd and H. van Wees. The maps fig. 2, 8, and 11 were designed by C. de Marco; the fig. 10 was drawn by J. Denkinger; I would like to thank them too.

Bibliography

Alcock, S., 1993
Graecia capta. The landscape of Roman Greece, Cambridge.

Asher, A., 1840
The Itinerary of Rabbi Benjamin of Tudela, vol I. London – Berlin.

Bintliff, J., 1996
Interactions of theory, methodology, and practice, *Archaeological dialogues 3* (2), 246-255.

Braudel, F., 1993
The history of civilizations, New York.

Chang, C., 1992
Archaeological landscapes. The ethnoarchaeology of pastoral land use in the Grevena Province of Greece, in: J. Rossignol and L. Wandsnider (Hrsg.), *Space, time and archaeological landscapes,* 65-89, New York – London.

Clarkson, P. B., 1998
Archaeological imaginings: the contextualization of images, in: D.S. Whitley (ed.), *Reader in archaeological theory. Post-processual and cognitive approaches,* 119-130, London – New York.

Greenwood, M. J., 1985
Human migration: theory, models, and empirical studies, *Journal of regional sciences 25* (4), 521-544.

Gregory, T. E. and Kardulias, P. N., 1990
Geophysical and surface surveys in the Byzantine fortress at Isthmia, *Hesperia* 59, 467-511.

Haggett, P., Cliff, A. D. and Frey, A., 1977
Locational analysis in human geography, 2nd ed. London.

Hall, J. M., 1997
Ethnic identity in Greek antiquity, Cambridge.

Harvey, D., 1996
Justice, nature and the geography of difference, Cambridge, MA.

Heuzey, L. A., 1860
Le mont Olympe et l'Acarnanie, Paris.

Kunow, J., 1994
Zur Theorie von kontinuierlichen und diskontinuierlichen Entwicklungen im Siedlungswesen, in: C. Dobiat (Hrsg.), (=*Marburger Studien zur Vor- und Frühgeschichte,* Bd. 16), 338-352. Marburg.

Kardulias, P. N., 1994
Paradigms of the past in Greek archaeology, in: P. N. Kardulias (ed.), *Beyond the site. Regional studies in the Aegean Area*, 1-23. Boston.

Lang, F., 1994
Veränderungen des Siedlungsbildes in Akarnanien von der klassisch-hellenistischen zur römischen Zeit, *Klio* 76, 239-254.

Lang, F. in press
Method for the functional analysis of medieval sites from the Stratiké-Surface-Survey-Project, Acarnania (Western Greece), in: J.L. Bintliff and D. Tsougarakis and E. Tsougarakis (eds.), *New approach to medieval and post-medieval Greece.*

Mahler, A., 1998
Herakles als Vermittler von mythischem Andachtsraum und realem Georaum. Versuch einer historischen Ökologie der mediterranen Landschaft, Eggingen.

Mitchell, W. J. T., 1994
Imperial landscape. In: W.T.J. Mitchell (ed.), *Landscape and power,* 5-34. Chicago.

Peet, R., 1998
Modern geographical thought. Oxford.

Rackham, O., 1996
Ecology and pseudo-ecology. The example of ancient Greece, in: *Shipley and Salmon*, 16-43.

Raeder, J., 1990
Bonner Jahrbücher 190, 631-636.

Rapoport, A., 1990
Systems of activities and systems of settings, in: S. Kent (ed.), *Domestic architecture and the use of space. An interdisciplinary cross-cultural study,* 9-20. Cambridge.

Rapoport, A., 1994.
Spatial organisation and the built environment, in: T. Ingold (ed.), *Companion encyclopedia of anthropology,* 460-502. London – New York.

Schlanger, S. H., 1992
Recognizing persistent places in Anasazi settlement systems, in: J. Rossignol and L. Wandsnider (eds.), *Space, time and archaeological landscapes,* 91-112. New York – London.

Schwandner, E.-L., 1995
Archäologischer Anzeiger, 783-786.

Shipley, G., 1996
Ancient history and landscapes histories. In: *Shipley and Salmon,* 1-5.

Shipley, G. and Salmon, J. (eds.), 1996
Human landscape in classical antiquity. Environment and culture. London – New York.

Strauch, D., 1996
Römische Politik und griechische Tradition. Die Umgestaltung Nordwest-Griechenlands unter römischer Herrschaft. München.

Strehlow, T., 1970
Geography and the totemic landscape in central Australia: a functional study, in: R. Berndt (ed.), *Australian aboriginal anthropology.* Nedlands.

Tilley, C., 1994
A phenomenology of landscape. Places, paths and monuments. Oxford.

Some News about Inscriptions from Northwestern Greece:

Preliminary Remarks on Recent Epigraphical Work in the Museums of Thyrion and Agrinion

Klaus Freitag

Under the direction of the 6th Ephorate of Prehistoric and Classical Antiquities, Dr. Lazaros Kolonas, an international team was formed a few years ago to study the epigraphical material from ancient Acarnania. The general objective is to collect and study all the epigraphical evidence from northwestern Greece. Members of the team include Prof. Dr. Claudia Antonetti from Venice, Prof. Dr. Peter Funke from Münster, Prof. Dr. Klaus Hallof from the "Inscriptiones Graecae" in Berlin and Prof. Dr. Hans-Joachim Gehrke from Freiburg. The work concentrated at first, of course, on the two most important museums in Acarnania, the archeological collections in Agrinion and Thyrion. Under the supervision of the researchers already mentioned my colleague Dr. Daniel Strauch and I began recording the Greek and Latin inscriptions in the museum of Agrinion in September of 1996. In September of 1997 I was able to study the epigraphical material in the museum of Thyrion with the help of some of my colleagues from Münster.[1*]

In my paper I would like to examine three points.

1. First of all I would like to present a short overview of epigraphical research in northwestern Greece.

2. In the second part I will give a concise report on the work in the museums in Agrinion and Thyrion.

3. Finally I will briefly present and provisionally classify some new and not yet published inscriptions from Acarnania which are important with respect to the history of northwestern Greece in the late Hellenistic and Roman periods.

I would like to stress explicitly that I can only give you what we call in German a "Werkstattbericht", that is a "workshop report", in the true sense of the word. The work in the two museums is now mostly finished. At present we are involved in processing and interpreting the individual epigraphical texts. We have also developed an epigraphical database which, in addition to the work on the squeezes and the photographs, will assist us further with the interpretation and documentation of the epigraphical material.

Please allow me to give you a brief review of the epigraphical research in Acarnania and Aitolia:

In 1897 the *Inscriptiones Graecae* IG IX, 1 was published. The editor, Wilhelm Dittenberger, collected and edited the already published inscriptions from Phocis, Locris, Aitolia, Acarnania and the Ionian Islands.[2] Since the beginning of the 20th century, the archeological and epigraphical investigations of Greek researchers in Thermos and other parts of Acarnania and Aitolia – Georgios Soteriadis and Konstantinos Romaios[3] should be mentioned here in particular – helped considerably to increase the number of historically relevant inscriptions many times. In the years following, the epigraphical research of northwestern Greece has been inseparably connected to the name Günther Klaffenbach (1890-1972). After the reorganization of the *Inscriptiones Graecae* by Ulrich von Wilamowitz-Moellendorf, the urgently needed second edition of the ninth volume of the *Inscriptiones Graecae* (IG IX, 1[2]) should include 4 fascicles. G. Klaffenbach already began preparing the new inscription volumes in 1919. He traveled widely in northwestern Greece and contacted Greek archeologists and epigraphists. He was already able to publish the Aitolian volume in 1932.[4] This fascicle contains 171 inscriptions in contrast to the 39 Aitolian inscriptions found in *Inscriptiones Graecae* IX 1 of 1897. On behalf of the Prussian Academy of Sciences Klaffenbach undertook further journeys in Phocis, Locris, Aitolia, Acarnania and the Ionian Islands in 1933 and 1934. Klaffenbach published the results of his research trips in the transactions ("Sitzungsberichte") of the Academy.[5]

The IG-volume with the Acarnanian inscriptions (IG IX 1², 2) appeared in 1957.[6] This volume contains a total of 398 inscriptions which were found in Acarnania; in contrast to the 99 inscriptions of the first edition which was edited by Dittenberger, the amount of epigraphical material has increased considerably. The volume with the inscriptions from West-Locris (IG IX 1², 1, 3) finally appeared in 1968. In spite of the difficult working conditions in the former German Democratic Republic and the political isolation, Günther Klaffenbach set a high standard in the three volumes of inscriptions from northwestern Greece. All the volumes contain informative fasti and extensive indices. So far the fascicle *Inscriptiones Graecae* IX 1², 1, 4 with the inscriptions from the Ionian Islands has yet not been published. One still has to depend on the 1897 *Inscriptiones Graecae* volume by Wilhelm Dittenberger which I have already mentioned.[7] In the museums in Agrinion and Thyrion we were able to find most of the inscriptions which Klaffenbach had included, and so we could study them once again. The inscriptions which could not be found there are either still on site, could not be examined by Klaffenbach himself, or have been lost in the course of time. Due to the careful and extremely productive activities of the appropriate Greek administration of antiquities and the responsible ephoroi, especially Eu-

thymios Mastrokostas[8], Petros Themelis, I. A. Papapoustolou, Lazaros Kolonas, as well as many others, a large number of new inscriptions from the whole nomos have been discovered since 1957.

Allow me to comment a bit on our work in the museum of Agrinion. Agrinion, a town of about forty thousand inhabitants, is the capital of the eparchy of Trikhonidhos and the largest city in the nomos. It was almost completely rebuilt after an earthquake in 1887. The site of ancient Agrinion has been located above the village of Megali Khora, 4 km northwest of the modern town. There is an important archeological museum here. The museum contains finds from the district of Aetoloacarnania ranging from the prehistoric to the Roman periods. It was erected in 1969. Our interest was concentrated on the epigraphical material, but of course other very important archeological items are also on exhibition.

In the museum in Agrinion we were able to study 141 inscriptions (about half of the inscriptions came from Acarnania, the other half from Aitolia). In principle a large number of inscriptions from sites in the whole nomos were collected. In recent years the museum of Agrinion has mostly kept material from central and southern Acarnania and west Aitolia. For example, inscriptions from Stratos are now exhibited or kept in the museum. The material is so extensive that one can no longer exhibit all the blocks of inscriptions in the museum itself; the material must be left in the archives and in the forecourt of the museum. In particular the newer material and the smaller fragments with remains of inscriptions are kept in the archive.

All the inscriptions were critically examined. All the stones in the museum of Agrinion were described and measured in a precise manner. In the case of the important new inscriptions and the historically important inscriptions already published, a first reading was done on the stone. At least one squeeze was made of each inscription and photographs were also taken.

In the museum there are some significant, not yet published inscriptions whose publication and interpretation are of great historical importance.

In this context let me mention only two longer and almost completely preserved manumission inscriptions from Gavalou, the ancient Trichonion. Due to the naming of eponymous officials, these are of particular importance for our view of the history and chronology of Aitolia in the second century BC, among other things.

There are two milestones from the Roman period in the museum which come from a place called Rhonghia in the vicinity of modern Stamna. Stamna is located on the left side of Acheloos south of Angelokastron. The earlier of the two milestones was made under the emperor Trajan (114-115 AD) and indicates a distance of 25 Roman miles. The later milestone was put up under Carus, Carinus and Numerianus (283 AD) and Constantius I. and Maximinian (293-305 AD).

Another milestone in Greek comes from Drymos, more precisely from a place called Kefeli. By means of the reference to C. Julius Verus Maximinus Thrax and his son of the same name the stone can be dated as belonging to the period of about 235-238 AD. The milestone from Drymos is now in the museum of Thyrion. These inscriptions were published by Kornelia Axiote.[9]

Taken as a whole, these inscriptions show only too clearly that Roman roads already existed in Acarnania in the first century AD and that they were then repaired under Trajan. These milestones provide us with a surprising glimpse into the Roman infrastructure in northwestern Greece of the Roman period. There was an important public road here which connected Nikopolis with Kalydon and the Gulf of Corinth. This road went from Actium, the port of Nikopolis, to Drymos which was 2 kilometers from the southern coast of the Ambrakian gulf. As some still unpublished Latin and Greek inscriptions from the museum in Thyrion show, an Asklepios shrine and probably a larger Roman settlement were located here as well.

The further course of the road from Drymos to Stamna is a point of controversy. Claudia Antonetti, for example, thinks these milestones marked a Roman road from Vonitsa to modern Amphilochia.[10] According to Kornelia Axiote the road did not lead to Amphilochia; rather it turned south directly in the area of Drymos, then led across a ford of the river Acheloos to the ancient site near Stamna. From here one could travel along the road to Calydon and the Gulf of Corinth.

The town of Thyrion, formerly Hag. Vasilios, lies on the northern slope of Mt. Bergandi. The present village is in the area of the important Acarnanian polis Thyrrheion, an ancient city surrounded by 10-kilometer long walls near the Ambrakian gulf. The museum was build in 1962. The museum contains a lot of archeological material from the ancient polis Thyrrheion dating form the classical to Roman periods. The epigraphical material consists of many funerary stelae and other material which comes primarily from the cemeteries of ancient Thyrrheion, from the area of the ancient Anaktorion and from the region of modern Vonitsa.

The work in the museum of Thyrion, the ancient Thyrrheion, produced even more results in terms of epigraphy. If you leaf through the Acarnania volume of the *Inscriptiones Graecae* by G. Klaffenbach, you find that 139 of the altogether 368 Acarnanian inscriptions collected there come from Thyrrheion and the surrounding area. In the interim more than 100 additional inscriptions from Thyrrheion have been reported in *Deltion* and *Ergon*. In September 1997 we could record a total of 291 inscriptions. Thus the number of unpublished or only provisionally published inscriptions in the museum is considerable.

The variety of the epigraphical material is remarkable: The museum exhibits the well-known Roman-Aitolian treaty of alliance from 212 BC, which G. Klaffenbach published in 1954, as well as the famous treaty of alliance between Rome and Thyrrheion from 94 BC. I will treat this Foedus below in greater detail. A Proxenie decree of the Acarnanian federation which was recently published by P. Funke, H.-J. Gehrke and L. Kolonas was also found in Thyrrheion.[11] This honorary decree for a Roman named G. Baebius not only gives us an insight into the history of Acarnania in its conflict with Rome in the second century BC, but also provides us with important historical information about the political situation of the Acarnanian federation in the late Hellenistic period.

Some other largely fragmentary decrees from Thyrrheion, which are probably from the late Hellenistic period, are among the newly discovered inscriptions. They are particularly important because they name city officials who were unknown up until now. Thus we learn that Prytanes and Grammateis acted as eponymous officials in Thyrrheion. Promnamones and Sympromnamones are mentioned as magistrates in the Acarnanian city of Thyrrheion for the first time.

There are also numerous lists of priests and cult officials from Thyrrheion which are interesting from a religious-historical point of view because cult officials are named, for example Hierophoros, Mageiros, etc. Several dedications, some of which are again unpublished inscriptions, give some indication of the entire spectrum of the divinities worshiped in Thyrrheion: Among others, the inscriptions mention Aphrodite with the exceptional epitheton Stratagis, Hermes, Pan, Priapos, Hermes, a cult of Herakles, as well as the cult of Zeus Melichios and of Zeus Xenios.

The epitaphs from the Hellenistic period are particularly numerous. Although it is a rather thankless task to record and publish these hundred epitaphs, we still think that this material will definitely be useful in view of future onomastical and prosopographical research[12], also in historical terms.

A new fragment of the alliance (foedus)

between Thyrrheion and Rome, which I have already mentioned, can be found in the museum of Thyrrheion. The naming of the consuls, the praetor urbanus and the praetor perigrinus makes it possible to date this inscription exactly – the year is 94 BC (Inscriptiones Graecae IX, 1², 2, 242). The upper part of the inscribed stele has been known for a long time. Günther Klaffenbach discovered this inscription in 1934 as a spoil built into a house in Thyrrheion. Klaffenbach published this inscription in the Acarnanian volume of the Inscriptiones Graecae.[13] This fragment was brought to the museum of Thyrion after the archeological collection was set up. A second fragment belonging to the inscription was discovered later and was brought to the museum in Thyrion in 1963; its inventory number is 14. Unfortunately no further information can be found concerning the exact site of the discovery of this fragment in the environs of Thyrion. This fragment was reported by E. Mastrokostas in 1963 in the Archaiologikon Deltion, but it has not yet been published.[14]

We are now in the process of preparing this fragment for publication. Now at least the treaty of alliance between Thyrrheion and Rome includes a total of 20 lines. The already published fragment contains the only completely preserved prescript of a treaty of alliance between Rome and a state in eastern Greece. The prescript closes with the naming of envoys from Thyrrheion who had traveled to Rome prior to the negotiations. The new fragment which is part of the inscription helps us get a further insight into the individual modalities of the agreement. In terms of the modalities of the agreements in the other treaties between Rome and smaller cities in eastern Greece, it is immediately striking that they are virtually identical. For this reason it is not difficult to reconstruct the new text.

We find here a declaration of permanent "friendship and alliance" (filia kai summachia) between Rome and the people of Thyrrheion which is to last forever on land and on sea; it adds that there should be no wars between the two parties. After

226

that there is a passage which states that neither party, neither the Romans nor the people of Thyrrheion, should allow enemies to pass through its land or through territory it controls.

In addition, the next provision prohibits assisting potential enemies by supplying grain, weapons, money and ships. The inscription breaks off here. Other standard provisions are missing: Each party must assist the other if an enemy starts a war against one of them. Another clause which is missing permits the amendment of the treaty by agreement of both parties. A treaty between Rome and a Greek state concludes by regulating the place where the text is exhibited (*pinax summaxias*) in Rome and the allied city.

In addition to the great historical significance of the inscription we would like to point out that with the help of the inscription it might be possible to reassess the epigraphical supplements and some other problems concerning the foedera between Rome and other Greek states which have long since been published and are preserved solely as fragments. With the help of the treaty from Thyrrheion together with the well-preserved treaty of alliance between Rome and the Thracian Maroneia[15], it may be possible to reconsider the language and formulas in other treaties, for example the treaties with Astypalaia (Sherk 1969, No. 16) and Mytilene (IG XII 2, 35).

Another important and still unpublished inscription from Thyrrheion which was discovered only a few years ago records a Roman senatorial decree in Greek translation from Rouga. The inscription stone had been used as a threshold in a house and is now stored temporarily in Vonitsa. Rouga, the site of the discovery of the inscription, is the name of a small peninsula near Vonitsa, approximately 6 km from Thyrion as the crow flies. From an archeological point of view it is interesting to note that the remains of an ancient paved road have been found near Rouga which obviously connected the coastal settlement and a small harbor with ancient Thyrrheion.

Lazaros Kolonas, who is the responsible ephoros for our region, reported this exceptional new find for the first time in 1995.[16] Unfortunately this extensive inscription which is formulated in several columns is in bad condition so that we have considerable problems with the reconstruction of the text.

The dating of the inscription is also problematic. Since the prescript naming the Roman officials is preserved in only a very fragmentary condition, it is not possible to date the inscription by means of the named eponymous officials. We will only be able to make some headway by using formal dating criteria such as the character of the letters, the inscription form and by means of other content-oriented considerations. The shapes of the letters, the inscription form and also the terminology suggest a dating in the second half of the second century or the first decades of the first century BC. As far as the content is concerned, a long-term conflict between the people of Thyrrheion and the Nesiotai, the "island inhabitants", is the subject of the inscription. The parties to the conflict had sent legations to Rome and accused each other there of diverse offenses. Among other things the Nesiotai complain that, contrary to previous senatorial decrees, they were attacked by the people of Thyrrheion at night and subsequently had to accommodate an occupational force in their city.

In the brief time allotted to me here I cannot treat all the philological, prosopographical and historical problems connected with this inscription. Above all else, three questions are of special importance, and we hope that we will be able to find answers to these questions, at least in part, in the course of our epigraphical and historical work.

Who are the Nesiotai and where is the polis of the Nesiotai located?

On the basis of the inscription, how can the relationship between the Nesiotai, the people of Thyrrheion and an Acarnanian federation which is still possibly in existence be described? How is the new *senatus consultum* from Rouga temporally and textually related to the treaty of alliance between Thyrrheion and Rome from 94 AD?

About 60 years after the conclusion of the treaty of alliance between Thyrrheion and Rome Octavian/Augustus founded the victory city Nikopolis in memory of his decisive naval victory over Antonius and Cleopatra. In an epigram of Antipatros of Thessaloniki, a contemporary of Augustus, Thyrrheion is named among the cities which were annexed to Nikopolis.[17] The rest of the ancient authors do not even mention Thyrrheion. During the period of time we worked there in the museum we were struck by the relatively large number of epitaphs from the Roman period, some of which were of excellent quality. In addition there is a multitude of other archeological remains in the collection from all areas of life which must certainly be dated as belonging to the same period. As a result it seems to us that a critical reevaluation of the thesis that Thyrrheion was deserted after the founding of Nikopolis is imperative. In reality the reorganization of northwestern Greece after 30 BC in terms of settlement policy evolved in a far more complex manner than that suggested in the summarizing and disparate source material.

Let us summarize what has been presented: All in all, we were able to study 141 inscriptions in the museum of Agrinion and 291 inscriptions in the collection in Thyrion. In 1996 and 1997 we were thus able to study and document a total of 432 Greek and Latin inscriptions from northwestern Greece. Most of the material has been at least provisionally published. The responsible ephori announce new epigraphical finds regularly in preliminary reports in *Archaiologikon Deltion*. About 10% of the inscriptions have not yet been published. This paper could not be anything more than a "workshop report" as I have already said. We do think, however, that a comprehensive revision of the epigraphical material in the museums of Agrinion and Thyrion is quite a worthwhile undertaking. The epigraphical research can help expand our knowledge of the ancient history of northwestern Greece in many facets and in a decisive way, not only with regard to the Classical and Hellenistic periods, but also for the second and first century BC and the Roman period. In the end we may be able to place our historical hypothesis on more solid ground.

Notes

NOTE 1★
I would like to thank L. Kolonas very much, also in the name of my colleague D. Strauch, for generously giving us permission to study the inscriptions in the museums of Agrinion and Thyrion. We would also like to express our special thanks to the local directors and staff of the museums. Without their energetic support and assistance the epigraphical work could never have been finished on site in such a relatively short amount of time.

NOTE 2
Dittenberger 1897.

NOTE 3
Romaios 1918, 105-124

NOTE 4
Klaffenbach 1932

NOTE 5
Klaffenbach 1935. Klaffenbach 1936. Klaffenbach 1939, 189-209. Klaffenbach 1954. See Toulomakos 1995, 193-199.

NOTE 6
Klaffenbach 1957.

NOTE 7
Strauch 1997, 209-254. Mela & Preka & Strauch 1998, 281-303.

NOTE 8
Mastrokostas 1965, 152-159. McCamp, 1977, 277ff.

NOTE 9
Axiote 1986, 186-205.

NOTE 10
Antonetti 1986, 39-72.

NOTE 11
Funke & Gehrke & Kolonas 1993, 131-144.

NOTE 12
Antonetti 1996, 149-155.

NOTE 13
Bernhardt, 1971, 72ff. Baranowski 1982. Sherwin-White 1984, 66ff. Gruen 731-744. Ferrary 1990, 217-235. Derow 1991, 261-270. Kallet-Marx 1995. Avram 1996, 491-511.

NOTE 14
E. Mastrokostas, AD 18 B 1 (1963) [1965] 148, Strauch, 1996, 135 and 370.

NOTE 15
Triantaphyllos 1983, 419-449. Loukopoulou, 1987, 101-110. Stern 1987, 501-509.

NOTE 16
L. Kolonas, AD 45, 1990 (1995), 140.

NOTE 17
Anth. Pal. IX 553.

Bibliography

Antonetti, C., 1986
L´Acarnania in epoca imperiale: contributi epigrafici, *Epigraphica* 48, 39-72.

Antonetti, C., 1996
La diffusione dei nomi romani in Etolia e in Acarnania e la presenza romana nella regione, in: A. D. Rizakis (ed.)., *Roman onomastics in the Greek east. Social and political aspects*, Athens/Paris (Meletemata 21.) 149-155.

Avram, A., 1996
Der Vertrag zwischen Rom und Kallatis (CIL I (2) 2, 2676), in: *Hellenismus. Beiträge zur Erforschung von Akkulturation und politischer Ordnung in den Staaten des hellenistischen Zeitalters.* Akten des Internationalen Hellenismus-Kolloquiums, hrsg. v. B. Funck. Tübingen 491-511.

Axiote, K., 1986
Ρωμαικών δρόμοι της Αιτωλοακαρνανίας, *AD* 35, 1980, 186-205.

Baranowski, D. W., 1982
Treaties of Military Alliance between Rom and Hellenistic States in the Last three Centuries B.C., Diss. Toronto

Bernhardt, R., 1971
Imperium und Eleutheria. Die römische Politik gegenüber den freien Städten des griechischen Ostens, Diss. Hamburg

Derow, P. S., 1991
Pharos and Rom, *ZPE* 88, 261-270.

Dittenberger, W., 1897
Vol. IX. *Inscriptiones Graeciae septentrionalis voluminibus VII et VIII non comprehensae. IG IX 1 Pars. I. Inscriptiones Phocidis, Locridis, Aetoliae, Acarnaniae, insularum maris Ionii.* Edid. Guilelmus Dittenberger, Berlin 1897.

Ferrary, J.-L., 1990
Traités et domination romaine dans le monde hellénique, in: M. Liverani e C. Zaccagnini (edd.), *I trattati nel mondo antico. Forma, ideologia, funzione,* Roma 217-235.

Funke, P., Gehrke, H.-J. & Kolonas, L., 1993
Ein neues Proxeniedekret des Akarnanischen Bundes, *Klio* 75, 131-144.

Gruen, E. S., 1984
The Hellenistic World and the Coming of Rome, Vol. 2, Berkeley.

Kallet-Marx, R. M., 1995
Hegemony to Empire. The development of the Roman Imperium in the East from 148 to 62 B.C. Berkeley ect.

Klaffenbach, G., 1932
IG IX 1 2 Pars I. (ed. altera): *Inscriptiones Phocidis, Locridis, Aetoliae, Acarnaniae, insularum maris Ionii. Fasc. 1. Inscriptiones Aetoliae.* Edid. Guentherus Klaffenbach, Berlin 1932.

Klaffenbach, G., 1935.
Bericht über eine epigraphische Reise durch Mittelgriechenland und die Ionischen Inseln. SB Berlin.

Klaffenbach, G., 1936
Neue Inschriften aus Ätolien, SB Berlin.

Klaffenbach, G., 1939
Zur Geschichte Ätoliens und Delphis im 3. Jahrhundert v. Chr., *Klio* 32, 189-209.

Klaffenbach, G., 1954
Der römisch-ätolische Bündnisvertrag vom Jahre 212 v. Chr., SB Berlin.

Klaffenbach, G., 1957
IG IX 1 2 Pars I. (ed. altera*): Inscriptiones Phocidis, Locridis, Aetoliae, Acarnaniae, insularum maris Ionii. Fasc. 2. Inscriptiones Acarnaniae.* Edid. Guentherus Klaffenbach 1957.

Loukopoulou, L. D., 1987
Provinciae Macedoniae finis orientalis: The Establishment of the Eastern Frontier, Hatzopoulos, M. B., and Loukopoulou, L.D. (edd.), *Two Studies in ancient Macedonian Topography*, Athens, 101-110.

Mastrokostas, E. I., 1965
Inschriften aus Ätolien, Akarnanien und Westlokris, *AM* 90, 152-159.

Mela, P. & Preka, K., & Strauch, D. 1998
Die Grabstelen vom Grundstück Andrioti auf Korkyra, *AA, 281-303*.

McCamp, I. 1977
Inscriptions from Palairos, *Hesperia* 46, 277ff.

Romaios, K. A. 1918
ANA THN AKARNANIAN, *AD* 4, 105-124.

Sherk, R.K. 1969
Roman Documents from the Greek East. Senatus consulta and Epistulae to the Age of Augustus, Baltimore.

Sherwin-White, A. N. 1984
Roman Foreign Policy in the East 168 B.C. to A.D. 1, Norman

Stern, J. 1987
Le traité d´alliance entre Rome et Maronée, *BCH* 111, 501-509.

Strauch, D. 1997
Aus der Arbeit am Inschriften-Corpus der Ionischen Inseln: IG IX 1²,4, *Chiron* 27, 209-254.

Strauch, D. 1995
Römische Politik und Griechische Tradition. Die Umgestaltung Nordwest-Griechenlands unter römischer Herrschaft, München.

Toulomakos, J. 1995
ΕΡΑΝΙΣΜΑΤΑ, 1. G. Klaffenbach´s epigraphische Forschungsreise in Mittelgriechenland, *TEKMHRIA* 1, 193-199.

Triantaphyllos, D. 1983
Συμμαχία Ρωμαίων και Μαρωνιτών, *Thrakike Epeteris* 4, 419-449.

The Cults of Apollo in Northwestern Greece

Chryseis Tzouvara-Souli

The purpose of our paper is to present all the sanctuaries of Apollo[1] in the areas of northwestern Greece, to discuss their cult affinities and to point out the existence of the worship of Apollo from Archaic times to the foundation of Nicopolis (31 BC).

The most famous sanctuaries and cults of Apollo can be found not only in the Corinthian colonies of northwestern Greece or in the areas affected by Corinthian influence (Ambracia, Apollonia, Corcyra, Leucas, Anactorium, Thermos, Calydon, Buthrotum, Amantia, Oricum) but also in other Epirotic sites such as Molossian Orrao and Dodona.

One of the main deities who were worshipped in Corinth was Apollo, whose cult is evident from the 7th century BC when a temple was built in honour of the god on the Holy Hill[2], through the Roman period, when the temple was reconstructed.[3]

Our information about the antiquity of the cult in Corinth comes from Herodotus (3. 52) and Pindar (Olymp. 13). According to a note of Will,[4] Apollo played a significant role in the abolition of tyranny in Corinth.

It is plausible that Apollo, originally protector of the tyrants,[5] might have played a major role in the history of the town as Archegetes and Agyieus,[6] who led the Corinthians to far-away colonies, and later as Pythios Soter who sent away the tyrants and according to Pindar re-established "Eunomia, Themis, and Dike".

The parallel cult of Apollo as Archegetes, Agyieus and Pythios Soter in the Corinthian colonies of Epirus (Ambracia and Apollonia) and in Corcyra, is one piece of evidence of the very close cult relations between Corinth and her colonies.[7]

In particular, Apollo recieved a special worship in Ambracia,[8] the most important colony in Epirus, which always kept up close relations with its mother city.[9]

According to literary evidence and archaeological finds, Apollo was worshipped as Agyieus, that is the god who protects the road.[10]

As far as the worship of Apollo in Ambracia is concerned, the reference of Athanadas,[11] a historian of the 4th century BC, is very indicative.

Athanadas refers to a quarrel between Apollo, Artemis and Heracles for the possession of the town and the intervention of the local hero Cragaleus. The tradition is also mentioned by Nicander and Antoninus Liberalis (4. 7).[12] Nilsson,[13] referring to the above passage, believes that Cragaleus was a local hero, who was displaced by Heracles,[14] and that the tradition is based on the worship of baetyl,[15] the symbol of Agyieus in Ambracia.

The frequent depiction of baetyl on the coins and the sealed tiles of the town from the Hellenistic period is evidence that Agyieus was the protector of Ambracia

Fig. 1. Tile from Ambracia of the 3rd / 2nd century BC with the inscription ΠΟΛΙΟΣ and baetyl.

and that this cult played an important role in the town.

The baetyl is found on many coins of Ambracia dating from the second half of the 5th century BC through the Roman period. More specifically, it is represented together with Athena Chalinitis on the back of the silver staters of the town in the years 456/426 B.C and 360/333 BC.[16]

After 238 BC, this symbol became the main image on the back of most coins from Ambracia, while the main deities of the town, that is to say Athena, Apollo, and Dione, are depicted alternately on the front.[17]

The baetyl of Agyieus also decorates the tiles of the temples and the public buildings of Ambracia and is accompanied by one of two inscriptions, either [Δ]ΑΜΟ[Σ]ΙΑ or ΠΟΛΙΟΣ and the initials of the town ΑΜΒΡ.[18] (Fig. 1).

The postarchaic temple of Arta is asso-ciated with the cult of Apollo.[19] The iden-tification of the temple with the most im-portant sanctuary of Ambracia, which was dedicated to the cult of Apollo Pythios and Soter, is confirmed by a stele of the 2nd century BC.[20]

This stele bears an inscription, which concerns a treaty defining of the bound-aries between two neighbouring towns, Ambracia and Charadros. The small part of the epilogue of the passage, which has been saved, includes an oath to the gods for the faithful observance of the terms of the treaty, placing special emphasis on the invocation of Soter. This must be Soter Pythios Apollo,[21] according to the invoca-tion of the god in a passage by Antoninus Liberalis IV. 7: Ἀμβρακιῶται δ'Ἀπόλλωνι μὲν Σωτῆρι θύουσι.[22]

Archaeological data, however, also sup-ports the attribution of the temple to the cult of Apollo. To be more specific, in the

Fig. 2. The base with trime-rous construction from the cella of the post Archaic temple of Apollo in Ambracia.

234

Fig. 3. The inscribed Corinthian Stele of the middle of the 6th century BC with a baetyl in a burial monument in Ambracia.

rear of the cella there is a base with a tri-partite construction and incised signs of a circle, which was used for the support of the symbol of the worshipped deity, i.e Pythios Apollo or Agyieus[23] (Fig. 2). Moreover, the base which supported the baetyl on the silver and bronze coins of Ambracia, is represented in the same way.[24]

A similar monument was found in Corinth, the metropolis of Ambracia, which supported the baetyl, the symbol of the god who led the colonists to the distant colonies.[25] It consists of a large circular pedestal, which is placed on a rectangular foundation near a street.

As the drawings of the architect of Elgin, Ittar, have shown[26] the monument consisted of more columns or drums of columns, a fact which allows us to associate it with the baetyl of Apollonia. As well, its dating according to recent archaeological research to the classical period,[27] and its position near a street support the attribution of the monument to the cult of Apollo Agyieus. This aspect is also reinforced by the finding of a stone baetyl near the temple of Asklepius in Corinth.[28]

Another argument, which testifies to the importance of the Agyieus cult in Corinth and the special significance of the baetyl, is the depiction of a baetyl in a burial stele[29] (Fig. 3). This stele has been erected by the Corinthians in a common burial monument (The Polyandrion of Ambracia), because they wanted to honour the dead from a naval-battle which took place near the Arachtus river after the mid-6th century BC between Corinthians and Ambracians one one side and Corcyraeans on the other.[30]

As well the other archaeological finds from Ambracia such as bronze coins from 238/168 BC with a radiate head of Apollo in front and on the other side Apollo naked, radiate, advancing right with bow in left hand and quiver with arrow at his back and in the field the inscription AM/BP, testify the importance of the cult.[31]

Another bronze coin from Ambracia dated to the same period 3rd /2nd century BC shows in its front a radiate or laureate head of Apollo and on the back a naked Zeus advancing right with thunderbolt in his raised right hand and an aegis in his left with the initial AM/BP.[32]

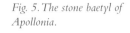
Fig. 5. The stone baetyl of Apollonia.

Fig. 4. Bronze coin from Athamania, dated to 190 BC, with head of the god laureate depicted on the obverse and bucranium and the inscription ΑΘΑΜΑΝΩΝ on the reverse.

To the same period, 3rd/2nd century BC, belong the inscribed stelai from Ambracia dedicated to many gods and goddesses, among them Apollo.[33]

As the archaeological data testify the cult of Apollo spread from Ambracia to the neighbouring areas like Athamania. The bronze coins from Athamania dated to 190 BC depict the head of the god laureate in front and on the back bucranium and the inscription ΑΘΑΜΑΝΩΝ[34] (Fig. 4).

The cult of Apollo was also important in Apollonia,[35] which was named after the god. In this city there are two stone baetyls. They were the symbol of the town. One of them has been preserved almost intact (Fig. 5) and is found near the Odeum of the town and the temple of Artemis,[36] while the other is in pieces and stands on a pedestal in front of the 4th century BC town wall.

The continuous representation of the baetyl on the coins[37] of Apollonia from the end of the fifth century BC to the Roman period is of great interest. The archaeological finds lead to the conclusion that Apollo Agyieus was the protector of the Apollonians and that his symbol, the baetyl, was the symbol of the town (Fig. 6).

One of the temples of Apollonia from the Archaic period has been attributed to the cult of Apollo.[38] The god was worshipped in Apollonia together with Artemis as in Corinth and the Corinthian colonies (Ambracia, Corcyra, Syracuse, also in Thermos and Calydon), according to philological and epigraphical evidence and the archaeological data,[39] and his cult was not prior to the period of colonization.[40]

The cult of Apollo spread from Ambracia and Apollonia to the neighbouring areas and it was well accepted by the other Epirote tribes.

Recent discoveries have shown that Agyieus was worshipped in the Molossian settlement Orrao,[41] which was surrounded by walls and which has been recently identified with the ruins of Ammotopos. A piece of a tile which was found in Orrao bears a representation of a baetyl on a biconcave base and the two letters MO, representing the initial letters of the tribal designation Molossos.[42]

Ambracia, a neighbouring town where there was considerable worship of the god, is regarded as the most probable place of the origin for this cult.

The cult of Agyieus, based on coin evidence, is attested in Oricum from the 3rd/2nd century BC. The baetyl is represented on a laurel wreath with the inscription ΩΡΙΚΙΩΝ on the back of bronze coins of the 3rd/2nd century BC.[43]

A baetyl with the inscription ΑΜΑΝΤΩΝ is represented on 2nd century BC bronze coins from the town which bear

Fig. 7. Statue of Apollo in Buthrotum from the Roman Period.

on the front the head of Artemis. Due to the close and friendly relations between Oricum and Amantia, Apollonia is considered as the most probable place of origin for the cult.[44]

It is probably due to the same reasons that Agyieus was worshipped in Olympi,[45] which was identified with the ruins of Mavrove, to the northeast of Aulon. The baetyl is represented on the back of 3rd and 2nd century BC bronze coins from the town with the inscription ΟΛΥΜΠΙΑ/ΣΤΑΝ, while the front is decorated with the head of Apollo.

It is also to a Corinthian influence that we must attribute the cult of Apollo in Buthrotum,[46] a region where many protocorinthian and Corinthian sherds were found, and where the peninsula Examili probably served as a Corinthian base.

Statues[47] of the god (Fig. 7) were found together with statues of Dionysos in this town. Ugolini dates them to Roman times, but Hammond suggests that these statues are evidence of a most ancient cult to the gods mentioned above in Buthrotum. As well, in Buthrotum, other deities whose cult has been detected in Corinth, were also worshipped.[48]

All the above mentioned data have shown that the cult of Apollo in Epirus is centered in the Corinthian colonies and it is from there that it spread to the neighbouring areas and influenced other tribes in Epirus.

Apollo was particularly worshipped in Dodone, as is certified by the oracular tablets of the 4th century BC, which refer to Themis and Apollo, together with Zeus Naios and Dione Naia:[49]

[Ζεῦ Νάιε καὶ Διώνα να]ῖα, Θέμι καὶ Ἀπόλλωνι [σωτ]ηρίας καὶ Τύχας ...].

From the rest of the finds which give

proof that there was a cult of Apollo in the sanctuary, a bronze statuette of Apollo is of greatest interest.[50] This statuette is dated to the middle of the 6th century BC and was a dedication to the sanctuary of Dodone by Etymocleidas according to the engraved inscription.[51]

The picture of the cult of Apollo at the sanctuary of Dodone is completed by an archaistic metal sheet from a cuirass, which has depicted on it the quarrel between Heracles and Apollo for the Delphic tripod.[52] (Fig. 8)

It is not clear, however, if the cult of Apollo at the sanctuary of Dodone is due to Corinthian influence or if it is due to

Fig. 8. The quarrel between Heracles and Apollo for the Delphic tripod in archaistic sheet, of metal of cuirass from the sanctuary of Dodona.

Fig. 9. Bronze base votive shoes with engraving inscription to Apollo Corcyraeus from the temple of Apollo on Mon Repos at Corcyra.

the nature of the god who is also worshipped in other oracular sanctuaries.[53]

It is known that Corinth from early times showed interest in northwestern Greece and its foundation myth indicates the relationship between Corinth and the oracle of Dodone.[54] According to a commentator on Pindar (Nem. 7. 155a) Aletes, who later became king of Corinth, asked for a prophecy from Zeus of Dodone and occupied the town which he named "Corinth of Zeus" in honour of the god who gave him this prophecy.[55]

Regardless of the origin of the cult of Apollo at the sanctuary of Dodone, the god was also worshipped as Molossos.[56] This adjective proves the significance of the cult in the Molossian tribe to which Dodone belonged.

Returning to the Corinthian colonies in northwestern Greece, where Apollo was especially worshipped, Corcyra,[57] the biggest and most important colony, should also, and even more so, have honored its protector and founder god. Indeed, according to archaeological data, the god was worshipped from the sixth century

BC until the Roman period. His cult probably took place alongside that of Pythios Apollo in the same sanctuary. Pythios Apollo is the god who helped the Corinthian colonies to throw off the tyranny and restore the democratic regime.

A column of the 7th/6th century BC, triangular in shape with an inscription ΜΥΣ ΜΕ ΙΣΑΤΟ, is connected with the cult of Agyieus as small clay votive shoes show.[58]

However, according to inscriptions, Apollo was worshipped in Corcyra as Corcyraeus. This cult is connected with a small, open-air sanctuary of the 6th/5th century BC on the N.A. side of the hill of Mon-Repos near the large sanctuary of Hera.[59] The kind of offerings to the god found here testify to his warlike nature.[60] Among them postarchaic clay bust of the god or priests of the god.[61]

From the other votives at the sanctuary a marble *perirrhantirium* with the inscription [ΑΠΟΛΛ]ΟΝ is of great interest, while on the rim of a phiale dated from the beginning of the 5th century BC one can read the dedicatory inscription to Apollo Corcyraeus.[62] The same inscription is engraved on the bronze foot of a tripod and found on another category of offerings as well.[63] It concerns bronze shoes: one of them is a micrographic sandal while the other two are bronze coated, normal sized, wooden shoes. On one of them the dedicatory inscription to Apollo Corcyraeus is preserved[64] (Fig. 9).

Parallel to the warlike character of Apollo, the god was associated in Corcyra with the Nymphs and was worshipped as Nomios Apollo according to Apollonius

Fig. 10. The temple of Apollo of the 7th century BC in Thermos.

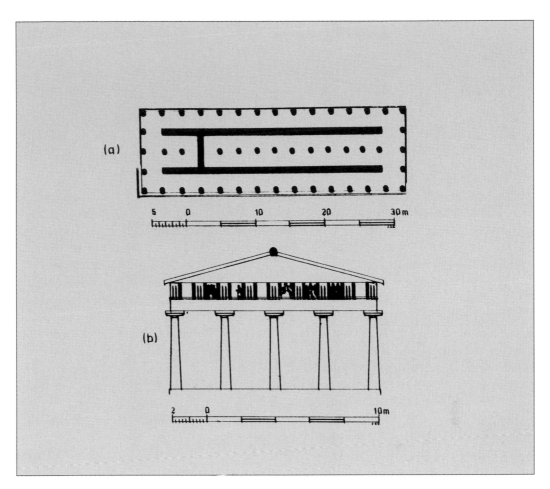

Rhodius (4. 1217-1219): Dörpfeld, Rhomaios and Calligas tried to locate the sanctuary.[65]

According to Apollonius Rhodius, 4. 1216 Apollo received an analogous worship in Oricum.[66]

In the study concerning the cult of Apollo in Northwestern Greece we must include two important sanctuaries of the god in Thermos and Calydon, situated in an area which was influenced by Corinth.[67]

The temple of Apollo in Thermos of Aetolia, dated to the last quarter of the 7th century BC (Fig. 10), was built in the place of other buildings of the Mycenaean and Geometric times. It preserves important samples both of the Corinthian and of native art.[68]

The activity of the Corinthian artists in northwestern Greece, during the 7th century BC as well as that of the natives, is demonstrated by the architectural decoration dated to the end of the 7th century

BC, of the small temple of Lyceios Apollo in Thermos, and by that of the temples in Calydon and Corcyra.[69]

Concerning the epithet of the god, Thermius, which is testified by the inscriptions that were found in the sanctuary of Apollo,[70] several opinions have been expressed: K. Rhomaios' opinion[71] has been predominant and it is indeed accepted by more recent researchers. Relying on the archaeological data, he attributes an inflammatory character to the god. And indeed the excavations that took place at the geometric sanctuary of Apollo in Thermos, gave evidence of the celebration of sacrifices of that kind.[72]

So it seems that a native cult preexisted the one of Thermius Apollo, which, however, must have come under the influence of Corinth, by the end of the 7th century BC, when Corinth colonizes northwestern Greece.[73] This opinion is supported by the archaeological finds which attest to the Corinthian artistic influence on the

Fig. 11. Inscribed plaque of the 6th century BC with the name Apollo Laphrius from Calydon.

regions of Aetolia, as well as by the cult epithet of Apollo, Lyceios.[74]

The surname Lyceios Apollo was found in an inscription from the end of 3th/beginning of the 2th century BC, which was found near the large temple in Thermos.[75] This inscription made it possible to associate the small temple of the Archaic Period, from around 600 BC, on the eastern part of the sanctuary of Apollo, with the worship of Lyceios Apollo.[76]

This surname Lyceios is also connected with Dionysos in Corinth. Here Apollo was worshipped since the Archaic period, and as Pausanias tells us (2. 2. 6), there were wooden statues of Dionysos with the surnames Lyceios and Bacchius at the Agora in Corinth.[77] The fact that these wooden statues (xoana) were placed close to one of Artemis, shows the common origin of the myths and the existence of the same kind of ecstatic cult for both gods.[78]

The god must have been worshipped in a similar way in Thermos, where, near the temple of Lyceios Apollo, there existed a small temple of Artemis from the 6th century BC, as it is clear from its terracotta decoration.[79]

Rhomaios identifies a bronze statuette from the end of the 7th century BC, which was found in the temple of Apollo, as the goddess Artemis whom he considers as an important deity in Thermos and Aetolia in general.[80]

Relationships between Dionysos and Artemis from the Archaic period up to the Roman one, are also attested in Calydon,[81] next to Thermos. The two main

gods of Calydon, Apollo Laphrius and Artemis Laphria were worshipped together with Dionysos (Paus. 4. 31. 7 and 7. 18. 8) in two temples, from the beginning of the 6th century BC.[82] The epigraphical evidence and the archaeological finds confirm the identification of the temples.[83]

In Calydon, together with Artemis, Apollo was already worshipped from the 6th century BC, as an inscribed stele of the 6th century BC, a kind of horos, attests. On this appears the name of Apollo Laphrius in the Corinthian alphabet[84] (Fig. 11). We are also told about the cult of the god by Strabo (10. 2. 21), who refers to the sanctuary as being one of Laphrius Apollo.[85]

The cult of Apollo in Leucas is probably associated with the Corinthian colonists, since Leucas is also Corinthian colony.[86] According to the literary evidence (Thuc. 39. 4. 2, Strab. 10.2, Greek Anth. 6. 251) and the archaeological data, the god was worshipped from the 5th century BC until the Roman period, with the name Leucatas and a temple was founded in his honour.[87] The depiction of the god on coins of the 4th and 2nd century BC is due to the particular worship which Apollo received in Leucas.[88]

As well, other cults of Corinthian origin are also testified to in Leucas; one of them is the cult of Athena, which according to a dedicatory inscription from the 6th century BC on a bronze helmet, belongs to the Archaic period.[89]

The silver staters of Leucas representing Pegasus and Athena Chalinitis dated to the end of the 6th century BC show the very strong influence of Corinth.[90]

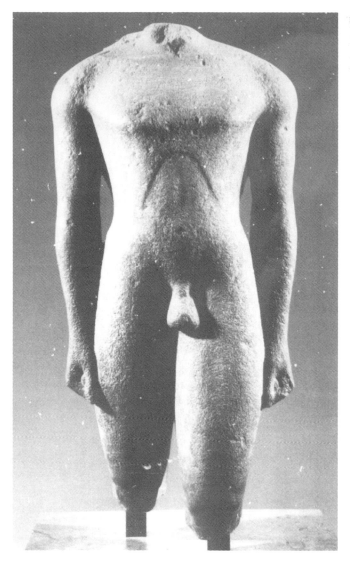

Fig. 12. The Kouroi of the 6th century BC from the temple of Apollo in Anactorium.

The picture of the Corinthian origin of many of the cults in Leucas is completed with the cult of the Nymphs and the other deities, Hermes, Pan, Silenoi and Satyrs as is shown by the study of archaeological material from caves in the island.[91]

Another cult of Apollo, is the one of Actius Apollo[92] which is investigated in Corinth. The god owes his name to the sanctuary in Actium, "the mouth of the Ambracian gulf" according to Strabo (10. 2. 7).[93]

Actius Apollo, god of navigation, was first worshipped in Anactorium,[94] a colony that the Corinthians founded around 625 BC, at the side of Ambracian gulf together with other colonies, such as Sollium and Heracleia.

In honour of Apollo the colonists es-

tablished a sanctuary, known to Thucydides (1. 29. 3), who also gives its topography.[95] The early worship of Actius Apollo is also testified to by archaeological finds and especially by the Kouroi of the first half of the 6th century BC, which belonged to the ancient temple.[96] (Fig. 12)

The *Actia* were celebrated in honour of Actius Apollo from at least the 4th century BC onwards. From the 3rd century BC, about 216 BC, the Acarnanians undertook the conduct of the games, after an agreement with Anactorium, by which the charge of the sanctuary of the Actius Apollo, was transferred to the Acarnanians.[97]

Moreover, the significance of the cult of Actius Apollo is attested to by the consular inscription of the 2nd century BC which mentions the god's priests, and by the frequent depiction of Apollo on silver coins of Anactorium from the 4th century BC as well as on bronze ones of the 3rd century to the 2nd century BC.[98]

The cult of Actius Apollo probably spread from Anactorium to the neighbouring areas like Ambracia as the archaeological data testify. In the bronze coins from Ambracia dated to 3rd/2nd century BC the head of young Heracles in a lion's skin is depicted on the front and on the back Apollo Actius is seated with bow in right hand and the initial AM/BP in the field.[99]

Actius Apollo was worshipped also in Thyrreium according to the silver coins of the 2nd century BC with the beardless head of Achelous on the obverse and Apollo Actius naked, seated in a throne, on the reverse. The god holds in right hand a string bow and the elbow rests on a support. On the field the inscription ΘΥΡΡΕΙΩΝ.[100]

The archaeological data do not testify to Apollo's cult in Cassope.[101] This town's close connections with the neighbouring areas like Ambracia, Anactorium and Leukas, where, as we know, Apollo received a special cult, permit us to consider it probable that Apollo was worshipped in Cassope.[102]

On basis of the more ancient bronze coins of Cassope 342/340,[103] where a snake is depicted on the reverse, Franke,[104] trying to interpret this cult symbol in association with Apollo's cult, draws on Aelian's information (Aelian, *NA*, 11. 2). According to Aelian, during the annual Epirote festival in honour of Apollo a virgin priestess was offering food to snakes. But nothing relates this information to Cassope and to Apollo, especially.

It is also known from the archaeological data and the literary evidences that the cult of Actius Apollo continued until the Roman period in the same sanctuary.[105] However, when Nicopolis was founded by Octavian in 31 BC, Apollo became the city's protector, since Octavian attributed his victory to Actius Apollo.[106]

The hill found today in the northern part of the village Smyrtoula, is identical

with the hill where Octavian established his headquarters before the naval battle. He dedicated the hill to Apollo after his victory (Strab. 7. 7. 5) and had "a Victory monument" erected. Moreover, he ordered this "Victory monument" decorated with the spoils, the rams of the enemy boats, a statue of Apollo and other dedications (Dio Cassius 51. 1. 3, Suet. *Aug.* 96. 2).[107]

At the same time, he reorganized the *Actia,* the local festival of Acarnanians in order to perpetuate the historical victory of Actium.[108]

The presence of Actius Apollo on the coins[109] from the beginning up to the end of the functioning of the town's mint, must be due to the great cult that Apollo received in Nicopolis.

On the coins from Nicopolis the god is presented nude, standing, often on a base with a bow in his left hand and a torch or Nike (Victory) in his right hand, while on the Roman coins he is depicted differently as a chitharoedos with a long chiton.

Actius Apollo, who was already engraved on the first coins of the town, coins which were cut immediately after 28 BC, seems to be a copy of an archaic statue or is at least intended as a depiction of an archaic one.[110] (Fig. 13)

Fig. 14. Actius Apollo on the bronze coin from Nicopolis, dated to the reign of Caracalla, with branch and arrow and in front head of the town.

Fig. 15. Leucatas Apollo in a bronze coin from Nicopolis, dated to the reign of Traianus, with the inscription ΑΠΟΛΛΩΝ ΛΕΥΚΑΤΑΣ.

With slight variations the god is depicted on the coins of the periods of Iulia Domna and Caracalla, of Philip the Second, of Gallienus and Saloneina[111] (Fig. 14). The researchers' opinions, however, differ as to which epithet should be attributed to Apollo on the coin.[112]

More specifically Franke[113] claims that it depicts the cult statue of Apollo Leucadius and not the Actian one, as has been accepted by other researchers. He mainly bases his opinion on the depiction of the god on a unique bronze coin from Nicopolis dated from the period of Traianus which bears the inscription Leucatas Apollo[114] (Fig. 15). The god is represented on a round base with his head turned to the left and his hair tied and a quiver on his shoulder. In his left hand he holds an arrow and in his right a torch.[115]

Franke[116] also accepts that the worship of Leucadius Apollo was neither replaced nor assimilated to the cult of Actius Apollo, as it had been claimed, but was transferred to Nicopolis, where it survived for a long time, and this is demonstrated by the depiction of the god's cult statue on the coins of the town.

The question then is why did the people of Nicopolis prefer to depict Leucadius Apollo instead of Actius, the god that they mostly worshipped? On the base of Ovid's *Heroides* 15, 165-166 Sutherland accepts as probable the identification of the two cults, Actius's and Leucadius

Apollo's, as the same.[117] Because of this, a certain confusion in the representation of their cult statues must be considered as possible. We accept that Leucadius Apollo must have been worshipped in a major way in Nicopolis, as is shown by a coin of Traianus with the inscription *Apollo Leucatas* and also by the literary evidence, which associates Leucadius with the sea battle off Actium, e.g. Propertius 3. 11. 69: *Leucadius versas acies memorabit Apollo.*[118] Besides, the god's depiction on the coins of Nicopolis is justified as Leucatas Apollo was worshipped in Leucas which was synoecised with Nicopolis.[119]

Apollo was probably also worshipped as Agyieus, as is shown by two marble fragments of a baetyl, which were found in Nicopolis.[120]

One of these is preserved under the Number 865 in the Archaeological Museum of Nicopolis and has not been published. Its height is 0,44m and the diameter of its base is 0,11m. The cone, the top of which is missing, comes down to a wider base with two concaves. (Fig. 16) The irregularity of the base shows that it has been detached from a pedestal. This means that the baetyl of Nicopolis matches the usual depiction of Apollo's symbol, as it appears on the coins from the Epirote towns and on the sealed tiles of Ambracia. It also resembles the stone baetyl of Apollonia.

The worship of Apollo Agyieus was

transferred to Nicopolis either from neighbouring Ambracia because of the synoecism or more probably from Apollonia because of Augustus' wishes.[121] It is known that Octavian was introduced to this cult in the towns of northwestern Greece and especially in Apollonia, where he lived for a long period. Since this town was associated with some important events of Octavian's life, it is natural, as Picard-Schmitter[122] observes, that he adopted the symbol of the town and this symbol was Apollo's baetyl, that is the baetyl of the god with whom he chose to be identified.

We can also say that Octavian's preference for this god is made obvious by the fact that on the Palatine Hill he dedicated a temple to Apollo and decorated it with the god's symbols.[123] Among these symbols is the baetyl which became a popular subject in Roman art during imperial times. The worship of Agyieus in Nicopolis must be associated with Actius Apollo.[124] We are led to this conclusion by H. Küthmann's note which tells us that Actius Apollo, who is depicted on the silver staters and demistaters of the Koinon of the Acarnanians (300-167 BC), rests his left elbow on a column, which he interprets as Agyieus' baetyl.[125] For this reason, he considers necessary the association of Actius Delphinius-Agyieus Apollo of the coins, comparing them with the coins of Megara, where a mingling of Apollo Agyieus and Delphinius is reported.[126]

As far as we know, however, Agyieus' symbol is not depicted on the coins of Nicopolis. But the existence of two stone baetyls in Nicopolis attests to the significance of the cult, which was well received even in Rome.[127]

Summing up, we would like to suggest that Apollo received a special worship in the region of northwestern Greece and mainly in its Corinthian colonies. His cult spread from these colonies to the neighbouring regions and was well received among the most important tribes. The respective cults of Apollo as Archegetes, Agyieus and Pythios Soter, in Ambracia and Apollonia as well as in Corcyra, proves

the existence of the strong cult ties of between Corinth and these towns. Apollo was the protector of Ambracia as well as of Apollonia and his symbol, the baetyl, was also the symbol of these towns. His cult stems from the Archaic period and is associated with the colonization of both towns. It is worth mentioning that Apollo did not have any other cult epithets of a native origin, either in Ambracia or in Apollonia, in contrast with Corcyra, where he was also worshipped as Corcyraeus.

The same statement can be made about the epithets of the god in the remaining regions of northwestern Greece, which we included in our paper, where the god was worshipped as Actius, Thermius, Laphrius and Leucatas. These names emphasize not only the significance of the cult but also the joint influence of the native peoples and the colonists. At the same time these names testify that Apollo's cult existed before the arrival of the Corinthian colonies and that it was influenced by Corinth after these colonies were founded.

The spreading of the cult in the Epirote and the Acarnanian towns is due to these towns' proximity with the Corinthian colonies, but also to the nature of Apollo, the god who was associated with prophecy.

When, however, Octavian Augustus compelled most of the inhabitants of Epirus and Aetolo-acarnania to be synoecized into his new city, Nicopolis, the cult of Apollo took a new dimension. As is to be expected, the inhabitants of the new town took with them the cults of their gods. In that way Apollo, the god of the colonists, became the protector of Octavian, and a contributor to the naval battle of Actium. For this Apollo was awarded by the Emperor himself and was worshipped even in Rome. Octavian founded a temple in honor of Apollo on the Palatine hill and decorated it with the cult symbols of the god, among them the baetyl, which was to become a popular subject in Roman Imperial Art.[128]

Notes

NOTE 1
For the cult of Apollo generally, see Burkert 1985, 143-149 and p. 483 in W. Apollo. See also W. Lambrinudakis, Ph. Bruneau, Ol. Palagia, M. Daumas, G. Kokkorou-Aleuras and El. Mathiopoulou-Tornaritou, "Apollon", LIMC II/1, München 1984, p. 183-327 with older bibliography.

NOTE 2
For the temple of Apollo of the 7th century BC, see Salmon 1984, 59-62, 78-79, 98-99 and for the chronology, Robinson 1976, 217-218. See also Stillwell 1932, 115f, R. Lisle 1955, 28 and Salmon 1984, 180.

NOTE 3
Sakellariou-Faraklas 1971, 143, §538 and Lisle 1955, 28.

NOTE 4
Will 1955, 410-412 and Vokotopoulou, 1975, 410-411.

NOTE 5
See Salmon 1984, 219, who believes that the temple of Apollo was established at the time of Cypselos, tyrant of Corinth for the protector god.

NOTE 6
For the cult of Apollo Archegetes, see Dunbabin 1948, 9, 51, 177, 181, 194, Kalliga 1978-79, 61.

NOTE 7
See Tzouvara-Souli 1987-1988, 99f, eadem 1992a, 91-95.

NOTE 8
For Ambracia see recently Tzouvara-Souli 1992b with older bibliography and for the recent excavations in Arta I. Andréou, ADelt 42 (1987), 1992, B₁ Χρον., p. 308-315, Karatzeni ibidem, 315-318 and Petropoulou ibidem, 318. See also Andréou 1993, 91-101, idem 1997, 17-35, A. Douzougli, ADelt 47 (1992), 1997, B₁ Χρον. 243-261, Karatzeni – Pliakou, ibidem., 262-264, Karatzeni 1994 264-270, Pliakou, ibidem., 271-273 and Sarri, ibidem., 273-278. See also Douzougli, ADelt 48 (1993), 1998, B₁ Χρον., p. 268-273, Pliakou, ibidem., 274-275, Angeli, ibidem., 275-278 and Kontogianni, ibidem., 278-281.

NOTE 9
For the relationship between Ambracia and Corinth, see Salmon 1984, 271f., 276f. and 394f. See also Graham 1964, 137f.

NOTE 10
Grammarians and lexicographers define the word Agyieus as an epithet for Apollo, but chiefly as a pointed column or obelisk and altar situated in front of the gates, see Harpocration s.u. Αγυιάς, Sudas s.u. Αγυιαί, Steph. Byzantius s.u. Αγυιά. Hesychios s.u. Αγυιεύς and Etymologicum Magnum 15,29f. See also J. E. Harrison, Themis, Cambridge 1912 (1963), 406, M. Nilsson, GGr RI³, München 1967, 203 and note 3.

NOTE 11
For Athanadas, see F. Jacoby, FGr H IIIb (Text) (303), Leiden 1955, 10-11.

NOTE 12
For Antoninus Liberalis, see M. Papathomopoulos, Antoninus Liberalis, Les Metamorphoses, Paris 1968, XIV.

NOTE 13
M. Nilsson, Studien zur Geschichte des alten Epeiros, Lund 1909, 20 and note 1.

NOTE 14
For the cult of Heracles in Ambracia and for his temple, see most recently Karatzeni 1994, 292f, idem, 1997, 233f. See also Tzouvara-Souli 2000, 112-118.

NOTE 15
The word baetyl is of unknown etymology, see P. Chantraine, Dictionnaire étymologique de la langue grecque, Histoire des Mots, Paris 1968 under the word baetyl. According to Zunth, Classica et Mediaevalia 8 (1946), 169-219 the term is a Mediterranean religious one equivalent to the Semitic term, bethel, which means "house of God". See Elena di Filippo Balestrazzi, Quaderni di archeologia della Libia 8 (1976), 180 note 38. For Agyieus generally see also Fehsentz, 1993, 126-196, Elena di Filippo Balestrazzi op.cit., 109-191 idem "Apollo Agyieus" LIMC, 327-332, and especially for the cult of Agyieus in Epirus, Tzouvara-Souli 1984, 427f.

NOTE 16
For the silver staters of Ambracia which depict Athena Chalinitis with different symbols see B. Head, Corinth, Colonies of Corinth, London 1889 (Bologna 1963), 104f, Ravel 1928, 26-34, 109, SNG Cop Epirus-Acarnania 1948, n. 3-10. C. Kraay, "The Earliest issue of Ambracia", QT 1977, 35-52, idem, "The Coinage of Ambracia and the preliminaries of the Peloponnesian War", QT 1979, 37-66 with new evidences and Th. Martin, Sovereignty and Coinage in Classical Greece, Princeton 1985, 239-295. See also Elena di Filippo Balestrazzi etc., op. cit., 127 with reference to the interpretation of the three part construction of the baetyl.

NOTE 17
For the baetyl's representations of these years, see Gardner 1963, 94, n. 1-14, B.V. Head, Historia Numorum, Oxford 1911, 320, 39, SNG Cop n. 21-25, Franke 1961, 324f. See also Tzouvara-Souli 1984, 430-431, M. Oikonomidou, Συμβολή στη μελέτη της κυκλοφορίας των χάλκινων νομισμάτων της Αμβρακίας, Phigos 1994., 282-283 and pl. 286-287 and recently Douzougli, ADelt. 47 (1992), 1997, 256, N. 3 and pl. 74a: 2b. These coins came to light from the recent excavations in Arta and from Hellenistic level, Douzougli, op. cit., 253 and note 33.

NOTE 18
For the tiles with baetyl from Ambracia, see P. R. Franke, op. cit., 312 n. 8 (pl. 61 (5), n. 7, pl. 61 (8). See also D. B. Thompson, Ptolemaic Oinochoai and Portraits in Faience, Oxford 1973, 63-64 note 11, I. Vokotopoulon,

ADelt 22 (1969), B₂, p. 342, pl. 247a, and A. Douzougli, *ADelt.* 47 (1992), 1997, *op. cit.,* 251, pl. 73d.

NOTE 19
For the temple and its association with Apollo, S. Dakaris, *ADelt* 20 (1965), Χρον. B₂, p. 345, *idem, ADelt* 21 (1966), Χρον., 278., Vokotipoulou 1975, 153, idem, *ADelt* 32 (1977), Χρον. B₁, 145. For the dedication of the temple to the cult of Apollo Pythios – Agyieus see Tzouvara-Souli 1984, 434-435.

NOTE 20
For the Stele, see P. Cabanes-J. Andréou 1985, 499-544: See also I. and H. Andréou, *ADelt* 41 (1986), Χρον., 101-102.

NOTE 21
For the cult of Soter Pythios Apollo generally in Corinth and Corinthian Colonies, see Will 1955, 410-411. See also Salmon, 1984, 73, 219-220 and for the temple of Pythios Apollo in Corinth, Robinson, 1976), 217-218 and Salmon 1984, 180, Williams, 1978, 88-89.

NOTE 22
See note 21.

NOTE 23
For the pedestal, see Vokotopoulou, *ADelt* 24 (1969), Χρον. B₂, p. 247. See also Tzouvara-Souli 1984, 32-33. For the same construction in Ambracia, connected with the baetyl see recently A. Douzougli, *ADelt* 47(1992), 1997, B₁ Χρον., 253 and note 32.

NOTE 24
For the coins of Ambracia, see Gardner 1963, pl. 18 n.1.

NOTE 25
For the cult of Apollo in Corinth from the Archaic period, Will 1955, 235f., 401f., Lisle, 1955, 25, 28, 82 and 101.

NOTE 26
For the monument, see Sakellariou-Faraklas 1971 143 §538, O. Broneer, "Cults in the Corinthian Agora", *Hesperia* 11 (1942), 153-154 and R. L. Scranton, Monuments in the Lower Agora and North of the Archaic Temple, *Corinth* I, 3 (1951), 83.

NOTE 27
Charles K. Williams II – Pamela Russel, "The circular Monument", *Hesperia* 50 (1981), 20.

NOTE 28
Ch. K. Williams II – P. Russel, *op. cit.,* 20.

NOTE 29
El Adreou, *ADelt* 41 (1986), Χρον. 104-105 and especially I. Andréou, Τα Επιγράμματα του Πολυανοδρίου της Αμβρακίας, *ADelt* 41 (1986), Meletai, p. 426-427.

NOTE 30
For the monument and the inscription, see J. Bousquet, "Deux (pigrammes Grecques". (Delphes, Ambracie), *BCH* 116 (1992), 596-606. See also Ag. P. Mathaiou, "Αμβρακίας Ελεγείον", horos 8-9 (1990-91), 271-277 and 303-310. Cf. El. and I. Andréou, Τα Επιγράμματα της Αμβρακίας και τα απαράδεκτα μιας ερμηνείας, *ADelt* 43 (1988), Meletai, 110-113.

NOTE 31
For the coins, see Gardner 1963, 95, N. 20-22, pl. 18.4.

NOTE 32
For these coins, see Gardner 1963, 95 N. 23-28 and SNG Cop Epirus-Acarnania (1943), N. 31-34. SNG, Grèce, Collection R. H. Evelpidis, II, p. XLVIII, N. 1777-1780. See also M. Oikonomidou, Phigos 1994, 282 and 288, A. Douzougli, *ADelt* 47 (1992), 1997 *op. cit.,* 255-256 N. 2 and Note 34.

NOTE 33
For the stele, see Tzouvara-Souli 1979, 1979, 19, fig. 8b and p. 44. See also *eadem.* 1992, 162-165.

NOTE 34
For the coins, see P. Franke 1961, 25-26, pl. 2 V23-32, P. 26-37 and for the cult of Apollo in Athamania see Tzouvara-Souli 1994, 54-55.

NOTE 35
For Apollonia and the relationship with Apollo, see Scymn. 438 in GGM I, 214, Plinius *HN* 3. 145 and Paus. 5. 22. 34. See Hammond 1967, 426, Will 1955, 518 f., Ceka 1982, *idem.* 1988, 86, Cabanes 1993, 7-20.

NOTE 36
For the baetyls in Apollonia, see A. Kahn, "Apollonia", *Archaeology* 14 (1961), 162, P. Franke, "Albanien im Altertum", *Antike Welt* 14 (1983), Sondernummer, 41, fig. 83 and p. 54 fig. 102. For the temples of Artemis, see M. Korkuti, Shqiperia Arkeologike. Tirane 1971, 13 n. 68, fig. 68, Sk. Anamali, "Santuari di Apollonia", La Magna Grecia e i grandi Santuari della Madrepatria, Atti del Trentunesimo Convegno di Studi sulla Magna Grecia, Taranto 4-8 Ottobre 1991, Taranto 1992, 127 f., See also in the same Atti, 127f: N. Ceka, "Santuari dell'area Illirico-Epirotico", who says that the temple belongs to the cult of Apollo.

NOTE 37
For the coins, see B. Head, HN² (see note 17), 314, Gardner 1963, 59, n. 49-53 (pl. 12 n. 9) and p. 60 n. 50-51, pl. 12 (n. 12). See also David R. Sear, *Greek coins and their values,* London 1966 (1975), n. 1887, Ceka 1972, 62 and p. 105, Collection R. Évelpidis, SNG Grèce, Louvain 1975, p. XL VI, n. 1710, 1714, 1715, 1716.

NOTE 38
See note 36.

NOTE 39
Chr. Tzouvara-Souli 1993, 67-68.

NOTE 40
Cf. Halic Myrto's view, Konsiderata me Obeliskum e Apolonisë, *Monumentet* 1 (1988), 81-86 with reference to the illyrian origin of the cult of Agyieus.

NOTE 41
For Orrao see P. Cabanes-J. Andréou 1985, 499f and 753-757. For the ancient settlement in general, see N. G. L. Hammond, *BSA* 48 (1953), 134-140, *idem* 1967, 154-156, Hoepfner – Schwandner 1986, 109-110, fig. 107 and Dakaris 1986, 108-146.

NOTE 42
Dakaris 1986, 413, pl. 41g.

NOTE 43
For Oricum, see N. G. L. Hammond 1967, 129, 385, 419, 494-495 and for the geographical position of Oricum on the sea road towards the Corinthian colonies, see R. Beaumont, Greek influence in the Adriatic sea before the fourth century BC, *JHS* 56 (1936), 165.

For the coins, see Gardner 1963, 99, pl. 31 n. 31, B.V. Head, HN² (see note 17), 316. See also R. Évelpidis SNG Grèce, Louvain 1975, p. XLVII, n. 1751 and 1752. For the other cults in Oricum of Corinthian origin see Tzouvara-Souli 1979, 13, 16, 36, 42, 59-60 and 82 f.

NOTE 44
For Amantia generally, see Sh. Gjongecaj, "Le monnayage d'Amantie", Iliria VII-VIII, 1977-1978, 83-112 and P. Cabanes, "Recherches Archéologiques en Albanie 1945-1985", *RA* 1986, F1, 126. For the coins Ceka 1972, 129-130 and Sh. Gjongecaj, op. cit., 104f., who observes that Artemis of Amantia was worshipped in a similar way to Apollo, *op. cit.*, p.105.

NOTE 45
For the Greek origin of the town, see F. Papazoglou, "Politarques en Illyrie" *Historia*

35 (1986), 438f and N.G.L. Hammond, "The Illyrian Atintani, the Epirotic Atintanes and the Roman Protectorate", *JRS* 79 (1989), 17.

For the coin, see L'Arte Albanese nei Secoli: Museo Nazionale Preistorico Etnografico "Luigi Pigorini" Piazzale Marconi n. 14. Roma Eur. Febbraio-Aprile 1985, Roma 1985, 72 n. 273,3 and Ceka 1988, 275n 144b.

NOTE 46
For Buthrotum, see L. Ugolini, *Albania Antica* I, Roma-Milano 1927, 153f, N.G.L. Hammond 1967, 474, 514, 552.

NOTE 47
Encicl. Ital. Append 2 (1938-48), 108, L. Ugolini, L'Acropoli di Butrinto, *Albania Antica* III, Roma 1942, p. 81f and Hammond 1967, 110.

NOTE 48
For the other cults of Corinthian origin from Buthrotum, see Tzouvara-Souli 1979, 11-12, *eadem* 1987-1988, 105 with older bibliography.

NOTE 49
For the inscription on leaden oracular tablet from Dodone, see S. Dakaris, *Prakt.* 1967, 49 n. 57 and J.-L. Robert, *REG* 82 (1969), 473 n. 348, 5, Cabanes 1976, 333, 550 n. 22.

NOTE 50
For the statuette, see Vokotopoulou, 1995, 142, 155, 162, 163 and pl. 53γ.

NOTE 51
For the inscription, see L. Jeffery, The Local Scripts of Archaic Greece, Oxford 1961, 228-229. See also Tzouvara-Souli 1992, 118-120 with older bibliography.

NOTE 52
For them, see D. Euangelidou, *Prakt.* 1930, 67-68, fig. 10 and for the other similar scenes from Dodone, see C. Carapanos, *Dodone et ses ruines*, Paris 1878, 33, 188 and

Pl. XVI, 1. See also E. Künze, "Archaische Schildbänder", *Olympische Forschungen* II (Berlin 1950), 116-117 and Beil. 9 (2) cf. S. Dakaris, "Το Ιερόν της Δωδώνης", *ADelt* 16 (1960), 7 note 7 who dates them to the 3rd century BC

NOTE 53
For the cult of Apollo in Delphi and other oracular sanctuaries, see Parke – Wormell, 1956, 3f. 51, 286f. 344, 369, 374. See also Parke 1967a, 30f., 68, 95, 97, 137f. See also M. Nilsson, GGR RI, München 1967, p. 544-547, Burkert 1985, 115, 117, 144 and Fonterose 1978, 90, 94-100, 151-156, 163-164, 179, 218, 233-234.

NOTE 54
Parke 1967b, 129f., Will 1955, 284-286, who believes that the relationship between Dodona and Corinth is dated from the Prehistoric times. See also Vokotopoulou 1975, 148.

NOTE 55
About the foundation of Doric Corinth and the interpretation of the myth, see Salmon, 1984, 39f., 46, 49 and 52. See also H. W. Parke, 1967b130.

NOTE 56
According to Lycophron, Alexandra, 426 "ότι ὁ Ἀπόλλων ἐν Μολοσσίᾳ τιμᾶται" (G.M. Mooney), New York 1979, 426 (Tzetzes), Ad Lycophron, 426. See also Hammond 1967, 798 (Index I). For the cult of Apollo, see Aelian., *NA*, XI.2 and Bickel 1930, 279-303, Hammond, 1967, 400, Franke 1961, 58f. See also Fr. Quantin, Aspects Épirotes de la vie religieuse antique, *REG* 112 (1999), 83 and Notes 103-107.

NOTE 57
For the history of Corcyra generally, see Preka-Alexandri 1994, 16f and for the cult of Apollo in Corcyra, Tzouvara-Souli 1993, 68 with older bibliography. See also about the cult of Agyieus Apollo in Corcyra, Tzouvara-Souli 1984, 439-441.

NOTE 58
J. Six, "Der Agyieus des Mys", *AM* 19 (1894), 340f., C. A. Rhomaios, "Les Premières fouilles de Corfou", *BCH* 49 (1925), 130.

NOTE 59
See P. Kalliga, *ADelt.* 23 (1968) B₂ Χρον., 309-313.

NOTE 60
G. Dontas, Οδηγός Αρχαιολογικού Μοσείου Κερκύρας, Αθήναι 1970, 51, P. Kalliga, *ADelt* 23 (1968), B₂ Χρον., 309-313 and pl. 249 (MR 1126). For other finds MR 1125, MR 966, 987 and 988. Between them a votive shield pl. 249a and a clay chariot (MR 856).

NOTE 61
P. Kalliga, *ADelt* 23 (1968), B₂ Χρον.,310-311 (pl. 250 á-â).

NOTE 62
P. Kalliga, *ADelt* 23 (1968), B₂ Χρον., 311. These finds are in the Archaeological Museum of Corcyra, numbers MR 934, MR 808, MR 685.

NOTE 63
P. Kalliga, *ADelt* 23 (1968), B₂ Χρον. p. 313 Archaeological Museum of Corcyra, numbers MR 938, 937, (pl. 253a) MR 936 and for the tripod *op. cit.,* 311 pl. 251 γ-δ.

NOTE 64
(MR 936) See Π. Καλλιγά, *op. cit.* in note 63, 313, pl. 253 ϐ, γ.

NOTE 65
P. Kalliga, *op. cit.* in note 63, 312. See also K. Rhomaios, Les Premières fouilles de Corfou, *BCH* 49 (1925), 217.

NOTE 66
See also M.Nilsson, GGr RI, München 1967, 536.

NOTE 67
For the Corinthian influence in these areas, see Tzouvara-Souli 1991, 151f with older bibliography. See also Antonetti 1990, 269.

NOTE 68
For the excavations in Thermos, see G. Sotiaridis, AEphem 1900, 171-211, K. Rhomaiou, Εκ του προιστορικού Θέρμου, ADelt 1 (1915), 225f and recently, I. A. Papapostolou, Η Ανασκαφή του Θέρμου, Πρακτικά Α' Αρχαιολογικού και Ιστορικού Συνεδρίου Αιτωλοακαρνανίας, Αγρίνιο, 21-22-23 Οκτωβρίου 1988, Αγρίνιο 1991, 139-143. See also Antonetti 1990, 169f and I. A. Papapostolou, Οι νεώτερες έρευνες στο Μέγαρο Β του Θέρμου, ΔΩΔΩΝΗ, ΚΣΤ'1 (1997), Μνήμη Σωτήρη Δάκαρη, Ιωάννινα 1997, 328 note 1. For the metopes of the temples see recently Antonetti 1990, 167 and 173f.

NOTE 69
For them, see Will 1955, 580 and note 5 with older bibliography. See also Salmon 1984, 61, 120, 121., Antonetti 1990, 167f.

NOTE 70
For the inscriptions, see G. Sotiriadi, AEphem 1905, p. 80 and Sylloge, 443, 45. See also K. Rhomaios, Απόλλων Θέρμιος, ΕΕΦΣΑΠΘ 2 ★1932), p. 25. For the temple and the inscriptions dedicated to Apollon Thermius, see recently Antonetti 1990, 169f. and 200-204 and for the cult of Apollo in Thermos from the Archaic period until the Hellenistic, Antonetti 1990, 170f and 198f.

NOTE 71
K. Rhomaios, Απόλλων Θέρμιος, *op. cit.* in note 70, 25f.

NOTE 72
About these see K. Rhomaios, *ADelt.* 10 (1926), p. 27f. and *idem* Απόλλων Θέρμιος, *op.cit.* in note 70, 23f. Cf. I. A. Papapostolou, *op. cit.* in note 68, 336-339. See also Antonetti 1990, 209f· who connects these sacrifices from the Bronze Age first with Mother Goodess and then with Apollo. The cult of Thermius Apollo continues in the Classical and Hellenistic periods according to the inscriptions and the games, named θερμικά: about these see Antonetti 1990, 197f.

NOTE 73
See Tzouvara-Souli, 1991, 152. Cf. Antonetti 1990, 209-210 and for different opinion about the cultic surname Thermius, see Antonetti 1990, 200f.

NOTE 74
About the temple of Apollo Lyceios. See Antonetti 1990, 185f, and 204f.

NOTE 75
IG, IX, I 1.81. See also G. Soteriadis, Επιγραφαί Θέρμου, *ADelt* 1 (1915), 56 and K. Rhomaios, Απόλλων Θέρμιος, *op.cit.* in note 70, 25.

NOTE 76
K. Rhomaios, Έρευναι εν Θέρμο, *ADelt* 2 (1916), 179f. and 186f., *idem, Prakt.* 1932, 56. For the cult of Lyceios Apollo in Thermos, see L.V. Borelli, *EAA*, t.VII, 827 (W. Thermos). For the temple of Lyceios Apollo, see also Cl. Antonetti 1990, 185f and p. 204f and for the cult of Lyceios in other cities like Thebes, Corinth, Sicyon, see Antonetti 1990, 204f with reference to ancient sources and archaeological data.

NOTE 77
For the ancient cult of Dionysos in Corinth, see Lisle 1955, 56 and note 146.

NOTE 78
See Lisle 1955.,20f.Will 1955, 216f.

NOTE 79
K. Rhomaios, Αρχαίον ιερόν παρά τον Ταξιάρχη της Αιτωλίας, *ADelt* 10 (1926), 32f., C.V. Borrelli *EAA*, t.VII, 827.

NOTE 80
K. Rhomaios, Εκ του προιστορικού Θέρμου, *ADelt* 1 (1915), 271-272, fig. 39 and for the cult of Artemis in Thermos K. Romaios, *ADelt* 10 (1926), 32f.

NOTE 81

For Calydon, see L.V. Borrelli *EAA* 4 (1961), 305-306 (W. Kalydon) with older bibliography. For the cults in Calydon see Dyggve-Poulsen 1948, 297 f., 340f. and Simon 1969 (1985), 105. See also Antonetti 1990,. 253f.

NOTE 82

K. Rhomaios, Αι ελληνοδανικαί Αναοκαφαί της Καλυδώνος, *ADelt* 10 (1926), App., 39f. For the cults in Calydon see also Antonetti 1990, 253f. and for the temples, Antonetti 1990, 245-253.

NOTE 83

K. Rhomaios, *ADelt* 10 (1926), p. 39f. and Dyggve-Poulsen 1948, 335. See also L. H. Jeffery, *The Local Scripts of Archaic Greece*, Oxford 1961, 226, 277 n. 9.

NOTE 84

K. Rhomaios, *ADelt*. 10 (1926), Append. p. 39 fig. 14, Dyggve-Poulsen 1948, 340 and fig. 309 and for the inscription L. Jeffery, *op. cit.*, p. 227 n. 5. See also Antonetti 1990, 249,n. 885 and p. 258.

NOTE 85

For the cult of Laphrius Apollo in Calydon, see K.Rhomaois, *ADelt* 10 (1926). Append p. 39 and Dyggve-Poulsen 1948, 340f. and recently Antonetti 1990, 245f. and 258f with discussion about the different opinion for the surname Laphrius and Laphria and the origin of the cult in northwestern Greece and mainly in Calydon.

NOTE 86

For the colonization in northwestern Greece, see J. G. O'Neill, *Ancient Corinth*, Baltimore 1930, 148f.,Will 1955, 517f., Graham 1964, 118, J. B. Salmon 1984, 209f. I. Malkin, *Religion and Colonization in Ancient Greece*, Köln 1987, 285 n. 104.

NOTE 87

For the cult of Apollo Leucatas, see also Oberhummer 1887, 223f, A. B. Cook, Zeus, I. p. 344-346, Dörpfeld 1965, 271f

and Rodogiannis 1980, 237f., M. Nilsson, GGrRI, 109f, *idem* GGrRI, 475 and Burkert, *Greek Religion*, 1985 (Stuttgart 1977), p. 83 and note 72.

NOTE 88

For the coins, see Gardner 1963, 178 N. 68-76, pl. 28 (11-13) and 186-187 N. 170-191, pl. 29 (5-6).

NOTE 89

For the inscription, see L. Jeffery, *The Local Scripts of Archaic Greece*, Oxford 1961, 227, 229, fig. 44 (N.1) and M. Guarducci, *Epigrafia Greca* I, Roma 1967, 293-294, fig. 138.

NOTE 90

B.V. Head, BMC, Corinth, Colonies of Corinth, London 1889 (Bologna 1963), 125-134, pl. 34, N. 180, pl. 35 (1-16), pl. 36 (1-25). See also Graham 1964, 121 and Salmon 1984, 271.

NOTE 91

P. Kalliga, *ADelt* 23 (1968), B2, p. 321 and recently, Tzouvara-Souli 1998, 371-436.

NOTE 92

For the cult of Actius Apollo, see recently Tzouvara-Souli 1998-99, 169f.

NOTE 93

J. B. Salmon 1984, 209f. and for the name of the temple Polyb. 4. 63. 4.

NOTE 94

For the Anactorium, a Corinthian colony, see Salmon 1984, 209f. and for Sollium and Heracleia Salmon 1984, 213 and Pharakla 1991, 221-227.

NOTE 95

For the sanctuary, see Habicht 1957, 98f., 501-504, and W. M. Murray 1982, 266f. See also J. Pouilloux, *Choix d' inscriptions Grecques, Textes, traductions et notes*, Paris 1960, 108 N. 29, I. G. IX I², 2, 583.

NOTE 96

For the Kouroi M. Collignon, "Torses archaiques en marble provenant d'Actium" *GA* 11 (1886), 234-243, pl. 29 and for the date of Kouroi E. Buschor, Frühgriechische Jünglinge, 1950, 43f, Habicht 1957, 100 and note 1, G. M. Richter, *Kouroi, Archaic Greek Youths*, London 1960, 60, 66 n. 40, fig. 154-156, pp. 85-86, fig. 255-257 and Kl. Wallenstein, *Korinthische Plastik des 7 und 6 Jahrhunderts vor Chr.*, Bonn 1971, 147 n. 34 (Paris, Louvre, MNB 766), Cf. G. Dontas 1997, 121-130.

NOTE 97

For the ancient Actia, see Sarikakis 1965, 146 and notes 1-5. See also Habicht 1957, 109. See also IG IX. F, 2, 563.

NOTE 98

For the consular inscription, see G. Klaffenbach, IG IX, 1, II, N. 208, 209, 1-4 and for the silver coins, see F. Imhoof-Blumer, "Die Münzen Akarnaniens", Wien 1878, 58-63, B.V. Head, *BMC,* "Corinth Colonies of Corinth" London 1889 (Bologna 1963), 115, n. 5, and pl. 31 (n. 5), *idem*, p. 116, N. 8 and pl. 31 (N. 8). See also C. Kraay, *Archaic and Classical Greek Coins,* London 1976, 125f. For the bronze coins, see P. Gardner, BMC Thessaly to Aetolia, op. c., p. 171 N. 3, pl. 27 (N. 11).

NOTE 99

For the coins with Acarnanian types, see Gardner 1963, 95 n. 15-17 and pl. 18 (N. 3), SNG Cop 30. SNG, Grèce, II, *op. cit.,* p. XLVIII N. 1773-1775, M. Oikonomidou, *Phigos* 1994,. 282, 286 and A. Douzougli, *ADelt* 47 (1992) 1997, *op. cit.,* 256 N 4, Note 35 and pl. 74d.3b.

NOTE 100

For the coins, see Gardner 1963, 193, N. 12, 13, pl. 30 (N. 1).

NOTE 101

See Tzouvara-Souli 1994, 122 and Dakaris. 1971, p. 86 § 319.

NOTE 102
For the cults in Cassope generally, see Tzouvara-Souli 1994, 107-135 and for the cult of Apollo in Cassope *ibidem* 112-113 and 122.

NOTE 103
For the coins, see Gardner 1963, 98 n. 1, Franke 1961, 69, pl. 5 V 1-3, R 1-4 and Dakaris 1971 56 § 204 and p. 65 § 237.

NOTE 104
P. Franke 1961, 58f.

NOTE 105
For the rule of Apollo in Actium, see Propertius 4. 6.29f., Verg. *Aen.* 8.698f. See also Gagé, 1955, 499f., Sarikakis 1965, 146 and note 6, D. Kienast, Augustus, Prinzeps und Monarch, Darmstadt 1982, 375 f. and note 93, Jucker 1982, 82 and note 2. See recently Isager, 1998, 399-411.

NOTE 106
For the cult of Apollo in Nicopolis, see Tzouvara-Souli 1987, 170f.

NOTE 107
For the hill and the monument, see A. Philadelpheus, Ἀνασκαφαί Νικοπόλεως, *AEphem* 1913, 235, Gagé, 1936, 53-54, D. Kienast, *op. cit.* in note 105, p. 354 and Murray-Petsas, 1989, 62-85. For the inscription, see H. Oliver, "Octavian's inscription at Nicopolis" *AJPh* 90 (1969), 178-182 and Murray-Petsas 1989, 62-85; cf. Zachos in this volume.

NOTE 108
For them Sarikakis 1965, 147 and Oikonomidou-Karamesine 1975, 42-43 with older bibliography.

NOTE 109
For the coins Oikonomidou-Karamesine 1975, 46f., 57, 87-88.

NOTE 110
Oikonomidou-Karamesine 1975, 46 and 63, pl. 1. See also L. Lacroix, *Les reproductions de Statue sur les monnaies grecques,* Liège 1949, 64, fig. 11 (N. 14).

NOTE 111
For the copies, see Oikonomidou-Karamesine 1975, 46, 47, 106, 117, 119, 120, 160, 164-165, pl. 37, 54 and 63.

NOTE 112
About this, see Tzouvara-Souli 1987, 176-177 with older discussion.

NOTE 113
Franke 1976, 159-163. Cf. Oikonomidou-Karamesine 1975, 46, who connects it with Actius Apollo.

NOTE 114
For the coin with the inscription ΛΕΥΚΑΤΗΣ ΑΠΟΛΛΩΝ, see F. Imhoof-Blumer, *Monnaies Grecques*, Paris-Leipzig 1883, 141, Franke 1976, 160 note 10. See also Karamesine-Oikonomidou 1975, 47 and 80, pl. 13 (N. 21).

NOTE 115
See above note 114.

NOTE 116
Franke 1976, 162.

NOTE 117
C.H.V. Sutherland, "Octavian's Gold and Silver Coinage from 32 to 27 BC", *Quaderni Ticinesi* 5 (1976), 151. See also Gagé 1936, 48.

NOTE 118
See above notes 105-106 and for the connection of Leucadius with Actium see Isager 1998, 399-411.

NOTE 119
For the cult of Apollo Leucatas in Leucas see (Thuc. 39. 4. 2. and Strab. 10. 9). See also Oberhummer 1887, 223f.and 254. K. Kraft, *Zur Münzprägung des Augustus,* Sitzungsber. der Wiss. Gesellschaft an der Johann Wolfgang Goethe-Universität Frankfurt/Mainz, Band 7 (1968), Nr. 5.216 and H. Prückner, "Das Budapest Aktium-Relief", Forschungen und Funde: *Festschrift Bernhard Neutsch* (Innsbruck 1980), 360.

NOTE 120
For the cult of Apollo Agyieus in Epirus, see Tzouvara-Souli 1984, 427-442 and for the baetyls from Nicopolis see these with Numbers 762 and 865 of the Archaeological Museum of Nicopolis.

NOTE 121
For them, see Tzouvara-Souli 1987, 177-178.

NOTE 122
Picard-Schmitter 1971, 76f,

NOTE 123
For the temple, see Picard-Schmitter 1971, 77 and for his decoration G. Carettoni, "Terracotte "Campana" dallo scavo del Tempio di Apollo Palatino": *Rend Pont Acc.* 44 (1971/72), 123f. and *idem*, "Nuova Serie di Grandi Lastre Fittili, "Campana,"," Bd A Ser.V, vol. 58 (1972), I, 75-78. About this see also E. Simon, *Augustus*, München 1986, 128f and 253-254, pl. 6-7.

NOTE 124
About this, see Tzouvara-Souli 1987, 178 with older bibliography.

NOTE 125
H. Küthmann, Actiaca: *Jbz Mus Mainz* 4 (1957), 78.

NOTE 126
For the coins from Megara B.V. Head, HN, 393, L. Anson, *Numismata Graeca*, p.V, London 1914, p. 15, pl. III, N. 96 and H. Küthmann, "Actiaca", *op. cit.*, in note 125, 76-78, pl. 12, N. 6.

NOTE 127
See above notes 122-123.

NOTE 128
See above note 122-123.

Bibliography

Andréou, J., 1993
Ambracie, une ville ancienne se reconstitue peu à peu par les recherches", *L'Illyrie méridionale et l'Épire dans l'antiquité*: Actes du IIe colloque international de Clermont-Ferrand réunis par Pierre Cabanes (25-27 Octobre 1990), Paris, 91-101.

Andréou, J., 1997
Η Τοπογραφία της Αμβρακίας και η πολιορκία του 189 π.Χρ., Αφιέρωμα στον N.G.L. Hammond, Παράρτημα Μακεδονικών αρ. 7, Θεσσαλονίκη, 17-35.

Antonetti, Cl., 1990
Les Étoliens. Image et religion, Paris.

Aphieroma Hammond, 1997
Αφιέρωμα στον N. G. L. Hammond, Παράρτημα Μακεδονικών αρ. 7, Θεσσαλονίκη.

Bickel, E., 1930
Apollon und Dodona, *Rh.Mus.* 79, 279-303.

Burkert, W., 1985
Greek Religion, Cambridge, Mass.

Cabanes, P., 1976
L'Épire de la mort de Pyrrhos à la conquête romaine, Paris.

Cabanes, P., 1993
L'apport des sources littéraires à l'onomastique d'Épidamne – Dyrrhachion et Apollonia d'Illyrie, *Grecs et Illyriens dans les inscriptions en langue grecque d'Épidamne – Dyrrhachion et d'Apollonia d'Illyrie*, Actes de la Table ronde internationale (Clermont-Ferrand, 19-21 Octobre 1989), Paris, 7-20.

Cabanes, P. et Andréou J., 1985
Le réglement frontalier entre les cités d'Ambracie et de Charadros, *BCH* 109, I, Études, 499-544.

Ceka, H., 1972
Question de Numismatique Illyrienne, Tirana.

Ceka, N., 1982
Apolonia e Ilirise, Tiranë.

Ceka, N., 1988
Albanien. Schätze aus dem Land der Skipetaren, Mainz.

Dakaris, S., 1971
Cassopaia, Athens.

Dakaris, S., 1986
Το Όρραον. Το σπίτι στην αρχαία Ήπειρο, *AEphem*, 108-146.

Dakaris, S., 1987
Η ρωμαϊκή πολιτική στην Ήπειρο, Νικόπολις Α', Πρακτικά Α' Διεθνούς Συμποσίου για τη Νικόπολη (23-29 Σεπτεμβρίου 1984), 11-21.

Dörpfeld, W., 1965
Alt-Ithaka I. Ein Beitrag zur Homer-Frage, (1927) Osnabrück.

Dontas, G., 1997
Σκέψεις, προβλημεατισμοί και προτάσεις για την γλυπτική της Κέρκυρας στους αρχαικούς και τους πρώιμους κλασικούς χρόνους, Έπαινος Ιωάννου Κ. Παπαδημητρίου, Αθήναι, 121-130.

Dunbabin, T. J., 1948
The Western Greeks, Oxford.

Dyggve, E. und Poulsen, F., 1948
Das Laphrion, København.

Fehsentz, V., 1993
Der Antike Agyieus, *JdI* 108, 126-196.

Fiedler, M., 1999
Leukas. Wohn und Alltagskultur in einer nordwestgriechischen Stadt, in Hoepfner, W. (ed.), *Geschichte des Wohnens in 5000 v. Chr. – 500 n. Chr. Vorgeschichte-Frühgeschichte – Antike*, 412-416, Stuttgart.

Fontenrose, J., 1978
The Delphic Oracle. Its responses and operations, London.

Franke, P., 1961
Die antike Münzen von Epirus, Wiesbaden.

Franke, P., 1976
Apollo Leucadius und Octavianus, *Chiron* 6, 159-163.

Gagé, J., 1936
Actiaca, Mélanges d'Archéologie et d'Histoire 53.

have already argued, this act of cult transfer appears to have played an important role in consolidating Augustus' large scale synoecism policy in Achaia. Pausanias and Strabo indirectly refer to great efforts made by Augustus to turn the then dwindling city of Patras into a grand Roman colony by resettling people in Patras who were living in villages and towns in the chora of Patras and on the Aetolian coast (Paus. 7. 18. 7; Strabo 10. 2. 21). Surveys and archaeological investigations in the regions collectively point to major territorial reorganizations in the Late Hellenistic and Early Imperial period. Thus, the total number of sites increase dramatically in this period in the coastal region around Patras while the number of sites decreases in the same period in Aetolia.[1] On the whole cult transferal now seem to have been a common phenomenon accompanying Roman synoecism in Greece and they seem at least sometimes to have constituted a deliberate tactic of domination.[2]

Of special interest for this paper is the way in which the transferal of Artemis Laphria and Dionysos from Kalydon to Patras, implied that two originally sub-urban cults became urban during a synoecism process. In fact, a closer look at synoecisms and sanctuaries in Achaia and Aetolia in the Archaic, Classical and Hellenistic periods will show that sanctuaries often changed "territorial status" during synoecisms. In this sense, the study highlightens the way in which Augustan cult transfer policy was in fact deeply rooted in earlier practices.

The location of cults in the LG – Early Archaic period (ca. 860–600 BC)

It is possible to roughly distinguish three types of cult on grounds of their location.[3]

First, to judge from strayfinds, surveys and excavations, the following cults lay outside, but relatively close to nucleated habitation: the Laphrion hill-sanctuary in Aetolia is situated outside the western main gate of the Classical-Hellenistic city-

walls of Kalydon at a distance of about 300 m and about 1 km from the acropolis.[4] According to strayfinds and tomb-distribution, the latter formed a centre of habitation already in Mycenaean-Archaic times.[5] Moreover, it should be recalled that Kalydon is one of the five Aitolian cities mentioned in the ship-cataloque (Il. 2. 638-640).

Perhaps a cult existed at the spring in Kryoneri approximately 4 km from Kalydon, though the evidence is confined to a Geometric bronze double-axe and bird in the Museum of Agrinion.[6] It should, nevertheless, be remembered that the spring is alluded to in the story of the maiden Calirrhoe and the priest of Dionysos, Coressus, told by Pausanias (7. 21. 1-5). Since Miss Benton noted some Neolithic, LHII-III and Geometric sherds on the slope of Mt Varassova, there may indeed once have existed a small habitation.[7] It is not impossible though, that the bronze finds should be understood as a rural cult in relation to Kalydon (see below).

The sanctuary in Kallipolis lies 150 m to the south of the Classical-Hellenistic fortification wall[8] and again survey-finds have proved the existence of a prehistoric and Iron Age settlement in the area of the Classical–Hellenistic city.[9]

At Araxos in Achaea, a bench interpreted as an altar and its associated finds is situated dirctly ouside the eastern entrance of the Mycenaean fortification wall on the very edge of the steep rocky hill. Again, the area within the fortification wall is rich in both prehistoric material and also Classical-Hellenistic. The early cult was therefore clearly placed on the fringe of the inhabited hill.[10]

Directly above the Classical-Hellenistic city of Aigeira, a construction interpreted as a Geometric naiskos lies partly above, partly integrated into settlement remains which are surrounded by a fortification wall dated to the LHIIIC period. Due, however, to the slightly different orientation of the building in relation to the LHIIIC settlement, it is regarded as post-dating the latter. On the whole, it is the impression of the excavator that no habi-

Fig. 2. The location of
Kalydon and Patras.

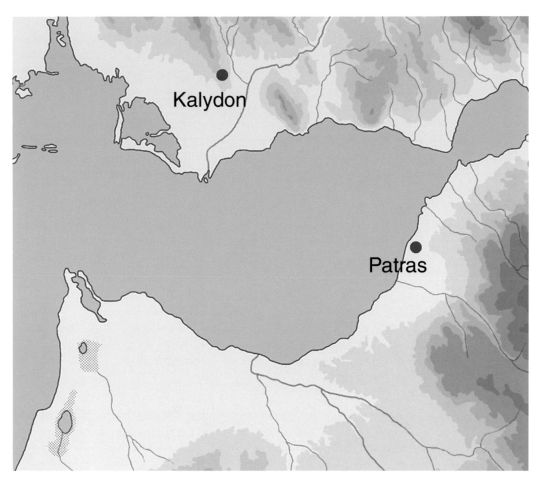

tation took place inside the Mycenaean fortification wall after the end of the Bronze Age, rather the site was given over to religious practices.[11] This indeed appears to be the case when its "successor", an Early Archaic, Doric temple, was constructed next to the building on top of the LHIIIC buildings.[12]

The relation of the earliest cult in Lousoi – which lies on the border between Arkadia and Achaea – to the settlements is not known with certainty archaeologically. In the ode by Bacchylides (born 521 or 524 BC), Lousoi is a spring which is clearly situated in wild nature (Bacchyl. *Epin*. 10 (11), 92-112) while Polybius, writing in the 2nd century, speaks of citizens of Lousoi (Polyb. 4. 18. 11) and according to Pausanias there once was a city called Lousoi, although he could not even locate its ruins (Paus. 8. 18. 8).

The second category consists of evidence for cults lying at some distance from nu-

cleated habitation and therefore seemingly "rural": The sanctuary at Lebenou (Charvati) is situated 4 kms as the crow flies from the city of Stratos[13] which lies at the Acheloos river in Acarnania but – in Woodhouse's words[14] – "is bound up with the history of Aetolia". A further site of interest is Pazaropoulos near Stratos at which place a monolithic column of 7th century BC date came to light.[15] The Lebenou sanctuary, which has been excavated recently was apparently the richest and most longlived of those so far found in the vicinity of Stratos. Moreover, this city appears also to have formed an early habitation centre, since the Greek-German survey has recently proved Stratos to be the sole site in the Stratiké plain to be continously inhabited from Geometric to Roman times. Other sites in the plain were at the most inhabited during four ceramic phases.[16] Returning to the site of Kryoneri on the coast, this may – as stated above – instead belong in this category, if

Kalydon was a nucleated habitation comparable to Stratos.

Like the Lebenou-sanctuary, Thermon was a long lived cult place. Moreover, its character appears to have undergone great changes through time from hero cult to league sanctuary.[17] Throughout this period, the relation of the sanctuary to the surrounding settlement pattern is not clear. In Classical-Hellenistic times, Thermon lay in between two groups of important cities, one of which consisted of Koronto, Pamphia, Metape, Trichonion and Akrai in the south, the other of Phistyon, Ambrakia and Thestiai in the northwest while none is known in its immediate surroundings.[18] It is certainly not unlikely that future investigations will prove several of these cities to have an Iron Age history. Especially extensive Early Iron Age cemeteries have already been found at Gavalou and Lithovouni identified with respectively Trichonion and Akrai.[19]

The relations of the Pitsa-cave[20] and the important sanctuary found at Rakita in Achaia to a settlement-pattern is not certain either. It deserves, however, to be mentioned that the former lies in between two important Classical-Hellenistic cities, Aigeira and Pellene, which are already mentioned by Homer (*Od.* 15.249-255)[21] and Aigeria lies, as mentioned above, below a Mycenaean stronghold. With regard to the large Geometric-Early Archaic, elliptical temple with peristyle found in Rakita, the building lies on a highly important route of communication along the Selinous river valley.[22] This route connected the central Peloponnese with central Greece – as confirmed through ceramic finds in Lousoi, Rakita, Aigion and Delphi – and it connected western Achaea with Eastern Achaea – and thus the two Homeric landscapes Bouprasion and Aigaleos. In particular, it served as the main road between the two Classical-Hellenistic cities Pharai and Rhypes as is also indirectly to be understood from Strabo who says that the territory of Rhypes was held by the people of Aigion and Pharai (Strabo 8.7.5). Both of the two cities have pro-

duced Geometric and Archaic material.[23] Mycenaean and Geometric tombs have moreover been found at several sites along this route, but so far not in the immediate vicinity of Rakita.[24]

The third category consists of evidence – very slight – for a cult situated more centrally in relation to important nucleated habitation. On the hill of Haghia Triadha, now known to be the site of Aetolian Chalkis, Mastrokostas found a fragmentary, primitive terracotta of a horseman.[25] Later excavations point to the existence of an important Geometric and Archaic settlement on the hill and the existence of a temple at least in the Classical period if not earlier. It probably stood in the area of the Haghia Triadha basilica the foundations of which crown the hill today.[26] In Aigion, a curved wall fragment from an apsis building was found at Dodekanison Street 4. The function of the building is, however, not known. Several Geometric tombs have been found in the vicinity.[27]

In conclusion, there are signs of two perhaps three basic types of sanctuaries in Aetolia and Achaia: 1. Cults placed on the fringe of inhabited land, 2. Cults located at some distance from a main area of habitation and (perhaps) 3. Cults placed more centrally in relation to an important habitation. It needs to be added though that the most substantial evidence for this pattern stems from the 7th century BC. As regards this period, it is intriguing to notice that cults characterized by elaborate or substantial architecture all belong to type 1. and 2. being situated in places which with reasonable certainty can be said to lie *outside* nucleated areas of habitation: Thermon (three, perhaps four temples are known: two or three smaller naiskoi, one long and narrow temple ("temple C"), all with elaborate terracotta roof-decoration including metopes with figural scenes probably of Corinthian workmanship, see above), Kallipolis (long and narrow temple, the socalled megaron B, very similar to temple C in Thermon), Kalydon (Geometric apsisbuilding? Geometric altars?[28]

"building H" (small ante-temple?) with the later, socalled "red roof";[29] the "Bunte Dach" belonging to a hypothetical 7th century BC predecessor to the Classical Artemis temple)[30], Rakita (a long and narrow elliptical temple with wooden peristyle on stone bases, see above) and Aigeira (Geometric naiskos? long and narrow 7th century temple, see above).

The location of cults in the Late Archaic period (ca. 600–500 BC)

The evidence for cults in this period ranges widely from single finds indicating cult activity to large sanctuaries, and the characters of well-documented cults differ from flimsy, open-air structures to temples with wooden peristyles covered by tile roofs with refined and delicate fictile decoration. All in all, a survey of the evidence for cults has shown that even though the evidence and the nature of the cults vary greatly, their location largely falls into three categories which are similar to those defined above.

The first category, tentatively called 'sub-urban', consists of eigth places of worship all of which are situated on the slopes of hills (six cases) or on the edge of hilltops (two cases). According to sherd material and the like, several of these hills were inhabited, and in the Classical period – with only one possible exception – they became strongly fortified cities. All cults continued after the erection of fortification-walls and all are situated just outside these or at the walls themselves:

- Western slopes of Palaiokastro: Spolaita (Kolonas 1991, 1992)
- Kallipolis: Hill sanctuary (see above)
- Kalydon: Laphrion-hill (see above)
- Kato Chrysovitsa (ancient Koronto?) (fortification not certain): Sykia spring[31]
- Stratos: Old Zeus temple (Schwandner – Kolonas 1996)
- Araxos (the Mycenaean fortification wall was reused): Altar (see above)

- Lousoi (ancient city not located): Sanctuary of Lousoi (Mitsopoulos-Leon 1992; Mitsopoulos-Leon und Ladstätter 1997)
- Perhaps Aigeira (Hyperasia; the Late Geometric and Archaic settlement is not located): Archaic temple on Mycenaean acropolis (see above).

The second category consists of thirteen places of worship which lie in "rural" areas in the sense that settlements in these areas never developed into important or fortified cities. Thus, as became evident from the surveys made by Bommeljé-Doorn (1987), Morgan-Hall (1996), and Lang (this volume) cults may lie close to graves, farmsteads and other settlement remains indicating that they were situated in landscapes which were never really desolate. As just stated, however, the decisive difference from the previous category is that the immediate surroundings of the sanctuaries in this category never developed major, important cities. In addition, almost all of these "rural" cults continued in use even after the emergence at some distance of fully developed, recognizable cities in the 5th and 4th centuries BC, and often were lavishly repaired. The cults in question are shown in Fig. 3. In addition to these, the cult on Mt Oite (Pyra) should be mentioned connected through legend as it is with the city Trachis.[32]

The third category consists of evidence for 'urban' cults, that is cults located centrally in relation to nucleated settlements which later became cities. As mentioned the evidence is very evasive. An Archaic bronze statuette of Zeus Fulgur is said to be from Ambrakia at which place scanty remains of what may be an acropolis wall have been observed.[33] The exact location of the statuette in relation to these ruins is, however, not known. At the site identified as the acropolis of Helike in Achaea, the foundations of two small temples were excavated which are dated to the Archaic or Classical period.[34] In Chalkis fragments of Archaic perirranteria and louteria are a relatively common feature in floating layers stemming from the acropolis, but their function need not be purely sacred.[35]

All in all, the erection of shrines with elaborately decorated tile-roofs is a characteristic feature of the 6th century: Kalydon (two stone-built temples: temple A and a hypothetical temple known among other things from the so called "Blassgelbe Dach", metopes, reused stoneblocks)[36], Lepenou (small oikos or in antis temple with metope decoration)[37], probably Zakonina (terracotta *kalypter* with female protomes)[38], Taxiarches (two small in antis temples with kalypter with silen's head and male heads; see above), Thermon (reparations of existing temples, erection of Apollo Lykeios shrine?; see above) and perhaps Lousoi ("Ostbau")[39], Stratos (an old Zeus-temple erected in this period contemporary with the Lebenou temple dated to around 550 BC ?), Santameri ("archaic" stonebuilt temple with metopes and triglyphs; see above), Nikolaikon (architectural terracotta of sphinx or gorgon; see above).

Again, as in the previous period, it is interesting that the most solid evidence for investment in sacred architecture stems from cults located outside nucleated settlements.

The Classical and Early Hellenistic period (ca. 500-250 BC)

The majority of cults established in earlier periods continued into Classical and to some extent even into Hellenistic times. In addition, quite a number of stone temples were built in this period. Most of these temples are only known from stray finds of architectural members, but a few are well preserved and the general impression is that many were built during the 5th and 4th centuries BC. Due to the erection of city walls and the growing monumentalization of urban functions in the Classical-Early Hellenistic period, three categories of cult now become distinct: urban, suburban and extra-urban.

Dealing first with the suburban cults, it is noticeable that several cults which began in the Archaic period, are not only still visited, but their shrines become repaired or even replaced by new temples in the 4th century (Kalydon, Kallipolis, Lousoi, Stratos). On the whole, suburban sanctuaries may become monumentalized through the building of propyla, storerooms and other facilities obviously meant to accomodate a growing number of visitors, votives and cult equipment (Kalydon, Lousoi). In addition to the old cults, new cults were established right outside the city-walls as e.g. the cultic remains at Grana outside the southwestern corner of the city-wall of Stratos.[40] Even new temples, sometimes housing fine cult images, appeared right outside the city-walls (Kallipolis: Demeter and Kore (see above), Makynia;[41] Malevros[42]; the "Asclepeion" and the statues of the "Muses" found near Gavalou (ancient Trichonion)[43], and probably outside Neromanna (ancient Phistyon?)[44] and Palaiokatunon (ancient Krokyleion).[45] It is true that the Zeus cult in Stratos, and apparently the Aphitou-Aphrodite-Enyalos-Artemis-cult at Araxos literally became built into the city-walls and thus ceased to be strictly speaking "sub-urban" cults in the sense defined above. On the other hand, their location at the very border of the city in a raised position with a commanding view over the surrounding plains establishes the temples as much more oriented towards the countryside than towards the city making it difficult to classify them categorically as urban. The rich votive deposit found about 250 m to the north of the area identified as ancient Pharai perhaps belongs in the category of suburban sanctuaries.[46] The only exception to the general impression of flourishing suburban sanctuaries, is the cult at Spolaita outside the walls of Palaiokastro (ancient Agrinion?), which appears to have died out at the end of the 4th century, but this cult was never characterized by fine architecture (see above). The list is accordingly:

Fig. 3. The distribution of Archaic (600-500 BC), "rural" cults (green dots) in Aetolia and Achaea in relation to major Classical-Hellenistic cities (red squares).

1. Stratos
2. Palaiokastro
3. Malevros
4. Ano Vlochos (Thestiai)
5. Paravola (Boukastion)
6. Neromanna (Phistyon)
7. Ambrakia
8. Kato Chrysovitsa (Koronto?)
9. Sitarolona (Pamphia?)
10. Analipse
11. Lithovounion (Akrai?)
12. Analipse (Metapa?)
13. Gavalou (Trichonion)
14. Papadates (Akrai?)
15. Angelokastro (Arsinoe)
16. Lepenou
17. Site in tobacco-field 4 kms to the northwest of Stratos[87]
18. Kryo Nero
19. Taxiarches[88]
20. Zakonina (Palaiokarya)[89]
21. Koniska[90]
22. Chrysovitsa[91]
23. Thermon[92]
24. Pharai
25. Tritaea
26. Keryneia (Helike)
27. Aigion
28. Aigeira
29. Pellene
30. Santameri[93]
31. Nikolaika[94]
32. Rakita (Ano Mazarakis)
33. Pitsa-cave
34. Patras
35. Dyme
36. Rhypes
37. Elis
38. Kynaithra
39. Kleitor
40. Lousoi.

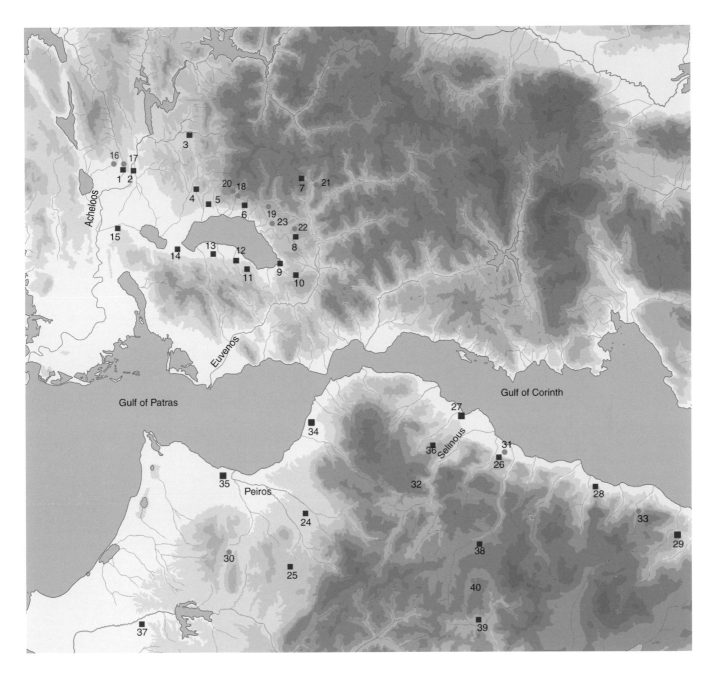

- Palaeokastro: Cult near Spolaita
- Kallipolis: 1. Demeter and Kore and 2. "old" cult
- Kalydon: The Laphrion hill.
- Kato Chrysovitsa (ancient Koronto?): Sykia spring
- Stratos: Hellenistic cult at Grana
- Araxos: Aphitou-Aphrodite-Enyalos-Artemis-cult
- Lousoi (city not identified): Sanctuary of Lousoi
- Aigeira: "Cult on Mycenaean acropolis"
- Malevros: Architectural members outside fortification wall
- Neromanna (ancient Phistyon): Architectural members (?) near Neromanna
- Palaiokatunon (ancient Krokyleion): Architectural members nearby
- Makynia: "temple" outside fortification wall
- Pharai: votive deposit

The "rural" sanctuaries lying at some distance from fortified, important cities also flourished in the Classical-Early Hellenistic period, as alluded to above and their distribution is shown in Fig. 4. Thus, Archaic cults continued at Lebenou and in the valley between Lebenou and Stratos, at Kryo Nero, Taxiarches, Pyra, Thermon, Rakita, and Pitsa. Moreover, new, elegant temples are built in the countryside at some distance from the fortified cities. These are first and foremost the temples at Velvina[47] and those known from temple-blocks reused in a church at Mokista near Thermon and near Neromanna (ancient Phistyon)[48], on the Varassova mountain near Chalkis in Aetolia,[49] and in a church in the territory of the site identified as Tritaea in Achaea.[50] Moreover, temples are known to have existed from the high-classical pedimental sculptures found at the Velvitsianico river in Achaea,[51] the tiles, blocks and sherds found at the Larisa river at Riolos[52] and the inscriptions (mentioning Demeter) and votive material found at Kopoulia near Petrochorio.[53] There are also remains from a small Hellenistic "rural" sanctuary at Haghios Ioannis near Dyme[54] and to the southwest of Patras.[55]

Less certain remains from "rural" temples and cults are those observed by Woodhouse at Frangoscala and Haghios Vlasios near respectively the fortified site of Malevros and Kolopyrgos in Aetolia.[56] Also, the fine, Early Classical female bronze statuette found in the town Kainourgion some kilometres from the impressive and huge fortified city at Ano Vlochos (ancient Thestiai) is so far the only evidence for cult activity here.[57]

It ought to be noted that some of these "rural" sanctuaries are known to have been situated close to Classical-Hellenistic minor settlements or farmsteads (for intance at Lebenou, Kopoulia and outside Patras), indicating that this may have been the case with many other "rural" cults. Since, however, several "rural" cults are characterized by fine shrines and temples which were lavishly repaired or even rebuilt in the city-state period, these cults can hardly be said to have served a purely local function comparable to e.g. the parish churches of our time. Rather, it is likely that they enjoyed support and were the object of worship from people living in the nearest cities. They are thus "rural"

in the sense that they – *apart* from their local function – also served as "extra-urban" sanctuaries in relation to cities farther away.

The third category of sanctuaries, the urban cults, consists of a handful of cases. In Aetolia, columns, triglyfs, simablocks and the like have been found inside the fortified kastro of Malevros (5th century),[58] of Lithovounion (Akrai? Pol. V.13);[59] furthermore on the Haghia Irini peak of Pleuron[60] and in floating layers stemming from the "acropolis" of Chalkis (4th century).[61] In Achaia, a small temple destroyed by an earthquake in the second or first century BC was excavated at the place probably to be identified as the acropolis of Helike[62] and as is well-known several well-preserved temples, which have been excavated in the market place in Aigeira, date to the Early Hellenistic period.[63]

In conclusion, it is interesting to observe that contemporary with both an increasing monumentalization of urban functions and a large scale building of city-walls, non-urban cults continue to leave behind the most conspicious traces and by far the most costly temples still appear outside city-walls. In fact, largescale, truly urban temple constructions are hard to trace in the archaeological record until the Early Hellenistic period.

The location of sanctuaries: a general conclusion

For several reasons, the early Aetolian and Achaean cults point to communities which are too developed to be characterized as simply "dispersed settlements" as is sometimes the case in recent scholarly literature.[64] First, at several places there is a high degree of continuity in cult activity, lasting several centuries (e.g. Kalydon, Lebenou, Kallipolis, Thermon, Taxiarches, Sykia spring, Rakita, Araxos, Aigeira, Lousoi, Pitsa). Even from the Late Geometric/Early Archaic period, there is evidence for a pattern comprising "nucleated

Fig. 4. The distribution of Classical-Hellenistic, "rural" cults (green dots) in relation to Classical-Hellenistic major cities (red squares) in Aetolia and Achaia.

1. *Stratos*
2. *Palaiokastro*
3. *Malevros*
4. *Ano Vlochos (Thestiai)*
5. *Paravola (Boukastion)*
6. *Neromanna (Phistyon)*
7. *Ambrakia*
8. *Kato Chrysovitsa (Koronto?)*
9. *Sitarolona (Pamphia?)*
10. *Analipse*
11. *Lithovounion (Akrai?)*
12. *Analipse (Metapa?)*
13. *Gavalou (Trichonion)*
14. *Papadates (Akrai?)*
15. *Angelokastro (Arsinoe)*
16. *Treis Ecclesies (Phana?)*
17. *Pleuron*
18. *Kalydon*
19. *Chalkis*
20. *Makynia*
21. *Naupaktos*
22. *Eupalion*
23. *Kallion*
24. *Trachis (Herakleia)*
25. *Kolopyrgos*
26. *Lebenou*
27. *Site in tobaccofield near Stratos*
28. *Frankoscala*
29. *Haghios Vlasios*
30. *Kainourgion*
31. *Kryo Nero*
32. *"Near" Neromanna*
33. *Mokista*
34. *Taxiarches*
35. *Thermon*
36. *Mt. Oité: Pyra*
37. *Molykrion*
38. *Church on Varassova mountain*
39. *Dyme*
40. *Patras*
41. *Rhypes*
42. *Aigion*
43. *Keryneia (Helike)*
44. *Aigeira*
45. *Pellene*
46. *Kynaithra*
47. *Kleitor*
48. *Tritaea*
49. *Elis*
50. *Pharai*
51. *Haghia Ioannis near Dyme*

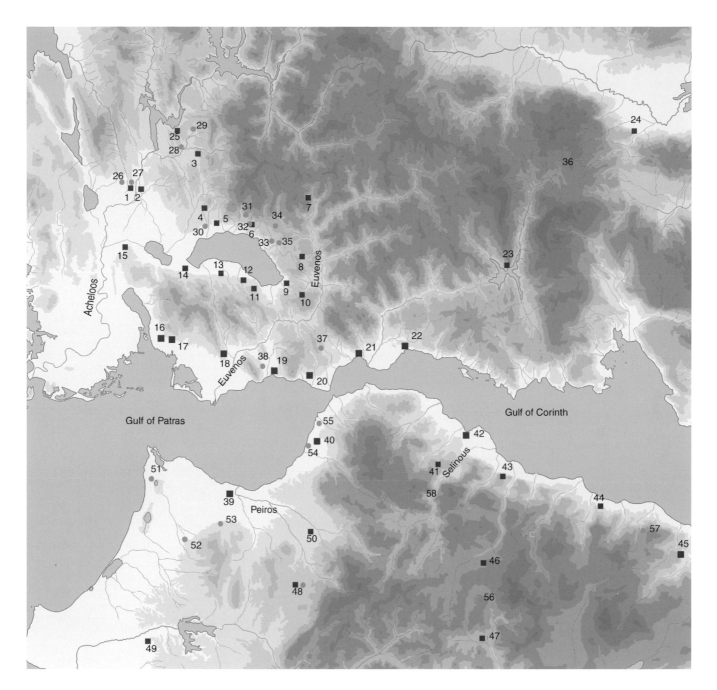

hill-habitation – cult situated at its fringe"
which becomes relatively distinct during
the Late Archaic period. In the Classical-
Hellenistic period these hill-settlements
develop into a series of fortified cities
with suburban sanctuaries. In fact, the
apparently persistent lack of priority in
the Archaic period, and even to some
extent in the Classical period, of distinct
urban cults should not necessarily be interpreted as a sign of lack of urbanization.
Rather, the distinct suburban sanctuary
may be revealed to be a characteristic of

Western Greek urban organization. Second, there are signs in the Archaic period
of a more developed pattern consisting of
"nucleated habitation – cult at its fringe –
cult in its territory" (Stratos, Kalydon?,
Aigeira/Pellene?). Third, the cult buildings
at several sites in the 7th and early 6th centuries BC already appear too sophisticated
to be the result of "dispersed settlement"
(e.g. Kalydon, Thermon, Lebenou,
Stratos?, Rakita). In fact, a largescale temple building programme appears to have
taken place in the 6th century BC involv-

ing among other things the erections of elaborate shrines in Stratos and Kalydon. These indications of a society organized on a more advanced level than has sometimes been thought are supported by recent excavations in Chalkis that point to the existence of town-planning in the Archaic period.[65] On the whole, scholars from especially Germany and Austria have recently drawn attention to evidence of early (Archaic) signs of a more advanced society in Northwestern Greece. For instance they have pointed to a possible Archaic lighthouse at Vigla (the harbour of Palairos),[66] to late Geometric and Archaic votives, burials, and architectural fragments from Elis indicating settlement and central administration well before 471 BC, when Elis is said to be founded[67] and to written evidence for well-developed political organizations and polis-imitating structures already in the Early Classical period.[68]

On the other hand, it has to be admitted that the cults described above present an uneven picture. Large scale investments in cultic architecture seem to be confined to particular areas, such as highly important routes of communication between inland and the coast (e.g the Selinous river valley and confluence of rivers in the Euvenos river), to the coastal region with its constant exposure to sea traffic, and to natural border zones (e.g. the Acheloos, Euvenos and Mornos rivers). The lack of finds and cults in large parts of the mountainous regions point to isolation, remoteness and backwardness. In other words, there is likely to have existed a high degree of discrepancy between levels of development among Aetolian-Achaean communities in one and the same period. Synoecisms may have taken place relatively early in one area, while dispersed settlements continued in other regions. Rural cults visited by people from scattered communities in the vicinity may have changed status when synoecisms took place, in the sense that they became extra-urban sanctuaries in relation to the new nucleated settlements and cities. Likewise, cults lying at the fringe or at some distance from a habitation may have become urban when the settlement expanded during synoecism (compare Stratos, Araxos).

Written sources

In many ways, a quick scanning of the written sources for synoecism processes in Achaia add to the impression just gained from the archaeological remains, even though a direct connection between the two types of sources is rarely to be found.

Homer mentions five places in a region called "Aigaleos" all of which were situated in the eastern half of Achaea and later became important cities: Pellene, Hyperasia (later called Aigeira), Aigai, Helike and Aigion (*Il.* 2. 573-75). He refers to a district, "Bouprasion", in the western half of the region (*Il.* 2. 615; compare Strabo 8. 3. 8), perhaps to be located between the Mycenaean strongholds at Araxos and Chlemoutsi.[69] Herodotos (1.145) gives the earliest and most complete list of cities in Achaea. This list comprises twelve cities: Pellene, Aigeira, Aigai, Boura, Helike, Aigion, Rhypes, Patras (Patrees), Pharai (Pharees), Olenos, Dyme, Tritaia. In naming twelve cities, Herodotos is no doubt guided by his view that the Ionians of Asia Minor originated from the northern Peloponnese and, accordingly, by his wish to explain why the Ionians restricted membership of the Panionion to twelve cities.[70] Nevertheless, later authors give more or less the same list of cities[71] and archaeology has so far not demonstrated that the list is distorted.

The synoecism processes of Dyme and Patras have especially caught the interest of scholars. According to Thucydides (5. 52. 2), Alkibiades tried to persuade the inhabitants of Patras to extend their city walls down to the sea. This event can be placed in 419 BC and implies that Patras at this time was a fortified city. According to Strabo (8. 3. 2), Patras was formed by seven demes and Pausanias (7. 18. 2-6) gives a lengthy description of the foundation myth of the city. These passages have led scholars to reconstruct two synoecism waves prior to the Augustan one. The earliest consisted of the unification of the villages Aroe, Antheia and Mesatis to form Patras and apparently took place in the area of Aroe in the Late Archaic or Early Classical period. During the second wave, dated to the 5th century BC, the villages of Boline, Argyra and Arba were incorporated into Patras.[72]

With regard to Dyme, Strabo (8. 3. 2) records, that Dyme was formed by eight demes one of which was the *polichne* Teuthra. Apart from being mentioned by Herodotus, the city figures in the naval battle between the Athenian and the Peloponnesian fleet near Rhion[73] and was liberated by Epaminondas,[74] indicating that by the 5th and 4th centuries BC, the city of Dyme had been formed. Its city walls appear, however, to stem from the 3rd century BC.[75] As in Patras, a later synoecism also seems to have taken place since Strabo (8. 7. 4) tells that the inhabitants of Olenos were transferred to Dyme for which reasons Olenos lay in ruins in his time. Other communities, such as Larisa, mentioned by Strabo (9. 5. 19) are likely to have been incorporated as well.

In this context it is interesting to observe that each of the communities swallowed up by Dyme and Patras possessed cults which either became transferred to or copied by the new city or continued to be worshipped in their original places by people in the new city. Thus, the following cults were worshipped in Pausanias' time and had obviously been moved from the communities of Aroe, Mesoa, and Antheia to Patras: an Artemis Limnatis cult originating in Mesoa,[76] an Artemis Triklaria cult originally located at the Meilichos river east of Patras (and perhaps to be identified with the pedimental sculptures found at the Velvitsianiko river mentioned above) at which place it functioned as a common precinct for Aroe, Antheia and Mesoa and was related to a cult for Dionysos with the surname Aesymnetes;[77] and, finally, a cult for Dionysos worshipped as respectively Mesateus, Antheus and Aroeus.[78]

In some cases, however, cults of the old communities appear to have continued in their original location and thus to have functioned as a kind of extra-urban sanctuary in relation to the new city of Patras. For instance, Athenaeus refers to a "cup-bearing Demeter" worshipped in the neighbourhood [chora] of Antheia,[79] while Artemis Limnatis and Artemis Triklaria seem from Pausanias' decription still to be connected to their original locations. In addition, the oracular Demeter and Gaia spring-cult at the harbour of Patras, described by Pausanias,[80] without a doubt precedes the formation of Patras. Originally, it was therefore a "rural" cult in relation to one of the old communities in the area of Patras, perhaps the one known to have existed on the slopes of the acropolis of Patras (Aroe?). Even in Classical times, the city of Patras was probably confined to the area of the Venetian city southwest of the acropolis.[81] With the expansion of Patras toward the sea in Late Hellenistic times, however, the Demeter and Gaia sanctuary changed in status to a suburban cult.

With regard to Dyme, Strabo (8. 3. 11) saw a temple for Artemis "Nemydia" [82] in the village Teuthea, while near the ruins of Olenos he saw "the notable temple of Asclepius" (8. 7. 4), and Pausanias noted "a temple of Larisaean Athena" by the Larisus river (7.17. 5). These sanctuaries must originally have been related to the old communities of Antheia, Teuthea and Larisa (if there was a village of this name[83]), but their relation no doubt shifted after the formation of Dyme during which Olenos and Teuthea were swallowed up by Dyme.

A close parallel to this situation is found in Strabo's and Pausanias' description of Pellene. Strabo (8. 7. 5) mentions a village [kome] called Pellene between Pellene and Aigion which – as we can gather from his description – was the seat for the Theoxenia in honour of Apollo mentioned already by Pindar.[84] Further, Pausanias (7. 27. 8-11) refers to Poseidion, probably a sanctuary for Poseidon, a sanctuary for Mysian Demeter sixty stades distant to Pellene and near it a sanctuary of Asclepius called Cyrus. All of these three cult places clearly functioned as extra-urban sanctuaries in relation to the new city of Pellene in Strabo's and Pausanias' time. Before, however, the synoecism of Pellene they belonged to small demes, the names of which are reflected in their epithets. Again, as was the case with cults near Dyme and Patras, their status as extra-urban sanctuaries in relation to important cities was a recent one which arose as a result of synoecism. Probably, the cluster of highly important suburban sanctuaries for Artemis, Dionysos, Athena and Hermes, which Pausanias saw directly outside the main gate to Pellene (8. 27. 1-4), and the Eileithyia cult (8.27.8) located immediately inside the gate also predate the synoecism of Pellene and were perhaps related to the deme of Poseidion, which Pausanias mentions after the Eileithyia cult and describes as located below the gymnasium.[85] In that case we are faced with a close parallel to the characteristic 6th century phenomenon revealed by archaeology. That is a case in which cults are situated on the fringe of a habitation that later developed into an important city.

Finally, Pausanias' remark on Lousoi (8. 18. 8) and Phelloe (7. 26.10) offers a good example of the way in which sanctuaries kept changing territorial status, even in much later times and how in fact extra-uban sanctuaries are often a late development. As already mentioned, Pausanias has heard of a city Lousoi, but states that in his time the sanctuary of Lousoi lies on the border (orois) of Kleitor. This suggest that the sanctuary had changed relation from Lousoi (suburban?) to Kleitor and become extra-urban in relation to the latter. With regard to Phelloe, Pausanias says that a straight road lead from Aigeira to the town (polisma) of Phelloe which was not always inhabited.[86] In view of the unstable settlement at Phelloe and its inferior political status, the sanctuaries for Dionysos and Artemis, which Pausanias saw in this community, must therefore for long periods have functioned as extra-urban cults in relation to the city of Hellenistic Aigeira.

Conclusion

Throughout the Geometric-Early Hellenistic period, rural sanctuaries or sanctuaries lying on the fringe of nucleated settlements are a characteristic phenomenon in Aetolia and Achaea. In fact large scale building programmes of temples and restaurations of older temples are best attested in rural sanctuaries, and not least suburban ones. Even when cities appear, non-urban sanctuaries, continue to dominate the archaeological picture although they may change status and become "extra-urban" in relation to one particular city. In many cases, the votive material and inscriptions prove the rural cults to be in honour of Artemis, Dionysos or Demeter. For these reasons, sanctuaries in Aetolia and Achaea cannot always be classified permanently as "urban", "surburban" or "extra-urban". These conclusions are by no means meant to challenge the current view on the "extra-urban" sanctuary as highly significant for the development of Greek city-states as argued by de Polignac (1984, 1995). Rather, attention has been drawn to the fact that, at least in Aetolia-Achaea – an area not treated by de Polignac in detail – the maintainance of unprotected cults outside habitation centres and later outside city walls was regarded as vital for the new cities. Written sources have been seen to supplement this impression, as Artemis, Dionysos and Demeter cults indirectly can be shown to be the oldest and most important cults in Patras and Dyme, and probably Pellene as well and to originate in smaller rural communities preceding the synoecims leading to the formation of these cities.

It is with this background that Augustus' transfer of the suburban cult of Artemis Laphria and Dionysos at Kalydon to the acropolis of Patras has to be understood. It was a political act, highly sensitive towards the significance which non-urban, and not least sub-urban cults had always played for the Aetolians and the Achaians, not least during synoecism processes.

Notes

NOTE 1
Bommeljé & Doorn 1987, 22 fig. 2.3;
Rizakis 1989; Alcock 1993, 132-145, 175-
177; Petropoulos and Rizakis 1994; lack of
Roman finds in Aetolian Chalkis: Eiring
1998, 259 and 2000; Dietz and
Moschos1998.

NOTE 2
Alcock 1993, 172-214.

NOTE 3
It is beyond the aims of this paper to give a
more detailed description of the sites mentioned. Instead, references are given to main
publications and descriptions of the sites.
For supplementary literature I refer to the
works by Antonetti 1990, Rizakis 1995,
Osanna 1996.

NOTE 4
Dyggve 1948, pl. 38.

NOTE 5
Bommeljé & Doorn 1987, 86-89; personal
observation.

NOTE 6
Kirsten 1941a, 116.

NOTE 7
Benton 1931/32, 238-39; this material formerly gave rise to the false identification of
the site with Chalkis.

NOTE 8
Themelis 1998; Mazarakis Ainian 1997,
135-136 with references.

NOTE 9
Vroom 1993, 133.

NOTE 10
Mastrokostas 1966; Mastrokostas 1967;
Daux 1964, 760-762; Rizakis 1992, 103-
107.

NOTE 11
Alzinger 1983, 37, fig. 2a; 1985, 430; compare Gogos 1986/87 and Mazarakis Ainian
1997, 164-166.

NOTE 12
Alzinger 1985, especially 446, and figs. 27,
41-42.

NOTE 13
AA 1994, 605-07; AA 1995, 783-786;
Kolonas 1998.

NOTE 14
Woodhouse 1897, 169.

NOTE 15
French 1992-93, 24.

NOTE 16
Lang 1994, 246; Lang this volume.

NOTE 17
Kawerau and Sotiriadis 1902-08; Papapostolou 1993, 1995, 1996; Mazarakis Ainian
1999.

NOTE 18
Compare Pritchett 1989, 126-140.

NOTE 19
Dekoulakou 1982; Stauropoulou-Gat-
si1986, 1997; Pritchett 1989, 132, 134.

NOTE 20
Orlandos 1965; PEC, 715.

NOTE 21
Hyperasia and Pellene and Gonouessa. The
location of Gonouessa is not certain, and it
is still discussed whether Gonouessa is the
same as Donouessa as stated by Pausanias
(7. 26. 2-3), see Rizakis 1995 no. 335 for
summary; compare Paus. (4.15.1) who at-
taches the city-ethnic Hyperiseus to a person called Ikaros, who won the foot race at
Olympia in 688 BC)

NOTE 22
Petropoulos 1997, 172-175; Blackman
1997-98a.

NOTE 23
Rizakis 1995, 193-94.

NOTE 24
Roman tiles and cooking vase-fragments
are reported from the modern village
Rakita and from the Haghia Paraskeui
church (Petropoulos 1997, 175).

NOTE 25
Mastrokostas 1969a, 320, pin. 228 c. The
bronze double axe reported by Bommeljé-
Doorn 1987, 112 as stemming from Kato
Vassiliki (Haghia Triadha) is reported by
Mastrokostas to have been found in Ano
Vassiliki (1969c, 320-321).

NOTE 26
Houby-Nielsen, Moschos and Gazis 2000.

NOTE 27
Papakosta 1990, 120-121, 122 fig.10; Morgan and Hall 1996, 176-179 for summary.

NOTE 28
Poulsen and Dyggve 1927, 36; Dygge 1948,
267-269.

NOTE 29
Dyggve 1948, 62, 270 n. 2.

NOTE 30
Dyggve 1948, pl. 16 A-P.

NOTE 31
Woodhouse 1897, 247; Rhomaios 1923c.

NOTE 32
Pappadakis 1922; Béquignon 1937, 210; for
the connection in myth between Mt. Oita
and Trachis, Malkin 1994, 227-230; for the
location of Trachis, see Pritchett 1989, 118-
121, 1991, 199-204.

NOTE 33
Rhomaios 1923a; Bommeljé & Doorn 1987, 76; Antonetti 1990, 224.

NOTE 34
Petropoulos 1998, 133, fig. 7.

NOTE 35
e.g. Dietz 1998, fig. 26:7 and fig. 32:7; Houby-Nielsen, Moschos and Gazis 2000, fig. 14.

NOTE 36
See Dyggve 1948.

NOTE 37
AA 1995, 785 figs. 2-3.

NOTE 38
Rhomaios 1923b; Kirsten 1941, 116.

NOTE 39
Mitsopoulos-Leon und Ladstätter 1997, 88-89.

NOTE 40
Kolonas 1996, 163.

NOTE 41
Kolonas 1994, fig.1.

NOTE 42
Woodhouse 1897,174-175 and personal observation 1994.

NOTE 43
Stauropoulou-Gatsi 1997, 148; Antonetti 1990, 238-240.

NOTE 44
Woodhouse 1897, 196-198.

NOTE 45
Woodhouse 1897, 376; for fortification: Bommeljé & Doorn 1987, 90-91.

NOTE 46
Rizakis 1995 no.160.

NOTE 47
Orlandos 1927; Knell 1973.

NOTE 48
Woodhouse 1897, 205-206 and photo opposite p. 206; Antonetti 1990, 227-228. If the temple is contemporary with reused inscriptions mentioning Artemis Hegemone, it may be Roman and not Hellenistic (see also Antonetti 1990, 227-8).

NOTE 49
Paliouras 1985, 41, 64, 68.

NOTE 50
Rizakis 1995 no. 282.

NOTE 51
Trianti 1991; Rizakis 1995 no. 254.

NOTE 52
Rizakis 1992, n. 77 p. 220.

NOTE 53
Lakari 1991, 244-45.

NOTE 54
Lakari 1991, 244.

NOTE 55
Papapostolou 1987, 134, pl. 37a; Petropoulos and Rizakis 1994, 198, n. 27 and no. 139 on fig. 1.

NOTE 56
Woodhouse 1897, 174-175; 289.

NOTE 57
Kirsten 1941; Mastrokostas 1969c, 318, pin. 226 a-b.

NOTE 58
Rhomaios 1927, 9.

NOTE 59
Woodhouse 1897, 259-260.

NOTE 60
Woodhouse 1897, 124.

NOTE 61
Houby-Nielsen, Moschos and Gazis 2000, fig. 7.

NOTE 62
Petropoulos 1998, 133, fig. 7.

NOTE 63
Alzinger 1989 and Bammer 1996 with references.

NOTE 64
For Achaea, see Morgan and Hall 1996.

NOTE 65
Dietz et al. 2000.

NOTE 66
Kolonas – Faisst 1992.

NOTE 67
Eder – Mitsopoulos-Leon 1999.

NOTE 68
Funke 1987, 1997 and this volume with references.

NOTE 69
Kirk 1985 on *Il.* 2. 615.

NOTE 70
Morgan and Hall 1996, 168.

NOTE 71
Strabo 8. 7. 4; Skylax 42; Polybius 2. 41; Paus. 7. 6. 1.

NOTE 72
Curtius 1851, 437, 453; Moggi 1976, 92-93; Rizakis 1995, no. 250.

NOTE 73
Thuc. 2. 84, 3-5; Diod. 12. 48. 1.

NOTE 74
Xen. 7. 1. 41-43; Diod. 15. 75. 2.

NOTE 75
Rizakis 1992, 81-84.

NOTE 76
Paus. 7. 20. 7-9.

NOTE 77
Paus. 7. 20.1.

NOTE 78
Paus. 7. 21. 6.

NOTE 79
Athen. XI. 460 d.

NOTE 80
Paus. 7. 21. 11-13; Herbillon 1929, 27-32;
Osanna 1996, 118-120.

NOTE 81
Rizakis 1998, 46, fig. 3.

NOTE 82
Probably rather "Limnatis"; see to Rizakis
1995, no. 522.

NOTE 83
Compare the recent finds of Hellenistic
houses and graves at Riolos: Petritaki 1993,
164-166.

NOTE 84
Schol. Pind. *Ol.* 9. 146; Rizakis 1995 nos.
531.

NOTE 85
For the significance of Artemis, Demeter
and Dioysos in early cults of Achaea:
Lafond 1991; Osanna 1996, 303-312.

NOTE 86
For a possible identification with the site
Seliana, see Rizakis 1995 no. 333 and Os-
anna 1996, 271-272.

NOTE 87
AA 1994, 606; AA 1995, 783-84 and Lang
this volume.

NOTE 88
Rhomaios 1929.

NOTE 89
Rhomaios 1923b; Kirsten 1941, 116; Bommeljé & Doorn 1987, 100; Antonetti 1990,
235.

NOTE 90
Rhomaios 1927, 6-7, eik. 3.

NOTE 91
Bronze (warrior?) statuette from Chrysovit-
sa-village (Rhomaios 1923c, 61).

NOTE 92
Summary: Fiehn 1934; Antonetti 1990,
151-210; Kuhn 1993; Mazarakis-Ainian
1997, 125-136.

NOTE 93
Mastrokostas 1969b, 216.

NOTE 94
Petropoulos 1998, fig.11; Blackman 1997-
98b, 40, fig. 13.

Bibliography

Alcock, S. E., 1993
Graecia Capta. The landscapes of Roman Greece. Cambridge.

Alzinger, W., 1983
AIGEIRA-HYPERASIA/
Peloponnes 1982, *ÖJh* 54, Beiblatt, 35-40.

Alzinger, W. et al., 1985
Aigeira-Hyperesia I, *Klio* 67, 388-451.

Alzinger, W., 1988
Hyperesia-Aigeira. Der Wandel eines Heiligtums von spätmykenischer bis in klassische Zeit, in: *Πρακτικά XII Διεθνούς Ζυνεδρίου Κλασικής Αρχαιολογίας, Αθήνα, 4-10 Σεπτ., Δ, Αθήνα,* 20-23.

Alzinger, W., 1989
Was sah Pausanias in Aigeira? Archäologische und litterarische Dokumente, in: Walker and Cameron (eds.) 1989, 142-145.

Antonetti, C., 1990
Les Étoliens. Religion et image (Centre de Recherches d´ Histoire Ancienne 92. Annales littéraires de l´Université de Besancon, 405). Paris.

Bammer, A., 1996
Aigeira. *ÖJh* 65, 33-38.

Benton, S., 1931/32
The Ionian Islands, *BSA* 32, 213-246.

Béquignon, Y., 1937
La Vallée du Spercheios. Des Origines au IV siecle. Paris.

Blackman, D., 1997-98a
Elike project, *ARepLond,* 40.

Blackman, D., 1997-98b
Ano Mazaraki (Rakita) Patron. *ARep Lond,* 39-40.

Bommeljé, S. and Doorn, P.K., 1987
Aetolia and the Aetolians. Towards the interdisciplinary study of a Greek region. (Studia Aetolica 1). Utrecht.

Curtius, E., 1851
Peloponnesos: eine historisch-geographische Beschreibung der Halbinsel I. Gotha.

Daux, G., 1964
Cronique des fouilles 1963: Araxos, *BCH* 88, 760-762.

Dekoulakou, I., 1982
Κεραμεικού 8ου και 7ου π.Χ. από τάφους Αχαΐας και Αιτωλίας, *ASAtene* 60, 219-236.

Dietz, S. and Moschos, I., 1998
Excavations at Haghia Triadha, 1996, in: *FPR,* 282-286.

Dietz et al., 2000
The Greek Danish Excavations in Ancient Chalkis in Aetolia, 1999, *ArchRepLond* (forthcoming).

Dyggve, E., 1948
Das Laphrion. Der Tempelbezirk von Kalydon. Mit einem Beitrag von Frederik Poulsen (Det Kongelige Danske Videnskabernes Selskab. Arkæologisk-Kunsthistoriske Skrifter, Bind 1 nr. 2). København.

Eder, B. – Mitsopoulos-Leon, V., 1999
Zur Geschichte der Stadt Elis vor dem Synoikismos von 471 v.Chr.: Die Zeugnisse der geometrischen und archaischen Zeit, *ÖJh* 68, Beiblatt, 2-39.

Eiring, J., 2000
The Registration Process for Finds from Haghia Triadha, in: *SPR,* 247-251.

Fiehn, K., 1934
Thermos, *RE,* 2423-2444.

French, E. B., 1992-93
Stratos. *ARepLond,* 24.

Funke, P., 1987
Zur Datierung befestigter Stadtanlagen in Aitolien. Historisch-philologische Anmerkungen zu einem Wechelverhältnis zwischen Siedlungsstruktur und politischer Organisation, *Boreas* 10, 87-96.

Funke, P., 1997
Polisgenese und Urbanisierung in Aitolien im 5. und 4 Jh. v. Chr., in: Hansen (ed.) 1997, 145-188.

Gogos, S., 1986/87
Kult und Heiligtümer der Artemis von Aigeira, *ÖJh* 57, Beiblatt, 108-139.

Hansen (ed.), M. H., 1996
Introduction to Inventory of Poleis. Acts of the Copenhagen Polis Centre, vol. 3, Copenhagen.

Hansen (ed.), M. H., 1997
The Polis as an Urban Centre and as a Political Community (Symposium August, 29-31, 1996; Acts of the Copenhagen Polis Centre vol. 4), Copenhagen.

Herbillon, J., 1929
Les Cultes des Patras avec une proso-pographie Patréenne, Baltimore- London – Oxford.

Hägg, R. (ed.), 1999
Ancient Greek Hero Cult. Proceedings of the Fifth International Seminar on Ancient Greek Cult, organized by the Department of Classical Archaeology and Ancient History, Göteborg University, 21-23 April 1995. Stockholm.

Houby-Nielsen, S., Moschos, I. and Gazis, M., 2000
Excavations on the hill of Haghia Triadha, in *SPR,* 225-245.

Isager, J. (ed.), 2001
Foundation and Destruction. Nikopolis and Northwestern Greece. Aarhus

Kawerau, G. und Sotiriadis, J., 1902-08
Der Apollotempel zu Thermos, *Antike Denkmäler* II, 5, Berlin.

Kirk, G. S., 1985
The Iliad. A Commentary. Cambridge. 1985.

Kirsten, E., 1941
Bericht über eine Reise in Aitolien und Akarnanien, *AA,* 99-119.

Knell, H., 1973
Der Artemistempel in Kalydon und der Poseidontempel in Molykreion, *AA,* 448-461.

Kolonas, L., 1991
Αρχαϊκό αγροτικό ιερό στη Σπολαϊτα Αιτωλοακαρνανίας, in: *Πρακτικά Α Αρχαιολογικού και Ιστορικού συνεδρίου Αιτωλοακαρνανίας, Αγρίνιο, 21-22-23 Οκτωβρίου 1988,* 162-168.

Kolonas, L., 1992
Σπολαϊτα Τριχωνίδας, *ADelt* 42, (1987), B, 177-179.

Kolonas, L., 1994
Η αρχαία Μακύνεια μετά τις πρόσφατες αρχαιολογικές έρευνες, Ναυπακτιακά, τ. ΣΤ᾽ (1992-93), 79-87.

Kolonas, L., 1996
Επιφανειακή έρευνα στρατικής γής, *ADelt* 46, B:1 (1991), 163.

Kolonas, L., 1998
Σπάθαρη Λεπενούς, *ADelt* 48 (1993), B, 141, pin. 48a.

Kolonas, L. – Faisst, G. W., 1992
Eine neuentdeckte Akropole in Akarnanien – Vorläufiger Bericht, *AA,* 561-572.

Kuhn, G., 1993
Bau B und Tempel C in Thermos, *AM* 108, 29-47.

Lafond, Y., 1991
Artémis en Achaïe, *REG* 104, 410-433.

Lakari, M., 1991
Αγροτικοί οικισμοί οτη Δυμαία χωρα: η περίπτωση του Πετροχωρίου, in: Rizakis (edt.) 1991, 241-246.

Lang, F., 1994
Veränderungen des Siedlungsbildes in Akarnanien von der klassich-hellenistischen zur römischen Zeit, *Klio* 76, 239-254.

Lang, F., 2001
The Dimensions of Material Topography, in: Isager (ed.) 2001.

Malkin, I., 1994
Myth and Territory in the Spartan Mediterranean. Cambridge.

Mastrokostas, E., 1966
Ανασκαφή του τείχους Δυμαίων, *ADelt* 19, B:1 (1964), 187-190.

Mastrokostas, E., 1967
Ανασκαφή του τείχους Δυμαίων, *ADelt* 20, B:2 (1965), 224-227.

Mastrokostas, E., 1969a
Χαλκίς, *ADelt* 22, B:2 (1967), 320 pin. 228 c.

Mastrokostas, E., 1969b
Σανταμέρι, *ADelt* 22, B:1 (1967), 216, pin. 156 f-g.

Mastrokostas, E., 1969c, Καινούριου, *ADelt* 22, B:2 (1967), 318, pin. 226 a-b.

Mazarakis Ainian, A., 1997
From Rulers' Dwellings to Temples. Architecture, Religion and Society in Early Iron Age Greece (1100-700 B.C.) (SIMA 121). Jonsered.

Mazarakis Ainian, A., 1999
Reflections on hero cults in Early Iron Age Greece, in: Hägg 1999 (ed.), 9-36.

Mitsopoulos-Leon, V., 1992
Artémis de Lousoi. Les fouilles autrichiennes, *Kernos* 5, 97-108.

Mitsopoulos-Leon, V. und Ladstätter, G., 1997
Lousoi. Österreichisches Archäologisches Institut, Grabungen 1997, 82-92.

Moggi, M., 1976
I Sinecismi interstatali greci. Pisa. 1976.

Morgan, C. and Hall, J. 1996
Achaean Poleis and Achaean Colonization, in: Hansen (ed.) 1996, 164-232.

Orlandos, A. K., 1927
Παράρτημα του Αρχαιολογικού Δελτίου του 1922-25: Ανασκαφαί εν Μολυκρείω της Αιτωλίας, *ADelt* 9 (1924-25), 55-64.

Osanna, M., 1996
Santuari e culti dell' Acaia antica. Napoli.

Palagia, P. and Coulson, W. (eds.), 1998
Regional Schools in Hellenistic Sculpture. Proceedings of an International Conference held at the American School of Classical Studies at Athens, March 15-17, 1996 (Oxbow Monographs 90). Oxford.

Paliouras, A. D., 1985
Βυζαντινή Αιτωλοακαρνανία. Συμβολή στη βυζαντινή και μεταβυζαντινή μνημειακή τέχνη. Αθήνα.

Papakosta, L., 1990
Αίγιο, *ADelt* 40B (1985), 120-123.

Papakosta, L., 1991
Παπατηρήσεις σχετικά με την τοπογραφία του αρχαίου Αίγιο, in: Rizakis 1991, 235-240.

Papapostolou, I. A., 1987
Οδός Ζακύνθου (μεταξύ οδών Κύπρου και Πέντε Πηγαδιών), *ADelt* 34 B:1 (1979), 134, pin. 37a).

Papapostolou, I. A., 1993
Θέρμος, *Ergon*, 44-58.

Papapostolou, I. A., 1995
Θέρμος, *Ergon*, 36-39.

Papapostolou, I. A., 1996
Θέρμος, *Ergon*, 57-62.

Pappadakis, N. G., 1922
Ανασκαφή της Πύρας της Οίτης, *ADelt* 5 (1919), 25-33.

Petritaki, M., 1993
Ριόλο. Θέση Καταρράχια, *ADelt* 43, B (1998), 164-166.

Petropoulos, M., 1991
Τοπογραφία της χώρας των Πατρών, in: Rizakis 1991, 249-258.

Petropoulos, M. and Rizakis, A. D., 1994
Settlement patterns and landscape in the coastal area of Patras. Preliminary report. *JRA* 183-207.

Petropoulos, M., 1997
Νεώτερα στοιχεία από την ανασκαφή γεωμετρικού ναού στο Μαζαραράκι (Ρακιτα) Πατρών, in: *Πρακτικά του Ε Διεθνούς Συνεδρίου Πελοποννησιακών Σπουδών (Αργος - Ναύπλίον 6-10 Σεπτεμβρίου 1995)*, τόμος Β, Αθήναι, 165-192.

Petropoulos, M., 1998
Κερύνεια Αιγιαλείας, *ADelt* 48, B (1993), 132-139.

Polignac, F. de, 1984
La Naissance de la cité grecque. Paris.

Polignac, F. de, 1995
Cults, territory, and the origins of the Greek city-state. Translated by Janet Lloyd. Foreword by Claude Mossé. Chicago and London.

Poulsen, F. und Rhomaios, K., 1927
Erster Vorläufiger Bericht über die dänisch-griechischen Ausgrabungen von Kalydon (Det Kongelige Danske Videnskabernes Selskab. Historisk-filosofiske Meddelelser XIV, 3) København.

Pritchett, W. K., 1989
Studies in Ancient Greek Topography. Part VI. Berkeley – Los Angeles – London.

Rhomaios, K., 1916
Θερμος, *ADelt* 1 (1915), 46-49.

Rhomaios, K., 1923a
Αμπρακιά, *ADelt* 6 (1920-21), 169-170, eik. 3-6.

Rhomaios, K., 1923b
Ζακόνινα, *ADelt* 6 (1920-21), 170.

Rhomaios, K., 1923c
Κόραι της Αιτωλίας, *ADelt* 6 (1920-21), 60-98.

Rhomaios, K., 1927
Παράρτημα του Αρχαιολογικού Δελτίου 1922-1925, *ADelt* 9 (1924-25), 1-12.

Rhomaios, K., 1929
Αρχαίον ιερόν παρά τον Ταξιάρχην της Αιτωλίας, *ADelt* 10 (1926), 1-33.

Rizakis, A. D., 1989
La Colonie romaine de Patras en Achaie: Le temoignage epigraphique, in: Walker and Cameron (eds.) 1989, 180-186.

Rizakis, A. D. (ed.), 1991
Achaia und Elis in der Antike (Meletimata 13). Athen.

Rizakis, A. D., 1991
Αρχαιολογικές Ερευνες στην Αχαΐα, in: *Τόμος Τιμητικός Κ.Ν. Τριανταφύλλου I* (Patras 1990), 510-513.

Rizakis, A. (ed.), 1992
Paysages d' Achaie I. Le bassin du Peiros et la plaine occidentale (Meletimata 15). Athen.

Rizakis, A. D., 1995
Achaïe I. Sources textuelles et histoire régionales (Meletimata 20). Athen.

Rizakis, A. D., 1998
Achaïe II. La cité de Patras: Épigraphie et Historie (Meletimata 25). Athènes.

Schwandner, E.-L. – Kolonas, L., 1996
Beobachtungen am Zeusheiligtum von Stratos, *IstMitt* 46, 1996, 187-196.

Stauropoulou-Gatsi, M., 1986
Πρωτογεωμετρικό νεκροταφείο Αιτωλίας, *ADelt* 35, I, 1980-83, 102-130.

Stauropoulou-Gatsi, M., 1997
Γάβαλου (αρχαίο Τριχώνιον), *ADelt* 47 (1992), 148.

Themelis, P., 1998
Attic Sculpture from Kallipolis (Aitolia): a Cult Group of Demeter and Kore, in: Palagia and Coulson (eds.) 1998, 47-59.

Trianti, T., 1985
Ο γλυπτός διάκοσμος του ναού στο Μάζι της Ηλείας. Αθήνα.

Walker, S. and Cameron, A. (eds.), 1989
The Greek Renaissance in the Roman Empire. Papers from the Tenth British Museum Classical Colloquium (BICS 55). London.

Woodhouse, W. J., 1897
Aetolia. Its Geography, Topography, and Antiquities (Reprint 1978). New York.

Vroom, J., 1993
The kastro of Veloukovo (Kallion): a note on the surface finds, *Pharos* I, 113-146.

Ancient authors

Athenaeus: The Deipnosophists with an English translation by Charles Burton Gulick, Ph.D. London: William Heinemann Ltd and Cambridge, Mass: Harvard University Press. 1955.

Pausanias: Description of Greece.III. With an English Translation by W.H.S. Jones. The Loeb Classical Library. London – New York. 1961.

Strabo: The geography of Strabo. IV. With an English translation by Horace Leonard Jones. The Loeb Classical Library. London – New York. 1927.

Abbreviations used in this paper

FPR
Dietz, S., Kolonas, L., Moschos, I. and Houby-Nielsen, S. (eds.) 1998 Surveys and Excavations 1995-1996. A Preliminary Report, *ProcDIA* 2, 233-318.

PEC
Stillwell, R. (ed.) 1976 The Princeton Encyclopedia of Classical Sites. Princeton – New Jersey.

SPR
Dietz, S., Kolonas, L., Houby-Nielsen, S. And Moschos, I. (eds.) 2000 Greek–Danish Excavations in Aetolian Chalkis 1997-1998. Second Preliminary Report, *ProcDIA* 3, 215-301.

Authors' addresses

Epimel.Anthi Angeli
12 Ephoria of Prehistoric
and Classical Antiquities,
Platia 25 Martiou,
GR–45221 Ioannina, Greece

Professor Neritan Ceka,
R.Jul Variboba P.3/9,
Tirana, Albania

Dr. Klaus Freitag
Seminar für Alte Geschichte,
Universität Münster.
Domplatz 20-22,
D-48143 Münster, Germany

Professor Peter Funke,
Seminar für Alte Geschichte,
Universität Münster.
Domplatz 20-22,
D-48143 Münster, Germany

*Lecturer Konstantina
Gravani-Katziki,*
Phil.School, Dep.of Archaeology,
University of Ioannina,
Dourouti,
GR–45221 Ioannina, Greece

Dr. Susanne Houby-Nielsen
Klassiska Institutionen,
Sølvegatan 2,
SE-22362 Lund, Sweden

Assoc. prof. Jacob Isager,
Department of Greek and Roman
Studies,
University of Southern Denmark,
Campusvej 55,
DK-5230 Odense M, Denmark

Epimel. Vivi Karatzeni,
12 Ephoria of Prehistoric
and Classical Antiquities,
Platia 25 Martiou,
GR–45221 Ioannina, Greece

Epimel. Ioulia Katsadima,
12 Ephoria of Prehistoric
and Classical Antiquities,
Platia 25 Martiou,
GR–45221 Ioannina, Greece

Dr.Franziska Lang
Institut für Altertumswissen-
schaften,
Universität Rostock,
Universitätsplatz 1,
D-18055 Rostock, Germany

Dr. Melissa Moore,
Department of Archaeology,
Boston University,
675 Commonwealth Avenue
Boston MA 02215, USA

Epimel.Giorgia Pliakou,
12 Ephoria of Prehistoric
and Classical Antiquities,
Platia 25 Martiou,
GR–45221 Ioannina, Greece

Dr. Ernst-Ludwig Schwandner,
Deutsches Archaeol. Institut,
Podbielskiallee 69,
D-14191 Berlin, Germany

Dr. Carol A. Stein,
Department of Archaeology,
Boston University,
675 Commonwealth Avenue
Boston MA 02215, USA

*Assoc. prof. Chryseis
Tzouvara-Souli,*
Phil.School, Dep.of Archaeology,
University of Ioannina,
Dourouti,
GR–45 221 Ioannina, Greece

Professor James Wiseman,
Department of Archaeology,
Boston University,
675 Commonwealth Avenue
Boston MA 02215, USA

Dr. Konstantinos Zachos,
12 Ephoria of Prehistoric
and Classical Antiquities,
Platia 25 Martiou,
GR–45221 Ioannina, Greece